STATE OF THE WORLD'S CITIES 2012/2013

Prosperity of Cities

Routledge
Taylor & Francis Group

UN⊕HABITAT

earthscan
from Routledge

First published 2013 by Routledge for and on behalf of the
United Nations Human Settlements Programme (UN-Habitat)

Simultaneously published in the USA and Canada
by Routledge
711 Third Avenue, New York, NY 10017

Routledge is an imprint of the Taylor & Francis Group, an informa business

Copyright © United Nations Human Settlements Programme, 2013

All rights reserved

United Nations Human Settlements Programme (UN-Habitat)
P.O. Box 30030, Nairobi, Kenya
Tel: +254 20 7621 234
Fax: +254 20 7624 266/7
Website: www.unhabitat.org

DISCLAIMER

The designations employed and the presentation of the material in this report do not imply the expression of any opinion whatsoever on the part of the Secretariat of the United Nations concerning the legal status of any country, territory, city or area, or of its authorities, or concerning delimitation of its frontiers or boundaries, or regarding its economic system or degree of development. The analysis, conclusions and recommendations of this report do not necessarily reflect the views of the United Nations Human Settlements Programme or its Governing Council.

The Report is produced with official data provided by governments and additional information gathered by the Global Urban Observatory. Cities and countries are invited to update data relevant to them. It is important to acknowledge that data varies according to definition and sources. While UN-Habitat checks data provided to the fullest extent possible, the responsibility for the accuracy of the information lies with the original providers of the data. Information contained in this Report is provided without warranty of any kind, either express or implied, including, without limitation, warranties of merchantability, fitness for a particular purpose and non-infringement. UN-Habitat specifically does not make any warranties or representations as to the accuracy or completeness of any such data. Under no circumstances shall UN-Habitat be liable for any loss, damage, liability or expense incurred or suffered that is claimed to have resulted from the use of this Report, including, without limitation, any fault, error, omission with respect thereto. The use of this Report is at the User's sole risk. Under no circumstances, including, but not limited to negligence, shall UN-Habitat or its affiliates be liable for any direct, indirect, incidental, special or consequential damages, even if UN-Habitat has been advised of the possibility of such damages.

HS/ (paperback)
HS/ (hardback)

ISBN13: 978-0-415-83888-7

Design and layout by Bounford.com, Cambridge, UK.
Printed by Bell & Bain Ltd., Glasgow.

Index by Margaret Binns

British Library Cataloguing in Publication Data
A catalogue record for this book is available from the British Library

Library of Congress Cataloging in Publication Data
A catalog record has been requested for this book

Secretary-General's Foreword

Our world today is predominantly urban. Cities can be prime driving forces of development and innovation. Yet the prosperity generated by cities has not been equitably shared, and a sizeable proportion of the urban population remains without access to the benefits that cities produce.

The 2012/2013 State of the World's Cities Report, "Prosperity of Cities", introduces a notion of prosperity that looks beyond the confines of economic growth that have dominated development policy and agendas for many years. It examines how cities can generate and equitably distribute the benefits and opportunities associated with prosperity, ensuring economic well being, social cohesion, environmental sustainability and a better quality of life in general.

As the world continues to grapple with the impact of an economic crisis, which has triggered a series of other crises, we are also witnessing valiant and creative attempts at different levels, by different actors, to seek solutions. Despite the challenges they face and, indeed, the dysfunction that prevails in many urban areas, cities have a central role to play in contributing to national and global recovery. And as the world seeks a more people-centred, sustainable approach to development, cities can lead the way with local solutions to global problems.

I commend the findings of this timely report to scholars, policy makers, development planners and all others interested in promoting prosperous towns and cities.

Ban Ki-moon
Secretary-General
United Nations

Foreword

This is a time of crises. This is also a time for solutions. Indeed, the world is currently engulfed in waves of financial, economic, environmental, social and political crises. Amidst the turmoil, however, we are also witnessing valiant and creative attempts at different levels and by different actors to seek for solutions.

The State of the World's Cities Report 2012/2013 presents, with compelling evidence, some of the underlying factors behind these crises that have strongly impacted on cities. It shows that a lopsided focus on purely financial prosperity has led to growing inequalities between rich and poor, generated serious distortions in the form and functionality of cities, also causing serious damage to the environment – not to mention the unleashing of precarious financial systems that could not be sustained in the long run.

The Report proposes a fresh approach to prosperity, one that is holistic and integrated and which is essential for the promotion of a collective well-being and fulfilment of all. This new approach does not only respond to the crises by providing safeguards against new risks, but it also helps cities to steer the world towards economically, socially, politically and environmentally prosperous urban futures. In order to measure present and future progress of cities towards the prosperity path, the Report introduces a new tool – *the City Prosperity Index* – together with a conceptual matrix, the *Wheel of Urban Prosperity*, both of which are meant to assist decision makers to design clear policy interventions.

To varying degrees of intensity, cities have been hit by different crises. However, this Report tells us that cities can also be a remedy to the regional and global crises. When supported by different tiers of government, and in the quest to generate holistic prosperity, cities can become flexible and creative platforms to address these crises in a pragmatic and efficient manner. Prosperity, in this sense, can be seen as a Pharmakon – both a cause of the problem and a remedy. As per this ancient Greek construct, when used properly, it can help decision-makers to steer cities towards well-balanced and harmonious development.

In this Report, UN-Habitat advocates for a new type of city – the city of the 21st century – that is a 'good', people-centred city, one that is capable of integrating the tangible and more intangible aspects of prosperity, and in the process shedding off the inefficient, unsustainable forms and functionalities of the city of the previous century. By doing this, UN-Habitat plays a pivotal role in ensuring that urban planning, legal, regulatory and institutional frameworks become an instrument of prosperity and well-being.

This is a time of solutions to the numerous challenges that confront today's cities. If we are to take measures that will make a difference to the lives of the billions of people in the world's cities, and to future generations, we need sound and solid knowledge and information. This Report provides some of these crucial ingredients. I am confident that it will serve as a useful tool in the necessary redefinition of the urban policy agenda at local, national and regional levels. I do believe also that it will provide valuable insights in the search for urban prosperity and related policy changes in the years ahead.

The Report is a bridge between research and policy, with inputs from more than 50 cities, individual scientists and institutions, particularly the Directorate-General for Regional Policy from the European Commission, and other partner institutions around the world that participated actively in the preparation of this study. I would like to thank them for their immense contribution. I would also like to thank the Government of Norway for its financial support.

The partnerships that have evolved during the preparation of this report are part and parcel of, as well as critically essential in, creating the building blocks of a more sustainable prosperity, one that is shared by all. UN-Habitat is determined to sustain and consolidate such partnerships as we collectively chart a better future.

Joan Clos
Under-Secretary-General,
United Nations Executive Director, UN-Habitat

Introduction

As the world moves into the urban age, the dynamism and intense vitality of cities become even more prominent. A fresh future is taking shape, with urban areas around the world becoming not just the dominant form of habitat for humankind, but also the engine-rooms of human development as a whole.

This ongoing evolution can be seen as yet another assertion, albeit on a larger scale, of the time-honoured role of cities as centres of prosperity. In the 21st as in much earlier centuries, people congregate in cities to realize aspirations and dreams, fulfil needs and turn ideas into realities.

Prosperity in this broader, organic sense transcends narrow economic success to encompass a socially broad-based, balanced and resilient type of development that combines tangible and more intangible aspects. Taken in this multi-dimensional sense, urban prosperity tightens the links between individuals and society with their everyday environment, i.e., the city itself. Amidst multiple challenges facing cities today, a focus on poverty reduction and/or responses to the economic crisis is gradually shifting to a broader and more general understanding of the need to harness the transformative dynamics and potentials which, to varying degrees, characterize any city anywhere in the world.

How to rekindle momentum, optimize regenerating potential, enhance strategic position in the international business sphere, polishing both image and appeal – in other words, how to foster prosperity – has become the main thrust behind urban development. In this endeavour, every city will inevitably find itself on its own specific and unique historic course. Still, a common set of conditions can be found prevailing in all cities, which enable human beings to flourish, feel fulfilled and healthy, and where business can thrive, develop and generate more wealth. These conditions mark out the city as the privileged locus of prosperity, where advancement and progress come to materialize.

This Report focuses on the notion of prosperity and its realization in urban areas. More specifically, this Report advocates a shift in attention around the world in favour of a more robust notion of development – one that looks beyond the narrow domain of economic growth that has dominated ill-balanced policy agendas over the last decades.

The gist of this Report is the need for transformative change towards people-centred, sustainable urban development, and this is what a revised notion of prosperity can provide. This focus on prosperity comes as institutional and policy backgrounds are in a state of flux around the world. Prosperity may appear to be a misplaced concern in the midst of multiple crises – financial, economic, environmental, social or political – that afflict the world today. It may appear as a luxury in the current economic predicament. However, what this Report shows with compelling evidence is that the current understanding of prosperity needs to be revised, and with it the policies and actions deployed by public authorities. UN-Habitat suggests a fresh approach to prosperity, one that reaches beyond the sole economic dimension to take in other vital dimensions such as quality of life, infrastructures, equity and environmental sustainability. The Report introduces a new statistical instrument, the City Prosperity Index, measuring the prosperity factors at work in an individual city, together with a general matrix, the Wheel of Urban Prosperity, which suggests areas for policy intervention.

As the privileged locus of prosperity, the city remains best placed to deal pragmatically with some of the new, post-crisis challenges. With adequate backing from higher tiers of government, the city appears as a flexible, operational, creative platform for the development of collaborative agendas and strategies for local responses to the global crisis.

Cities can offer remedies to the worldwide crises – if only we put them in better positions to respond to the challenges of our age, optimizing resources and harnessing the potentialities of the future. This is the 'good', people-centred city, one that is capable of integrating the tangible and more intangible aspects of prosperity – in the process shedding the inefficient, unsustainable forms and functionalities of the previous century or so – the city of the 21st century.

This Report comes at a transitional juncture in the international agenda: in the wake of the 'Rio + 20' conference on the environment and development, and ahead of a fresh, updated Habitat Agenda due in 2016 (Habitat III). Against this background, this UN-Habitat Report calls on countries and cities to engage with a fresher notion of prosperity in their respective agendas. Prosperity involves a degree of confidence in the foreseeable future. As the world recovers from one of its worst-ever economic crises and a variety of interrelated predicaments, we must find a new sense of balance and safeguard against risks of further turmoil. With dominant roles in economic, political and social life cities remain critical to setting our nations on a more inclusive, productive, creative and sustainable course.

Acknowledgements

CORE TEAM

Director: Oyebanji O. Oyeyinka

Coordinator: Eduardo López Moreno

Task Manager: Ben C. Arimah

Statistical Adviser: Gora Mboup

Principal Authors: Eduardo López Moreno,
Ben C. Arimah, Gora Mboup, Mohamed Halfani, Oyebanji O. Oyeyinka

Research: Raymond Otieno Otieno, Gianluca Crispi, Anne Amin

City Prosperity Index: Gora Mboup, Wandia Riunga, John Obure

Editor: Thierry Naudin

SUPPORT TEAM

Contributors: Wandia Seaforth, Obas John Ebohon,
Cecilia M. Zanetta, Kaushalesh Lal, Dina K. Shehayeb,
Olumuyiwa Alaba, Sai Balakrishnan, Maria Buhigas,
Christopher Horwood

Statistics: Omondi Odhiambo, Joel Jere, Julius Majale,
Wandia Riunga, John Obure, Anne Kibet, Wladimir Ray, Kaushalesh Lal

Maps: Maharufa Hossain, Jane Arimah

Administrative Support Team: Beatrice Bazanye, Anne Idukitta,
Elizabeth Kahwae, Jacqueline Macha, Mary Dibo

UN-HABITAT ADVISORY AND TECHNICAL SUPPORT

Elkin Velasquez, Laura Petrella, José Chong, Claudio Acioly, John Hogan,
Raf Tuts, Ana Moreno, Alioune Badiane, Mariam Yunusa, Roi Chiti, Axumite
Gebre-Egziabher, Kibe Muigai.

INTERNATIONAL ADVISORY BOARD

Patricia Annez; Mark Redwood; Billy Cobbett; Lamia Kamal-Chaoui; Edgar
Pieterse; Amin Y. Kamete; Smita Srinivas; Alfonso Iracheta; Yu Zhu; Dina K.
Shehayeb, Inga Klevby, Maha Yahya, Javier Sanchez-Reaza.

FINANCIAL SUPPORT

Government of Norway

SPECIAL TECHNICAL CONTRIBUTION

Directorate-General for Regional and Urban Policy (European Commission),
various background documents from experts: Zoé Buyle-Bodin, Corinne
Hermant-de Callataÿ, Christian Svanfeldt, Birgit Georgi, Antonio G. Calafati,
Celine Rozenblat, Moritz Lennert, Gilles Van Hamme, Maciej Smêtkowski
and Uwe Neumann.

ADDITIONAL CONTRIBUTIONS:

Thematic Background Papers:

Brian H. Roberts; Pengfei Ni; Robert M. Buckley and Achilles Kallergis; David
Simon, Michail Fragkias, Robin Leichenko, Roberto Sánchez-Rodríguez,
Karen Seto and Bill Solecki, Susan Parnell and Matthew Sharp; Ivan Turok.

City Reports for policy analysis:

Latin America and the Caribbean: Francisco Perez Arellano (Guadalajara);
Ana Raquel Flores (Ciudad Del Este); Vladimir Morales Gonzalez
(Valparaíso);Flávio José Nery Conde Malta (Santos); Ibarra Rolando
Mendoza (Panama City); Oscar Bragos (Rosario); Tito Alejandro Alegría
Olazábal (Tijuana); Grethel Castellanos (Santo Domingo); Haydée Beltrán
Urán (Medellín); Isabel Viana (Montevideo); Miguel Coyula (Havana);
Carlos Foronda (La Paz); Alberto José Tobío (Guarenas); Luis Delgado
Galimberti (Lima); Alain Philippe Yerro (Fort-De-France).

Africa: Femi Olokesusi (Accra, Ibadan and Lagos);Yeraswork Admassie
(Addis Ababa); Hany M. Ayad (Alexandria); Madani Safar Zitoun (Algiers);
Albino Mazembe (Beira); Aldo Lupala (Dar es Salaam); Faustin Tirwirukwa
Kalabamu (Gaborone); Rosemary Awuor Hayanga (Johannesburg);
Allan Cain (Luanda); Godfrey Hampwaye and Wilma Nchito (Lusaka);
Alfred Omenya (Nairobi); C. Fernandez (Praia).

Asia and Arab States: Saswati G. Belliapa (Bangalore); Francisco L.
Fernandez (Cebu); Yanping Liu and Yuehan Wang (Chongqing); Amelita Atillo
(Davao); Pelin F. Kurtul (Gaziantep); Dung D. Dzung (Ho Chi Minh City);
Satyanarayana Vejella (Hyderabad); Syed Shabih ul Hassan Zaidi. (Lahore);
Lan Jin and Yanping Liu. (Shenzhen); Centre for Livable Cities (Singapore);
Omar Khattab (Kuwait City); Ali Shabou, Nashwa Soboh, Kamal Jalouka,
Deema Abu Thaib, (Aqaba and Amman); Sinan Shakir A. Karim (Basra);
Mona Fawaz and Nisrene Baghdadi (Beirut); Ahmedou Mena (Doha); Darim.
Al-Bassam and Jalal Mouris (Dubai); Dara al Yaqubi (Erbil); Falah Al- Kubaisy
(Muharrak); Rana Hassan and Ismae'l Sheikh Hassan (Saida).

Input to boxes:

Michael Cohen, Cilla Ng, Inga Klevby, José Chong, Zeltia Gonzales,
Estefania Villalobos, Laura Petrella, Alexy Romero Garcia C., Dennis
Mwaniki and Francisco Perez Arellano.

Design and page layout:

Bounford.com (UK)

Front cover pictures

Equity and Social Inclusion: © Meunierd/Shutterstock.com
Quality of Life: © 2012 Peter Herbert/fotoLIBRA.com
Infrastructure: © Paul Smith/Panos Pictures
Productivity: © Atul Loke/Panos Pictures
Environmental Sustainability: © Anne-Britt Svinnset/Shutterstock.com

Back cover picture

© Claudio Zaccherini/Shutterstock.com

Contents

Boxes

Figures

Tables

Statistical Annex

Overview and Key Findings

A fresh future is taking shape, with urban areas around the world becoming not just the dominant form of habitat for humankind, but also the engine-rooms of human development as a whole. Initially understood as a transitional process, urbanization has become a positive force for transformation that makes countries more advanced, developed and richer, in most cases.

Today, as many centuries ago, human beings regroup together in order better to exchange, learn, produce, enjoy and protect each other. Moving to a city or staying in a city is in itself an objective desire to have a better life. The fostering of prosperity has been one of the main reasons that explain the existence of cities. They are the places where humankind realizes ambitions, aspirations and dreams, fulfil yearning needs, and turn ideas into realities.

Urban prosperity takes different forms and characterizations. Each individual city, depending on its own stage of socioeconomic development, history and culture, can be seen as giving its own unique interpretation of prosperity, including in the way it is shared among the population. Still, it is possible to find a common set of conditions that enable urban residents to flourish, feel happy and healthy, and in which business can thrive, institutions develop, and physical spaces become more integrated and diverse.

In this sense, the city is the home of prosperity. It is the place where human beings find satisfaction of basic needs and essential public and private goods, where commodities can be found in sufficiency and their utility enjoyed. Cities are where material and immaterial aspects of life are realized, providing contentment and happiness and increasing the prospects of individual and collective well-being. However, when prosperity is absent or confined to some groups, when it is only enjoyed in some parts of the city, when it is used to pursue vested interests, or when it is a justification for financial gains for the few in detriment of the majority, the city becomes the arena where the right for a shared prosperity is fought for.

RE-THINKING URBAN PROSPERITY
The Pursuit of Prosperity in a Time of Crisis
Never before had humankind faced cascading crises of all types as have affected it since 2008, from financial to economic to environmental to social to political. Soaring unemployment, food shortages and attendant price rises, strains on financial institutions, insecurity and political instability, among other crises, might well on their own call into question the relevance and even the viability of a Report on prosperity. This proliferation of risks might even challenge the conventional notion of 'Cities as the Home of Prosperity', i.e. where, by definition, 'successful, flourishing, or thriving conditions' prevail.

As people in the latter part of 2011 gathered in Cairo's Tahrir Square or Madrid's Puerta del Sol, in front of London's St Paul's cathedral or in New York's Zuccotti Park, they were not only demanding more equality and inclusion; they were also expressing solidarity with fellow citizens that are part of the '99 per cent' (the vast majority) as opposed to the 'one per cent' (the tiny proportion of people with vastly disproportionate shares of wealth and power). From a symbolic point of view, these actions came as attempts to build bridges over social, political and cultural differences; more practically, though, and as earlier in Tunisia, these movements highlighted the inherent risks of ill-balanced growth or development policies, and their failure to safeguard prosperity for all.

As a result of lopsided development notions and policies, instead of being places of opportunities and prosperity, cities all-too-often have become places of deprivation, inequality and exclusion. In too many parts of the developing world, unequal access to opportunities and resources has pushed many people into *favelas*, *bidonvilles*, *Katchi Abadis* or *campamentos* (as slums are known). In Europe as in other parts of the developed world, new forms of social exclusion, marginalization and poverty are emerging, such as infrastructure-poor suburbs, immigrant poverty, young people at risk, and the vulnerable elderly.

Throughout history, cities as seats of power have served as arenas for protests and the recent social movements are no exception. Demographic concentrations in dense urban spaces allow critical masses of protestors to congregate and air new ideas, highlighting cities' role as sounding boards for positive social change.

Cities: Remedy to the Global Crises
If anything, the recent crises have demonstrated that cities around the world are, to varying degrees of intensity, exposed at least as much to the destructive as to the more beneficial effects of international markets, including social and political repercussions. In this sense, these crises did more than highlight the transformative role of cities; they also showed that they are in a better position, at

least notionally, to address regional and global crises. For that purpose, there is a need to confer a more vigorous role to cities with a strong support from various tiers of government. Cities need to be put in better positions to respond to the challenges of our age, optimizing resources and harnessing the potentialities of the future.

With this reinvigorated support, cities can act as remedies to the global crises in a number of ways:

- Acting as flexible and creative platforms that can develop responses in a pragmatic and efficient manner;
- Boosting production in the real sector of the economy at local level, with attendant employment and income generation;
- Acting as the fora where linkages, trust, respect and inclusive responses are built;
- Preparing local actions that can be structured and included in national agendas for more efficient, flexible results and more beneficial effects;
- Negotiating with local stakeholders and forging new partnerships and social pacts which, in turn, can strengthen national governments;
- Aligning central and local government expenditures at city level in order to maximize benefits and impacts;
- Devising a number of safeguards against a variety of evolving socioeconomic risks, prioritizing investment in social security nets and local/regional infrastructure, with a view to securing longer-term growth;
- Deploying safeguards against the risks international markets may bring to bear on local socioeconomic conditions, and adopting redistributive policies in close collaboration with central governments.

Re-Thinking Urban Prosperity

A poverty-stricken plumber in Hyderabad (India), a factory worker in Bogotá (Colombia), a middle manager in Madrid (Spain), a businessman in Fortaleza (Brazil), a car mechanic in Nairobi (Kenya) – all five will have aspirations to prosperous lives. However, prosperity means different things to different people around the world. Whatever the individual perception, regardless of culture and civilization, prosperity refers to a sense of general and individual socioeconomic security for the immediate and foreseeable future, which comes with the fulfilment of other, non-material needs and aspirations.

Yet, the prevailing view continues to confine prosperity to the realm of economics; a limiting view that shuts out other dimensions that are integral to human well-being and necessary for individual and collective fulfilment.

If anything, the 2008 financial crisis has amplified the need to include other, non-economic dimensions in the understanding and measurement of prosperity.

This edition of the *State of the World's Cities* report calls on countries and cities to engage with a fresher notion of prosperity in their respective agendas – one that transcends the narrow confines of an accumulation-driven model that benefits only a few to the detriment of the majority. It proposes a new notion that looks beyond the narrow domain of economic growth that has dominated ill-balanced policy agendas over the last decades. Prosperity in this broader, organic sense encompasses a socially broad-based, balanced and resilient type of development that combines tangible and more intangible aspects. This fresh notion is more holistic and integrated, including other vital dimensions such as quality of life, adequate infrastructures, equity and environmental sustainability.

The gist of this Report is the need for transformative action in favour of the people-centred, sustainable urban development which a revised notion of prosperity can provide. This focus on prosperity comes as institutional and policy backgrounds are in a state of flux around the world. It is expected that this new approach to prosperity will put cities and countries in a better position not just to respond to the effects of the crisis and provide safeguards against new risks, but also to steer the world towards economically, socially, politically and environmentally urban futures.

However, for this notion of prosperity to be implemented at city level, there is a need to reconsider the existing model of urban development, introducing major changes in the form and function of the city – an approach that re-shapes urban space through appropriate planning and design, creating a city at a human scale where diversity, connectivity, and physical integration are all inter-woven, and prosperity is shared. This new urban space requires a different type of city.

Promoting the City of the 21st Century

In this Report, UN-Habitat advocates for a new type of city – the city of the 21st century – that is a 'good', people-centred city, one that is capable of integrating the tangible and more intangible aspects of prosperity, in the process shedding the inefficient, unsustainable forms and functionalities of the city of the previous century. UN-Habitat plays a pivotal role in ensuring that urban planning, legal, regulatory and institutional frameworks become an instrument of prosperity and well-being.

The city of the 21st century transcends the form and functionality of previous models, balancing lower energy costs with a smaller ecological footprint, more compact form, and greater heterogeneity and functionality. This city safeguards against new risks and creates conditions for a higher provision of public goods, together with more creative spaces for imagination and social interaction.

The city of the 21st century is one that:
- Reduces disaster risks and vulnerabilities for all, including the poor, and builds resilience to any adverse forces of nature;
- Stimulates local job creation, promotes social diversity, maintains a sustainable environment and recognizes the importance of public spaces;
- Creates harmony between the five dimensions of prosperity and enhances the prospects for a better future;
- Comes with a change of pace, profile and urban functions and provides the social, political and economic conditions of prosperity.

Conceptualizing Prosperity

Prosperity implies success, wealth, thriving conditions, and well-being as well as confidence and opportunity. In general terms, a prosperous city offers a profusion of public goods and develops policies and actions for sustainable use, and allows equitable access to 'commons'. In this Report, UN-Habitat conceptualizes urban prosperity as follows:
- First, a prosperous city contributes to economic growth through productivity, generating the income and employment that afford adequate living standards for the whole population;
- Second, a prosperous city deploys the infrastructure, physical assets and amenities – adequate water, sanitation, power supply, road network, information and communications technology, etc. – required to sustain both the population and the economy;
- Third, prosperous cities provide the social services – education, health, recreation, safety and security, etc. – required for improved living standards, enabling the population to maximize individual potential and lead fulfilling lives;
- Fourth, a city is only prosperous to the extent that poverty and inequalities are minimal. No city can claim to be prosperous when large segments of the population live in abject poverty and deprivation. This involves reducing the incidence of slums and new forms of poverty;

- Fifth, the creation and (re)distribution of the benefits of prosperity do not destroy or degrade the environment; instead, the city's natural assets are preserved for the sake of sustainable urbanization.

In order to measure present and future progress of cities along the prosperity path, the Report introduces a new tool – the *City Prosperity Index* – together with a conceptual matrix, the *Wheel of Urban Prosperity*; both of which are meant to assist decision-makers with the design of effective policy interventions.

The 'Wheel of Urban Prosperity'

Prosperity, as defined by UN-Habitat, is a social construct that materializes in the realm of human actions. It builds deliberately and conscientiously on the objective conditions prevailing in a city at any time, wherever located and however large or small. This is a broader, wide-ranging notion that has to do with well-balanced, harmonious development in an environment of fairness and justice.

UN-Habitat's notion of prosperity takes in all urban functions as subsumed under five main categories: productivity, infrastructure, quality of life, equity and environmental sustainability. Since shared, balanced development is a crucial feature of prosperity, none of the dimensions must prevail over the others and all must be kept roughly 'equal' – for the sake of a smooth 'ride' on the path of prosperity. In practice, of course, it is a rare city where the five dimensions will be found equal at any point in time, and this is where policy interventions will be called for, as suggested graphically by the conceptual matrix of the *Wheel of Urban Prosperity*.

UN-Habitat's 'wheel of prosperity' symbolizes the well-balanced development of the five dimensions of prosperity, the current condition of which is measured through the City Prosperity Index (CPI).

The 'outer rim' of the wheel absorbs the cumulative forces transmitted through the 'spokes' – the five dimensions of prosperity. It provides some level of direction and symbolically contributes to guide the city towards a more prosperous path.

The spokes are the five dimensions of prosperity. In most cases, they interact and influence each other through various, quasi-automatic linkages along the periphery or 'outer rim'. For example, as a city develops infrastructure, it will also enhance prospects for economic expansion and enhance quality of life. Likewise, when a city pursues pro-poor policies and equitable development, this will also enhance the chances of higher productivity and improved environmental protection. Interactions and inter-influences between the 'spokes' can also occur at the centre of the wheel, where they are more policy-determined.

The hub at the centre of the wheel brings together the urban power functions (e.g., public authorities, laws, regulations and institutions, urban planning, civil society, trade associations, special agencies, etc.) associated with the five 'spokes'. In this role, the 'hub' represents human agency in all its embodiments. It holds the five 'spokes' together and endeavours to maintain their balance and symmetry, with four interrelated roles: (i) ensuring the prevalence of *public* over any other kind of interest; (ii) controlling the direction, pace and momentum of the 'wheel'; (iii) ensuring balanced development of the five 'spokes' and associated synergies; and (iv) in a two-way relationship, absorbing and amortising any 'shocks' transmitted by the 'spokes'.

This Report suggests that it is for the city of the 21st century to pursue shared, integrated prosperity, keeping the 'wheel' well balanced with mutually reinforcing spokes through a dynamic hub. UN-Habitat introduces a new statistical instrument, the *City Prosperity Index*, to measure the prosperity factors at work in individual cities, which pinpoints areas for policy intervention.

The City Prosperity Index

Cities can take different paths to prosperity. Still, UN-Habitat has developed an index that measures the current status of cities vis-à-vis the five dimensions of prosperity, as conceptualized by UN-Habitat. This index also measures government actions and policies in the pursuit of prosperity, and the outcomes of these policies. The index provides an indication of how solid or weak are the prosperity factors available to any individual city.

However, UN-Habitat's 'City Prosperity Index' (CPI) does not only provide indices and measurements; it also enables decision-makers to identify opportunities and potential areas of action along the path of prosperity.

The CPI includes various indices and indicators for each dimension of prosperity, with specific indices computed into one single metric that measures advancement along the road of prosperity. This information is relevant to decision-makers and important for prosperity-oriented public policy-making.

The CPI is composed of the five dimensions (the 'spokes' in the 'wheel') of urban prosperity. For the calculation of specific indices, the CPI includes various components partially covered in other measures such as the Green City Index, the Ecological City Index and the Livable City Index, which are further disaggregated into various variables and sub-indices. The CPI also relies on the Human Development Index (HDI), which goes into the computation of the 'City Human Development Index' (CHDI). The CPI has been designed in such a way that additional information and data can be incorporated when calculating the index. This degree of adaptability makes it possible to bring the more important city-specific variables and space-related indicators into the index.

The UN-Habitat City Prosperity Index is unique in the world for two reasons: (i) it focuses on individual *cities*, as opposed to countries, and (ii) it is concerned with prosperity as measured across *five dimensions*, of which the local economy is only one, as opposed to the sole business environment. The resulting CPI values can be regrouped in six distinct brackets that range from cities with '*very solid*' prosperity factors to those where those factors are found to be '*very weak*'.

In broad terms, the classification by CPI values results in regional brackets with various cities in the developed world featuring solid prosperity factors (CPI: 0.900 or higher), with a majority of African cities with very weak readings constituting the last two groups (CPI: 0.600 or below). In between, a large number of Asian and Latin American cities make up the third and fourth groups (with CPI values of 0.700–0.799 and 0.600–0.699, respectively).

The classification of cities according to the six different CPI groups shows the following characteristics:

Group (by prosperity factors)	Characteristics	Cities
Cities with very solid prosperity factors (0.900 and above)	■ Strong integration of the 5 dimensions of prosperity. ■ High production of goods and services, strong economic fundamentals, high productivity. ■ Urban power functions (good governance, urban planning, laws, regulations and institutional frameworks) work fairly well, creating safe and secure environments.	Vienna, Warsaw, Milan, Barcelona, Copenhagen, Zurich, Amsterdam, Auckland, Melbourne, Tokyo, Paris, Oslo, Dublin, Helsinki, Stockholm, London, Toronto, New York.

Group (by prosperity factors)	Characteristics	Cities
Cities with solid prosperity factors – first category (0.800–0.899):	■ The dimensions of prosperity are connected, generating a self-reinforcing, cumulative momentum. ■ Relatively strong institutions, responsive legal and regulatory frameworks. ■ Large availability of public goods.	Ankara, Mexico City, Guadalajara, Bucharest, Shanghai, Almaty, São Paulo, Moscow, Seoul, Prague, Athens, Budapest, Lisbon.
Cities with solid prosperity factors – second category (0.700–0.799):	■ Show 'less coordinated', ill-balanced development in the 'spokes'. ■ Institutions, legal and regulatory frameworks and urban management practices are undergoing consolidation.	Casablanca, Cairo, Manila, Johannesburg, Jakarta, Cape Town, Beijing, Yerevan, Kyiv, Bangkok, Amman.
Cities with moderate prosperity factors (0.600–0.699):	■ Wider discrepancies among the 5 dimensions of prosperity. ■ Institutional and structural failings. ■ Less balanced development. ■ Neat divide between rich and poor.	New Delhi, Yaoundé, Guatemala City, Ulaanbaatar, Phnom Penh, Nairobi, Mumbai, Chisinau, Tegucigalpa.
Cities with weak prosperity factors (0.500–0.599):	■ Production of goods and services is still too low. ■ Historic structural problems, chronic inequality of opportunities and widespread poverty. ■ Inadequate capital investment in public goods. ■ Lack of pro-poor social programmes.	Lusaka, Dar es Salaam, Harare, Dakar, Addis Ababa, La Paz, Accra, Lagos, Kampala, Dhaka, Kathmandu, Abidjan.
Cities with very weak prosperity factors (below 0.500):	■ Dysfunctional systems, institutional failings. ■ Sluggish economic growth, widespread poverty and destitution. ■ Post- or ongoing conflict countries.	Monrovia, Conakry, Antananarivo, Bamako, Niamey.

THE PROSPERITY OF CITIES
The Five Dimensions of Prosperity

This edition of the *State of the World's Cities* report presents a fresh perspective on prosperity based on five dimensions – productivity, infrastructures, quality of life, equity and environmental sustainability. In the pursuit of prosperity urban authorities must understand the various interlinkages and interdependencies between these five dimensions. Well-targeted interventions in one of the dimensions of prosperity will have multiplier effects in the other dimensions. Urban power functions ensure shared, balanced development, which is a defining feature of prosperity. Taken individually, the most important features of each of these dimensions are outlined below.

Productivity and the Prosperity of Cities

■ Urban areas contribute disproportionally to national productivity. However, the structural productivity of cities will at least in part rest upon an efficient supply of serviced land and reliable infrastructure, including transport, power, water and sanitation as well as information/communication technologies. Cities at earlier stages of development must look to enhance transport connectivity, including to markets, providing the population with access to adequate healthcare and basic education.

■ Concentrations of populations, infrastructure, economic, social and cultural activities can lead to substantial benefits and efficiency due to agglomeration and scale economies. Agglomeration economies give cities a competitive advantage and benefit densely populated urban areas.

■ The sound operation of any city (traffic and emergency management, transportation, waste collection/disposal and other services) has a crucial role to play in support of social and economic activities.

■ Cities where exchange of ideas and innovation are encouraged will be better able to tap into the growth dynamics that fuel the creation of social and intellectual capital, thereby contributing to prosperity. However, it is worthy of note that top performing cities derive their strengths not just from their status as global economic powerhouses, or from sophisticated infrastructure and innovation mechanisms, but also from their ability to enhance quality of life.

Urban Infrastructure: Bedrock of Prosperity

- Prioritizing infrastructure must feature in any long-term economic and social development and environmental protection strategy. Prosperous cities are those that have vastly improved the range and quality of their infrastructure.
- As they meet infrastructure requirements, cities signal that provision of public goods is high on the local political agenda. However, infrastructure needs proper maintenance if the initial investment is to pay off and the benefits are to endure over time.
- Consistent and targeted investments in transport and communication infrastructure are a major factor behind urban prosperity. It is in the best interests of cities to develop sustainable public transport, which will have positive repercussions on all dimensions of prosperity.

Quality of Life and Urban Prosperity

- Cities that are committed to quality of life are almost always also committed to enhanced productivity and equity, emphasizing the strong relation between these dimensions.
- Cities that give priority to the notion of public space, providing green areas, parks and recreation facilities, demonstrate a commitment to improved quality of life. Such cities are also likely in the process to enhance community cohesion and civic identity.
- Access to public spaces does not only improve quality of life, it is a first step to civic empowerment, paving the way for a broader, deeper institutional and political space.
- Effective public safety is a fundamental 'common good' that enhances quality of life for all, and is a major foundation for urban prosperity.

Equity and the Prosperity of Cities

- Inequalities are becoming steeper. Paradoxically, this has occurred as wealth rose enormously around the world. However, equity has a significant impact on economic performance, since the greater the degree of equity, the greater the chances of a fuller, more efficient use of available resources, including skills and creative talent.
- Prosperity thrives on equity, which involves a lowering of barriers on individual/collective potential, expansion of opportunities, and strengthening of human agency and civic engagement. When equity is embedded in urban development strategies, efficiency is enhanced, asset utilization becomes optimal, productivity improves, and social cohesion is strengthened.

- More equitable cities have greater chances to be more prosperous, too; but prosperity does not happen all by itself, or as a logical consequence of economic growth. Promoting equity is a dual endeavour: (i) providing the conditions that enable every individual and social group to realize their full potential and harness the collective benefits and opportunities that cities offer; (ii) removing any systemic barriers that discriminate against any individual or social group.
- When prosperity remains an elusive proposition for a majority of the population, the prospects of social unrest or full-blown conflicts increase, since the majority's claims are nothing but demands for effective human dignity.
- There is no substitute for government leadership to address issues of equity, with civil society playing advocacy, support and complementary roles.

Environmental Sustainability and the Prosperity of Cities

- Environmentally sustainable cities are likely to be more productive, competitive, innovative and prosperous. These cities are able to draw a healthy balance between economic growth and the environment, in the process facilitating integrated development and resilience.
- Urbanization and economic growth are inevitable; if matched with appropriate and effective policies and governance, the environmental consequences are manageable.
- Cities must build those financial and other institutions required to achieve environmental sustainability, otherwise economic growth will fall short of ensuring shared prosperity.
- Environmentally sustainable cities are more compact, energy-efficient, clean and less polluted, more accessible, and offer better transport choices.
- Investments in renewable energies could generate more employment and income for urban households. Waste management and recycling can be a huge source of employment in developing countries.

POLICIES FOR PROSPEROUS CITIES
Factors Promoting Prosperity

UN-Habitat opinion surveys and policy analysis have identified a number of factors that can create a favourable environment for cities to prosper. These factors are mediated by the local context, and as such, their effects may vary across cities and regions. A clear understanding and appreciation of these factors is important in reorienting the policies, supporting structures and mechanisms that can affect the prosperity of cities. These eight factors are the following: effective urban planning and management; decentralization polices and appropriate institutions; a system that creates equal opportunities for all; participation of civil society; elected local officials; a favourable business environment; access to basic amenities; and public transport and mobility.

Effective urban planning and management: This has been perceived by local experts surveyed by UN-Habitat as the most important factor behind a favourable environment for urban prosperity. The five dimensions of prosperity will give any city a grip on an otherwise largely uncontrolled urbanization process. Against a background of rapid urbanization, urban planning is a necessity not a luxury, as demonstrated, in the many cities where it has been lacking, by the proliferation of slum and squatter settlements, spiralling poverty, inadequate infrastructure and deteriorating environmental conditions – all of which are inconsistent with prosperity. Evidence shows that when planned and well managed, with distributive mechanisms in place, urbanization can reduce poverty. Urban planning and appropriately developed institutions and regulations also have major roles to play, improving equity through the capture and redistribution of rising land values. Moreover, effective urban planning can encourage more compact, efficient and sustainable development, with the benefits of economies of scale and agglomeration.

Decentralization and appropriate institutions: Decentralization policies emerge as the second important factor enhancing urban prosperity. Local experts see it as the most important factor in Latin America and the Caribbean. The perceived effect of decentralization in Arab States appears to lag behind other regions. The highly centralized governance structure in this region undermines the efficiency of municipal authorities, obstructs political participation and erodes the relationships between the citizenry and public authorities. In Africa, the degree of decentralization varies significantly across countries: it is high in South Africa and Uganda, but only moderate in Kenya, Ghana, Nigeria, Rwanda and Namibia. Many Asian countries have made remarkable progress with decentralization, such as Indonesia and the Philippines. The one lesson from this diversity of experiences and circumstances is that for decentralization to be effective and strengthen urban authorities' commitment to prosperity, it must be matched by fiscal devolution. It is also clear that decentralization works well when backed by strong commitment and support from central government.

A system that creates equal opportunities: A system that guarantees equal opportunities for all is the third important factor underlying the prosperity of cities. The more egalitarian a city, the more prosperous it is to become. The importance of such a system is most pronounced in Arab States compared with other regions, perhaps due to the fact that this sub-region is one of the most egalitarian in terms of income distribution in the developing world (Gini coefficient of 0.36). For a city to be truly prosperous, it must deploy systems that will ensure equal opportunities for all, especially the more vulnerable – the poor, women, children, the elderly, youth and the disabled. On the contrary, highly unequal cities are a ticking time bomb waiting to explode. A system that creates equal opportunities for all can use redistributive policies that give priority to low-income groups and areas (e.g., Venezuela's massive investment in healthcare and education, with the provision of over 8,000 clinics in the *barrios* or universal pension schemes in Botswana, Lesotho, Mauritius and Namibia). Another alternative will be conditional cash transfers (e.g., Brazil's *Bolsa Família* scheme, which benefits 11.1 million families, and has contributed to reducing poverty and inequality).

Civil society participation: Policies that promote the participation of civil society are perceived by local experts as the fourth most important factor behind enhanced urban prosperity. Participation of civil society has the potential to empower communities, build social capital, lead to better design of urban projects, and allow for citizens' concerns to be incorporated into development strategies. The perceived importance of participation of civil society varies across regions. It is seen by local experts as the second most important factor in Latin America and the Caribbean, while in Arab States it ranks only fifth. Asia provides a classic example of a participatory planning process with the People's Campaign for Decentralized Planning in the State of Kerala (India), which was launched in 1996. Lessons from various countries suggest that successful civil society participation is dependent upon certain preconditions such as: (i) a political system that encourages active citizenship and is committed to equity and remedial action; (ii) a legal basis for participation; (iii) available resources in terms of skilled and committed professionals, as well as well-resourced and empowered local governments; and (iv) informed and organized communities and stakeholders.

A favourable business environment: Cities with favourable business environments and entrepreneurial cultures are more likely to be prosperous than others. A business-conducive environment is needed for a vibrant private sector, attracting and retaining investment (including foreign direct), creating jobs and improving productivity – all of which are important for the promotion of growth and for expanded opportunities for the poor. In Asia, a favourable business environment is perceived as the most important factor promoting prosperity, as demonstrated by Singapore. Other Asian countries that rank high with respect to the ease of doing business include Hong Kong, Korea, Thailand, Malaysia and Japan. In Africa, countries such as Mauritius, South Africa, Rwanda, Tunisia and Botswana also have a good record enabling business environment. In recent years, Rwanda has undertaken reforms to streamline business procedures, create a favourable legal framework, reduce bureaucracy, and improve service delivery in order to promote both domestic and foreign investment.

Impediments to the Prosperity of Cities

Based on the UN-Habitat local expert survey, the seven main impediments to urban prosperity are the following: poor governance and weak institutions; corruption; lack of appropriate infrastructure; high incidence of slums and poverty; high costs of doing business; low levels of human capital; and high crime rates. The hard-won prosperity gains made by cities can be jeopardized or eroded by these impediments.

Poor governance and weak institutions: The impact of poor governance and weak institutions on urban prosperity appears to be more pronounced in Africa and Arab States, where over 40 per cent of experts cite this factor as the single most important impediment. Indeed, in these cities, as in many others in developing countries, the institutions required for urban prosperity, if they exist, are weakly developed. Institutional inadequacies take the form of weak (if not altogether lacking) legal and institutional frameworks, disregard for the rule of law, poor enforcement of property rights, excessive bureaucracy, and proliferation of corrupt practices, among others. All these are incompatible with urban prosperity.

Corruption: Corruption is considered by local experts as the second most important hindrance to enhanced urban prosperity. The negative effects vary across cities and regions. While corruption on a grand scale has (as might be expected) the most devastating impact, corruption in any form undermines confidence in the fairness of government, the rule of law and economic stability. In Arab States, corruption is the joint first factor along with poor governance and weak institutions; in Asia it is perceived as the second most serious impediment; and in Latin America and the Caribbean, it is rated as the third most important. Corruption can be detrimental in a variety of ways: acting as a deterrent to foreign direct investment; undermining the ability of city authorities to provide fair municipal services; distorting infrastructure spending in various ways that are not beneficial for the urban poor; and causing poor delivery of urban services.

Inadequate infrastructure: Inadequate infrastructure is a major impediment to the prosperity of cities. The impacts of deficient infrastructure appear to be more pronounced in Asian and African cities and less so in Arab States. Cities with deficient infrastructure can be adversely affected on many fronts. For instance, inadequate water and sanitation facilities will lead to deterioration of the urban environment, increasing the disease burden on the urban poor. Deficient infrastructure can raise the costs of doing business in urban areas and reduce firm productivity by as much as 40 per cent. Besides denting trade and competitiveness, inadequate infrastructure often leads to congested roads and poor transport facilities, which all act as serious hindrances to any city's prosperity.

High incidence of slums and poverty: Cities with high incidence of slums are an indication of lopsided prosperity. Slum dwellers are often stigmatized on account of their location and are often discriminated against in terms of access to public and social services, as well as employment. Large concentrations of slums impose enormous burdens on urban authorities that often lack the political will and resources to provide even the most basic services, with implications for the prosperity of cities. Rather than being proactive in their approach to urban development, cities with large concentrations of slums are likely to adopt a reactionary and fragmentary approach to urban development, which tends to be expensive in the long run.

Poorly developed human capital: Low levels of human capital and skilled labour can hinder urban prosperity. Education is essential not just for nurturing but also for attracting talents, and bolstering innovation. Availability of highly-skilled human capital in turn attracts and generates innovative and knowledge-based industries. Attracting and cultivating talents has become common practice for cities in the pursuit of prosperity. From New York to Boston, London to Vienna, Dubai to Singapore, or Bangalore to Shenzhen, many cities can illustrate this phenomenon. The cities' large proportions of high-skilled workers, nurtured through their vocational education system, have been crucial for city prosperity.

High crime rates: Crime emerges as another major impediment to the prosperity of cities. No city can claim to be truly prosperous if it is crime-ridden and the population lives in a perpetual state of insecurity. Crime is a major deterrent to domestic and foreign investment and can cause capital flight. In Africa, more than 29 per cent of business people report that crime was a significant investment constraint. In South Africa, a survey of major cities showed that around 25 per cent of respondents were reluctant to allow their children to walk to school, while 30 per cent stopped using public transportation. In large Latin American cities, high numbers of murders deter people from working evenings and at night. In Jamaica, crime has a pernicious effect on national tourism and is often cited as a major reason for the country's weak economy.

All these factors have implications for local economies, quality of life and the attractiveness of public spaces, on top of lost opportunities for socioeconomic advancement that are so crucial for the prosperity of cities.

Policies Promoting Prosperity

UN-Habitat policy analysis identifies three major types of action to promote urban prosperity:

1. Innovations to support the transition to the City of the 21st Century.
2. Urban planning and design for prosperity.
3. Empowering laws and institutions for urban prosperity.

Various other policies and actions are certainly needed, the specific nature of which will vary from one city to the next. In this endeavour, and given the holistic nature of prosperity, effective coordination of municipal authorities with local and central government has a pivotal role to play.

Innovations to support the transition to the City of the 21st Century: Creativity and innovation involve a variety of areas that range from technology to institutions, organizations and modes of operation to information and knowledge, finance and human development. Although increasingly viewed from the sole economic perspective, innovations can flourish in many areas such as developing and managing urban life, renewal of social institutions, improved urban policies, development of knowledge networks, etc.

Creativity and innovation are largely influenced by six main types of factors: (i) locational advantages (i.e., economies of agglomeration and 'positive externalities'

at regional scale); (ii) knowledge networks; (iii) cultural factors; (iv) the economic environment; (v) organizational factors; and (vi) State/government interventions (i.e., policies, incentives, institutions). The cities and countries best placed for economic growth and prosperity are those that invest in building knowledge and innovation institutions and related systems with strong support from both public authorities and the private sector.

Innovation is a creative capital that is brought to bear on various dimensions of development and prosperity, in the process unleashing undeveloped potential and making fuller use of local resources and assets. The culture of creativity must be embedded in the way cities operate. Therefore, it is not just for government or business, but also for communities and the public at large, to mobilize their own powers of imagination. In practice, all of this requires well-adapted physical environments, which in turn have to do with urban economies and better urban planning. From a more institutional point of view, support to knowledge exchange and networking is another way of stimulating creative capital, along with favourable conditions for research and development. As for the productive sector, creative stimulation can also derive from economies of agglomeration and an entrepreneur-friendly environment.

The transformative power of innovation is closely linked to the various components of prosperity – productivity, infrastructure, quality of life, equity and environmental sustainability. Innovation can contribute to any of these dimensions, or respond to the supporting institutions and policies at the core of these dimensions, steering the course of the city along the path of prosperity and sustainable development.

Urban planning and design for prosperity: In the midst of ongoing demographic, socioeconomic or environmental cross-currents, cities must reassert control over their destinies with reinvigorated urban planning and design, for the sake of shared prosperity and harmonious development.

If urban planning is to be in a better position to address the shortcomings of the Global Standard Urbanization Model of the 20th century, both theory and practice must come under serious review to 'rescue' the discipline from its role as a mere technical tool, restoring it to its rightful position in the public sphere. However, efficient urban planning requires a reinvigorated notion that can really contribute to the pursuit of shared prosperity, and for that purpose four conditions must be met: (i) restoration of public confidence; (ii) repositioning of urban planning in decision-making; (iii) deployment of the fullness of its functions across the five dimensions of shared prosperity; and (iv) support for these functions with adequate financing.

As a decision-making tool, urban planning must better defend the 'public' against the menace of ever-expanding 'private' interests and its consequences: shrinking public spaces and reduced provision of public goods, which in turn affect more collective, intangible dimensions, such as quality of life, social interaction, cultural identity and social values. Interdependencies and interactions among the five 'spokes' in the 'wheel of urban prosperity' (productivity, infrastructure, quality of life, equity and environmental sustainability) can be deliberately enhanced (as opposed to being allowed to occur all by themselves) through the strategies and interventions that are part and parcel of urban planning. More specifically, it is in the power of a well-planned decision or well-calibrated choice in one dimension of prosperity – for example, the design of a street supporting multimodal transport as part of the infrastructure development of the city – not just to make that particular part of the urban space more accessible or pedestrian-friendly, but in the process also to improve productivity (shops, street-trading, etc.), quality of life and social inclusion.

UN-Habitat calls for a fresh, different type of urban planning and design – one that has the power to transform urban landscapes and expand existing enclaves of prosperity across the entire city. UN-Habitat proposes a reinvigorated notion of urban planning, one that comes with a new value system that relies on effective institutions, well-adapted laws and regulations, sustainable urban solutions and active civic involvement in public affairs. This type of planning signals a paradigm shift towards a new urban pattern – the city of the 21st century: a city that can better respond to the challenges of our age, optimizing resources to harness the potentialities of the future; a people-centred city, one that is capable of transcending the inefficient, unsustainable GS20C model, in the process integrating and nurturing the five dimensions of urban prosperity as defined in this Report. UN-Habitat's reinvigorated notion of urban planning involves sustainable use of, and equitable access to, the 'commons' through appropriate policies and schemes. It also gives any city tighter public control over the use of land, and contributes to the change in form and function of cities based on sustainable development principles. Acting from the 'hub' of the 'wheel for prosperity', urban planning can identify strategies and plan for optimal production of public goods,

in the process contributing to social capital, enhancing sense of place, safety and security, integrating social groups (e.g., youth), and increasing the economic value of the areas where these goods are provided.

Prosperous cities must plan and implement a variety of technical solutions to improve functionality and achieve sustainable urban forms. Although solutions can vary according to local conditions, UN-Habitat has identified a number of key interventions in various areas, including: increase population density to sustainable levels; encourage social diversity and mixed land-use; devise multimodal mobility strategies; plan infill development and guided expansion; and promote livable public spaces and vibrant streets.

Empowering laws and institutions for urban prosperity: The success of some of the cities as highlighted in this Report is based on specific combinations of laws, regulations, institutions and processes. In almost all cases, advances along the five dimensions of prosperity are either accelerated or impeded by existing bodies of laws and regulations, the strength of enforcement, as well as by the configuration, capacity and flexibility of the institutions responsible for steering urban development.

In recent years, there has been a resurgence of policy reviews and scholarly studies striving to address the normative and organizational underpinnings of urban change. As part of this change, it is clear that legal and institutional systems are part of the hub that drives the 'wheel of urban prosperity', supplying the laws and regulations that support and shape the five 'spokes', adjusting them over time as conditions, needs and fresh risks may require. In this process, business, academia, civil society – non-governmental and grassroots organizations, trade unions and professional associations, political parties, etc. – all need to contribute to the design and enforcement of these laws and regulations, including strong institutions, to make sure that the city moves along the path of prosperity. Laws that are adapted to the requirements and expectations of the city of the 21st century and the associated institutional set determine the very genesis of the modern city.

Laws, regulations and institutions as factors of restraint, opportunity and action, act as the levers that can optimize the social function of property and balance it out with private rights and assets. They can revitalize 'Rights to the Commons' and expand the public realm. As cities work on the five dimensions of prosperity, there also occurs a progressive expansion in the size of the commons. More amenities are brought into collective use and more access is provided, enabling larger numbers of urban residents to use and enjoy shared spaces, services and facilities. Rules and regulations constitute a key instrument in urban management and development. They generally steer and circumscribe planning and construction. Indeed, statutes, ordinances and regulations are the bases for the guidelines and standards regulating spatial layouts and construction designs. The same applies to institutional relationships, functional allocations and authority designation, besides resource distribution. The legal framework in turn enables civic organizations and community activities. Equally significant is the overall manner in which legal-regulatory and institutional frameworks delineate the public and private spheres and guide the interaction between and within them in the everyday workings of the city. The capacity for a city to maintain extensive and quality shared spaces and facilities provides a good indication of its degree of prosperity.

The review of regulatory frameworks is of particular importance for those cities in the developing world that have long operated with externally derived standards and codes, who must also tend to effective implementation and enforcement capacities. This calls not only for major institutional restructuring, but also for a revision of zoning and building codes to support urban reforms, not to mention squatter regulation and slum upgrading. In addition, cities today must provide accommodative measures, allowing for progressive construction, smaller plot sizes and multiple variants of land tenure with higher densities. Similarly, utility standards must be adjusted, and new development financing channels devised, in the face of inequity and exclusion.

Part One

Re-thinking
Urban Prosperity

© Ragma Images/Shutterstock.com

© Denis Mironov/Shutterstock.com

Conceptualizing Urban Prosperity

THE CITY IS THE HOME OF PROSPERITY

Cities are where human beings find satisfaction of basic needs and essential public goods. Where various products can be found in sufficiency and their utility enjoyed. Cities are also where ambitions, aspirations and other intangible aspects of life are realized, providing contentment and happiness and increasing the prospects of individual and collective well-being.

However, when prosperity is absent or restricted to some groups, when it is only enjoyed in some parts of the city, when it is used to pursue specific interests, or when it is a justification for financial gains for the few to the detriment of the majority, the city becomes the locus where the right to shared prosperity is claimed and fought for.

> **POLICY** It is in every city's interest to adopt organically integrated types of development and prosperity that transcend the narrow confines of an accumulation-driven model that benefits only a few to the detriment of the majority.

PROSPERITY: A MISPLACED CONCERN IN THE MIDST OF CRISES?

Never before has humankind as a whole faced cascading crises of all types as have affected it since 2008, from financial to economic to environmental to social to political. Soaring unemployment, food shortages and attendant price rises, strains on financial institutions, insecurity and political instability, among other crises, might well on their own call into question the relevance and even the viability of a report focused on prosperity. This proliferation of risks might even challenge the conventional notion of 'Cities as the Home of Prosperity', i.e. where, by definition, 'successful, flourishing, or thriving conditions' prevail.

Ill-balanced development notions and policies have meant that, instead of being the locus of opportunity and prosperity, cities all-too-often have become places of deprivation, inequality and exclusion. In too many parts of the developing world, unequal access to opportunities and resources has pushed vast numbers of people into *favelas*, *bidonvilles*, *katchi abadis* or *campamentos*, as slums are known. In Europe, new forms of social exclusion, marginalization and poverty are emerging, such as infrastructure-poor, immigrant poverty, young people at risk, and more vulnerable elderly.[1]

As people in the latter part of 2011 gathered in Cairo's Tahrir Square or Madrid's Puerta del Sol, in front of London's St Paul's cathedral or in New York's Zuccotti Park, they were not only demanding more equality and inclusion; they were also expressing solidarity with fellow citizens that belong with the '99 per cent' (the vast majority) as opposed to the 'one per cent' (those with vastly disproportionate shares of wealth and decision-making capacity). These movements highlighted the inherent risks of ill-balanced growth or development policies, and their failure to safeguard prosperity for all. Throughout history, cities as seats of power have served as stages for

> A focus on prosperity as conventionally understood seems, at best, an unnecessary luxury in a time of crisis. At worst prosperity can be seen as a harbinger of yet another single-minded pursuit of purely economic prosperity that might bring the global economy to the brink again.

4

Box 1.1.1

Crises, cities and prosperity

The financial crisis: Borrowing, borrowing, borrowing

Prominent scholars such as Joseph Stiglitz ascribe the 2008 financial crisis to rising income inequalities in countries around the world. In the face of stagnating real earnings, those households in the lower- and middle-income brackets were forced into more and more borrowing in order to maintain or improve living standards. With financiers experimenting with risky schemes at the other end of the credit chain, this situation led to a spate of defaults and, ultimately, the financial crash of 2008. The double irony of this crisis is that it originated in the efforts of a supposedly sophisticated financial system to give low-income categories a much-desired access to housing finance – and a foothold in prosperity.

The democratic crisis: 'We are the 99 per cent!'

The recent crisis is more than just an economic one. More fundamentally, it has exposed a number of risks to social justice, fairness, participation and, ultimately, democracy. Systematic decision-making in favour of those better-off is, in itself, a form of democratic deficit, and one that has led to popular movements like New York's *Occupy Wall Street*. The movement 'calls for a society organized around the needs, desires, dreams, of the 99 per cent, not the one per cent' The other major uprisings of 2011 – the Arab Spring in North Africa and the Middle East, and Spain's own Indignados – were also motivated by similar demands for better and deeper democracy as essential for overall prosperity. These protests highlighted the fact that economic growth was a necessary condition for prosperity, though insufficient on its own: social and political inclusion is vital for prosperity.

The environmental crisis: The convergence of climate change and urbanization

The current pattern of urbanization both in developed and developing countries converges on one and the same model: low density-based suburbanization. Land speculation is associated with indiscriminate conversion of rural land to urban uses in the peripheries; this phenomenon combines with a growing reliance on individual motor vehicles and new-fangled middle-class lifestyles to expand urban areas way beyond formal city boundaries. A variety of economic agents can typically be found behind this trend, including real estate developers, home- and road-builders, national and international chain stores, among others, more often than not with support from banks and finance houses. Wasteful expansion of cities in endless peripheries is a major factor behind climate change. Beyond the physical threats from climate change, some cities stand to face an array of additional risks related to the provision of basic services and public goods (water supply, physical infrastructure, transport, energy, etc.), affecting industrial production, local economies, assets and livelihoods. Climate change may have ripple effects across many sectors of urban life, affecting the potential for prosperity of the more vulnerable populations: women, youth, children and ethnic minorities.[2]

May 1 2012 saw protests in many cities around the globe. In New York City, labour union members marched in support of the Occupy Wall Street activists campaigning against the chaos in the financial sector.

© A Katz/Shutterstock.com

Box 1.1.2

Ghost towns, vacant homes: wasted prosperity

What sowed the seeds of the 2008 world financial crisis was an unusual combination of sustained economic growth and low interest rates. The resulting sense of prosperity and optimism might have been legitimate (some respected economists saw a 'new golden age' opening up), but in the USA and elsewhere the financial sector needed higher interest rates to maintain or boost profits. Home loans to low-income ('sub-prime') households provided an opportunity for higher yields, and the US guarantee mechanism made securities based on sub-prime home loans an attractive proposition for US and foreign investors – good returns and no apparent risk, especially when enhanced by sophisticated derivative instruments. The whole structure unravelled when low-income borrowers defaulted *en masse* on their badly structured home loans: interest payments stopped on both loans and bonds, which became largely worthless, the financial sector was destabilized around the world, a credit crunch began and a global recession with it.

This happened at a time when, in both developed and emerging countries, the numbers of built houses and mortgage loans had reached historic levels, in the process expanding peri-urban areas far beyond previous limits. As a result, the bursting of the property 'bubble' reverberated around the world, from San Francisco to Mexico to Dublin to Madrid to Cairo and to Shanghai.

In 2007, Spain and Ireland built many more houses than any other European country.[3] In Spain alone, it is estimated that some seven million units were built between 2001 and 2010, while the population grew 5.2 million during the same period,while over that same period, house prices more than doubled.[4] In Mexico, the housing sector grew 12 per cent in 2004, more than four times the country's overall growth rate that same year.[5] In Egypt, since the 1980s, many urban developments have sprung up on desert land. In the Greater Cairo area, for instance, eight cities in particular have become the focus of massive investment, speculative interest, territorial expansion and grandiose urban planning.[6]

Evidence shows that in nations like Angola, Egypt, Mexico or China, what had originally been planned as new housing opportunities for the medium- to low-income segments (including rural migrants in China) turned out as quality developments which high prices and dependence on new roads and motor vehicles made inaccessible to the initial targets. In these cases, the failure lay both in poor urban planning and the misidentification of the target population. Uncontrolled, quick-profit oriented property market growth has left behind sprawling, badly planned peri-urban developments where millions of housing units have remained vacant once the property bubble burst. In North America, repossessed houses represent masses of capital and ruined dreams, lying out there unused and useless, abandoned, wasted.

In Europe as a whole, Spain stands out with the highest number of vacant houses – with contrasted figures that refer to three up to six million units. In Ireland the celebrated 'Celtic Tiger' has left behind more than 2,800 'ghost estates' – urban developments where an important proportion of the houses are vacant or unfinished, according to a 2010 government survey.[7] In the United States, about 11 per cent were unoccupied in 2011.[8] The situation is not any different in Latin America. In Mexico, five million houses were vacant in 2010, or 14 per cent of the housing stock.[9] In Brazil, 6.1 million houses were vacant in 2010.[10] In China and Egypt, the situation is even more alarming with many developments or 'ghost towns' unoccupied or partially occupied.

Although data is scant, evidence shows that, in addition to vacant houses, China is no stranger to the 'ghost town' phenomenon either. For example, Kangbashi, a satellite town of Ordos, Inner Mongolia, was planned for one million but had a much smaller population in 2010;[11] with many of the houses remaining empty despite 90 per cent of them having been purchased.[12] And it would seem there are many other developments sub-occupied in China. For example, Chenggong, a newly developed area in the southern city of Kunming (Tianjin), remains poorly occupied five to 10 years after completion.[13] In urban Egypt, the proportion of vacant urban housing units is reported to be in excess of 20 to 30 per cent of the housing stock.[14]

Oversupply is a major factor behind housing vacancies. Property and land speculation results in unaffordable prices. Uncontrolled or permissive urban and regional planning (often linked to corruption) is another factor. Cultural factors can also come into play. In countries as diverse as Spain, Ireland and China, housing purchases for investment, together with a tradition of small-scale letting,[15] encourage owners to maintain vacant properties regardless of actual demand.

Around Cairo (as in countries like Mexico), lack of infrastructure, public services and social amenities in new suburban areas is another factor behind high vacancy rates, along with high commuting costs. Based on research by Mexico's National Housing Fund Institute for Workers (INFONAVIT),[16] it would appear that more than one third of vacancies in the country is related to lack of basic services, and another third to excessive commuting times to/from work, school etc., as also happens in China's own new towns. In Mexico, insecurity and inadequate housing designs are other factors, which also testify to poor overall planning. Easy credit has turned into a crunch and the fake prosperity associated with the property/housing 'bubble' leaves a legacy of evictions and indebtedness, instead of comfort and valuable capital, with a once thriving construction sector and millions of workers left to stall. Millions of housing units stand vacant while thousands of households are evicted from their homes because they default on mortgage payments. Lending institutions sit on vast stocks of vacant new homes with limited market value, while evicted or low-income households are consigned to inadequate, insecure housing conditions. In Spain, the number of evictions has tripled since 2007. In Ireland, vacant houses could be used to reduce the deficit of housing for those in need.

Box 1.1.3

When streets amplify claims: the 'Arab Spring'

When Mohamed Bouazisi, a 26-year-old street vendor in Sidi Bouzid (Tunisia), doused himself in petrol and scratched a match, little did he know that his tragic act would set ablaze a number of cities along the southern and eastern Mediterranean shores, in the process toppling some well-established governments. The unfortunate young man also shed the cruellest possible light on the punishing lack of socioeconomic opportunities many youths his age are so familiar with in that part of the world: a graduate who took to street vending in a bid to survive, Bouazisi had been arrested for lack of a permit and his goods destroyed.

This lack of perspectives highlights the ill-balanced type of 'prosperity' which this Report is looking to redress. Among other positive features, Tunisia is known both for having eradicated slums and for its young, well-educated workforce, but so far economic opportunities have been inequitably shared, to the sole benefit of a number of vested interests.[17] This is for lack of the political and other institutions that ensure inclusion, equal distribution of wealth among various groups, and respect for cultural diversity.

Bouazisi was one in the more than 100 million 15- to 29-year-old cohort who contribute up to 30 per cent to the Middle East and North African population.[18] This so-called 'youth bulge' in the region's demographic profile reflects the lag between rapidly declining mortality and a slower decrease in fertility rates. With the scarcity of (especially quality) jobs, average unemployment in the region – 25 per cent – is nearly double the worldwide rate of 13 per cent. As usual, averages conceal significantly higher numbers: in Algeria and the Palestinian Territories, unemployment is the plight of 40 per cent of the active population. In Algiers, Tunis, Cairo or Tripoli, more than 50 per cent of the unemployed are first-time job seekers – the highest of any region of the world. This reflects a significant mismatch between education (especially secondary) and labour markets.

In these capitals as in secondary cities and towns from January 2011 onwards, the street became the natural forum as the chain of protests spread across the region. Being spaces for flows and movement, streets and squares emerged as the privileged locus where people can do more than express grievances: they can forge identities and enlarge solidarities (including across borders). In this somewhat chaotic, spontaneous process, people come to recognize their mutual interests, shared feelings and aspirations. Cities leave their spatial imprints on the nature of social struggles, where politics evolves from a 'micro-' to a 'macro-dimensional' nature, transcending wealth, power and privilege. As Bouazisi might have hoped, what has come to be known as the 'Arab Spring' showed how cities can act as catalysts for cooperation and sharing.

protests and the recent social movements are no exception. Demographic concentrations in dense urban spaces allow critical masses of protestors to congregate and air new ideas, highlighting cities' role as sounding boards for positive social change. This points to another of the promises of a prosperous city – not just a more productive socioeconomic use of space and the built environment, but also one that safeguards the city's role as a public forum where plans and policies can be discussed and challenged for the sake of a more prosperous society.

CITIES: REMEDY TO THE GLOBAL CRISES

If anything, the recent crises have demonstrated that cities around the world are, to varying degrees of intensity, exposed at least as much to the destructive as to the more beneficial effects of international markets, including social and political repercussions. In this sense, these crises did more than expose systemic market failures: they also highlighted major imbalances at the core of economic policy-making.[19]

When responding to such crises, national macroeconomic policies definitely have a major role to play through countercyclical public expenditure, strengthening bank supervision and financial regulations, introducing progressive income taxation, and reinforcing worldwide financial governance mechanisms, among other solutions.

However, responses to global crises must also allow for a vigorous role for cities. So far, cities have been perceived as the 'engines' of national economies and there is no reason to depart from that view. Indeed, city authorities find themselves, at least notionally, in a position to boost production in the real sector of the economy at local level, with attendant employment and income generation. If urban responses to economic crises are to be effective on a local scale with positive regional or national repercussions ('multiplier effects'), then efficient, multi-way institutional, policy and budget linkages are required between all relevant tiers of government. In this respect, proper alignment of central and local government expenditures at city level can facilitate transfers and their effective use by city authorities.

Far from undermining the role of cities as 'engines' of national economic development, the recent worldwide crisis has highlighted the evolving nature of the risks against which urban spaces must safeguard themselves, and their populations, and the same goes with the effects of climate change. Municipal authorities must also be aware

Cities are a remedy to the global crises. They provide ready, flexible and creative platforms that can mitigate the effects of regional and global crises in a pragmatic, balanced and efficient way. Cities can act as the fora where the linkages, trust, respect and inclusiveness that are part of any remedy to the crisis can be built. Acting locally in different areas and spaces, urban responses to the crisis can be structured and included in national agendas for more efficiency, with better chances of flexible responses and more beneficial effects. Although not immune to the divisive partisanship and ideologies that can paralyze decision-making, cities find themselves in more privileged positions than national governments to negotiate and agree on responses with local stakeholders. They can forge new partnerships and local social pacts which, in turn, can strengthen national governments in the face of global challenges.

POLICY Cities can devise a number of safeguards against a variety of socioeconomic risks. Municipal authorities can prioritize expenditures on social security nets, local/regional infrastructure and other types of development, with a view to securing longer-term growth while stimulating consumption and/or employment in the short term.

POLICY Cities can also deploy safeguards against the risks international markets may bring to bear on local socioeconomic conditions, deploying redistributive policies in close collaboration with central government in order to reduce income gaps and other local structural problems.

China: busy traffic on one of Beijing's boulevards. Wide avenues such as this bring a sense of space to city centres but increasing wealth has led to a massive growth in private car use, with attendant congestion and increase in greenhouse gas emissions.

© Yu Yang/Shutterstock.com

Box 1.1.4

Cities and global crises

The mismanagement of urban economies and finance as epitomized by the 2008 housing finance crisis in the USA has reverberated around the world. The subsequent economic crunch has, among other consequences, caused a fall in migrant worker remittances, and fiscal retrenchment has forced cuts in public spending on infrastructure, health and education in many countries.

Urban areas around the world have distinctly felt the pinch, what with rising numbers of redundancies and declining demand for goods and services of all kinds. From automakers in Detroit to urban shopkeepers in Buenos Aires or Nairobi, to factory workers in Shanghai to farmers in Brazil or Burkina Faso, millions have found themselves caught short.

In contrast, the highly urbanized economies of Argentina, Brazil, Chile, Colombia and Mexico have generally responded better to the global slowdown than the United States or Europe, as they activated their urban economies through focused spending and credit, together with stronger 'safety nets' for more vulnerable households.

Latin America highlights the problem with conventional economic stimulus through additional government spending: these blanket policies pay no attention to the specific locations where economic problems are occurring, or where consumption requires stimulus for a quick reactivation of maximal multiplier effects. Outside Latin America, no government spending has specifically targeted cities, thereby ignoring the spatial configurations of national and local economies and, more particularly, the way agglomeration economies might be energized by additional public expenditure.

Over time, economic growth is closely associated with the urban share of the population, and in all countries in the world nowadays more than half of GDP emanates from urban areas. As economies, too, become more urban, the relationship strengthens between the efficiencies and productivity of agglomeration economies, on the one hand, and location on the other hand. The essence of the process of value creation is to bring factors of production together in time and space. When associated with higher densities and proximity, industrial agglomeration reduces production costs and stimulates consumption by an ever more affluent urban labour force. Research in Brazil has found that productivity increased roughly one per cent for every 10 per cent increase in the number of workers employed in an industry or a city. This means that if the number of workers in a city rose from 1,000 to 10,000, productivity would increase by a hefty factor of 90.[20] Lessons from decades of practice and programme assistance should be reflected, rather than patently ignored, in governments' fiscal stimulus policies. The single major lesson of development assistance is that not only do local conditions matter, but they also win at the end of the day. Far from supply/demand charts, the space in which economic behaviour actually occurs is none other than shops, markets, factories, where production, commerce, and consumption occur, and in households where purchase decisions are made.

The central issue for policy and strategy is how best to support cities' efforts to stimulate and sustain the economic multipliers needed to generate employment and incomes. In this respect, infrastructure is a necessary though not a sufficient condition, and that is why local economic development strategies must cut across sectors. Once incentives and other conditions for productivity are in place, the distribution and sale of goods and services are the next steps.

that safeguards against newly emerging risks can take all sorts of forms, including incentives (e.g., higher wages for low-income workers), benefits (healthcare or retirement income schemes) and trust (e.g., avoiding corruption, or fair dealings with organized civil society). These safeguards can complement those of a more tangible nature, such as urban rehabilitation and transport- or climate-related infrastructure, which preserve the mutual benefits of productivity and socioeconomic well-being for businesses and residents alike.

RE-THINKING URBAN PROSPERITY

A poverty-stricken plumber in Hyderabad (India), a factory worker in Bogotá (Colombia), a middle manager in Madrid (Spain), a businessman in Fortaleza (Brazil), a car mechanic in Nairobi (Kenya) – all five will have aspirations to prosperous lives. However, prosperity means different things to different people around the world. Whatever the individual perception, regardless of culture and civilization, prosperity refers to a sense of general and individual socioeconomic security for the immediate and foreseeable future, which comes with the fulfilment of other, non-material needs and aspirations.

Yet, the prevailing view continues to confine prosperity to the realm of economics, a restrictive view that shuts out other dimensions which are integral to human well-being and necessary for

UN-Habitat presents a fresh perspective on prosperity based on five dimensions – productivity, infrastructures, quality of life, equity and environmental sustainability.

POLICY A fresh approach to prosperity is needed, not just to respond to the effects of the crisis and safeguard against new risks, but also to steer the world towards economically, socially, politically and environmentally prosperous urban futures.

individual and collective fulfilment. If anything, the 2008 financial crisis has amplified the need to include other, non-economic dimensions in the understanding and measurement of prosperity.

This Report introduces a new gauge for the degree of prosperity in the cities of the world. As developed by UN-Habitat, the City Prosperity Index combines the five dimensions of prosperity as understood in this Report and as subsumed in measurable indicators. The index pinpoints individual cities' strengths and weaknesses, in the process suggesting where policy action can address imbalances.

Re-thinking prosperity in those terms requires a shift away from the current dominant perspective, which is outdated and unsustainable on many grounds with its combination of cheap fossil fuel, heavy dependence on the motor car, highly segmented urban forms, socially and economically segregated spaces, endless urban peripheries that consume land, resources and in many cases natural protected areas – and all largely steered by private, not public interest.

POLICY Shared urban prosperity puts people first, values the tangible and intangible aspects of development, promotes inclusive economic growth, protects human rights, ensures enabling equitable development, cares for the natural environment, reduces disaster risks and vulnerabilities for the poor and builds resilience to adverse forces of nature. This new city – the city of the 21st century – creates harmony between the five dimensions of prosperity and enhances the prospects of a better future.

POLICY The 'good', people-centred city of the 21st century stimulates local job creation, promotes social diversity, maintains a sustainable environment and recognizes the importance of public spaces. It is a city that is all encompassing and accessible to everyone.

POLICY The city of the 21st century transcends the form and functionality set in previous centuries, balancing lower energy costs with a smaller ecological footprint, a more compact form, greater heterogeneity and functionality, safeguards against new risks, a higher provision of public goods, and a more 'human scale', together with more creative spaces for imagination and social interaction.

Prosperity involves a forward-looking perspective, a widely shared basic aspiration. It is also a process, one which, through adequate actions, safeguards and practices, together with support from appropriate institutions, has the potential to improve individual and collective well-being. Looking beyond the economic or financial dimension, prosperity in this sense includes other vital dimensions such as quality of life, adequate infrastructures, equity and environmental sustainability. Prosperity is about raising living standards; extending the outreach and quality of the public sphere; and providing ease and convenience in life and work routines. It is about a sense of balance and sharing across social spheres or lifestyles and, more personally, a sense of shared security, efficiency, comfort and aesthetics.

Those living in prosperous cities enjoy the benefits of standard public goods such as educational opportunities, health services, mobility, a safe environment and good quality physical capital, including adequate public spaces.[21] Similarly, prosperous cities safeguard residents against socioeconomic marginalization, contributing to a sense of belonging and 'social cohesion'. Moreover, prosperous cities come with positive side-effects in the form of non-market goods which, with well-devised safeguards from public authorities, can be made accessible to everyone. For example, European cities can differ greatly in terms of per capita consumption of *private* goods, but then not so much in terms of per capita consumption of *non-market* goods; this goes to show that prosperity, indeed, is not only about money. For instance, a resident of Frankfurt-am-Main, Germany, may enjoy a much higher income and consumption of private goods than fellow countrymen in Freiburg or Jena; still, each in their respective city will likely have access to the same amounts of non-market goods (e.g., pleasant urban landscapes, thanks to adequate planning/preservation policies). It is not uncommon for cities with lower incomes to provide higher amounts of non-market goods.[22] Prosperity is strongly linked to the production of public goods.

CONCEPTUALIZING PROSPERITY: THE UN-HABITAT APPROACH

Prosperity implies success, wealth, thriving conditions, and well-being as well as opportunity. In any urban setting, a key question will arise: What are the essential conditions and elements that are required for a city to thrive, or for an urban area to be described as prosperous, or for the well-being of the population? Put differently, what are the manifestations or outcomes of a prosperous city? In general terms, a prosperous city offers a profusion of public goods and develops policies and actions for a sustainable use of, and equitable access to, 'commons'.[23] More specifically, several elements which come to mind guide what constitutes the UN-Habitat conceptualization of urban prosperity.

First, a prosperous city contributes to economic growth through productivity, generating the income and employment that afford adequate living standards for the whole population. Second, a prosperous city deploys the infrastructure, physical assets and amenities – adequate water, sanitation, power supply, road network, information and communications technology, etc. – required to sustain both the population and the economy. Third, prosperous cities provide the social services – education, health, recreation, safety and security, etc. – required for improved living standards, enabling the population to maximize individual potential and lead fulfilling lives. Fourth, a city is only prosperous to the extent that poverty and inequalities are minimal. No city can claim to be prosperous when large segments of the population live in abject poverty and deprivation. This involves reducing the incidence of slums and new forms of poverty. Prosperous cities are equitable and socially inclusive. The benefits and opportunities that come with a prosperous city are equitably (re)distributed. A prosperous city ensures gender equality, protects the rights of minority and vulnerable groups, and ensures civic participation by all in the social, political and cultural spheres.

Fifth, the creation and (re)distribution of the benefits of prosperity do not destroy or degrade the environment;

instead, the city's natural assets are preserved for the sake of sustainable urbanization.

THE 'WHEEL OF URBAN PROSPERITY'

Prosperity, as defined by UN-Habitat, is a social construct that materializes in the realm of human actions. It builds deliberately and conscientiously on the objective conditions prevailing in a city at any time, wherever located and however large or small. It is a broader, wide-ranging notion that has to do with well-balanced, harmonious development in an environment of fairness and justice.

As described above, prosperity takes in all urban functions as subsumed in five main categories. Since shared, balanced development is a crucial feature of prosperity, none of the dimensions must prevail over the others and all must be kept roughly 'equal' – for the sake of a smooth 'ride' on the path of prosperity. In practice, of course, it is a rare city where the five dimensions will be found equal at any point in time, and this is where policy interventions will be called for, as suggested graphically by the profile of a city's specific 'prosperity index'. For instance, infrastructure may be well advanced but inaccessible to large portions of the population, therefore compromising the notion of equity. In other, frequent situations, a city may be economically efficient, enhancing job opportunities, but neglecting the natural environment.

Since socioeconomic conditions keep changing on a local and a broader scale, they will have an effect on one or more of the five dimensions of prosperity, and it will be for policy interventions to restore the balance. In

Table 1.1.1	
Defining a prosperous city	
A prosperous city is one that provides	
Productivity	Contributes to economic growth and development, generates income, provides decent jobs and equal opportunities for all through effective economic policies and reforms.
Infrastructure development	Provides adequate infrastructure – water, sanitation, roads, information and communication technology – in order to improve living standards and enhance productivity, mobility and connectivity.
Quality of life	Enhances the use of public spaces for the sake of community cohesion and civic identity, and guarantees individual and material safety and security.
Equity and social inclusion	Ensures equitable (re)distribution of the benefits of prosperity, reduces poverty and the incidence of slums, protects the rights of minority and vulnerable groups, enhances gender equality, and ensures civic participation in the social, political and cultural spheres.
Environmental sustainability	Values the protection of the urban environment and natural assets while ensuring growth, pursues energy efficiency, reduces pressure on surrounding land and natural resources, reduces environmental losses through creative, environment-enhancing solutions.

this endeavour, city authorities will find that the various interlinkages and interdependencies between the five dimensions can also be of a positive nature. For instance, provision of water and sanitation in informal settlements will improve both equity and quality of life, and even the environment. This points to the 'natural' or 'spontaneous' interdependencies between the five dimensions along the outer rim of the wheel. These can also be strengthened with a multiplier effect through deliberate, well-targeted interventions through the 'hub' of the wheel, i.e., the combined power functions at work in any city. For instance, building a school and a covered market next to a poor area is likely to have multiplier effects across the five dimensions of shared prosperity.

This goes to show that far from some new 'model' or 'utopia' or branding/marketing technique, UN-Habitat's 'wheel of prosperity' symbolizes the well-balanced development of the five dimensions, the current condition of which is graphically represented in the Wheel of Urban Prosperity (see below). The 'outer rim' absorbs the cumulative forces transmitted through the 'spokes' – the five dimensions of prosperity. At the centre is the 'hub' – the local urban power functions, with four interrelated roles: (i) ensuring the prevalence of *public* over any other kind of interest; (ii) controlling the direction, pace and momentum of the 'wheel'; (iii) ensuring the balanced development of the five 'spokes' and associated synergies; and (iv) in a two-way relationship, absorbing and amortising any 'shocks'

Figure 1.1.1

The Wheel of Urban Prosperity

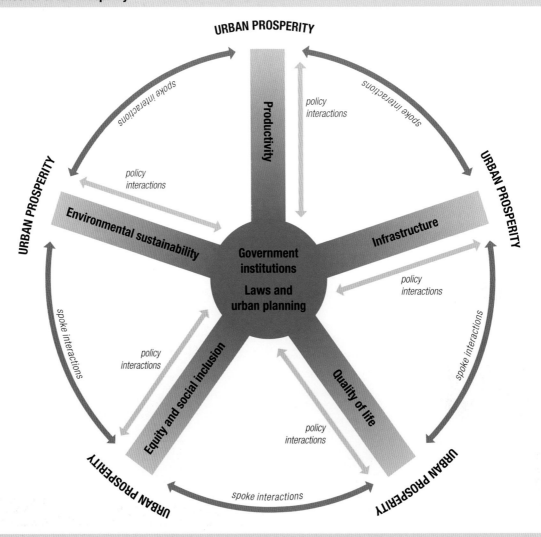

Source: UN-Habitat, 2012.

transmitted by the 'spokes'. The 'hub' brings together the power functions (e.g., laws, regulations and institutions, urban planning, civil society, trade associations, dedicated agencies, etc.) associated with the five 'spokes'. In this role, the 'hub' represents human agency in all its embodiments. It holds the five 'spokes' together and endeavours to maintain their balance and symmetry over time.

MEASURING PROSPERITY: ATTEMPTS, FAILURES AND PROGRESS

Prosperity remains one of humankind's most enduring pursuits across time and space. But it is only in the past few decades that decision-makers, academics, practitioners and populations have started to measure this important dimension of human development. This has been a journey of learning, trial and error. The adage *'what gets measured, gets done'* has injected a sense of urgency in the pursuit not just of prosperity *per se*, but also of an operational definition complete with specific indicators.

More than 70 years ago in 1937, the Nobel-winning metric of gross domestic product (GDP) was purported to be the 'mother of all statistics', capturing the notion of prosperity through any country's total production of goods and services. Although GDP spread rapidly and was widely accepted for decades, it is becoming more and more apparent that this aggregate is too narrow to provide the accurate measure of a society's overall well-being today. In

> The 'hub' is made up of the local urban power functions. These encompass the public sector (municipal and other institutions/agencies, as well as laws and regulations) and the non-public sector (civil society, private business etc.). They combine in a variety of ways according to local needs and conditions, with the synergies between them resulting in innovative institutional or policy practice that contributes to shared prosperity.

1972, the king of Bhutan declared he was interested in measuring 'Gross National Happiness' (GNH). In 1990, US economist Mahbub ul-Haq convinced future Nobel laureate Amartya Sen to create 'an index as vulgar as GDP but more relevant to our own lives'.[24] In 2006, China developed its own 'Green GDP Index', which seriously challenged the validity of the standard aggregate, once environmental aspects were factored in.[25] In 2009, Joseph Stiglitz called for an end to 'GDP fetishism' and, one year later, the British government announced that it would, for the first time, survey happiness in addition to purely economic measures.[26]

> **POLICY** The city of the 21st century seeks to achieve integrated prosperity, making the 'wheel' well balanced with mutually reinforcing spokes in a dynamic hub.

Fetching water in Debre Zeit city, Ethiopia. Quality of life and prosperity require an urban growth with commensurate infrastructure and basic services.

© Eduardo Lopez Moreno

Prosperity is a more complex notion, one that cannot be captured through straightforward indices that measure how much money people earn or how many cars they own. A 'prosperous' life includes other non-material, non-tangible dimensions, like having a voice in shaping the future of one's city, having meaningful relationships, belonging to supportive communities, and having the resources and capabilities to transform your dreams into concrete realities.

The ideas, aspirations and challenges of this early 21st century are different from those of the Great Depression era that was at the origin of the GDP measure. Ecological and environmental concerns have become central priorities for the way we shape our contemporary and future societies. Protection of human rights, advancement of democratic values – including women's empowerment – and respect of fundamental principles such as dignity and tolerance – all of these are part of a more inclusive and prosperous future. Equity is essential to higher prosperity and sustained urban development. Currently, GDP does not reflect any of these critical conditions.

The search for alternative measures of prosperity is an unprecedented and cutting-edge scientific endeavour. Studies have shown that even though income is an important determinant of subjective well-being, wealthier countries are no happier than poorer ones. 'Life satisfaction has remained more or less unchanged in most advanced economies over several decades in spite of significant economic growth'.[27] While income per capita has tripled in the USA since 1950, the percentage of people describing themselves as 'happy' has barely increased at all, and has even declined since the mid-1970s. 'In Japan, there has been little change in life-satisfaction over several decades. In the UK the percentage reporting themselves 'very happy' declined from 53 per cent in 1957 to 36 per cent today, even though real incomes have more than doubled'.[28] The so-called 'happiness paradox' has been empirically demonstrated by economist Richard Easterlin in a study of 19 developed and developing countries.[29] Many other studies have since corroborated what is now known as the 'Easterlin paradox', leading some countries and institutions to search for alternative indicators to measure societal progress.

Recent efforts have attempted to include these other dimensions of prosperity for a more accurate representation of societal progress. Table 1.1.2 presents a summary of these methods and approaches.

Simple pleasures, such as a stroll along the streets of Kathmandu, Nepal, indicate real, everyday prosperity.
© Dhoxax/Shutterstock.com

The notion of prosperity is still largely viewed as belonging in the realm of economics. However, it is also acknowledged that prosperity goes beyond material well-being and economic growth. Trying to integrate other tangible and less tangible human dimensions of development such as well-being and quality of life has been an ongoing story for more than 40 years, with efforts to create new matrices and approaches that add nuance to standard GDP.

Table 1.1.2
Measuring progress and prosperity

Human Development Index (HDI) **United Nations Development Programme** 1990	HDI combines indicators of life expectancy, educational attainment and income into a composite human development index. It is a single statistic that serves as a frame of reference for both social and economic development, ranking countries by level of "human development".
Genuine Progress Indicator (GPI) **Think-tank Redefining Progress** 1994	GPI was developed as an alternative system to GDP measurement. It is used as a more inclusive type of economics based on 'True Cost' economics, looking how increased production of goods and services has actually resulted in the improvement of welfare or well-being.
Measuring Sustainable Development **UNECE, OECD, EUROSTAT** 2005	This particular measure is structured around the concept of capital, as measured under four main dimensions – economic, natural, human and social – that all pertain to sustainability. The idea is to make this concept operational for public policies.
Prosperity Index **Regional Research Institute, USA** 2006	This index measures regional economic prosperity and tracks performance at city level, assessing competitiveness and identifying opportunities to improve business. Although based on economic prosperity, the index includes three main components: business, people and location.
Commission on the measurement of economic performance and social progress, France 2008	This Commission proposed to shift emphasis from measuring economic production to measuring people's well-being, against a background of sustainability. The Commission concluded that well-being is better assessed on the basis of income and consumption rather than production.
Legatum Prosperity Index **Legatum Institute, UK** 2008	The index purports to measure national prosperity based on wealth and well-being, using a composite indicator. It ranks 110 countries based on eight 'pillars of prosperity': economic conditions, entrepreneurship and opportunity, governance, education, health, safety and security, personal freedom, and social capital.
Redefining Prosperity **UN Sustainable Development Commission** 2009	Prosperity is redefined based on three aspects: a) fulfilment of material needs; b) the social and psychological dimensions that contribute to an enhanced sense of identity, meaning, belonging and hope; c) individual capability to flourish in more prosperous environments.
National Well-Being Accounts Index **New Economics Foundation, UK** 2009	The index measures social progress based on subjective well-being. It combines two types of data: personal (emotional well-being, satisfying life, vitality, resilience, self-esteem) and social well-being (supportive relationships, trust and belonging).
Global City Index (GCI) **Foreign Policy Magazine, Kearney & Chicago Council on Global Affairs** 2010	The GCI measures the international standing of cities along five dimensions: business activity, human capital, information exchange, cultural experience and political engagement. The index results in competitiveness rankings of cities in terms of business opportunities and economic innovation.
Sustainable Development Index **Department for Environment, Food and Rural Affairs, UK** 2010	This index combines four sets of data: sustainable consumption and production, climate change and energy, protecting natural resources and enhancing the environment, and creating sustainable communities. The index is a composite of a total 68 indicators.

Various sources, compiled by UN-Habitat, 2012.

Box 1.1.5

Perceptions, feelings and opinions about prosperity

Most cities nowadays depend on objective variables to guide policy-making. These variables are based on 'hard' statistics and 'cardinal' basic indicators, including inflation rates, gross domestic product (GDP) and foreign (direct or indirect) investment. Yet, for the sake of better-balanced policies, more and more cities are recognizing the need to include subjective variables for better policy-making, based on residents' perceptions, feelings and experiences – which are referred to as 'ordinal' measures. Perception surveys are particularly important in the current aftermath of a crisis that has eroded the trust of a vast majority of citizens in a broad range of institutions including business, the media and government.

Perception and customer satisfaction surveys can provide important signals, views and opinions of what citizens want or expect from political leaders – and they can do so almost in 'real time'. At a time when cities and governments find themselves under immense financial constraints, and important decisions must be made with limited information, the potential benefits of perception surveys have never looked higher. Using a variety of metrics, many cities have commissioned such surveys on major issues and used them to establish policy priorities. For instance, the City of Cape Town, South Africa, has commissioned an annual, independent customer satisfaction survey to gauge the perceptions of residents and businesses with regard to municipal service delivery. The survey is conducted through both face-to-face interviews and telephone conversations.[30] Such perception surveys provide an easy, proactive and cost-effective way of securing feedback from residents and business.[31]

When governments use these perceptions as a 'diagnostic' to identify, and respond to, areas of concern, they can reclaim legitimacy among the population. In a related development, a UN-Habitat perception survey of local experts (2011) recently revealed that a majority perceived that municipal authorities in 50 representative cities considered equity and environmental sustainability as the least important dimensions of prosperity, by comparison with productivity, quality of life and infrastructure. These findings suggest that city authorities must pay more attention to the equity dimension of prosperity in response to residents' concerns.

Perception surveys can alert public authorities not only to what citizens need and value, but also to what citizens want from different tiers of government – local, district/provincial or national. Since prosperity takes multiple dimensions, some tiers of government may find themselves in better positions than others when it comes to effective delivery. Regarding quality of life – in this Report, one of the five dimensions of prosperity – the experts surveyed by UN-Habitat survey agreed that, of all the different tiers of government, local authorities should be expected to implement adequate policies in areas like affordable public transport, well-planned public spaces, sports and recreational facilities, security and safety, and local socioeconomic development.[32] Indeed, those experts consider that local authorities are generally best placed to provide for safe, inclusive and environmentally sound neighbourhoods for improved overall quality of life.

Objective statistics and subjective perceptions may tell different stories, but together they represent an important metric of prosperity. For example, cities with steep income inequality (i.e., statistically, with Gini coefficients of 0.5 or higher) do not only reflect institutional and structural failures in income distribution, but their risks of social unrest are also higher. These risks can be further exacerbated by social and spatial perceptions of inequality, which can be heightened by belief systems and cultural norms. Unmet demands for a more balanced distribution of the benefits of prosperity can lead to popular frustration, and even to unrest. Conversely, a low degree of human development will bring a population to adapt their expectations to what they believe is possible in their circumstances.[33] Given these caveats, governments must combine subjective perceptions with objective variables to develop a more accurate understanding of the best ways of advancing urban prosperity. Taken together, 'soft' indicators (including perception surveys) and statistical measures ('hard' indicators) enable policy- and decision-makers better to understand both the (social and economic) state their cities are in, and the state (of mind) the populations are in.

THE UN-HABITAT 'CITY PROSPERITY INDEX'

Cities can take different paths to prosperity. UN-Habitat views development as a non-linear, non-sequential and complex process and recognizes that development paths are differentiated and unique.[34] Still, actions and policies implemented by governments to enhance prosperity and the outcomes of these policies can be measured to provide an indication of how solid or weak are the prosperity factors available to any individual urban area.

UN-Habitat's 'City Prosperity Index' (CPI) does not only provide indices and measurements; it also enables decision-makers to identify opportunities and potential areas of action along the path of prosperity. The CPI includes various indices and indicators that are relevant to urban areas and important for prosperity-oriented public policy-making.

Being based on the UN-Habitat concept of prosperity, the CPI includes the five dimensions (the 'spokes' in the 'wheel') of urban prosperity. The CPI includes various dimensions

Box 1.1.6

Cities and human development

Cities with high HDI values appear both as engines of positive change and as beneficiaries of prosperity. In the developing world, some urban areas are becoming so prosperous that they have closed the gap with, or even surpassed, the HDI of cities in developed nations. For example, Seoul, South Korea, features a HDI as high as 0.911, higher than that of many European cities, particularly the southern and eastern regions where HDI readings, though high, come under 0.900 in cities such as Lisbon, Athens or Warsaw.

UN-Habitat analysis shows that some cities in the developing world are becoming more prosperous (with higher HDI values), reflecting very significant progress on health and education, and at times even in the absence of sustained economic growth.

City and National HDI values

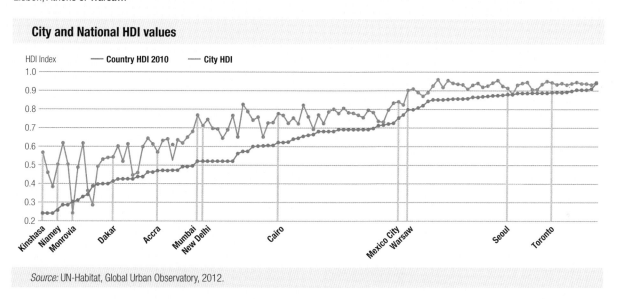

Source: UN-Habitat, Global Urban Observatory, 2012.

partially covered in other indices such as the Green City Index,[35] the Ecological City Index, and the Livable City Index. Each is further disaggregated into various variables and sub-indices. UN-Habitat has adopted an incremental approach to the development of this index. Two of the dimensions – productivity and quality of life – correspond to components of the Human Development Index (HDI), and have been used to compute the 'City Human Development Index' (CHDI). The three other dimensions – infrastructure, environmental sustainability and equity – are made of various key indicators as indicated in Table 1.1.3. Although more refinement is still needed in terms of what indicators are included in the index and the respective weightings thereof, those that have been selected offer the possibility of disaggregating the different dimensions of prosperity, in the process identifying policy intervention areas.[36]

Although in many cases the prosperity of a city will go hand in hand with that of the country, significant variations in CPI measures can be found in cities in the same country, and this goes to show that *national*

aggregates do not necessarily reflect what happens in different *regions* or *cities*. Most existing prosperity indices provide estimations for countries only (see Table 1.1.2). By comparison, the UN-Habitat City Prosperity Index is unique in the world for two reasons: (i) it focuses on individual *cities*, as opposed to countries, and (ii) it is concerned with prosperity as measured across *five dimensions*, of which the local economy is only one, as opposed to the sole business environment. The resulting CPI values can be regrouped in six distinct brackets that range from cities with '*very solid*' prosperity factors to those where those factors are found to be '*very weak*'.[37]

The Human Development Index (HDI) is typically higher in cities compared with relevant national averages. Indeed, cities are in general richer than the rest of any country. However, differences between city and country HDI measures are much steeper in nations with lower national HDI measures.

Table 1.1.3	
The UN-Habitat City Prosperity Index	
Dimensions	**Definitions/variables**
Productivity	The productivity index is measured through the city product, which is composed of the variables capital investment, formal/informal employment, inflation, trade, savings, export/import and household income/consumption. The city product represents the total output of goods and services (value added) produced by a city's population during a specific year (details of the methodology can be found in the CPI technical report).
Quality of life	The quality of life index is a combination of four sub-indices: education, health, safety/security, social capital and public space. The sub-index education includes literacy, primary, secondary and tertiary enrolment. The sub-index health includes life expectancy, under-five mortality rates, HIV/AIDS, morbidity and nutrition variables.
Infrastructure development	The infrastructure development index combines two sub-indices: one for infrastructure, and another for housing. The infrastructure sub-index includes: connection to services (piped water, sewerage, electricity and ICT), waste management, knowledge infrastructure, health infrastructure, transport and road infrastructure. The housing sub-index includes building materials and living space.
Environmental sustainability	The environmental sustainability index is made of four sub-indices: air quality (PM10), CO_2 emissions, energy and indoor pollution.
Equity and social inclusion	The equity and social inclusion index combines statistical measures of inequality of income/consumption (Gini coefficient) and social and gender inequality of access to services and infrastructure.

In broad terms, the classification of cities by CPI values results in regional brackets, with various cities in the developed world featuring solid prosperity factors (CPI: 0.900 or higher), with a majority of African cities with very weak readings constituting the last two groups (CPI: 0.600 or below). In between, a large number of Asian and Latin American cities make up the third and fourth groups (with CPI values of 0.700–0.799 and 0.600–0.699, respectively).

Cities with very solid prosperity factors (0.900 and above): In the world's most prosperous cities the five 'spokes' are well developed overall, with very little variations among them. Urban power functions such as good governance, urban planning, laws, regulations and institutional frameworks ensure that no

particular dimension of prosperity gains prevalence to the detriment of the others. Cities with very solid prosperity factors feature high volumes of goods and services as well

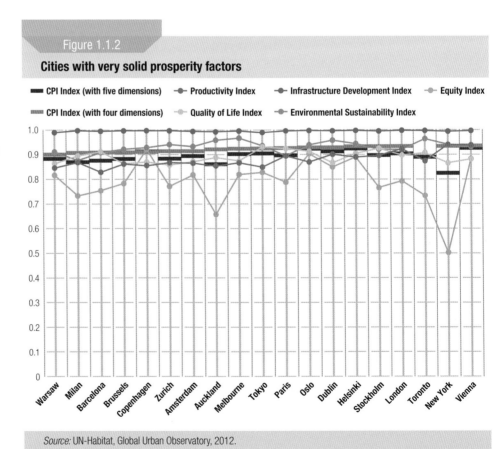

Figure 1.1.2

Cities with very solid prosperity factors

- CPI Index (with five dimensions)
- CPI Index (with four dimensions)
- Productivity Index
- Quality of Life Index
- Infrastructure Development Index
- Environmental Sustainability Index
- Equity Index

Source: UN-Habitat, Global Urban Observatory, 2012.

18

as strong economic fundamentals and high productivity. Their populations live longer and are well educated. Infrastructures are available and the environment is well managed. These cities are well governed and ensure safe, secure environments. It is clear that the five 'spokes' of urban prosperity are kept together in balance and at a right pace by a 'hub' that has the collective interest as its core.

All the cities in this group feature very high Gross National Incomes (GNI) per capita (from US$ 25,478 for New Zealand to US$ 58,810 for Norway) and they produce a substantial share of the country's GDP (e.g., Brussels – admittedly an exception – contributes as much as 46 per cent of Belgium's GDP). The economic power of some of these cities is comparable to that of many national economies. Estimated GDP equivalents in Tokyo and New York are similar to those of Canada or Spain, while London's GDP is higher than that of Sweden or Switzerland.

When the equity index is included in the CPI, the findings show that urban equity and prosperity are closely linked: not unsurprisingly, cities that do well on the first four dimensions of prosperity (with very solid prosperity factors) seem to be more equitable. In most cities of this group, inequality is relatively low, as reflected in low Gini coefficients (typically below 0.4, the exception being New York where inequality is significantly steeper (0.5)). When the equity dimension is taken into consideration, the CPI remains high for all cities (i.e., above 0.800), but only half remain with 'very solid' prosperity factors (i.e., CPI above 0.900).

Cities with solid prosperity factors – first category (CPI: 0.800–0.899): Cities in this bracket feature high CPI values. The five 'spokes' of prosperity are connected, generating a self-reinforcing, cumulative momentum along the path of prosperity. The minute variations between the 'spokes' is evidence of the efficiency of the 'hub', i.e., relatively strong institutions,

POLICY Despite their high production of goods and services, European cities are experiencing many crises –financial, employment and housing, among others – and it is expected that their respective CPI values will reflect this in the near future.

responsive legal and regulatory frameworks and large availability of public goods. Cities in Southern and Eastern Europe such as Lisbon, Athens, Warsaw, Budapest, Prague, Bucharest and Moscow feature in this bracket, along with others in Latin America and Asia: São Paulo, Mexico City, Almaty (Kazakhstan), Shanghai, Seoul and Ankara.

Cities with solid prosperity factors belong to countries with different stages of economic development and different HDIs, with Kazakhstan featuring the highest (0.884) and China, Turkey and Brazil the lowest (0.663, 0.679 and 0.699, respectively).

However, it is important to note that high inequalities in Moscow, Mexico City and São Paulo interfere with their performance in terms of prosperity. When the equity index is included in the CPI, both cities score below 0.800. This suggests that, although prosperity factors remain on the whole solid, they are somewhat weaker. While inequality is

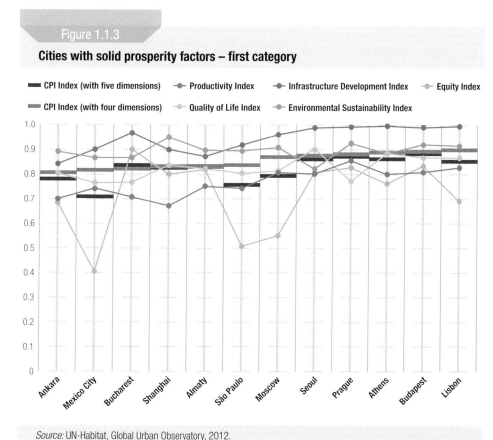

Figure 1.1.3

Cities with solid prosperity factors – first category

- CPI Index (with five dimensions)
- CPI Index (with four dimensions)
- Productivity Index
- Quality of Life Index
- Infrastructure Development Index
- Environmental Sustainability Index
- Equity Index

Source: UN-Habitat, Global Urban Observatory, 2012.

19

POLICY Cities in emerging economies such as Brazil or China combine high economic growth and strong infrastructure, and are expected to move faster along the path of prosperity – but then, for the sake of balanced development, they must tackle inequalities and environmental degradation. They also must look to improve quality of life through more ample provision of public goods.

historically entrenched in most Latin American cities, it is a recent phenomenon in Russia, in the extended aftermath of economic liberalization.

Cities with solid prosperity factors – second category (CPI: 0.700–0.799): This group is heterogeneous, with some cities showing a 'less coordinated', ill-balanced development in the 'spokes'. This comes as the result of institutions, legal and regulatory frameworks and urban management practices that are in the course of consolidation, and this is why they cannot hold together all the elements of the 'wheel' to operate with stability. Heterogeneity is also related to the stage of development of the relevant countries. Measured by HDI readings, significant variations occur between countries like Jordan (0.884) and Indonesia (0.600), for instance. Interestingly, the capital cities of these two countries do not feature such extreme variations in their respective HDIs (0.810 for Amman and 0.755 for Jakarta).

However, it is important to note that inequality is inconsistent with prosperity

as understood in this Report. When the equity index is included in the CPI, Cape Town and Johannesburg (which both feature very high Gini coefficients) drop from the bracket of cities with 'solid' prosperity factors and join the 'weak' or even 'very weak' group, with CPI values of 0.590 and 0.479 respectively.

Most of the cities in this group are located in Asia: Amman, Bangkok, Hanoi, Yerevan, Beijing, Jakarta and Manila. Four African cities also feature solid prosperity factors: Cape Town, Johannesburg, Cairo and Casablanca. Kyiv in Ukraine is the only city in Eastern Europe.

Box 1.1.7

Promising African cities

Among the 20 African cities included in UN-Habitat's CPI sample, Cape Town, Johannesburg, Cairo and Casablanca are the only ones featuring solid prosperity factors. Cairo's current political turmoil highlights the need for a more integrated pathway and more balanced growth with some dimensions (quality of life and infrastructure) progressing much faster than others (equity and social inclusion). Morocco, on the contrary, has embraced political change with a new constitution that enhances civil liberties and expands the notion of prosperity, which stand to benefit Casablanca and other cities. South African cities have experienced significant economic growth, but in the past two decades life expectancy has declined substantially, affecting quality of life.

Figure 1.1.4

Cities with solid prosperity factors – second category

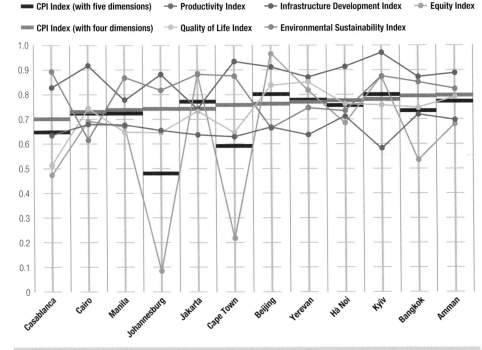

Source: UN-Habitat, Global Urban Observatory, 2012.

Cities with moderate prosperity factors (CPI: 0.600–0.699): The difference between 'solid' and 'moderate' prosperity factors lies in wider discrepancies among the values of the various components. This points to institutional and structural failures, as the 'hub' fails to keep the 'spokes' at a relatively same 'length'. Cities with less balanced development feature contrasted patterns, with a neat divide between rich and poor.

In Nairobi, prosperity is compromised by steep inequality (Gini coefficient: 0.59), causing its CPI value to drop from 'moderate' to 'weak' (0.673 to 0.593).

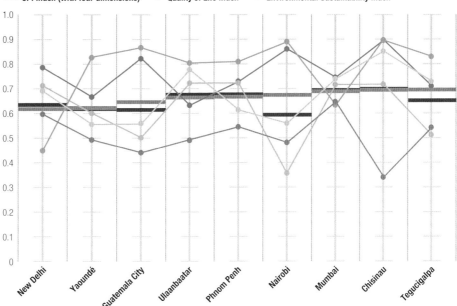

Figure 1.1.5

Cities with moderate prosperity factors

Source: UN-Habitat, Global Urban Observatory, 2012.

Cities with weak prosperity factors (CPI: 0.500–0.599): In most cities with weak or very weak prosperity factors, much remains to be done in terms of quality of life, infrastructure and the environment in most of the cities in this bracket. Production of goods and services is still too low, a reflection of underdevelopment. Historic structural problems, chronic inequality of opportunities, widespread poverty, inadequate capital investment in public goods, and lack of pro-poor social programmes are critical factors behind such low degrees of prosperity.

The city product of African cities in this bracket is low, as are the ratings for quality of life and infrastructure. Most of these cities perform better on the environment indicator (low emissions of fine particles (PM10)). Recent progress in Ghana in the economic and political

> Most of the cities in this bracket – Tegucigalpa, Nairobi, Phnom Penh, Ulaanbaatar, Guatemala City, Yaoundé, Mumbai and New Delhi – feature low HDIs (below 0.62). While in most cities a moderate CPI value is associated with a low city product, in the case of the two Indian cities the low CPIs mostly reflect poor environmental conditions.

Box 1.1.8

Low production, highly available public goods

Chisinau, the capital of Moldova, features a very low city product (0.34) that is almost half those of Mumbai (0.645) or New Delhi (0.596). Still, this combines with very high readings for quality of life (0.85), infrastructure (0.895) and clean environment (0.894), similar to those for much richer cities like Auckland, Brussels, London or New York. With a very modest economic base, the city has been able to deliver sufficient public goods to reach a moderate degree of prosperity. This goes to show that various dimensions of urban prosperity can be deployed even when economic growth remains relatively weak.

spheres looks certain to improve the CPI value for Accra, which at the moment is low (0.533) due to poor economic performance (0.347). Addis Ababa features relatively low in all CPI components, and this relative uniformity reflects a fair balance among the 'spokes' (0.52 on average). The city continues to make progress, thanks to higher investment in infrastructure and construction, manufacturing and tertiary activities. This in turn paves the way for job creation, and it is for central government to ensure that this economic model, which involves several dimensions of prosperity, retains both momentum and good synchronization.

Various cities/countries in this group have recently been marred by conflicts, political instability or economic crisis. The city product of Harare (0.246), not long ago a very vibrant economic centre, is almost as low as that of post-conflict cities like Monrovia (0.048), Antananarivo (0.171) or Conakry (0.133). In 2002, Zimbabwe recorded the lowest slum prevalence of the region, and one of the lowest of all the developing world (four per cent); poor governance, political instability and massive housing evictions in 2005 have raised that percentage to 17 per cent, mainly due to overcrowding; and yet, Harare features high infrastructure development (0.899), similar to that of emerging economy cities like Ankara, Manila, Mexico City or Mumbai. Quality of life in Harare is also very low, reflecting a dramatic reduction in life expectancy (to 1970s levels). Similar declines are also observed in the Democratic Republic of Congo, Lesotho, Swaziland or Zambia.

It is important to note that inequality further weakens the CPI values for Lagos, Harare and Lusaka. When the equity index is included in the CPI, all three cities move from 'weak' to 'very weak' prosperity factors (below 0.500).

Cities with very weak prosperity factors (CPI below 0.500): Cities in this bracket feature contrasted patterns among the sub-indices in the CPI. For some, the dispersion of index values across the 'spokes' reflects institutional and

The bulk of this bracket can be found in Africa: Abidjan, Accra, Addis Ababa, Dakar, Dar es Salaam, Harare, Kampala, Lagos and Lusaka. Also included are Dhaka, Kathmandu and La Paz.

Recycling is a vital service in modern cities.

© EGD/Shutterstock.com

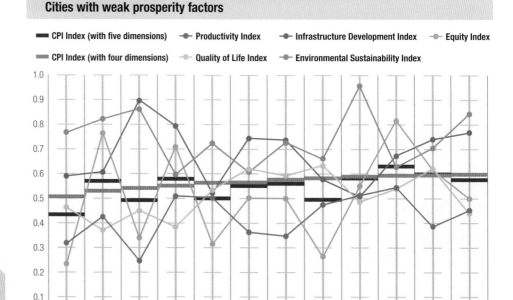

Figure 1.1.6

Cities with weak prosperity factors

- CPI Index (with five dimensions)
- CPI Index (with four dimensions)
- Productivity Index
- Quality of Life Index
- Infrastructure Development Index
- Environmental Sustainability Index
- Equity Index

Source: UN-Habitat, Global Urban Observatory, 2012.

22

Figure 1.1.7

Cities with very weak prosperity factors

- ▬ CPI Index (with five dimensions)
- ▬ CPI Index (with four dimensions)
- —●— Infrastructure Development Index
- —●— Environmental Sustainability Index
- —●— Productivity Index
- —○— Quality of Life Index
- —●— Equity Index

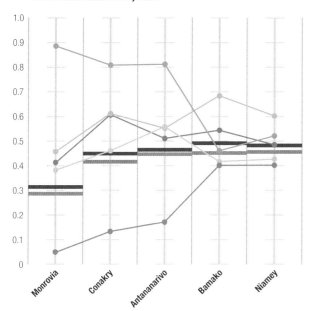

Source: UN-Habitat, Global Urban Observatory, 2012.

structural problems. For others, the five dimensions of prosperity do converge, if at very low values, a hallmark of dysfunctional systems, institutional failures, sluggish economic growth as well as widespread poverty and destitution.

There are only five cities with very weak prosperity factors (CPI below 0.500) in UN-Habitat's worldwide sample. The common feature of cities with very weak prosperity factors is that they have recently experienced various conflicts of varying degrees of intensity. In Bamako, Antananarivo, Monrovia, Niamey and Conakry, production, quality of life and infrastructure indicators are all very low.

POLICY More prosperous cities demonstrate the effective functioning of the hub in terms of urban power functions such as governance, urban planning, laws, regulations, and institutions.

El Alto, Bolivia: a large and poorly serviced part of greater La Paz, where the population is 80% indigenous.

© Eduardo Lopez Moreno

Box 1.1.9

Visualizing the 5 dimensions of the CPI

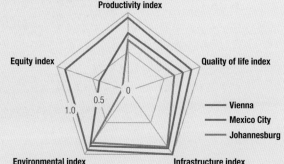

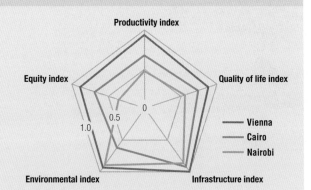

The two pentagons represent the five 'spokes' of prosperity as measured in five cities and the extent to which they are imbalanced/balanced in relation to each other. The radar-shaped graphs suggest where policy interventions are required. For instance, Nairobi (in the right-hand graph) performs well in terms of the environment and infrastructure, but less so on equity, productivity and quality of life. In Cairo, the situation is the reverse, as the environment appears to be the weaker point in an otherwise well-balanced pattern of prosperity – although at an overall lower level compared with Vienna. Similar interpretations can be derived from the pentagon to the left, which compares the relative performances of Mexico City and Johannesburg, again against Vienna's.

Endnotes

1   López Moreno, 2010.

2   UN-Habitat, 2011a.

3   Kitchin et al, 2010.

4   Banco De España, 2012.

5   Vassalli and Sánchez, 2009.

6   UN-Habitat, 2011c.

7   British Broadcasting Corporation, 2010.

8   U.S. Department of Commerce, 2011.

9   BBVA, 2011; INFONAVIT, 2011a.

10 Instituto Brasileiro de Geografia e Estadistica, 2010.

11 Yu, 2011.

12 Quartly, 2010.

13 Barboza, 2010.

14 UN-Habitat, 2011c.

15 Inurrieta Beruete, 2007.

16 INFONAVIT, 2011b.

17 The phenomenon had been highlighted nearly a decade earlier by the United Nations Development Programme (UNDP, 2002).

18 Assaad and Roudi-Fahimi, 2007.

19 United Nations, 2010a.

20 Spence et al, 2008.

21 Calafati, 2011.

22 *Ibid.*

23 Historically, water, biodiversity, knowledge and some other shared resources, including roads, sidewalks, highways and other public infrastructure, have been considered as 'commons'. 'Commons' are also intangible aspects such as clean environmental conditions, identity, cultural and symbolic spaces. More recently, from an institutional governance perspective, 'commons' are institutional arrangements such as 'spaces' for negotiation and participation, cultural norms and legal and statutory provisions.

24 Dickinson, 2011.

25 The outcome of China's 'green GDP' index was that if air pollution, water shortages, desertification, and depletion of fish stocks and wildlife were factored into its GDP calculation, the 2004 GDP would have been 511 billion yuan (US$ 66 billion), or three per cent lower (SEPA and NBS, 2006).

26 Dickinson, 2011.

27 Jackson, 2009.

28 *Ibid.*

29 Easterlin, 1973; 1974.

30 City of Cape Town, 2011.

31 Quantisoft, 2012.

32 *Ibid.*

33 Sen, 1979.

34 Oyelaran-Oyeyinka and Sampath, 2010.

35 Between 2009 and 2012, Siemens sponsored a series of publications on Green City from which the performance, with respect to urban environmental sustainability, of cities in different parts of the world can be assessed. An Ecological City Index was also developed in assessing the sustainability of the environment (S. Joss, D. Tomozeiu and R. Cowley, 2012: *Eco-city indicators – governance challenges*). In the quality of life aspect, the Livable City Index was also developed. The Economist Intelligence's Unit publishes annually a Global Liveability Report. Mercer also releases annually the Quality of Living Survey, comparing 221 cities based on 39 criteria (Mercier, 2011: *Quality of living survey*). Since 2007, the lifestyle magazine Monocle has published an annual list of livable cities.

36 Further compounding the problem of data dearth is the fact that most of the existing information was not collected in a uniform way to allow for comparisons of cities across countries and regions.

37 This classification has used data from multiple sources for the various components of the UN-Habitat Urban Prosperity Index, and this calls for a word of caution when interpreting some of these variations.

© Christian Als/Panos Pictures

Urban and Regional Trends

MORE THAN HALF OF THE WORLD POPULATION IS NOW URBAN

It is really remarkable that only one century ago, two out of 10 people in the world were living in urban areas. In the least developed countries, this proportion was as low as five per cent, as the overwhelming majority was living in rural areas. The world has been rapidly urbanizing since then and, in some countries and regions, at an unprecedented pace. It was only two years ago that humankind took a landmark step when, for the first time in history, urban outnumbered rural populations. This milestone marked the advent of a new 'urban millennium' and, by the middle of this century, it is expected that out of every 10 people on the planet, seven will be living in urban areas.

Interestingly, only 60 years ago or so (1950), the number of people living in urban centres was slightly higher in developed (54 per cent, or 442 million) as compared with developing countries. Today, of every 10 urban residents in the world more than seven are found in developing countries, which are also hosts to an overwhelming (82 per cent) proportion of humankind. Moreover, it is estimated that, between 2010 and 2015, some 200,000 people on average will be added to the world's urban population every day. Worth noting is that 91 per cent of this daily increase (or 183,000) is expected to take place in developing countries.

In the last quarter of 2011, the world population reached the seven billion mark. This historic event took place 12 years after the six billion mark. It took 123 years to double from one to two billion but 'only' 33 years to cross the three-billion threshold.[1] Although demographic growth is slowing down

across the world as a whole, it remains that the ever-shorter time it has taken to add one extra billion signals a major shift in both the pace and scale of global demographics.

It is almost certain that at some point in late 2011, the seven-billionth human was born in a developing country. This is where virtually all (93 per cent) of the world's population growth is happening today. Moreover, all future population growth is expected to take place in urban areas, and again nearly all of it in Africa, Asia and Latin America. Therefore, it is highly probable that the seven-billionth human was born in a city in any of these three regions.

These numbers highlight the extent to which the world population has increasingly come to live in urban areas. For all the clarity of these trends and the benefits that come with urbanization, too many governments still maintain ambivalent if not hostile attitudes to this process. In 2009, slightly over two-thirds (67 per cent) of countries in the world reported that they had implemented policies to reduce or even reverse migrant flows from rural areas to cities. Of an average 10 African governments, slightly over eight were found trying to stem rural migration.[2] However, contrary to common perception, migration from rural to urban areas is no longer the dominant determinant of urban population growth in developing countries. Today, natural increase accounts for some 60 per cent of that growth, and the transformation of rural settlements into urban places, a process known as 'reclassification', accounts for another 20 per cent or so.

Understanding current and prospective trends in urban demographic growth is fundamental if appropriate policies and strategies are to be designed and deployed to maximize the benefits of urbanization. This includes taking advantage of opportunities, devising better regional and urban policies, and planning for the future. In this chapter, every major region of the world is shown to feature unique development patterns that are analysed against the background of current trends and projections.

Urban Change in Developed Countries

URBAN POPULATION GROWTH IS NEXT TO STAGNANT

In the more advanced nations, urban population growth is next to stagnant (0.67 per cent on an annual average basis since 2010), which represents an additional six million or so every year. In Europe, the annual increase is only two million. By comparison, the aggregate annual population increase in six major developing-country cities – New Delhi and Mumbai (India), Dhaka (Bangladesh), Lagos (Nigeria), Kinshasa (Democratic Republic of Congo) and Karachi (Pakistan) – is higher than Europe's entire population. Population in North American cities was the least slow of all those in the developed world between 2005 and 2010, particularly in the United States (one per cent on average).

The growth, decline and prosperity of cities: There is no clear association between the demographic growth or decline of cities and their degrees of prosperity. Although population numbers have declined in a number of cities in Western Europe, Canada and New Zealand, this did not affect living standards, which in some cases even improved. On the other hand, and as might be expected, population declines in a number of cities in Eastern Europe and the United States of America are strongly associated with economic decay. The loss of economic momentum in Cleveland, Detroit and Buffalo (homes to the USA's declining automobile, steel and heavy industries, respectively) and the deterioration of inner city conditions (deserted residential areas and crumbling infrastructure) have all gone hand in hand with population declines.

> In the past 20 years, the proportion of European cities with declining populations is similar to those whose population growth rates are over one per cent.

> Cities must create capacities that will enable them to understand and anticipate trends as well as develop appropriate strategies to harness the growth and offset the decline of some areas or regions.

Population decline in the city proper can very often go hand in hand with rapid growth in peripheral areas, a phenomenon known as the 'doughnut effect'. For example, in Saskatoon, one of Canada's most dynamic and affluent economic hubs, migration and natural increase caused a 15 per cent population increase in peripheral municipalities between 1996 and 2001.[3] Likewise in the United States of America, there has been a continuous decline (minus 8.3 per cent between 2000 and 2010) in the population of affluent St. Louis, while neighbouring cities such as St. Charles and Jefferson increased their populations by 26.6 per cent and 10.8 per cent, respectively, during the same period.[4]

Growing cities are located in growing regions: Cities and the surrounding regions are typically interdependent economically and tend to share similar socioeconomic and demographic trends. In most North American cities, growing cities correspond to the most dynamic regions and those experiencing population losses are located in less dynamic regions. Canada is a case in point. Research found that between 1981 and 2001, two-thirds of smaller cities and towns with declining populations were located within declining regions, and 77 per cent of cities on a positive demographic trend were to be found in growing regions.[5] In contrast, in Western Europe the prosperity of entire regions is largely dependent on a primate conurbation and the concentration of services and manufacturing that comes with it. A study on the sustainability of 285 European regions conducted by the Berlin Institute in 2007/8, just prior to the financial crises, showed that cities like Reykjavík, Stockholm, Oslo, Zurich and Geneva were doing well, as did the regions where they are located. With their relatively unchanged, well-educated and well-nigh fully employed populations, these cities base their economic momentum on a combination of factors: they act as administrative and/or financial/economic as well as cultural capital cities, with high value-added activities (including communications, business services, high technologies, research, etc.),[6] and this momentum spills over across the (often largely urbanized) surrounding

> **POLICY** Regional and national urban planning through central government in collaboration with lower levels of governance and other key stakeholders plays a critical role in creating a system of cities and in determining the prosperity and growth of cities.

China, Ruili, Yunnan Province. Dai minority threshing rice harvest in fields which are gradually being swallowed by this booming border city.

© Mark Henley/Panos Pictures

Figure 1.2.1

Population density in Europe, 2001

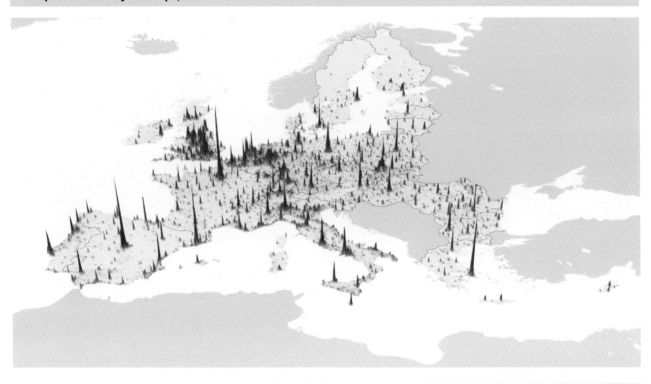

Source: ORNL LandScan – cartography DG REGIO, European Commission.

regions through manufacturing and ancillary (logistics, etc.) activities.

Cities in the north will continue to attract migrants: European urban areas, in particular, will continue to feature low fertility rates and rapidly aging populations. These demographic trends are unmistakable and point to overall demographic decline.

Between 2005 and 2010, net international migration counterbalanced the excess of deaths over births in 11 developed countries, while contributing twice as much to population growth in another nine countries.[7] With the ongoing economic crisis, the aggregate flow of immigrants to developed countries has slowed down from an annual 2.3 per cent average rate in 2000–05 to 1.7 per cent in 2005–10. Rising unemployment in some of the host cities/countries may cause governments to impose restrictions on increased immigration.[9]

In Italy, the dynamic, affluent northern industrial cities of Brescia and Reggio Emilia saw the share of immigrants in their populations increase from five and six per cent respectively in 2002 to 19.3 and 17.2 per cent in 2010.[10] Ireland's economic boom caused Dublin's foreign-born population to soar by over 300 per cent between 1991 and 2008.[11]

With the ongoing economic crisis, the aggregate flow of immigrants to developed countries has slowed down from an annual 2.3 per cent average rate in 2000–05 to 1.7 per cent in 2005–10.[12] Despite these current trends, it looks like enduring demographic and economic asymmetries between the North and South will continue to fuel international migration, as developed nations require foreign workers to address labour shortages and counter the effects of population aging on welfare systems.

In the European Union countries, it is projected that deaths would outnumber births from 2015 onwards, putting an end to population growth through natural increase. Positive net migration will be the only demographic growth factor until 2035.[8]

POLICY It would be in the best interests of European countries/cities to review immigration policies with a view to maximizing the benefits and reducing the more negative aspects of the phenomenon, with inclusionary social and political mechanisms to bring prosperity to all.

Box 1.2.1

Increased participation of European cities in networks

Large European cities in terms of both population and economic production, such as London and Paris, are characterized by their involvement in business networks across the continent and beyond. Other cities with higher GDP per capita, such as Amsterdam, Zurich, Brussels, Frankfurt, Dublin, Copenhagen and Stockholm, are also involved in important networks on account of their high concentrations of national and sub-regional banking, financial and business services. In contrast, those cities with high shares of manufacturing are associated with lower participation in international networks. Various Southern and Eastern European cities, including Athens, Rome, Madrid, Barcelona and Milan, appear to be relatively weak in terms of international networks despite their economic size. Some German cities also belong in this category, notably Berlin.

It must also be remembered that the primary sector (mining and agriculture) can also connect urban areas in developed countries to world markets through company headquarters, commodity exchanges and specialist services based in cities located next to production areas. This is the case with countries like Australia (mining) and Canada (mining and intensive cereal production).

Source: Moritz Lennert (2011), Cities in Networks, prepared for UN-Habitat

Urban Change in Developing Countries

DIVERGENT URBAN GROWTH PATTERNS

In the past decade, the urban population in the developing world grew an average 1.2 million people per *week*, or slightly less than one full *year*'s demographic growth in Europe's urban areas. Asia dominated the picture, adding 0.88 million new urban dwellers every week. Africa was the second largest contributor with an additional 0.23 million per week, dwarfing Latin America and the Caribbean's 0.15 million weekly increment.

Africa: The urban population is set to outstrip Europe's: In what promises to be one of the more remarkable forthcoming developments in the overall pattern of urbanization in Africa, the region's population is poised to outgrow both Europe's and Latin America's, which was the first region to become predominantly urban in the developing world. In 2025, the aggregate urban populations of Africa, Europe, Latin America and the Caribbean are expected to reach 642 million, 566 million and 560 million, respectively.

In the developing world, the pace of urban population growth rate has slowed down from just under three per cent in the year 2000 to 2.4 per cent in 2010, which is still three and a half times higher than the annual average population growth rate in developed countries.

Box 1.2.2

Africa, urbanization and positive change

It is only one century ago or so that the urban population in Africa was less than eight per cent of the total. Since then, many things have changed, some in a positive way.

Over the entire span of the 20th century, life expectancy increased from 24 to 52 years.[13] Education has become more widespread, with literacy rates in Sub-Saharan Africa rising from 23 per cent in 1970 to 65 per cent in 2010.[14] Gross domestic product per capita increased from 585 (1990) international dollars in 1913 to 1,368 in 1998.[15] By the end of the 20th century, Africa's population was 35 per cent urban.

Africa: the ongoing urban economic momentum in Africa is a result of a number of the typical factors of prosperity at work in other regions of the world, such as economies of agglomeration, location advantages, and diversification of the economic base, albeit all in nascent form.

Urbanization in Africa features a conspicuous degree of primacy, i.e., the concentration of significant proportions of the national urban population in one or a very small number of cities. Basic infrastructure and communication networks have undergone tangible improvements in many cities. Public transport still features as a major issue on the urban development agenda, while inequality and poverty remain at the heart of Africa's problems.

POLICY African cities must connect to regional and global business networks, enhance quality of life, improve basic infrastructure and communication networks, address public transport deficiencies and environmental conditions, and respond to inequality and poverty issues, if they are to turn into real engines of national growth and prosperity.

Asia: This region is also confronted by the same urban paradox as Africa. Despite high concentrations of population in large cities, the continent ranks among the least-urbanized regions in the world (45 per cent urban). The tipping point for 'urban Asia' is expected to happen earlier though (around 2020s).

POLICY Cities must give more attention to rising inequalities and the worrying trend of environmental degradation.

In an apparent paradox, by that same year, 2025, Africa will still be the least urbanized region in the world (45 per cent of the population).

Asia: Moving into the 'Urban Century'

Half of the world's urban population now lives in Asia. This region has accounted for about 65 per cent of the demographic expansion of all urban areas across the world since the beginning of the 21st century. Undoubtedly, this is the 'Asian Urban Century'.[16] Large population concentrations in mega-cities are to remain a prominent feature in urban Asia (today, seven out of the 10 most populous cities of the world are in this region). In the recent past, Delhi and Shanghai have joined the league of 'meta-cities', those massive conurbations of more than 20 million people. It is expected that by 2020, another three Asian cities – Beijing, Dhaka and Mumbai – will have reached the 20 million mark.

Asia's urban population growth rate remains sustained if somewhat slower at an annual estimated rate of 2.4 per cent (compared to 2.7 per cent between 2005 and 2010), second only to Africa's. On current trends, this slowdown should continue (to an average of 1.7 per cent in the early 2020s and below one per cent by 2050).[17]

No developing region has invested more than Asia in advanced knowledge infrastructure for economic development. A combination of public and private sector capital expenditure has provided the modern infrastructure required for industrial expansion, research and development, innovation and entrepreneurship, which in turn have enhanced the economic potential and competitiveness of so many cities in Asia. These, as a result, are rapidly shifting away from labour-intensive to high-technology industries and to the service-oriented sector. For instance, Cebu City in the Philippines is prospering on the back of business process outsourcing, where the number of jobs soared from 40,000 to 70,000 from 2009 to 2010.[18] Nowadays in Lahore, the capital of the Punjab Province of Pakistan, as many as 42 per cent of the workforce are employed in finance, banking, real estate and social services. In India, Bangalore, the capital of Karnataka State, is behind 32 per cent of the country's software exports and provides 25 per cent of jobs in the national information technology sector.[19]

This is only some factual evidence highlighting the main lesson from Asia, namely, that infrastructure development focused on improved productivity (and quality of life) has gone hand in hand with economic growth and urbanization, particularly over the last two decades. According to the UN-Habitat *State of Asian Cities Report*, the region contributed a solid 30 per cent of the world's economic output in 2008.[20] More specifically, the report noted that cities accounted for 80 per cent of Asia's gross domestic product, while only hosting slightly over 40 per cent of the region's total population. Increases in GDP per capita (as measured in constant year-2000 US dollars) has been spectacular in East Asia and the Pacific, with a 120 per cent surge between the year 2000 and 2010. By comparison, over that same period GDP per capita in Sub-Saharan Africa grew by 25 per cent, and only 22 per cent in Latin America and the Caribbean.[21]

Latin America and the Caribbean: Inter-city migration predominates: This is the most urbanized region in the world (80 per cent of the total population, compared with Europe's 73 per cent). The urban transition in this region was achieved in the early 1960s, or about 16 years before Western Asia (the second sub-region in the developing world to become predominantly urban), and 30 and 45 years respectively before Southern and North Africa (or, on current trends, some 70 years before the whole of Africa).

Still, and as in Africa and Asia, some of the foundations for improved prosperity have been emerging across Latin America and the Caribbean over the past few years. Most prominent among these are transport infrastructure and telecommunications, together with the provision of basic services and housing improvements. In some countries, better physical connectivity, enhanced communication

La Paz, Bolivia, sprawls ever higher up the mountain side. The metropolitan area, formed by the neighbouring cities of La Paz, El Alto and Viacha, is the most populous area of Bolivia.

© 2012 Robert Gilhooly/fotoLIBRA.com

Latin America and the Caribbean will be nearly 87 per cent urban in 2050, by which time the annual average pace of growth in the urban population is expected to slow down to 0.3 per cent. Some cities already see their populations shrinking. Latin America and the Caribbean stands out as the only region where migration between urban areas is a significant determinant of urban population growth, accounting for nearly 50 per cent and due to several factors, chief among them the pursuit of prosperity.

POLICY Latin American cities must become more productive and generate local jobs, and improve transport infrastructure and living conditions, short of which they will face prospects of population decline due to higher mobility from city to city. They must reduce entrenched inequalities while improving quality of life and environmental protection. More prosperous cities must articulate better their strategic advantages with national economic policies and enhance their creative capital to increase prosperity prospects.

POLICY Even though the region is more urbanized than Europe, GDP per capita (PPP) was nearly three times lower than the European Union's in 2010. The main reasons include chronic inequalities and mass poverty, insufficient infrastructure, poor public services, inadequate connectivity, poor governance and fragile institutions.

technologies at urban and regional levels, and improved quality of life, particularly in secondary cities, have contributed to reduce urban primacy. Today and as a result, small- and medium-size cities in the region are not only growing faster, but are also becoming destinations of choice for people who were living in larger agglomerations.

In many Latin American cities, economies have diversified through de-industrialization and the expansion of tertiary activities, particularly in the trade and service sectors, causing informal employment to soar, but the phenomenon has not yet been properly quantified.

CONVERGENT URBAN GROWTH PATTERNS

Cities are expanding in a discontinuous, scattered and low-density form that is not sustainable: A defining feature of cities in the developing world is an outward expansion far beyond formal administrative boundaries, largely propelled by the use of the automobile and land speculation. A large number of cities – whether in Angola, Egypt, Brazil,

China, or almost any other country – feature very land-consuming suburban sprawling patterns which often extend to even farther peripheries. A study on 120 cities shows that urban land cover has, on average, grown more than twice as much as the urban population. Similar urban trends can be observed in other parts of the world. For instance, in Mexico, the urban physical expansion of all urban areas over the past 30 years was estimated to be at around 7.4 per cent on an annual average basis, outstripping population growth by a multiple of nearly four.[22] In India, built-up areas grew faster than the population in nearly all of the largest cities, especially during the 2000–11 period in Greater Mumbai, Bangalore, Pune, Jaipur, and Kolkata. India's larger cities –particularly Bangalore, Hyderabad, and Surat – are sprawling at an accelerated pace, with the attendant decrease in densities outside their administrative boundaries.[23] Similar urban trends can be observed in other parts of the world. In Algeria, for instance, much of the urban expansion has taken the form of uncontrolled sprawl around Algiers, with many of the more affluent, car-owning residents migrating to the periphery. Between 1987 and 2008, the land area of the city increased by almost four per cent per year, compared with only 1.5 per cent for the population.[24] In the Saudi capital Jeddah, private developers in 2009 requested an allocation of over 20,000 hectares of land outside city boundaries, but municipal authorities were able to prove that only 17,000 hectares would be needed to accommodate requirements over the next 29 years, half of which could be located on vacant land within the city's existing boundaries.[25]

Cities are becoming endless expanses, with high degrees of fragmentation of the urban fabric that result in vast interstitial open spaces. At the periphery, residential neighbourhoods are characterized by low-density developments which, along with under-used spaces and fragmented built-up areas in the intermediate city-rings, are contributing to dramatic reductions in residential densities. In the developing world, it was

Most urban plans and regulatory regimes in the developing world have been incapable of preventing the conversion of rural land to urban use in city peripheries. As a result, the reclassification of settlements from 'rural' to 'urban' has become the second most significant determinant of urban population growth and expansion in the developing world today.

observed that the average built-up area densities declined in 75 out of the 88 sampled cities, or 6 out of 7, between 1990 and 2000. Densities shrank from an average 174 persons per hectare (p/ha) in 1990 to 135 p/ha in the year 2000. The most significant decrease took place in the sampled Asian cities, where the densities shrank from 217 p/ha in 1990 to 160 p/ha in the year 2000, or a 26 per cent decrease.[26] In the recent past, significant decreases in built-up densities in cities especially outside administrative boundaries have also been reported. Among many examples, cities such as Bangalore, Hyderabad and Surat (in India) reduced by more than half the built-up densities outside administrative boundaries between 2000 and 2010.[27]

POLICY Cities must accommodate demographic and spatial expansion, with a concomitant development of well-devised urban structures that would reduce transport and service delivery costs, optimize land use and support the deployment and/or protection of open spaces.

POLICY Better connectivity, mobility and accessibility and well-planned integration of land-use, density and transport have the potential to reduce energy consumption drastically, making cities more sustainable.

Box 1.2.3

Prosperity and urbanization: contrasted trends within regions

Urbanization is far from being homogenous within single large regions of the world. Even though regional averages are important to understand urban trends, conditions and projections and for the sake of comparison, they conceal large disparities across countries in the same region.

Levels of urbanization and rates of growth differ significantly when compared with the economic development of countries within the same region. In general, low-income economies are growing at least twice as fast as high-income economies, but their typical level of urbanization is less than half that of the more developed countries.

Intra-regional differences can be significant, though. For instance, Africa's urban population growth rate was on average 3.3 per cent in 2010, but variations among low- and high-income African economies were very significant: 30 countries that were ranked as 'poor' saw their urban populations grow at a very brisk pace (about four per cent) while nine countries in the 'upper middle-income' category grew at a more moderate rate of about two per cent from 2005 to 2010. It is well known that populations in less advanced countries grow much faster on average than those more advanced; but what this data shows is that, within the same region, some countries see their urban populations expand twice as fast as that of other countries, and the stage of development is a determinant factor behind this difference. While countries with the poorest economies will take around 18 years to double their urban populations, countries with the most advanced economies of the region will take more than double, considering that their urban growth rates are diminishing faster.

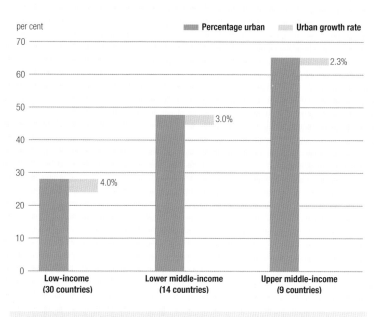

Africa: proportion urban and urban growth rate, 2010

Source: UN-Habitat, 2012.

This goes to show that the level to which a national population is urbanized reflects the degree of economic development. Understanding which cities are experiencing a demographic boom and which others are undergoing dramatic decreases in population is critical when it comes to designing urban policies that are apt to maximize gains, redress regional imbalances and (re)allocate capital expenditure for the sake of higher levels of prosperity and more sustainable urban and regional development.

NOVEL URBAN/REGIONAL CONFIGURATIONS AND PROSPERITY

Cities large or small have increasingly come to merge together to form new spatial configurations that typically take three principal forms: **mega-regions, urban corridors** and **city-regions**. Each on its own spatial scale, these three forms seem to act as nodes where global and regional flows of people, capital, goods and information combine and commingle, resulting in faster growth, both demographic and economic, than that of the countries where they are located. These new configurations are more and more spatially connected and functionally bound by their economic and environmental links, at times even socially and politically. They play an increasing role in the creation and distribution of prosperity far beyond their own specific geographic areas.

Large cities such as Bangalore, Mexico City or Cairo are found morphing into new spatial configurations in which they amalgamate other cities and towns of various sizes within their economic orbit. In other cases, two or more large cities, such as Mumbai and Delhi in India, São Paulo-Rio de Janeiro in Brazil, or Ibadan-Lagos-Accra in Africa, form transport corridors for the purposes of industrial development, business services or trade. Still in other cases, government creates planned 'supra-agglomerations' as part of a regional/national development strategy. This is the case in China, where the Guangdong Provincial Government recently announced the development of the Pearl River Delta mega-region, which would include nine large cities[28] with an aggregate surface area of 40,000 km², or 26 times that of Greater London.[29]

A critical mass of people, ideas, infrastructure and resources acts as a magnet for development, attracting migrants, private firms, investors and developers. All of this enhances the prospects for more employment opportunities, wealth creation, innovation and knowledge, which are all major factors of prosperity.

POLICY The challenge here is for local authorities and regional governments to design the development of cities in parallel with the development of regions, rather than treating both as isolated spaces, a process which involves innovative coordination mechanisms for urban/regional management and governance.

POLICY Considering the 'natural' or 'spontaneous' growth of these large urban configurations, cities and regions in the developing world must introduce regional planning strategies to mitigate any adverse side-effects and harness the opportunities and potentials that are concentrated in those large agglomerations.

Mexico City, a metropolis of over 20 million people.
© ecco3d/Shutterstock

Large urban configurations, as grouped in networks of cities, amplify the benefits of economies of agglomeration, increasing efficiencies and enhancing connectivity. They also generate economies of scale that are beneficial in terms of labour markets, as well as transport and communication infrastructure, which in turn increase local consumer demand.

Box 1.2.4

Large urban configurations differ across regions

Europe: Urban planning has had much more influence here than in any other region of the world. Located along major transport routes, novel urban configurations are specialized industrial and business centres, but with less dense populations than counterparts in developing regions. Many capital cities have moved from the 'regional' to the 'supra' cluster format.

Example: The so-called 'Blue Banana', a discontinuous corridor linking many West European cities from London to Milan. The area combines the highest concentrations of population and economic (especially banking/financial and manufacturing) centres in the whole continent.

North America: The main features here are massive investment in freeway systems and planned urban development with a dispersed pattern of urban settlement and specialized functions. Most cities in these configurations have populations of over one million, and the typical morphology is polycentric in terms of both urban form and economic structure. They rank among the largest in the world for aggregate surface area, about 18.9 million urban acres.

Example: The North-East mega-region including Boston, New York, Philadelphia, Baltimore and Washington D.C., which hosts 17 per cent (or about 52 million) of the US population and generates 21 per cent of the nation's GDP.

Asia: In newly industrialized countries, large agglomerations are more dispersed and less well planned. Densities are typically much higher – over 15,000/km^2 – but in city regions can be as twice as high, particularly in inner city areas. Large urban configurations are becoming more specialized, including industrial cluster development (high technology and traditional manufacturing) and services (health, education and transport).

Example: China's Hong Kong-Shenzhen-Guangzhou agglomeration is home to 120 million.

Africa: There are relatively few large urban configurations in Africa. They tend to be linear along corridors or coastal trading routes (e.g., the Abidjan-Accra-Lagos corridor) and major arterial roads between adjacent provincial cities (Johannesburg-Pretoria and Lagos-Ibadan). Typically they are not planned. Services are poor, as are transport infrastructure and logistics. Employment is driven primarily by trading, natural resources and low-level services. The typical pattern combines high population density in inner cities and low densities in outer areas.

Examples:
Cairo-Giza, the largest urban agglomeration in Northern Africa, home to 17.8 million.

The Cairo-Alexandria corridor is the largest mega-urban region (stretching over 225km), with export-oriented agriculture accounting for 40 per cent of the surface area.

The Ibadan-Lagos-Accra corridor spans over 600 km across four countries (including Benin and Togo) and is host to some 30 million.

Arab States: There are very few large urban configurations in Arab States. In the Near East, the evolution is from mono- to polycentric or diffuse urban corridor formats, especially in Iraq, Iran, Saudi Arabia and Turkey. In the Maghreb, large urban configurations develop along rivers, coastal areas and trade routes. Trans-border cities are expanding along highways and modern transportation networks, and as in Africa they tend to be linear along urban corridors.

Examples:
Tangier is emerging as a new Extended Metropolitan Region around what has become North Africa's largest container port.

The Kenitra-El Jadida corridor includes the cities of Casablanca and Rabat, Morocco's business and administrative capitals respectively, which are home to a combined 7.5 million people and generate half the country's GDP.

The Abu Dhabi-Sharjah free trade zone also includes Dubai and Ajman, with over 200 factories, more than 3.5 million residents and the largest container port in the region.

Latin America: Despite the fact that the region has the highest proportion of urban population in the world and except for a number of city-regions, large urban configurations are rather few. They are changing from a mono-centric pattern of development to polycentric and urban corridor forms. Those cities constrained by physical geography spread along main transportation lines and adjacent rural areas. Large cities are growing in a diffuse, low-density pattern with peripheral industrial development and housing.

The mega-region that stretches from São Paulo to Rio de Janeiro is home to 43 million people.

Sources: Brian H. Roberts (2011); UN-Habitat State of the Arab Cities Report (2012); Regional Plan Association and America 2050 (2012).

Box 1.2.5

Novel configurations: a typology

Mega-regions surpass mega- and meta-cities by population and economic output, combining large markets, skilled labour and innovation, and amalgamating several cities within the orbit of the overall region.

Example: Japan's Tokyo-Nagoya-Osaka-Kyoto-Kobe region, with a population close to 60 million.

Urban corridors: a number of urban centres of various sizes are connected along transportation routes in linear development axes that are often linked to a number of megacities, encompassing hinterlands. New developments in some fringe areas experience the fastest growth rates and the most rapid urban transformation.

Example: in Malaysia, the Kuala Lumpur-Klang corridor along the Klang Valley.

City-regions take on a larger scale than large cities, expanding beyond formal administrative boundaries to engulf smaller ones as well as semi-urban and rural hinterlands, and even merging with other intermediate cities, creating large conurbations that eventually form city-regions.

Examples: São Paulo, Brazil; Cape Town, South Africa; Bangkok, Thailand.

ENHANCING PROSPERITY IN LARGE URBAN CONFIGURATIONS: THE 5 DIMENSIONS

Large urban configurations concentrate many of the resources and opportunities that give substance to the five dimensions of prosperity: enhanced productivity, infrastructural development, quality of life, equity and social inclusion, and environmental sustainability.

Enhanced productivity: Planning large urban configurations as a 'portfolio' of functional and complementary areas of specialization can lead to more diversified economies, capitalizing on the comparative advantages of each city within the large agglomeration and developing a strong regional vision for the whole large configuration. For instance, in the Pearl River Delta mega-region in China, each of the cities capitalizes on its comparative strengths, and contributes to the overall prosperity of the large configuration.

Infrastructural development: Transport infrastructure improves connectivity and spatially integrates the networks

of cities that make up the urban/regional configuration. The large economically prosperous cities of Shanghai, Guangzhou and Beijing have invested in infrastructure to connect peripheral towns and enhance the large urban configuration. Beijing has extended 304 km of roads to link all 'administrative villages' to the city (2005). Shanghai has built 750 km of highways to integrate the rural hinterland (2007). Guangzhou has completed extensive networks of roads, electricity and water distribution to all neighbouring rural settlements with more than 100 residents (2007).[30]

Equity and social inclusion: The market-driven logic of scale economies can interfere with equitable distribution, such as unregulated land markets, spatial segregation, extreme income inequalities and uneven development. Speculative real estate development in many of these large urban configurations effectively excludes not only the poor, but even the middle class, from formal land markets, creating an

POLICY It is in a city's best interest to establish linkages with other neighbouring urban areas for the sake of complementary functions. This will help to develop a strong collective regional identity, in the process achieving greater economic momentum than if they remain in isolation.

POLICY Investments in transport infrastructure and related reforms, including finance and regulations, deliver major economic benefits, contributing to poverty alleviation and improving quality of life.

POLICY Cities and regional governments should encourage social and institutional innovations that can reduce socio-spatial inequalities; this can include tax revenue transfers among urban authorities within the large urban configuration, or revenue-sharing, or equalization grants.

POLICY More effective local and regional institutions, new linkages and alliances across the three tiers of government, together with a comprehensive vision with clear plans favouring inclusiveness, are all crucial for equitable development and prosperity.

India, Tirupur, Tamil Nadu. Workers at a textile factory in Tirupur. There are some 7,000 garment factories in the city, providing employment to close to one million people.

© Atul Loke/Panos Pictures

uneven patchwork of privilege and underprivilege across large urban areas.

Quality of life: When city leaders cooperate, rather than compete, in a number of areas (crime, poverty, social inequalities, transport systems, infrastructure), a more effective type of regional governance emerges that has direct implications on quality of life both inside and outside the large urban configuration.

Environmental sustainability: Environmental challenges transcend political/administrative boundaries. Yet, local authorities may find themselves with little power or resources to counter the damaging effects of growth on the environment, particularly in the face of the negative externalities generated by neighbouring cities.

POLICY Increasing evidence shows that interventions to promote quality of life have clear positive effects on the other dimensions of prosperity. Unsurprisingly, progress on the other dimensions of prosperity is found to enhance quality of life.

POLICY Looking beyond their own local interests and cooperating with the other jurisdictions involved, local authorities can improve competitive advantage while also preserving the environment.

POLICY Working together, cities in a large urban configuration are in better positions effectively to protect, manage, and plan for physical environment that span multiple jurisdictions.

POLICY The economic surpluses that large urban agglomerations derive from productivity gains can be channelled towards the protection of natural resources in the region, with the costs of maintaining these indivisible public goods equitably shared among the population.

LARGE URBAN CONFIGURATIONS FACE SPECIFIC RISKS

Large urban configurations come with a number of well-identified, specific risks: poor urban/regional planning, lack of coordination and deficient coping strategies in the face of social and fiscal disparities. Although these affect the whole population, the bulk of the risks fall disproportionately on the poor.

In most cases, large urban configurations in developing countries are not planned. Economic forces and spontaneous growth tend to sharpen spatial and social disparities, which are further compounded by

Table 1.2.1

Prosperity performance indicators of selected large urban configurations by regions (2008)

City	Country	Population (millions)	Typology	Metro Area Km²	PPKm²	Met GDP $Bn	GDP/Capita	GDP/C City to National Ratio
ASIA								
Tokyo	Japan	35.83	Urban Corridor	8,677	4,100	$1,479	$41,278	1.2
Seoul	South Korea	9.78	Mega City	959	10,200	$291	$29,755	1.2
Guangzhou	China	10.18	Urban Corridor	1,968	6,700	$143	$14,044	2.6
Hong Kong	China	7.28	Trans-Border	280	25,200	$320	$43,956	1
Singapore	Singapore	4.49	Trans-Border	463	9,700	$215	$47,884	1
Metro Manila	Philippines	13.5	Mega City	1,425	14,600	$149	$11,035	3.3
Mumbai	India	19.35	Mega City	1082	17,880	$209	$10,801	4
Istanbul	Turkey	12.6	Mega City	1,269	10,400	$182	$14,444	1.5
Tel Aviv	Israel	3.33	Urban Corridor	1516	5,900	$122	$36,684	1.3
OCEANIA								
Sydney	Australia	4.36	Urban Corridor	1,788	2,438	$213	$48,853	1.3
Melbourne	Australia	3.64	Urban Corridor	2,152	1,600	$172	$47,318	1.3
AMERICAS								
New York City	USA	19.18	Mega City	11,264	1,800	$1,406	$73,306	1.6
Los Angeles	USA	12.59	Urban Corridor	5,812	2,500	$792	$62,907	1.4
Mexico City	Mexico	21.16	Urban Corridor	2,525	7,400	$390	$18,428	1.5
São Paulo	Brazil	19.89	Urban Corridor	3,756	5,400	$388	$19,507	2
Rio de Janeiro	Brazil	11.89	Urban Corridor	2,123	5,600	$201	$16,905	1.7
AFRICA								
Cairo	Egypt	15.55	Urban Corridor	1,709	10,100	$145	$9,327	1.7
Algiers	Algeria	2.8	Mega City	453	7,800	$45	$16,071	2
Casablanca	Morocco	3.28	Sub National	1378	2,383	$33	$10,049	2.6
Johannesburg	South Africa	10.27	Mega City	2,525	3,000	$164	$15,972	1.5
Cape Town	South Africa	7.28	Mega City	2455	2,965	$103	$14,148	1.3
Lagos	Nigeria	10.58	Urban Corridor	997	9,500	$35	$3,309	1.5

Sources of data: GDP data from (Price Waterhouse Coopers, 2010), area data (Hove, 2010) adjusted on a density estimate and Google Earth urban area estimates.

inefficient use of land and other resources. Close links with world financial markets and the impacts of global and regional economic crises shape 'uneven geographies of development'.

Faced with the challenges and costs of addressing sustainability problems, many large urban agglomerations may choose to ignore quality of life and environmental issues, in the belief that these can be caught up with later. Large urban configurations that take this path run the risk of finding it increasingly difficult to attract investment, labour and skills. Economic growth may happen, but the risks of future disinvestments by firms and exit of some social groups could compromise future prosperity.

POLICY Addressing negative externalities will attract investment, labour and skills, in the process contributing to future urban prosperity.

GDP $m/Km²	Economic Drivers
$170	Services /Manufacturing/Government/Transport
$303	Manufacturing
$73	Manufacturing
$1,143	Advanced Services/Transport
$464	Advanced Services/Transport
$105	Advanced Services
$193	Advanced Services/Manufacturing
$143	Advanced Services/Manufacturing
$80	Advanced Services/Manufacturing
$119	Advanced Services/Transport
$80	Advanced Services
$125	Advanced Services/Transport
$136	Advanced Services/Transport
$154	Advanced Services/Gov/Manufacturing
$103	Advanced Services/Manufacturing/Transport
$95	Advanced Services/Gov/Manufacturing/Transport
$85	Advanced Services/Gov/Manufacturing
$99	Advanced Services/Gov/Manufacturing
$24	Manufacturing
$65	Advanced Services/Manufacturing
$42	Advanced Services/Manufacturing
$35	Advanced Services/Manufacturing

Endnotes

1   United Nations, 1999.

2   United Nations, 2010b.

3   Statistics Canada, 2001.

4   U.S. Census Bureau (n.d.) U.S. Census Bureau: State and County QuickFacts http:// quickfacts.census.gov/qfd/index.html

5   Statistics Canada, 2005.

6   Pierre Bourdieu views "the capital [city] as the locus where all forms of capital [resources] are concentrated" in Bourdieu P., Sur l'Etat – Cours au Collège de France 1989-1992, p. 162, Paris, 2012. For an in-depth analysis, see Bourdieu. Les effets de lieu (locus effects) in Bourdieu P. (ed.), La Misère du monde, pp. 159-167, Paris, 1993.

7   United Nations, 2010b.

8   Eurostat, 2008.

9   United Nations, 2010b.

10 ISMU Foundation – Projects and Studies on Multiethnicity, 2010.

11 City of Dublin, 2009.

12 United Nations, 2010b.

13 Maddison, 2001.

14 UNDP, 2010.

15 Maddison, 2001.

16 Mohan, 2006.

17 United Nations, Department of Economic and Social Affairs, Population Division (2012). World Urbanization Prospects: The 2011 Revision, CD-ROM Edition.

18 Fernandez, F.L., 2011.

19 Zaidi, 2011.

20 UN-Habitat and ESCAP, 2010.

21 World Bank Data: World Development Indicators & Global Development Finance, Online database last updated July 9 2012, http://data.worldbank.org

22 ONU-HABITAT and SEDESOL, 2011.

23 IIHS, 2011.

24 Safar Zitoun and Tabti-Talamali, 2009.

25 Jeddah Municipality, 2009.

26 Shlomo et al, 2010.

27 IIHS, 2011.

28 The nine cities are the following: Guangzhou, Shenzhen, Foshan, Dongguan, Zhongshan, Zhuhai, Jiangmen, Huizhou and Zhaoqing.

29 Roberts, 2011.

30 World Bank, 2009a.

Part Two

Dimensions of
City Prosperity

© Joyfull/Shutterstock.com

© Claudio Zaccherini/Shutterstock.com

Productivity and the Prosperity of Cities

Enhancing urban productivity is clearly desirable, as it improves competitiveness and, ultimately, the prosperity of any city. More productive cities are able to increase output with the same amounts of resources, generating additional real income that can raise living standards through more affordable goods and services. More specifically, the extra income and municipal revenue generated through productivity will enable any city to provide more, better services, such as housing, education and healthcare, social programmes and expanded infrastructure networks to support both productive and leisure activities. Raising urban productivity is not a goal in itself, but a critical starting point to provide residents with decent income for their basic needs and adequate living standards.[1]

Urban productivity refers to the efficiency with which a city transforms inputs into outputs. It is commonly defined as a ratio of a quantitative measure of output to a quantitative measure of input used.[2] From a classic economic perspective, the traditional factors of production – land, labour, and capital – are also considered the key inputs or resources associated with

Shenzhen, China: inside the factory of the biggest CCTV surveillance camera producer in China.

© Bartlomiej Magierowski/Shutterstock.com

urban productivity. More recently, non-tangible types of capital such as human, intellectual and social capital have increasingly been recognized as key determinants of urban productivity. Likewise, outputs have been traditionally seen from an economic perspective; but concomitantly with the emergence of more encompassing conceptualizations of development, the focus has gradually expanded in an attempt to capture non-economic urban dimensions. In this way, the concept of productivity has been explored in relation to broader notions of well-being, such as urban prosperity and quality of life, the opportunities cities offer to all residents and business, along with social cohesiveness and environmental quality.[3]

However, because of limited data, gross domestic product (GDP) per capita is commonly used as a proxy for urban productivity, with a city's GDP measuring local production of goods and services and the population serving as a proxy for inputs related to human capital. Despite its expediency, it is important to emphasize that GDP per capita falls short of a full reflection of the complex dynamics determining urban productivity. For example, the GDP per capita of a small city in an oil-producing country fully reliant on oil exports may look comparable to that of an innovation hub in a developed country, although the respective sources of wealth differ considerably. Likewise, GDP per capita says little about the way a city's productivity gains are distributed among residents in terms of employment and overall well-being. For instance, productivity growth in cities with *labour*-intensive economies will have a greater impact on employment than in *capital*-intensive urban economies. The city of Brussels, for example, shows that high GDP per capita income does not necessarily mean job opportunities for all. Although its GDP per capita is one of the highest in the world (over US$80,000 in 2008), Brussels experienced 15.9 per cent unemployment in 2009, or double Belgium's national average of eight per cent.[4]

RISING URBANIZATION AND INCREASING PRODUCTIVITY

As countries become more urbanized, both urban and national productivity will increase. As shown in Figure 2.1.1, rising urbanization and per capita income went hand in hand for the world as a whole over the past five decades. While the share of urban populations worldwide increased from 33 to 51 per cent between 1960 and 2010, per capita income increased by 152 per cent – from US$2,382 to US$6,006 – over the same period.[5]

However, as shown in Figure 2.1.2, the positive link between urbanization and national productivity holds mainly for high- and middle-income countries, signalling healthy urbanization dynamics fuelled by prosperous cities acting as magnets for rural migration. Low-income countries display a more mixed sort of trend. While these countries as a whole experienced a fast pace of urbanization from 1960 onward, GDP per capita remained largely unchanged, and even decreased, particularly between 1970 and the year 2000. This would suggest that, rather than being attracted by better economic opportunities in urban areas ('demand pull'), rural migrants were only seeking refuge from famine, war or other calamities in what is often

POLICY Cities are naturally more productive than rural areas, as they benefit from larger pools of labour and talent, together with concentration efficiencies for both producers and consumers, and a more fluid exchange of ideas and innovations.[6]

In OECD countries, GDP per capita is, on average, 64 per cent higher in urban areas than in rural areas. Similarly, in European cities with populations over one million, average GDP per capita is 25 per cent higher than in the EU as a whole, and 40 per cent higher than that of their home nations.[7]

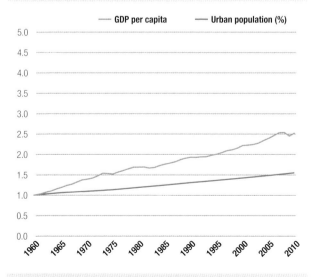

Figure 2.1.1

Urbanization and per capita GDP across countries as % of base year, 1960–2010

Source: UNDESA (2012) urbanization; World Bank (2012) GDP per capita.

Figure 2.1.2

Trends in urbanization and national GDP per capita – for various levels of income, 1960–2010

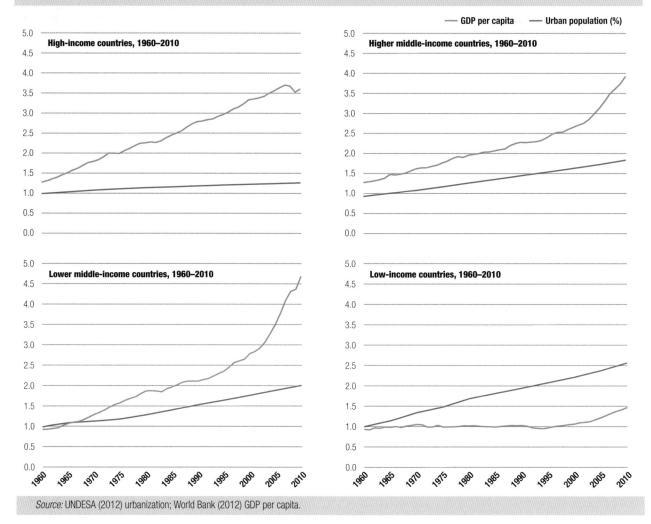

Source: UNDESA (2012) urbanization; World Bank (2012) GDP per capita.

The correlation between urbanization rates and productivity over the past five decades has also varied across and within regions, reflecting the multiplicity of factors affecting both phenomena.

referred to as 'supply push' urbanization.[8]

The experience of the USA, Brazil, China and Kenya illustrates some of the specific factors at work in individual countries. Figure 2.1.3 shows that in the USA, urbanization rates and per capita income moved together until roughly 1940, when urbanization reached close to 60 per cent. Thereafter, per capita income grew more rapidly, reflecting the productivity gains from improvements in manufacturing and services as well as infrastructure investments made during the inter-war years.[9]

Brazil, a higher middle-income country, underwent a seemingly similar growth-urbanization path until the late

1960s, when about half the population became urban. Thereafter, productivity neither grew significantly faster than urbanization, nor were productivity gains sustained, suggesting that urbanization alone may not guarantee continued productivity increases.

China, a lower middle-income country, experienced a gradual increase in urbanization rates and productivity until the late 1970s, when urbanization reached 20 per cent. After the opening up of the economy in 1978, productivity increased at a much faster pace – GDP per capita grew by a factor of roughly 15 between 1978 and 2010, while the percentage of the urban population increased by a factor of 'only' 2.4 during the same period.

Lastly, Kenya illustrates the experience of the limited number of low-income countries, mostly in Sub-Saharan Africa, where productivity growth was negligible even though urbanization rates continued to rise.[10]

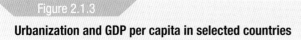

Urbanization and GDP per capita in selected countries

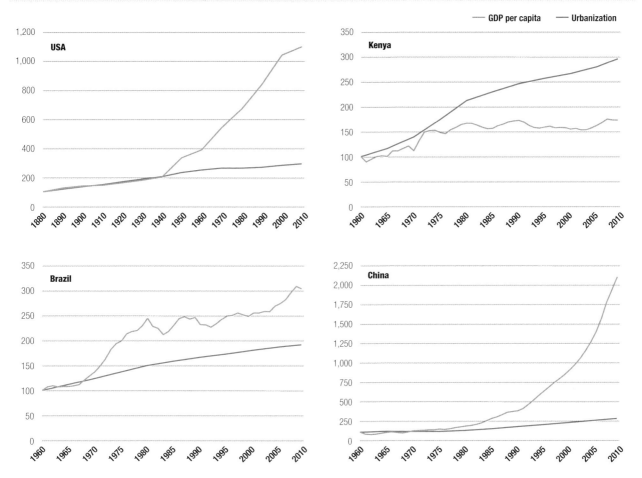

Note: Both time series are indexed to 100 in the initial year. The y value of each series shows the percentage change with respect to the base year. GDP per capita is in constant 2000 US$.

Source: UNDESA (2012) urbanization; World Bank (2012) GDP per capita.

Even where productivity did not improve hand in hand with urbanization, the dominant role of urban areas in national economic productivity is evident across countries. In other words, urban areas contribute disproportionately to national productivity. In the USA, New York City contributes about 10 per cent of the country's GDP and only 6.3 per cent of the total population. The 10 US cities with the largest GDP produce 36 per cent of the country's goods and services and 24 per cent of the total population.[11] São Paulo, Brazil's economic and financial capital, accounts for 10 per cent of the population, but 25 per cent of national GDP.[12] In China, the 53 metropolitan regions with populations over one million contribute about 62 per cent of national non-farm GDP and 29 per cent of the country's population. In Kenya, Nairobi, with 8.4 per cent of the country's population, accounts for almost 20 per cent of

national GDP.[13] Worldwide, the largest 100 cities accounted for around 30 per cent of the total production of goods and services in 2008, with the top 30 cities alone accounting for around 18 per cent.[14]

FACTORS AFFECTING URBAN PRODUCTIVITY

The factors affecting urban productivity are multiple and diverse in nature. Moreover, these factors intertwine in endless combinations both across cities and time, making it difficult to isolate their specific impact. City size is undoubtedly an important factor. As noted by the International Labour Organization, an expanding labour force and, depending on the rate of population growth and the age structure, labour force participation is an important source of growth. However, in the long run, it is labour productivity rather than labour *per se* that determines wage levels, prices and, subsequently, living standards.[15] Otherwise, how would a city such as New York produce the same amount of goods and services as 80 countries put together, and almost as much as Tokyo, which has twice its population? Or why would Lagos generate only a minor fraction – five per cent – of New York's own production of goods and services with a similar-sized population? Likewise, Paris' urban productivity is almost four times that of Istanbul, although both urban agglomerations have roughly the same population.[16] While some of the differences in productivity among cities of roughly the same size are explained by national factors, differences in productivity among cities of equivalent size can also occur within the same country. This is illustrated, for example, by Boston and Atlanta in the USA: with roughly the same population (4.2 million), Boston's productivity was 20 per cent higher than that of Atlanta in 2008 (see Figure 2.1.4).[17]

The factors determining urban productivity can be split into two broad categories: external factors that give cities additional comparative advantage, including national and regional factors; and city-level factors that affect the city's production function, such as physical infrastructure, growth management and human capital, together with innovative, entrepreneurial spirits.

EXTERNAL FACTORS

External factors largely lie beyond any city's orbit of influence. They include geographic location as well as regional and national comparative advantage (Table 2.1.1).

In terms of geographic location, coastal areas and river deltas have long been preferred locations for cities. Currently, 14 of the world's 19 largest cities are ports, which benefit from lower transportation costs and access to wider markets.[18] Natural beauty and warmer weather also give cities specific comparative advantages, and have served to spur the growth of resort cities around the world, from the French Riviera to Punta del Este (Uruguay), Eilat (Israel), Jurmala (Latvia) or Las Palmas (Canary Islands).

The importance of national comparative advantage is illustrated by the fact that, while 22 of the world's top 30 largest urban areas (by population) were located in emerging or developing economies in 2008, only seven emerging economy cities ranked among the top 30 in terms of urban GDP. The group included Mexico City, São Paulo, Buenos Aires, Moscow, Shanghai, Mumbai and Rio de Janeiro, but no Middle Eastern or African cities. The average GDP per capita of these emerging/developing country cities tends to be substantially smaller than that of developed cities (Figure 2.1.4).

Subsequent expansion in individual cities triggered the emergence of 'city clusters', spurring the growth of second-tier cities such as Tianjin, Shijiazhuang and Tangshan, which respectively developed around Beijing; Zhuhai, Dongguan and Foshan around the provincial capital of Guangzhou;

> Cities located in countries with well-educated labour forces, sound infrastructure, mature financial markets, stable political systems and firmly grounded market mechanisms feature higher productivity than those located in countries that do not offer these conditions.

> In China, national policies have played a key role in improved productivity in coastal cities. Three decades ago, China moved to promote economic growth in those cities through a combination of industrialization and financial incentives, putting them in a better position to compete for foreign investment and infrastructure spending.

Figure 2.1.4

Population, GDP per capita and total GDP for selected metropolitan areas (2008)

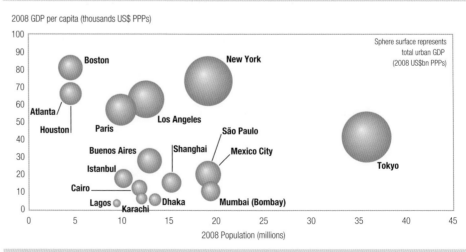

Source: Data from PricewaterhouseCoopers (2009)

Table 2.1.1

External factors determining a city's productivity

Geographical comparative advantage	**Physical attributes** Climate Location (e.g., ports, rivers) Natural endowments Soils Minerals Energy Natural beauty Archeological heritage
Regional comparative advantage	**Economic opportunities** Access to markets, investors and skills Regional hubs and/or clusters
National comparative advantage	**Level of development** Pool of labour, skills, scientific and technological capital Social conditions (e.g., poverty, inequality) Economic infrastructure **Institutional conditions** Sound institutions Sound governance Political stability Maturity of financial markets **Economic policies** Ease of doing business Investment attractiveness Macroeconomic stability **Vision** National leadership

and Suzhou, Wuxi and Hangzhou in close proximity to Shanghai. These city clusters generated agglomeration economies at the regional level, expanding opportunities for trade and enhancing their (and their entire region's) attractions for investors.[19] This cumulative effect has resulted in dramatic differences in productivity between coastal cities and their counterparts in the hinterland, with the growth differential surpassing six per cent, and the ratio of per capita fiscal revenues between the richest and the poorest provinces increasing from 2:1 to 19:1.[20]

CITY-LEVEL FACTORS AFFECTING URBAN PRODUCTIVITY

Cities play a key role in their own productivity, since many of the factors involved are typically found to play out within their jurisdictions. Some of these factors are intrinsic to all urban areas – occurring naturally, such as agglomeration and scale economies (Table 2.1.2). Other city-specific factors depend on the city's ability to capitalize on the natural productivity potential of agglomeration economies ('extrinsic city-specific factors').

Intrinsic city-level factors[21]

One of the most obvious factors determining urban productivity is population growth. As a city's population increases, so does the pool of workers and consumers.

Agglomeration economies are the benefits firms derive from locating near customers and suppliers in order to reduce transport and communication costs while securing access to large labour pools. In larger cities, workers benefit from a wider range of potential employers, which lowers the workers' risk of unemployment. Better matching between labour supply and demand results in greater flexibility, higher productivity and stronger potential for both workers and businesses. Cities also offer firms and residents access to a wider and better range of shared services and infrastructure.[22]

As firms locate close to others, either in other industries ('clustering') or within the same industry ('specialization'), they all benefit from lower transaction costs.[23] While concentrations of firms often begin spontaneously, they can evolve over time to become competitive in export markets, such as the manufacturing of surgical instruments in Sialkot, Pakistan; ceramic tiles in Santa Catarina, Brazil; cotton knitwear in Tirrupur, India; auto parts in Nnewi, Nigeria; wine in Cape Town, South Africa; metal working in the Suami Magazine in Kumasi, Ghana, as well as a variety of clusters in Kenya and South Africa.[24]

As hinted earlier, agglomeration economies also benefit densely populated areas within cities. For example, the original advantage of city centres in terms of lower transportation costs is enhanced over time as a result of agglomeration economies. Higher real estate prices capture these benefits, shaping the city's urban form as it grows not only horizontally but also

> The concentration of infrastructure, people, as well as economic, social and cultural activities, leads to substantial benefits and efficiency due to agglomeration and scale economies.

> **POLICY** Agglomeration economies give cities a competitive advantage over rural areas, as well as large over smaller cities. Agglomeration economies also benefit densely populated areas within cities.

Table 2.1.2	
City-specific factors determining a city's productivity	
Intrinsic (natural) productivity growth factors	**Economies of scale** Provision of urban services **Agglomeration economies** Matching Sharing Learning
Extrinsic productivity growth factors	**Technical efficiency** Structural efficiency Land management policies Space efficiency Infrastructure investment Taxation Disaster prevention Operational efficiency Day-to-day urban management Service delivery Emergency management **Institutional scaffolding** Sound local institutions (e.g., decentralization) Sound governance Ease of doing business **Quality of life** (quality of education, safety, cultural life, liveliness) Attractiveness to knowledge-based industries Attraction and retention of the 'creative class' **Learning-based efficiency** Creativity and innovation Research and development and technological development Entrepreneurship **Vision** Local leadership Local governance

vertically. In a city where market forces are at work, one can expect higher density areas to be the more productive.

Extrinsic city-level factors

As cities continue to grow, higher productivity comes to depend on other factors, such as the ability to maximize the technical efficiency of urban systems, both structural and operational. Effective management of agglomeration diseconomies – including congestion and rising input prices – enables the population and businesses to maximize their own productive potential.

The structural productivity of cities in part rests upon an efficient supply of serviced land and reliable infrastructure, including transport, power, water and sanitation, as well as information and communication technologies. These are critical enabling factors of urban development, providing basic inputs for productive activity and, if deficient, acting as a constraint to growth and private investment.

Buildings have significant roles to play in business productivity, and infrastructure is crucial to any efficient circulation of people, goods and information. Housing supplies could also be considered an important production input, as a suitable stock of housing that adequately responds to the demands of all socioeconomic groups is a prerequisite for an expanding and diverse workforce.[25] If flawed, land policies or speculative market forces can also introduce artificial distortions that interfere with the natural generation of agglomeration economies. Local urban experts in the Arab States and, to a lesser extent, in Africa and Asia, identify efficient urban planning and urban management as the most influential factor behind prosperity.

In turn, efficient supplies of physical infrastructure require sound land management policies and taxation systems that help internalize negative externalities. Also needed are adequate amounts of capital expenditure, which can prove a challenge as most urban services are 'public goods' that require long-term, large-scale public sector investments involving multiple tiers of government. As a result, they are often overlooked, particularly in developing countries, with attendant chronic infrastructure backlogs.

Several cities are actively expanding infrastructure as part of their development strategies. In an effort to make the most of the opportunities opened up by East Africa's fledgling common market, Kenya's capital, Nairobi, is developing transport and communications infrastructures, with tangible results in terms of efficiency and productivity in various economic sectors. Similar efforts are underway in Guadalajara, Mexico, in a bid to attract more high-technology firms (electronics and communications). As a result, production structures are undergoing

Lack of adequate infrastructure severely hinders the structural productivity of cities, limiting their capacity to achieve full potential. This has been the case in Mumbai where, despite serious attempts to create an international financial hub, the city's chaotic transport conditions, and high rents (twice those in Manhattan) have deterred leading financial companies from establishing operations in the city.[26]

POLICY The sound operation of cities, which encompasses traffic and emergency management, transport services, waste collection and other critical support to social and economic activities, has a major role to play in urban productivity.

New technologies offer opportunities for enhanced urban management, making cities more efficient and productive.

China: docks on the Huangpu river, which flows through the centre of Shanghai. The Huangpu is a tributary of the Yellow River, joining it just before that river flows into the East China Sea, and thus the port has developed as a major import/export hub.

© Claudio Zaccherini/Shutterstock.com

Figure 2.1.5

Factors hampering economic productivity as perceived by local experts

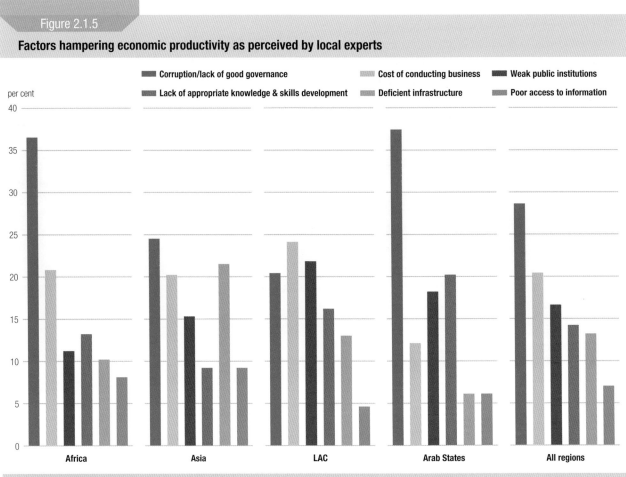

Legend:
- Corruption/lack of good governance
- Cost of conducting business
- Weak public institutions
- Lack of appropriate knowledge & skills development
- Deficient infrastructure
- Poor access to information

Source: UN-Habitat, City Monitoring Branch, *Policy Survey*, 2011.

> Cities that foster the exchange of ideas and innovations are able to tap into growth dynamics which fuel the creation of social and intellectual capital, thereby further contributing to productivity.

rapid change, and suburban landscapes with them.

In Rio de Janeiro, the newly established *Operations Centre* offers a glimpse of the way cities might be managed in the future.[27] This city-wide command centre for emergency situations uses real-time information from multiple departments and government agencies, Visual displays of data from various urban systems, including surveillance cameras, together with maps, news updates, information about incidents,

and even simulations, facilitate real-time monitoring and analysis. Although initially designed for forecasting floods and other emergencies, the Centre is also used for day-to-day management of urban functions. Similar projects have already been implemented in New York City and in Gauteng (South Africa).[28]

While physical factors are undoubtedly key determinants of productivity, local experts around the world emphasize the importance of 'soft' factors. Specifically, corruption and lack of good governance were identified as the most significant barriers to economic productivity by 25 per cent of the local experts surveyed by UN-Habitat (Figure 2.1.5). Additional factors included the high cost or difficulty of conducting business, weak institutions, insufficient knowledge and skills, deficient infrastructure and poor access to information.

With the decline of physical constraints on cities and communities as a result of technological progress in recent decades, creativity and innovation have arguably become major driving forces of productivity and economic growth in urban areas.

> POLICY Cities that educate, attract and retain creative individuals are more likely to prosper, as these individuals generate new ideas and products, and, in turn, also attract high-value added industries, including knowledge-based firms.

Some cities opt to showcase their tangible and intangible heritage and exploit their cultural identity in a bid to strengthen comparative advantage and to bring about social and economic transformation.[29] Doha, Qatar, for example, is developing education and arts as part of the city's new cultural vision.[30] Gaziantep in eastern Turkey has taken to use cultural heritage as a touristic asset for the purposes of enhanced prosperity. Heritage restoration and rehabilitation enhance quality of life while contributing to economic development.[31]

Talent, in turn, is a function of the quality of local school systems and higher education. Many cities in the developing world are faced with brain drain due to lack of local and national policies to retain highly qualified individuals. With the exception of Asia, where about half of the local experts perceive that cities are making efforts to retain talent, the proportions are alarmingly low in other regions. There are exceptions, though: Dubai, UAE, emphasizes higher education and training in engineering and information technologies.[32] In China, Chongqing has developed an ambitious training programme to support the transition of rural migrants from manual-based to skill-based types of work; by 2009, nearly one-third of migrants had benefited from the scheme.[33]

Some cities in developing countries have embraced the model of world-class innovation clusters, such as California's Silicon Valley or Boston's Route 128, in bids to become 'high-tech hubs'. Those that have met with success in this endeavour, such as India's Bangalore, owe it to the same basic factors: the presence of top-quality academic and research institutions as well as substantial public and corporate investment. However, some observers claim that the city needs to pay more attention to infrastructure development and to ensure that the benefits of growth are more evenly distributed across all the population.

Quality of life is rapidly emerging as a major asset in any efforts to attract and retain creative minds and businesses. It comes as no surprise that Toronto, San Francisco or Stockholm should consistently rank among the top performing cities in the world, since they are found as performing particularly well in a wide range of both economic and quality of life indicators such as

> Top performing cities derive their strengths not just from their status as global economic powerhouses or from sophisticated infrastructure, but also from their ability to enhance quality of life.[34]

> A city's existing talent pool is a major determinant of productivity. The more highly skilled a city's population, the more likely it is to attract more talent.

POLICY Offering an environment that is conducive to research and development enables cities to play significant roles in a knowledge-based economy. There is a direct link between R&D, technology and productivity.

crime levels, green areas, air quality and life satisfaction. Outside the more developed nations, Singapore, with a similar balance of quality of life attributes, also ranks among the top world cities and the highest among developing countries.

URBAN PRODUCTIVITY: SOME CHALLENGES
While China's urban population increased from 17 to 39 per cent within a span of 40 years (from 1963 to 2003), the same change in urban population took 120 years in Great Britain and 80 years in the USA.[35] Cities in more advanced countries are better positioned to capitalize on the agglomeration economies associated with population growth. This is not just because that growth is more manageable (typically around one per cent per year); but also because, as suggested by their high GDP per capita, these cities already have the physical and institutional support needed to capitalize on that demographic potential. Such capacities are generally not available in developing countries, leaving fast-expanding cities more exposed to the agglomeration diseconomies which prevent them from fully capitalizing on the productivity potential associated with sustained population growth (typically an annual rate of two to four per cent or more). Despite the difficulty, some cities, such as Shenzhen in China, have made remarkable progress (see box 2.1.1 on page 52).

However, not all cities are fully capitalizing on the gains of population growth. This is the case of Dhaka, the capital city of Bangladesh, the ninth largest city in the world. With an average annual population growth of 4.4 per cent between 1990 and 2008, Dhaka is one of

> The fast pace of urbanization in developing countries presents both challenges and opportunities for the productivity of cities.

Box 2.1.1

Shenzhen: capitalizing on the gains of urban growth

Until recently Shenzhen was one of the world's fastest growing cities. During the past 30 years or so, Shenzhen's GDP per capita ranked first among China's major cities – averaging a phenomenal 27 per cent annual growth in urban GDP. The gains from Shenzhen's fast pace of industrialization, urbanization and modernization have served to enhance living standards for the whole population, including incomes and living conditions. A new social security and public health insurance system has been successfully implemented. The city's Gini's coefficient has remained around 0.3, far less than that of the other cities on the mainland, denoting the city's efforts to achieve an equitable growth pattern.[36]

the fastest growing in Asia. While some of the population growth has only reflected recent expansion boundaries, the Dhaka region has long attracted migrants from rural areas looking for opportunities in the booming metropolis. They provide much-needed labour in rapidly growing sectors of the economy. Fuelled by the continuous growth in the financial, manufacturing and telecommunications sectors, annual GDP is an estimated US$75 billion.[37] At the same time, Dhaka's GDP per capita is the lowest of all megacities, suggesting that agglomeration diseconomies are likely to have offset a large proportion of the potential benefits associated with strong population growth. In other words, the productivity gains associated with such growth would have been remarkable if only Dhaka had been able to manage its expansion more effectively and distribute the benefits in a more equitable manner.

Unfortunately, Dhaka's experience does not seem to be the exception. Urban experts sampled in the UN-Habitat survey expressed scepticism over any effective (re)distribution of the benefits of urban prosperity: in Bangalore, Ho Chi Minh City and Chongqing, these benefits are perceived to be captured mainly by the educated class; in Alexandria and Nairobi, mostly by the wealthy; and largely by politicians in Santo Domingo, Dubai and Dar es Salaam. As shown in Figure 2.1.6, urban experts in all regions share the same grim assessment; only Asia suggests a slightly more positive outlook with 20 per cent of local experts saying that economic prosperity is evenly distributed, compared with 14 per cent in the Middle East and roughly seven per cent in Africa and Latin America.

HOW TO RAISE A CITY'S PRODUCTIVITY? SOME GENERAL POLICY GUIDELINES

There is not a single blanket prescription for enhanced urban productivity. While it is generally linked to stable macroeconomic conditions, sound institutions and adequate infrastructure, the focus of dedicated policy actions will depend on a city's level of development.

The management of urban growth is particularly important for rapidly expanding cities in the early stages of development for them fully to capitalize on the natural benefits of agglomeration economies and to reduce future inefficiencies.

Ineffective land management, inadequate spending on infrastructure, distorting taxation schemes and unduly cumbersome business regulations are detrimental to any city's structural productivity.

It is important to identify any barriers that prevent a city from maximizing its productivity potential. In this regard, reducing traffic congestion, enhancing mass transit options and providing efficient, reliable services are major determinants in any city's functional

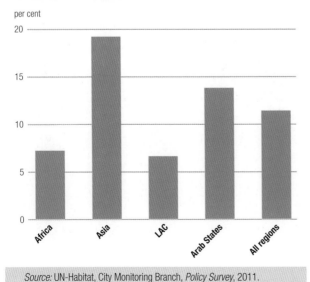

Figure 2.1.6

Perceptions of experts regarding the distribution of economic prosperity

per cent

POLICY Cities at the early stages of development must improve transportation for easier two-way access to markets, and make adequate healthcare and basic education available to the whole population.

Source: UN-Habitat, City Monitoring Branch, *Policy Survey*, 2011.

POLICY As cities progress along the development path, they ought to facilitate production processes, also address any technical and organizational inefficiencies that hinder structural and operational productivity.

POLICY The importance of sound governance structures to prevent corruption, together with strong local institutions and business-conducive regulations, cannot be overemphasized.

POLICY To enhance productivity, cities at all stages of development should seek support from a wide range of stakeholders and set in motion the process of desirable change.

China: the Hexi Corridor, part of the historical Silk Route, remains economically important.

© 2012 Edwina Sassoon/fotoLIBRA.com

productivity. In addition, cities at intermediate levels of development should also enhance their technological capacities with a sharper focus on higher education and training as well as ICT infrastructure.

In order to sustain higher wages and the associated standards of living, more advanced cities need to tap into innovation-driven productivity gains by supporting businesses' ability to compete based on more sophisticated and innovative production processes and products. While the factors at work are less easy to grasp than in the case of technical efficiency, experience from around the world points to the importance of supporting research and development in quality higher education and research institutions with both public and corporate investment.

Promoting an entrepreneurial spirit, particularly among youth, is a desirable strategy for any city, regardless of development level or economic strength. Similarly, far from being a desirable though ultimately dispensable aspiration, enhancing overall quality of life should be considered as essential to any economic development strategy, if a city is to attract creative people and businesses.

Leadership will always be a critical factor, be it collective, as exercised through sound governance systems, or individual, i.e. relying on a particularly inspiring politician or local figure. It takes leadership to change the prevailing urban paradigm and develop the transformative vision that will not just boost productivity of a city, or region, or even country, but also broadly distribute the associated benefits for the sake of shared prosperity.

Endnotes

1   Buyle-Bodin and Hermant-De Callataÿ, 2011.

2   OECD, 2001.

3   GDP per capita also has the added advantage of being consistently defined across nations, which makes it better suited for international comparisons.

4   Brussels' many commuters – roughly 360,000 coming from neighbouring regions of Flanders and Wallonia – also artificially raise its productivity (http://en.wikipedia.org/wiki/Economy_of_Belgium).

5   *World Bank Data: World Development Indicators & Global Development Finance*, Online database last updated July 9 2012, http://data.worldbank.org

6   UN-Habitat, 2010a.

7   European Commission, 2009.

8   Buckley and Kallergis, 2011.

9   *Ibid.*

10 *Ibid.*

11 PricewaterhouseCoopers, 2009.

12 Cities Alliance, 2006.

13 Kenya's 2008 GDP (PPP current International), total population, population in the largest city: World Development Indicators (2012); Nairobi's 2008 GDP (PPP): PricewaterhouseCoopers (2009).

14 PricewaterhouseCoopers, *Op. Cit.*

15 International Labor Organization, 2003.

16 OECD, 2006.

17 PricewaterhouseCoopers, 2009.

18 UN-Habitat, 2008.

19 ActiveUKChina, 2012.

20 UN-Habitat, 2008.

21 This section draws heavily from Turok, I. (2011) *Urban Employment and the Prosperity of Cities*. Background paper prepared for "State of the World's Cities Report 2012/2013".

22 As noted by Turok, see Jacobs, J. (1969) *The Economy of Cities*, London, Jonathan Cape; Jacobs, J. (1984) *Cities and the Wealth of Nations*, New York, Random House; Porter, M. (1998) 'Clusters and the new economics of competitiveness', *Harvard Business Review*, December, pp.77-90.

23 As noted by Turok (2011), Alfred Marshall (1920) was the first economist to recognize the benefits for firms of having access to a reservoir of information and ideas, skills and shared inputs; Marshall, A. (1920) *Principles of Economics* (8th edition), Macmillan, London. See also Duranton, G. and D. Puga (2004) 'Micro-foundations of urban agglomeration economies', in *Handbook of Urban and Regional Economics*, Henderson, V. and Thisse, J. (eds.) vol. 4, North Holland, Amsterdam, pp. 2063-117; and Venables, A. J. (2010) 'Economic geography and African development', *Papers in Regional Science*, 89(3), pp.469-483.

24 Adebowale, 2011.

25 Turok, 2011.

26 *Bloomberg Business Week*, April 23, 2011 as quoted by Buckley and Kallergis, 2011.

27 Rio's Operation Centre builds upon advanced technologies created by IBM Research labs around the world.

28 Astroman, 2011.

29 Spirou, 2011.

30 Mena, 2011.

31 Kurtul, 2011.

32 Al-Bassam and Mouris, 2011.

33 Liu and Wang, 2011.

34 PricewaterhouseCoopers, 2010.

35 China's urban growth rates: UNDESA (WUP): US' and Great Britain's urban growth rates: Buckley, R. and A. Kallergis (2011) *Op. Cit.*

36 Jin and Liu, 2011.

37 PricewaterhouseCoopers, 2009.

© Philip Lange/Shutterstock.com

Urban Infrastructure: Bedrock of Prosperity

Infrastructure is crucial for the development, functionality and prosperity of urban areas. It provides the foundation on which any city will thrive. Adequate infrastructure – improved water and sanitation, reliable and sufficient power supply, efficient transport networks and modern information and communication technologies (ICTs) – contributes to the sustainability and economic growth of urban areas, promotes the competitiveness of local businesses, improves labour productivity, enhances the investment climate in a city and contributes to its attractiveness. Physical infrastructure, such as roads, power and communication facilities, improves urban connectivity, which is essential to induce growth and reduce poverty. Cities that fail to provide adequate infrastructure are less likely to be prosperous and sustainable in terms of balancing socioeconomic development with environmental protection.[1]

Since inception in 2008 the global economic crisis has had a pernicious effect on the ability of cities to fund new infrastructure and maintain current stocks. In the USA for instance, Community Block Grants from the Federal Government to cities have been slashed by a quarter in the past two years.[2] Likewise,

Mexico: aerial view of Guadalajara.

© Jesus Cervantes/Shutterstock.com

Cities that have managed to attract investment and enhance competitiveness in a highly globalized economy are those that have vastly improved the range and quality of their infrastructure. Conversely, poor infrastructure is a major impediment to development, poverty reduction and improved standards of living.

Lujiazui City, China: high-speed trains substantially reduce transit times between cities, a 140 km journey taking only 30 minutes.

© ArtisticPhoto/Shutterstock.com

New York State faces a funding shortfall of US$80 billion needed to repair over one-third of bridges and other crumbling infrastructure.[3] In developing countries, frequent mismatches between the infrastructure requirements of urban areas and the ability of authorities to provide the requisite financial resources can exacerbate already poor living conditions through the proliferation of slums, unsanitary environmental conditions, and inadequate water and power supply.

There is a positive link between the provision of infrastructure and the level of urbanization. More urbanized countries tend to provide more infrastructures (Figure 2.2.1.). High levels of infrastructure and service provision in urban areas can partly be attributed to higher densification

Figure 2.2.1

Infrastructure provision is closely related to levels of urbanization

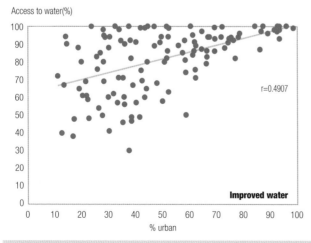

Access to water(%)

r=0.4907

Improved water

% urban

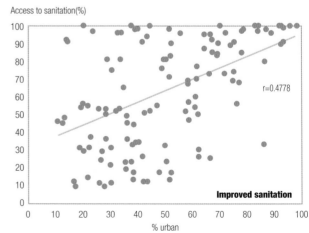

Access to sanitation(%)

r=0.4778

Improved sanitation

% urban

Source: WHO/UNICEF (2010); and World Bank Database (2010).

together with agglomeration and scale economies, which increase returns on investment. Moreover, the greater purchasing power and effective demand associated with urban areas will ensure cost recovery.

TRENDS IN THE PROVISION OF URBAN INFRASTRUCTURE: SIGNIFICANT REGIONAL VARIATIONS

Differences in infrastructure across regions have implications for the prosperity of cities and reflect a variety of factors, including levels of income or development, economic growth, pace of urbanization, technical capacities and political commitment. The lowest levels of infrastructure provision are to be found in urban Africa (average water and sanitation coverage is 89 and 69 per cent respectively; electricity: 69 per cent; paved roads: 28 per cent; fixed telephone lines: four per cent; cellphones and Internet connectivity: 57 and 10 per cent, respectively).

Asian cities have strongly invested in infrastructure development in the past few decades, achieving nearly universal provision of water, electricity and mobile telephone services. In particular, China has pursued

a conscious strategy of infrastructure-led growth since the 1990s. Investment in this area increased from 5.7 per cent of GDP in 1998 to 14.4 per cent in 2006.[4] During the same period, India increased infrastructure spending from 4.1 per cent to 5.6 per cent of GDP. The average for Latin America and the Caribbean is under two per cent of GDP,[5] compared with Africa's estimated 5–6 per cent.[6] In Latin America, public investment in infrastructure bore the brunt of fiscal adjustment, as it fell from more than three per cent of GDP in 1988 to about 1.6 per cent in 1998. Consequently, productive infrastructure such as roads, electricity and telecommunications – all of which are crucial for the prosperity of cities – now lags behind East Asia and China, in a reversal of the situation prevailing in 1980.

POLICY Infrastructure is the most common entry point to prosperity in cities. Prioritizing infrastructure is part of long-term socioeconomic development, and environmental protection for most cities.

Figure 2.2.2

Infrastructure coverage by region

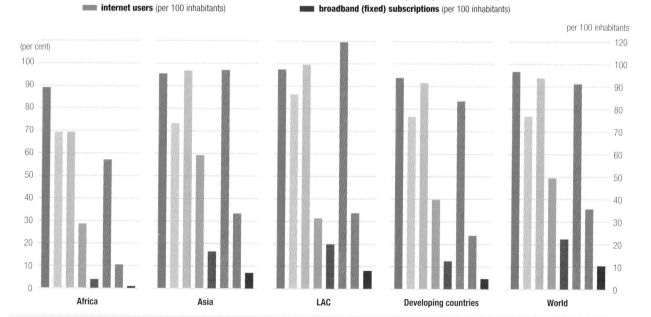

- ▪ **urban population with improved water** (per cent)
- ▪ **urban population with improved sanitation** (per cent)
- ▪ **urban population with electricity** (per cent)
- ▪ **paved roads as a proportion of total** (per cent)
- ▪ **fixed telephone lines** (per 100 inhabitants)
- ▪ **mobile cellular subscriptions** (per 100 inhabitants)
- ▪ **internet users** (per 100 inhabitants)
- ▪ **broadband (fixed) subscriptions** (per 100 inhabitants)

Source: WHO/UNICEF (2010); International Energy Agency (2010); International Road Federation (2009); ITU World Telecommunication/ICT Indicators Database (2010).

Box 2.2.1

Ranking of urban infrastructure

The local experts surveyed by UN-Habitat report that, across all developing regions, the least developed components of urban infrastructure relate to recreation, sanitation and urban transport, while the most developed is telecommunications. All of this has important implications for urban prosperity. For instance, the low priority given to recreational infrastructure implies that access to public spaces in many cities is limited, as indicated in Chapter 2.3 (Quality of Life). Similarly, the low priority given to urban transport has wider-ranging implications, in this case for intra- and inter-urban mobility.

Ranking (<1 = least developed; 5 = most developed)

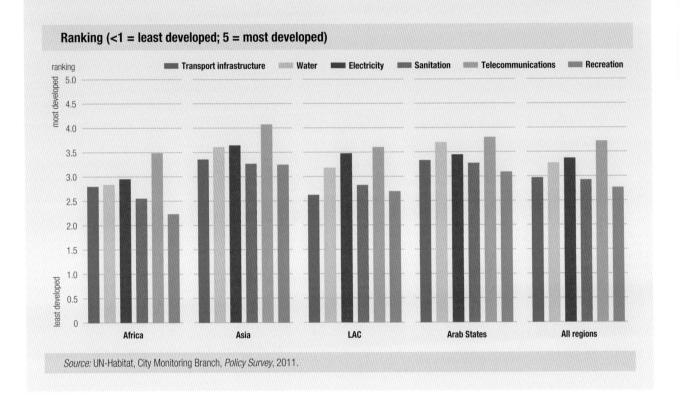

Source: UN-Habitat, City Monitoring Branch, *Policy Survey*, 2011.

There are remarkable inter-city differences in local experts' perceptions regarding the coverage and quality of urban infrastructure. These differences are discussed below with respect to water, roads and ICTs.

Water supply: when good governance changes the equation

Adequate water supply is essential for environmental sustainability and quality of life. Access to clean water reduces morbidity and mortality, and improves the productive abilities of the poor.

Water scarcity characterizes African cities: Although official statistics reveal that 89 per cent of the urban population in Africa is now enjoying improved water supply, a large majority of Sub-Saharan African cities experience regular water shortages. The UN-Habitat survey shows that 11 of the 14 African cities (79 per cent) under review are associated with such problems.

Experts concur that worst affected are Ibadan and Dar es Salaam, closely followed by Accra, Addis Ababa, Luanda, Lusaka, Lagos and Nairobi, which suffer chronic water shortages. Although 78 to 98 per cent of households in four of these cities – Accra, Lagos, Nairobi and Lusaka – benefit from improved access to water, most experts also identify them as experiencing severe water shortages. Interestingly, despite its semi-arid climate and location in a water-poor country, Gaborone experiences the lowest levels of water shortages among the African cities surveyed by UN-Habitat. This is partly because, through expanded water supplies and conservation measures, the city's water agency (Water Utilities Corporation) has put itself in a position to meet the demand, which is in excess of 20 million cubic metres per annum.[7] Similarly, drought-affected Algiers has in recent years overcome the problem of chronic scarcity through several water management initiatives.[8]

The water shortage pattern is more mixed in Asian cities: Half of the Asian cities in the UN-Habitat survey experience water shortages. Those with the more severe shortages are Cebu, Davao, Bangalore, Lahore, and Hyderabad. In Bangalore, water is supplied once in 46 hours for a period of 2–3 hours.[9] This trend had been observed by one analyst who noted that: 'no South Asian city can supply water 24/7 to its residents'.[10]

On the other hand, water scarcity is unknown in Singapore, according to all local respondents to the survey. Other cities where water shortages are perceived to be relatively insignificant include Chongqing, Gaziantep and Shenzhen.

Differences in shortage patterns across Asian cities have to do mainly with water governance. For instance, the Bangalore Water Supply and Sewerage Board faces several

> **POLICY** City authorities must systematically maintain infrastructure stocks to ensure that the benefits thereof are fully capitalized. It is in their best interest to improve coordination with various tiers of government for the design, provision and maintenance of infrastructure.

challenges, including: extension of its service area from 226 km² to 800 km² in 2007; high costs of production of water brought from a distance of over 100 km; dependence on State subsidies; user charges that have not been revised for about 10 years; and inadequate legislation on groundwater abstraction.[11]

Water shortage patterns vary significantly across Latin American cities: The UN-Habitat survey found that eight of the 15 cities under review in this region experienced serious water shortages, including Havana, Panama City, Guarenas (Venezuela), Lima, Ciudad del Este (Paraguay) and Guadalajara. Cities where water scarcity is perceived as 'moderate' are Tijuana, La Paz and Valparaiso; those without perceived water shortages are Medellín, Fort-de-France (French Antilles) and Montevideo.

Differences in shortage patterns across cities reflect

Saudi Arabia: an old water tower, a well-known feature in the city of Riyadh.

© Fedor Selivanov/Shutterstock.com

> The success of Singapore in meeting local water demand is down to effective water governance. The Public Utilities Board has developed a long-term strategy known as 'the Four National Taps' to ensure steady, sustainable supplies. The strategy entails using water from different sources: catchment, recycling, desalination and imports.

Many Arab cities are able to meet their water requirements because of the high political priority given to the provision of this public good.[12] City authorities have improved water security through increased supplies, demand management, conservation and desalination.[13]

local conditions and the state of water management. In 2011, Havana experienced its worst water shortage since 1961 due to the effects of drought and depletion of fresh supplies as well as a deteriorated network – about 70 per cent of the city's 3,158 km of pipelines are in poor condition, resulting in significant leakages.[14]

In contrast, regular supplies in Medellín reflect sound management by *Empresas Públicas de Medellín* (EPM), one of the most successful public utility companies in Latin America. In 2009, EPM launched the *Litros de Amor* scheme to provide free-of-charge water (a daily 25 litres per head) to economically poor households.[15]

Uneven water shortage patterns in Arab State cities: Despite their typical location in hyper-arid regions, Arab State cities generally do not suffer from severe water shortages. However, according to local experts, three of the surveyed cities are finding water supply a major challenge: Amman, Basra and Saida (Lebanon). In Amman, the situation is quite critical with supplies only once or twice a week.[16] In Basra, the supply falls short of around 33 per cent of the needs of the population.[17] Residents often complain about quality (taste, smell and colour).[18] Arab cities deemed

to be meeting their water needs include Aqaba, Doha, Al-Muharrak (Bahrain), Dubai, Kuwait City and Erbil.

Trends in road infrastructure

The road network will rank amongst any city's most prized assets, as it facilitates the movement of people and goods. Apart from access, road networks also form the basic grids for trunk infrastructure for water, sanitation and power supplies. Roads also contribute to effective mobility, which is crucial for the prosperity of any city. Congested roads and poor facilities for pedestrians are the most pervasive transport problems affecting cities in developing countries (Table 2.2.1). The UN-Habitat survey shows that to a large majority of experts – 96 per cent in Africa; 91 per cent in Asia; 88 per cent in Latin America; and 80 per cent in Arab States – traffic congestion is the main form of infrastructure deficiency plaguing cities in those regions, hindering free movement and making travel frustrating and time-consuming. The economic costs of traffic congestion are enormous: in the USA in 2010, a staggering US$101 billion was lost in productivity and wasted fuel, or US$713 per commuter;[19] and in Mauritius, traffic congestion in cities costs the economy 1.3 per cent of GDP.[20]

Road infrastructure remains poor in African cities: In most African cities, roads account for less than seven per cent of land area, compared with 25–30 per cent in developed country cities (Table 2.2.2).[21] In Kinshasa, Kampala and Ouagadougou, paved roads account for less than 12 per cent of the whole urban network. In many cities, the road

Table 2.2.1					
Infrastructure deficiencies as perceived by local experts in surveyed cities (per cent)					
Type of deficiency	**Africa**	**Asia**	**LAC**	**Arab States**	**All cities**
Congested roads	96.0	90.6	87.9	79.5	89.3
Poor facilities for pedestrians	89.2	73.4	79.2	42.7	74.3
Power outages	86.1	58.2	58.8	59.5	66.5
Flooding	75.7	59.5	77.1	33.9	65.0
Slow/unaffordable Internet connections	80.6	38.9	63.6	56.3	61.3
Leaking sewers	80.0	49.7	59.4	28.0	57.4
Shortages of potable water	73.3	40.5	55.0	36.7	53.5
Shortage of cooking gas/other sources of energy	55.6	29.2	31.7	14.2	34.6
Interrupted phone lines	51.5	22.3	28.0	31.7	33.9

Source: UN-Habitat, City Monitoring Branch, *Policy Survey*, 2011.

network has barely kept pace with urban growth: in Douala, for instance, it has remained unchanged for the past 20 years despite a doubling of the population, increased numbers of vehicles, and urban sprawl.[22] The dysfunctional nature of road infrastructure in Africa poses a major challenge to mobility and prosperity and is an important source of congestion. In addition to this, poor maintenance is a major problem: only 18.5 per cent of experts across African cities believe that infrastructure is systematically maintained.

However, some African cities have taken innovative steps to enhance mobility and tackle traffic congestion. Lagos introduced a Bus Rapid Transit (BRT) system in March 2008. This commuter-oriented service delivers fast, comfortable and cost-effective urban mobility. Currently in its first phase, the Lagos BRT covers a 22-km corridor, moving more than 200,000 passengers daily, which exceeds expected usage by 100 per cent.[23] In July 2010, South Africa's Gauteng Province launched the Gautrain, a state-of-the-art 80-km rapid railway. Built at a cost of US$3.8 billion, this is Africa's first high-speed urban train, linking the airport, Johannesburg and Pretoria. The Gautrain was designed to reduce road congestion, promote economic development and

provide alternative means of transport,[24] and began operations in July 2010, just before the opening of the 2010 FIFA World Cup, with service between Sandton Station and O. R. Tambo International Airport. Operations on the second phase linking Johannesburg and Pretoria commenced in August 2011. Gautrain takes less than 30 minutes to cover the distance between both cities,

> Road congestion, poor facilities for pedestrians, power outages and flooding are major infrastructural deficiencies, which adversely affect the prosperity of cities.

> A notable feature of the transport system in African cities is the virtual absence of state-operated/regulated public transport. The private sector is the major provider of transport services, often in the form of second-hand mini- and microbuses, shared taxis, and, more recently, commercial motorcycles.[25] The needs of pedestrians are hardly taken into consideration despite the fact that walking accounts for over 60–70 per cent of trips in cities such as Conakry, Douala or Kinshasa.[26]

Table 2.2.2

Characteristics of the road network in selected African cities

City	Length of road network (km)	Length of paved road network (km)	Paved roads as % of roads	Paved road density (metres per 1,000 pop)	Paved road density (km per km²)
Abidjan	2,042	1,205	59	346	2.1
Accra	1,899	950	50	339	2.8
Addis Ababa	–	400	–	129	0.7
Bamako	836	201	24	167	0.8
Conakry	815	261	32	174	2.3
Dar es Salaam	1,140	445	39	122	0.2
Douala	1,800	450	25	237	2.4
Kampala	984	118	12	170	0.2
Kigali	610	451	74	225	0.5
Kinshasa	5,000	500	10	63	0.1
Lagos	–	6,000	–	400	1.7
Lusaka	2,500	700	28	500	1.9
Ouagadougou	1,827	201	11	185	0.4
Average	–	–	33	318	1.7

Source: Kumar and Barrett (2008, p.24); figures for Lusaka were obtained for the local study prepared for this Report.

In major Asian cities, about 11 per cent of land space is devoted to roads, well below the 20–30 per cent rate common in US cities.[27] In Indian cities, the proportion varies from 21 per cent in Delhi to 11 per cent in Mumbai to five per cent in Kolkata.[28]

In India, public transport accounts for only 22 per cent of urban trips among ever-increasing numbers of private vehicles.[30] A greater proportion of these vehicles is concentrated in only a few cities: New Delhi, Mumbai, Kolkata and Bangalore, which together host five per cent of India's population but 14 per cent of registered vehicles.[31]

which by car could take up to two hours. With 100,000 passenger trips per day, Gautrain is expected to reduce the number of cars on the main highway by 20 per cent.[29]

Significant improvements in road infrastructure in Asian cities: In recent years, various Asian countries have embarked on ambitious programmes of road development and expansion. In 1997, India started the Golden Quadrilateral motorway to connect the country's largest cities – Kolkata, Delhi, Mumbai and Chennai. An east–west corridor has also been recently completed, not just improving connections between cities but also opening up the hinterlands. In China, cities have been at the forefront of massive infrastructure development with emphasis on new roads and subway systems. The urban road network more than doubled between 1990 and 2003,[32] largely contributing to urbanization and economic growth. Cities like Beijing and Shanghai have extended infrastructure to suburban areas in a bid to match spatial expansion. Beijing currently allocates 30 per cent of its construction budget to mass transit[33] and Shanghai spends 10 per cent of its GDP on infrastructure, of which 40 per cent is for transportation. Singapore's public transportation system is considered to be one of the best integrated and best planned in the world. In addition, adequate facilities are provided for pedestrians in the form of a safe and comfortable walking environment, which enhances quality of life.

Massive economic growth in Asia, particularly in China and India, has spurred spectacular increases in the numbers of motor vehicles. This has contributed to traffic congestion, air and noise pollution, road accidents and higher energy use in the region. In India, the number of passenger vehicles increased by 12.9 per cent between 2007 and 2008 as nine million motorized vehicles were sold over the course of a single year.[34] In China, the number of vehicles increased 10-fold between 1990 and 2002; of particular significance is the increase in the number of motorcycles and scooters, from just 200,000 in 1981 to 50 million in 2002. By 2009, China had over 91 million motorized two-wheelers – accounting for 51.2 per cent of the total number of motor vehicles.[35] Private vehicles account for over 76.8 per cent of total vehicles in China.[36] The situation is similar in India, where public transport accounts for only 22 per cent of urban trips, as increasing numbers of private vehicles ply the roads.[37]

However, the provision of transport infrastructure in Asian cities is not commensurate with increases in motor vehicles or travel demand. In India between 1951 and 2004, the number of motor vehicles grew from 300,000 to over 30 million – a 100-fold increase – while the length of the road network only increased by a multiple of eight – from 400,000 to 3.23 million km.[38] In Mumbai, Delhi, and Chennai, annual average travel demand increased by five, ten and seven per cent, respectively, but growth in roadway supply barely reached one per cent.[39]

In most Indian cities, infrastructure for pedestrians is lacking. This is confirmed by the UN-Habitat policy survey, which shows that a large proportion of local experts in Hyderabad and Bangalore are of the view that this type of infrastructure is poorly developed. This situation forces pedestrians to share crowded roads with fast moving vehicles. The end result is high ratios of accidents involving pedestrians – 50 per cent in Delhi and 80 per cent in Mumbai.[40] In China, most cities provide infrastructure for pedestrians and cyclists. This may account for the lower incidence of traffic fatalities involving pedestrians – just 25 per cent.[41] However, in recent years, walking and cycling amenities have been on the decline in Chinese cities, which are unable to cope with the increased numbers of users. It has been observed that: '*Many pavements and cycle lanes are eliminated or narrowed to accommodate more car lanes. Some streets and districts are now off-limits to cyclists.*'[42]

Latin America and the Caribbean features the highest rate of motorization of all developing countries: The region has five times as many cars as sub-Saharan Africa or Asia, and about twice as many as the Middle East or North Africa.[43] Motorization in the region increased from 100 vehicles per 1,000 in 1990 to 155 per 1,000 in 2005, before reaching 169:1,000 in 2008. Rising incomes, expanding middle classes, high levels of urbanization, an expanding local automobile industry, and availability of low-cost vehicles are the major forces driving motorization in Latin America and the Caribbean.

As a result, cities in the region experience severe traffic congestion. A great majority of local experts surveyed by UN-Habitat (over 80 per cent) report that the roads in their respective cities are congested. The situation in São Paulo is exceptional, with the world's worst traffic jams according to *Time* magazine; on May 9, 2008, traffic congestion extended over 266 km in greater São Paulo.[44] While the phenomenon affects all segments of the population, particularly the poor, the rich have resorted to helicopters to navigate the crippling traffic in the metropolis. Traffic congestion costs the city's economy US$2.2 billion a year in lost productivity.[45] Time spent in traffic also results in situations that affect quality of life. This is in addition to deteriorating air quality, traffic accidents, increased fuel consumption and the growth in emissions of greenhouse gases.

Cities such as Buenos Aires, Mexico City and São Paulo have witnessed overall declines in the shares of public transport. In São Paulo, public transport as a share of all trips declined from 46 per cent in 1977 to 33 per cent in 1997 and again to 29 per cent in 2001.[46] In Havana, the total number of public transport users declined from 3.5 million in 1991 to 540,000 in 2011.[47] In Guadalajara, use of private cars increased from 30 to 50 per cent of all trips between the years 2000 and 2010, while the number of public transport users declined from 60 to 30 per cent.[48] In Port of Spain (Trinidad and Tobago), despite the problems associated with private car-ownership and although a designated congestion-free east–west bus route had been made available, the use of public buses declined from 16.3 million users in 1990 to 6.4 million in 1998.[49] Factors behind these sharp declines include poor perceptions of public bus services; lack of information on availability, routes and schedules; crime

POLICY Cities must address road congestion problems that adversely affect their prosperity.

A trend closely associated with motorization in Latin American and Caribbean cities is the decreasing share of public transport. This has implications for the mobility of the poorer households.

Curitiba, Brazil: a tubular bus station and sleek, modern bus, part of the city's integrated transport system.

© Paul Smith/Panos Pictures

POLICY Cities should develop sustainable public transport solutions that can have positive effects on all the dimensions of prosperity.

and safety concerns; and the long distances that commuters have to walk to bus stops/terminals.

An indication of the infrastructure for sustainable road transport in Latin American cities can be gleaned from Table 2.2.3. In the selected cities, dedicated bus lanes (often in the form of BRT) amount to a combined 904 km, accounting for only 2.2 per cent of the 42,000 km of public roads used by buses. Bogotá and Curitiba feature the highest shares of dedicated bus lanes, with 1.1 per cent each of roads used by all forms of public transport; in the case of Bogotá, dedicated bus lanes account for 6.4 per cent of public roads used by this type of transport. In Bogotá and Curitiba, the dedicated bus lanes are part of the TransMilenio and BRT systems respectively, which now serve as the models for BRT across the world.

In many Latin American cities, facilities for non-motorized transport do not appear to rank high among priorities. The UN-Habitat survey shows that, with the exception of cities such as Fort-de-France, Santos and Medellín, a majority of local experts believe that pedestrian facilities are poorly developed. This is somewhat confirmed in Table 2.2.3, which shows Curitiba as the only city where the length of priority lanes for pedestrians is in double digits (19 km).

Cities in the Arab States have the highest rates of vehicle ownership: Over the past two decades, the Arab region has witnessed phenomenal growth in motorization. In 2008, the total number of motor vehicles reached 26.7 million – having grown at an annual average rate of 4.2 per cent between 1997 and 2008.[50] The region features one of the highest ratios of vehicle ownership in the developing world. For instance, in Bahrain, Kuwait, Qatar, the UAE and Oman, the ratios of motor vehicles per 1,000 population are 509, 507, 724, 313, and 225 respectively.[51] Factors behind this trend include the affluence occasioned by the region's oil-driven economic boom, strong preference for private cars, subsidized fuel, greater availability of car finance and lack of effective public transportation.

These high ratios have led to chronic traffic congestion. According to the UN-Habitat survey, with the exception of Aqaba (Jordan) most experts (over 75 per cent) are of the view that their respective cities experience chronic traffic congestion.

Conditions in Dubai typify those of other cities in Gulf Cooperation Council countries: with over one million cars, Dubai's car-ownership ratio of 541:1,000 exceeds those of London (345:1,000) and New York (444:1,000).[52] Being one of the fastest growing cities in the world with vehicle ownership increasing at a 12 per cent annual rate, it comes as little surprise that Dubai has become the most congested city in the Middle East. Commuting to and from work takes an average one hour and 45 minutes[53] and this congestion causes losses of US$1.3 billion, or 3.2 per cent of the city's GDP, every year.[54] In Amman, the number of privately-owned cars reached 544,974 in 2009, growing at the rate of 10 per cent per annum and accounting for 72 per cent of the total number of vehicles.[55]

The quality and maintenance of roads in Arab cities is high by comparison with other developing countries. However, even massive investment in road networks has not kept pace with the rapid increase in vehicle numbers. There

Table 2.2.3

Priority lanes for buses, cyclists and pedestrians in selected Latin American cities

Metropolitan area	Bus lanes (km)	Cycling (km)	Pedestrians (km)
Belo Horizonte	28	20.0	0.5
Bogotá	85	291.3	2.4
Buenos Aires	16	93.0	5.4
Caracas	0	14.0	2.2
México City	174	30.0	0.0
Curitiba	72	120.1	19.0
Guadalajara	0	0	2.5
León	15	54.3	1.2
Lima	34	59.0	1.7
Montevideo	0	8.4	1.0
Porto Alegre	43	0.0	0.7
Río de Janeiro	24	153.0	0.0
San José	0	0	1.0
Santiago	113	112.8	5.5
São Paulo	301	40.2	7.4
Total	904	996.1	50.5

Source: Corporación Andina de Fomento (2010) *Observatorio de Movilidad Urbana para América Latina,* Corporación Andina de Fomento.

are areas – particularly the suburbs which public buses do not serve – where commuters have no option but to use private cars. Therefore, providing alternatives to the car appears to be the most viable option. Several cities in the region are moving in this direction. For instance, the Dubai Metro commenced partial operations in September 2009. When fully operational in 2012, this underground railway is expected to reduce the number of cars on the road by as much as 30 per cent.[56] In 2010, the Greater Amman Municipality launched a US$175 million BRT scheme covering 32km in three busy corridors. When completed in 2012, capacity will reach 6,000 passengers per hour.[57]

Information and communication technologies (ICTs) and the prosperity of cities

Over the past decade, worldwide expansion in ICTs has been nothing short of phenomenal. For instance, in the sole mobile telephony area, the total number of subscriptions

Public transport systems are inadequate in many Arab cities. For instance, in Beirut, fewer than 10 per cent of commuters are served by public transport;[58] in Amman the corresponding figure is 14 per cent.[59]

increased from 962 million in 2001 to six billion in 2011 – resulting in a worldwide ratio of 867:1,000.[60] It is worth noting that developing countries account for over 75 per cent of global cellular telephone subscriptions. No other component of infrastructure has witnessed such spectacular growth. Advances in ICTs and liberalization of telecommunications markets have led to wealth creation and economic growth, with cities the major beneficiaries. ICTs play a major role in any city's competitiveness, productivity and prosperity as they facilitate innovation, efficiency and effective service delivery. Overwhelming

Figure 2.2.3

Telephone infrastructure in selected African cities

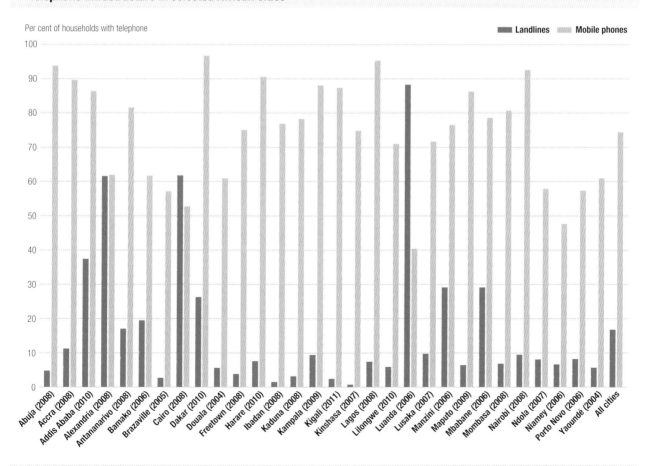

Source: UN-Habitat Global Urban Observatory Database, 2011.

Box 2.2.2

When cellphones provide pro-poor banking services

M-PESA is a cellphone-based service that facilitates financial transactions. With more than 15 million regular users in Kenya.[61] It provides mobile banking services to over 70 per cent of the adult population.[62] In particular, the network serves people in areas where established banks do not operate. For example, Nairobi's largest slum, Kibera, does not feature a single bank branch, but is host to over 40 M-PESA outlets.[63] Some 26 per cent of all users save money through their cellphones.[64] Moreover, the system empowers women, providing them with an unprecedented ability to store and manage their own monies.[65] Over time, M-PESA has evolved from a purely money transfer system into a platform that enables firms, non-governmental organizations, schools and hospitals to receive and make payments.

In 2010, M-PESA created over 30,000 jobs[66] in its 17,653 outlets.[67] By September 2011, 32,000 outlets were in operation.[68] The network is extensive enough to enable urban users to make remittances to family members in rural areas. In terms of money transfers, M-PESA processes more transactions locally than Western Union does around the world.[69] As at March 2011, the total value of transactions through M-PESA since inception stood at US$9.98 billion.[70]

Cellphone numbers surpass those of fixed lines in virtually all cities. In Kinshasa, there are 119 times as many households owning cellphones as fixed lines. In Lagos, Harare, Kampala and Mombasa, households are 12 times more likely to own cellphones than landlines.

Apart from facilitating connectivity and communication, cellphone networks also serve as catalysts for growth, contributing an estimated average US$56 billion, or 3.5 per cent of GDP, to the African economy every year,[76] and providing over five million jobs. The growth of cellular telephony has spurred many innovative applications, most notable of which is cellphone-based banking. The most successful among such services is M-PESA, which has revolutionized money transfers in Kenya and is contributing to financial inclusion for the poor (Box 2.2.2).

ICTs in Asian cities: Cellular telephony has also expanded dramatically in this region. India's four major cities – Delhi, Mumbai, Kolkata and Chennai – can boast cellphone connection rates of 138 per cent, 112 per cent, 102 per cent and 143 per cent respectively.[77] In Singapore, telecommunications infrastructure is highly developed. In 2010, the household fixed-line penetration rate was 103 per cent, and the mobile population penetration rate was 144 per cent, with 82 per cent of households having access to Internet.[78]

ICTs are major contributors to economic growth in Asia, accounting for US$485 billion, or 2.7 per cent of GDP; they also provide 11.4 million direct and indirect jobs – for each job created by a cellphone operator, eight additional ones are generated.[79] The major role played by the mobile telephone sector has seen it act as a buffer against economic recession in the region.

If any city must be seen as synonymous with ICTs in Asia it must be Bangalore. Often referred to as the *Silicon Valley of India* or the *IT Hub of Asia*, the Indian city stands out as India's dominant ICT cluster and the fourth largest in the world, accounting for more than 35 per cent of Indian software exports[80] and employing over one-third of its ITC professionals.[81] Bangalore has developed into a centre of high-technology research and production; 80 per cent of global IT companies operating in India have their research and development centres in Bangalore.[82] In 2007, more than 500 major international companies including Hewlett-Packard, Dell, IBM, and Accenture had operations in Bangalore.[83] The ICT sector has proved to be by far to the most vibrant of the city's economy; this is evidenced in the 176 per cent increase in the number of IT firms from 782 in 2000 to 2,156 in 2010.[84]

majorities of surveyed experts – 85 per cent in Africa; 96 per cent in Asia; 86 per cent in Latin America and the Caribbean; and 90 per cent in Arab States – rank telecommunications infrastructure as 'highly developed' or 'developed' in their respective cities.

In Africa, the total number of cellphone connections has grown by 30 per cent annually since 2001, and by 2011 over 60 per cent of the population was connected.[71] In Asia-Pacific, connections increased from 824 million in 2005 to three billion in 2011, making the region the largest cellphone market in the world.[72] In Latin America and the Caribbean, mobile connections have grown by 13 per cent over the past four years, reaching 632 million in 2011.[73] Remarkable growth rates have also been witnessed in the Middle East, where connections nearly doubled, from 177 million in 2007 to 334 million in 2011.[74]

ICTs in African cities: Cellphones have leapfrogged landlines in Africa by comparison with developed regions that had invested in landlines before moving to cellphone networks.[75] At least 90 per cent of households in Abuja, Accra, Dakar, Lagos, Luanda and Nairobi own cellphones; even where ownership appears to be relatively low, it hardly falls below 50 per cent of the population (Figure 2.2.3).

ICTs in Latin American cities: Cellphones are fairly widespread in the region. Urban areas in Brazil, Chile, Panama and Paraguay feature the highest connection rates, with at least 80 per cent of households owning cellphones.[85] In major Mexican cities, ownership varies between 66 and 84 per cent of the population. Compared with Africa and Asia, fixed lines are more developed in Latin American cities. For instance, between 41 per cent and 68 per cent of households in Mexico's major cities have fixed lines. Still, the cellphone sector contributes significantly to the region's economy: 1.7 per cent of regional GDP (or US$82 billion) in 2010. Increases in cellphone connectivity have also been found to boost GDP per capita, but this contribution is not linear, since the effect diminishes as saturation levels are reached. The industry also contributes to the region's public finances, with public authorities garnering US$48 billion in taxes and regulatory fees in 2010.[86] The economic contribution of the sector also included over 1.5 million jobs in 2010.

ICTs in Arab State cities: Urban ownership of cellphones in Arab States, especially Gulf Cooperation Council countries, is widespread. Penetration rates in Doha, Dubai, Amman, Kuwait, Muscat and Riyadh are in excess of 100 per cent (Dubai's is the highest in the world

with over 200 cellphones per 100 residents). This group of countries has invested in ITC-dedicated parks in a bid to boost socioeconomic growth and to diversify away from an oil-dependent to a knowledge-based economy. Several cities, including Dubai, Doha, Kuwait and Muscat, have used ITC to launch e-government initiatives. This has made it possible to make government services available online and enable cities to develop interactive or transactional websites, integrating functions across multiple government departments. This has reduced bureaucracy and improved overall efficiency of government agencies. The ICT sector plays a significant role in the region's economy. In the case of the UAE, the sector contributed 5.3 per cent to GDP in 2010, up from 4.1 per cent in 2007, and currently employs over 11,500.[87]

INFRASTRUCTURE DEVELOPMENT AND THE PROSPERITY OF CITIES

It is possible to identify the specific contributions adequate infrastructure can make to the prosperity of cities, but it must be remembered that they are interrelated and interact with one another in a variety of ways. As perceived by experts participating in the UN-Habitat survey, these contributions are the following (by order of decreasing

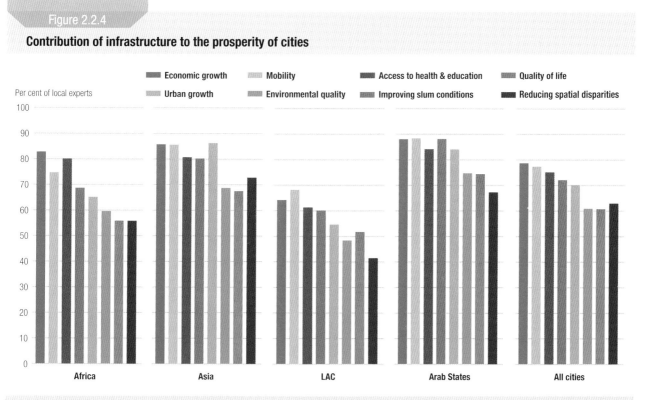

Figure 2.2.4

Contribution of infrastructure to the prosperity of cities

Source: UN-Habitat, City Monitoring Branch, *Policy Survey*, 2011.

importance): economic growth; facilitating mobility; improved access to health and education; improved quality of life; steering spatial expansion; environmental quality; improved slum conditions; reduced poverty and reduced spatial disparities. These are presented in Figure 2.2.4 for the four regions under review.

Economic growth: Infrastructure plays a crucial, supporting role in economic growth. At the same time, it is worth stressing that the reverse is true: economic growth also favours infrastructure through enhanced productivity and tax revenues. Experts surveyed by UN-Habitat view economic growth as the most important benefit attached to infrastructure and, if in an indirect sort of way, to the prosperity of cities (Figure 2.2.4). This finding echoes those in previous studies, albeit at a regional level, which confirm the intuitive notion that infrastructure has a positive impact on growth. Between 1990 and 2005, improved infrastructure contributed one per cent to per capita economic growth in Africa, and 1.2 per cent in Asia.[88] In Africa, the greatest impact has been attributed to telecommunications and, to a lesser extent, roads. In Latin America, infrastructure has had a recognized effect on economic growth, with telecommunications, transport

and power making stronger contributions than non-infrastructure capital.[89]

Facilitating mobility: Consistent and targeted investment in transport and communications infrastructure is a major factor underlying urban prosperity. Seamless movement within and between cities through efficient mass transit systems is essential to urban functionality and prosperity. Cities that have enhanced mobility through sustainable transport policies have reaped huge benefits across all dimensions of prosperity. In Bogotá and Curitiba, for instance, BRT enhances daily living conditions. In Bogotá, fast and reliable transport is now available to over 1.4 million passengers per day, in the process reducing traffic congestion.[90] Commuting times have been cut by 34 per cent and traffic fatalities by no less than 88 per cent, with greenhouse gas emissions reduced by an average 134,011 tons/year. In the case of Curitiba, 70 per cent of commuters use BRT to travel to work, cutting the number of motor vehicle commutes by an average 27 million a year. When compared with eight other Brazilian cities of

Alto, Bolivia: Congested road systems negatively impact productivity and quality of life.

© Eduardo Lopez Moreno

similar size, Curitiba uses 30 per cent less fuel per capita, with attendant reductions in air pollution. Curitiba's BRT serves over 1.3 million passengers a day, enabling them to spend only some 10 per cent of income on transport, or only a fraction of the national average.[91] In Lagos, BRT has attracted enthusiastic new patronage from those who previously avoided public transport.[92] The BRT system has resulted in a 30 per cent decrease in average fares, reduced average commuting time by 40 per cent and waiting time by 35 per cent. BRT has also created direct employment for 1,000 people, together with over 500,000 indirect jobs.

Access to healthcare and education: Infrastructure facilitates access to healthcare and education, which are essential components of human development and feature prominently among Millennium Development Goals. Sound health brings better-learning children and better-working adults – both being major assets to any city in the immediate and longer term futures. Education is also crucial to empowerment, reducing poverty and enhancing productivity. Cities with healthier, better-educated workforces are more likely to be productive and competitive. In metropolitan areas such as Istanbul and Mexico City, it has been shown that productivity can be hampered by the low skills of the working population.[93] Provision of healthcare and educational facilities in poor neighbourhoods can help reduce inequality.

Improving quality of life: Infrastructure can improve quality of life in a variety of ways, including enhanced safety and security, especially for youth and women, and expanded provision of public goods to enhance the city's appeal. With regard to youth, provision of training, sport and recreational facilities will not only make any city more attractive: it will also positively engage one of the most risk-prone segments of the population and deflect them away from a life of crime and deviant behaviour. In the Grants Pen area of Kingston (Jamaica), a newly created 'Peace Park' now provides young people with fresh recreational opportunities, contributing to a lower incidence of crime in the area.[94] Public spaces, including streets, need to be planned and designed in such a way that they enhance the safety and security of women.

Steering spatial expansion: Infrastructure can steer the spatial expansion of a city, facilitating more compact urban development and integrating different land uses. Compact urban forms are deemed to be efficient, inclusive and sustainable

POLICY Provision of infrastructure must take the needs of women into consideration.

in four different ways: (1) lower infrastructure costs; (2) improved access to services and facilities; (3) enhanced livelihoods for the urban poor; and (4) lower degrees of social segregation. Besides, higher densities enable cities to take advantage of agglomeration economies, which are crucial to prosperity. Singapore is planned as a compact city, with high-density residential and commercial developments around multiple transport nodes.

Environmental quality: In developing countries, many cities are characterized by inadequate water supply and squalid conditions in terms of sanitation. These two components of infrastructure are vital to improved – i.e., clean, pollution-free – environmental conditions in cities. Furthermore, flood-control infrastructure safeguards urban areas against erosion, flooding, landslides and disasters. Improved environmental quality in cities – particularly in slums and squatter settlements – is linked to reduced morbidity and mortality, greater productivity, improved livelihoods and reduced vulnerability for the poor. In Argentina, child mortality has declined by 14 per cent and 26 per cent in the poor and extremely poor municipalities respectively, following improvements in water distribution and quality.[95] For girls, access to improved water supply will have a beneficial impact on school attendance and performance, as they spend less time fetching water.

Improving slum conditions and reducing poverty: Infrastructure can contribute to the prosperity of cities through improved slum conditions and reduced poverty. Providing adequate infrastructure for roads, water, sanitation and electricity can reduce the health burden faced by slum dwellers, delivering major benefits in terms of environmental quality. Since the defining features of slums include lack of water, sanitation, etc., provision of infrastructure has a major role to play in any transformation of informal into formal settlements.[96]

Reducing spatial disparities: Infrastructure can reduce spatial disparities, particularly in sprawling, uncontrolled and largely un-serviced peri-urban areas. The provision of basic infrastructure and services will go a long way toward improving quality of life in these peripheral locations. Given that these locations are often inaccessible to public transport, connective infrastructure can integrate these areas into the main urban fabric.

POLICY Beneficiary communities must be fully involved in the design, provision and maintenance of infrastructure.

Endnotes

1 Choguill, 1996; Teriman et al., 2010.

2 Cooper, 2010.

3 Spector, 2011.

4 Lall et al,2010.

5 Fay and Morrison, 2005.

6 Foster and Briceno-Garmendia, 2010.

7 Toteng, 2008.

8 General Electric Power and Water, 2010.

9 Belliapa, 2011.

10 Harris, 2008.

11 Belliapa, 2011.

12 However, the region is the least provided in the world, with just 1.4 per cent of the planet renewable freshwater (Roudi-Fahimi et al, 2002).

13 The Arab State's Region is host to 65 of the world's 100 largest desalination plants (Pacific Institute,2011).

14 Latin American Herald Tribune, 2011.

15 López , 2011.

16 Shabou et al, 2011.

17 Karim, 2011.

18 Takechi, 2010.

19 Schrank et al, 2011.

20 African Economic Outlook, 2011.

21 Kumar and Barrett, 2008.

22 Kumar, 2011.

23 Lagos Metropolitan Transport Authority (n.d) *Bus Rapid Transit*, http://www.lamata-ng.com/brt.htm

24 Railway-technology.com (n.d) Gautrain rapid rail link, South Africa, http://www.railway-technology.com/projects/gautrain/

25 In 2007, Lagos had over 100,000 minibuses and 200,000 commercial motorcycles directly employing 500,000 people (Kumar, 2011).

26 Kumar and Barrett, 2008.

27 World Bank. 2002.

28 Pucher et al, 2007.

29 OSEC and Rainbow Unlimited GMBH, 2010.

30 HPEC, 2011.

31 Uddin, 2009.

32 The network increased from 95,000 to 208,000 km from 1990 to 2003 (Pucher et al, 2007).

33 McKinsey Global Institute, 2009.

34 Uddin, 2009.

35 Beijing Traffic Management Bureau, 2010.

36 *Ibid.*

37 HPEC, 2011.

38 Uddin, 2009.

39 Pucher et al, 2007.

40 Pucher et al, 2005.

41 Pucher et al, 2007.

42 *Ibid.*

43 Estimated from World Bank (2011)

44 de la Torre et al, 2009.

45 Canassa, 2008.

46 Vicentini, 2010; Luoma et al, 2010.

47 Coyula, 2011.

48 Perez, 2011.

49 Leung, 2009.

50 ESCWA, 2009.

51 World Bank, 2011.

52 Shariff, 2007; Raouf, 2009.

53 Gulf Talent, 2007.

54 Shariff, 2007.

55 Shabou et al, 2011.

56 Raouf, 2009.

57 Al-Rawashdeh, 2011.

58 Kollock, 2010.

59 Shabou et al, 2011.

60 International Telecommunication Union, 2010.

61 Safaricom, 2011.

62 IMF, 2011.

63 Morawczynski and Pickens, 2009.

64 Finaccess, 2009.

65 World Bank, 2010.

66 Vaughan, 2010.

67 Safaricom, 2010.

68 Safaricom, 2011.

69 IMF, 2011.

70 Safaricom, 2011.

71 GSM Association, 2011a.

72 GSM Association, 2011b.

73 GSM Association, 2011c.

74 GSM Association, 2011b.

75 Aker and Mbiti, 2010.

76 GSM Association (2011a) *Africa Mobile Observatory 2011*, GSMA, London

77 Philip, 2009.

78 Centre for Livable Cities, 2011.

79 GSM Association, 2011b.

80 Greater Bangalore Municipal Corporation (n.d) *Bengaluru City Profile*, http://bbmp.gov.in/

81 Government of Karnataka (n.d) *Bangalore Urban: the Silicon Valley of India*, from http://advantagekarnataka.com

82 Government of Karnataka, 2008.

83 BBC, 2007.

84 Government of Karnataka, 2011.

85 Fernández-Ardèvol, 2010.

86 GSM Association, 2011c.

87 Telecommunications and Regulatory Authority, 2011.

88 Calderón, 2008.

89 Calderón and Servén, 2003.

90 Hidalgo, 2008.

91 Goodman et al, 2006.

92 World Bank, 2009b.

93 OECD, 2006.

94 UN-Habitat, 2007.

95 Galiani et al, 2005.

96 Gulyani and Bassett, 2007.

Chapter 2.3

© Philip Lange/Shutterstock.com

Quality of Life and Urban Prosperity

For more than two millennia, quality of life has been part of philosophical discussions: abstract terms, metaphors, interpretations, theoretical positions have evolved over time with different perspectives, moving from the realm of ideas to the urban development agenda.

Today no one disputes that quality of life is essential for any city to prosper. The notion is increasingly popular with decision-makers, practitioners and urban populations alike. Everyone agrees on its importance, but everyone will also agree that this notion comes with different meanings and facets. Many efforts have been made to develop a policy-oriented definition, yet the essence of quality of life remains vague when applied to urban areas. For all these different views and understandings, the very basic notion remains largely similar both in the developed and the developing world: people in Jakarta, Naples, Los Angeles or Bogotá will, to a large extent, share similar concerns, including decent employment, material well-being, fulfilling family lives and sound health. Individuals and specific circumstances may mean that one of these factors comes to be valued over others; yet, as noted in the report by the French Government Commission on the Measurement of Economic Performance and Social Progress (2009), these factors constitute *'the most important features that give life its value.'*[2]

> "Quality of life is often tied to the opportunities available to people, to the meaning and purpose they attach to their lives and to the extent to which they enjoy the possibilities available to them".[1]

MEASURING QUALITY OF LIFE

Recently, efforts have turned from definition to scientific measurement of quality of life. To Nobel laureate Amartya Sen, quality of life is determined by the various opportunities open to individuals, and their freedom to choose from these.[3] Other conceptual approaches measure quality of life based on the notion of subjective well-being and on economic notions drawn from welfare economics.[4] Subjective measures of quality of life are premised on the argument that individuals are the best judges of their life conditions, and they 'provide valuable information about a crucial component of social change: the values, beliefs and motivations of ordinary citizens'.[5] The *World Values Survey* provides a very comprehensive subjective measurement of quality of life, which reflects representative individuals' beliefs and values in 54 countries around the world. The survey has a standardized questionnaire on religion, gender roles, work motivations, democracy, good governance, social capital, political participation, tolerance of other groups, environmental protection and subjective well-being.[6] More recent measurements of quality of life combine subjective and objective measures. In 2003, the European Environmental Agency investigated eight domains of individual life situations in 25 EU member states, ranging from economic situation, housing and employment to work-life balance, health, subjective well-being and perceived quality of life.[7] The international human resource consulting firm, Mercer, focuses on the quality of life of expatriates, taking in criteria such as availability of consumer goods, the economic environment, the natural, political and social environments as well as recreation amenities.[8] Also targeting business, the *Economist Intelligence Unit* has designed a Quality of Life Index using nine factors: material well-being, health, political stability and security, family life, community life, gender equality, political freedom, climate and geography, and job security.[9]

71

QUALITY OF LIFE: A SYNTHESIS OF ALL DIMENSIONS OF PROSPERITY

Quality of life underpins the functionality of cities: the notion is at the crossroads of all policies and actions,[10] and represents a synthesis of all the dimensions of prosperity. When a city generates employment and economic growth, quality of life improves. When a city designs better buildings and public spaces that provide attractive, secure, clean and durable surroundings, it is improving quality of life. When a city provides adequate public transport, it improves quality of life for both users and non-users. When a city raises levels of education and provides good healthcare, it ensures quality of life for the foreseeable future. And when a city reduces the use of environmental resources and becomes more energy-efficient, it also improves quality of life.

According to the UN-Habitat survey (2011), experts value assurances to live and work freely, good quality of education, adequate housing with basic services, and meaningful employment with decent income as the most important factors promoting quality of life and prosperity in their cities.

In Europe, a survey on perceived quality of life in 75 cities (2010) shows that 'the three most important issues for the city' were: educational facilities, job creation/reduce unemployment and the availability and quality of health services, among seven other alternatives, namely social services, housing conditions, air pollution, noise, public transport, infrastructure and safety.[11]

It remains that, as perceived by experts and residents in developing and developed countries alike, the quality of urban life is a broader concept that includes a full range of factors such as economic development, living standards, material progress and individual and collective well-being, which all are important dimensions of prosperity.

Experts from 50 cities consider quality of life as the second most important dimension promoting prosperity in cities, after infrastructure development.

POLICY It is in any city's best interest to promote public goods such as public transport, green areas, public spaces and 'urban commons' such as safety, security and political participation, in order to enhance quality of life and shared prosperity.

Figure 2.3.1

Perceptions about cities' most important problems (three most mentioned issues)

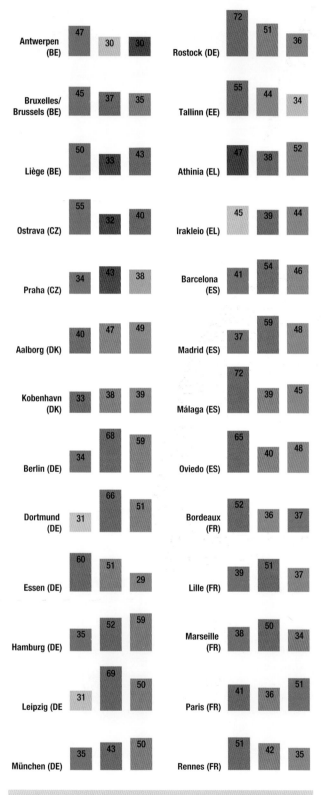

Source: Directorate-General for Regional Policy, European Commission, 2010.

72

Treating quality of life as a by-product

UN-Habitat survey results show that the more committed a city is to promote quality of life, the more the chances that the effects will be broad-ranging. There is a clear positive association between a high degree of commitment to address quality of life and the possibility of designing specific policies. Unfortunately, the opposite also applies, and many cities treat quality of life as a by-product or an 'after-effect' of policy interventions. Even where some cities perform well under other dimensions of prosperity, they fail to deliver better quality of life. Abidjan, Dakar, Dar es Salaam and Kampala provide good examples: they feature moderate or weak values on the 'City Prosperity Index', but rank much lower still for quality of life, which goes to show that this dimension cannot be considered just as an indirect or implicit component of any urban policy agenda.

A number of studies have shown that the various determinants of quality of life generate complex interactions and diverse causal relations. Sometimes, efforts to promote one element can have unexpected detrimental effects on other elements; for example, prioritizing economic growth *per se* can have damaging effects on the environment.

In other cases, positive linkages between these determinants are quite obvious; for instance, the provision of green open spaces brings

health benefits to the population. In some other cases, the relationship can be less evident; for example, individual housing choices may have environmental impacts that affect quality of life in a variety of ways.[12] All too often, cities do not clearly perceive the complexity of these interactions and assume that interrelations will always be positive. Several cities in Asia and the Arab States that are experiencing high economic growth are mostly focusing on infrastructure development in the pursuit of higher productivity and therefore higher incomes, assuming that this will lead to better quality of life in the long term. Generally, that is what happens, since economic growth increases purchasing power and demand for goods and services including education, entertainment, financial services and housing, which, in turn, not only create new employment opportunities but also contribute to higher quality of life. However, these infrastructures may not be accessible to the urban poor and may have also negative effects on the environment, thereby affecting quality of life.

However, UN-Habitat policy analysis shows that most surveyed cities in the developing world have no clear policies, actions or reliable procedures to deliver and improve quality of life to the whole population. With the exceptions of Singapore, Davao, Ho Chi Minh City and Chongqing in

> Social equity and quality of life go hand in hand. In practice, though, any policies and actions aiming at improved societal well-being largely depend on the political will of governments and the degree of participation of civil society organizations and, in particular, their degree of autonomy when it comes to advocating, upholding, and fighting for, the rights of all.

> **POLICY** Cities that focus only on economic development and provide services that are not public goods tend to further marginalize minority and vulnerable groups, thereby reducing their quality of life.

Accessibility, environmental sustainability and health: cyclists on dedicated cycle lanes in Copenhagen, Denmark.

© Anne-Britt Svinnset/Shutterstock.com

Figure 2.3.2

Perception of experts regarding their city's commitment to promoting quality of life

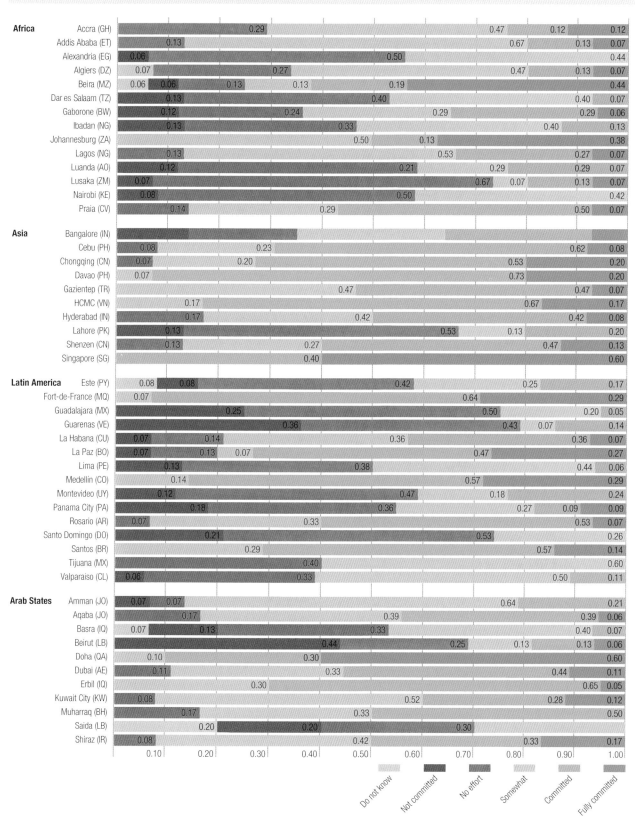

Source: UN-Habitat, City Monitoring Branch, *Policy Survey*, 2011.

Asia, Fort-de-France and Medellín in Latin America and the Caribbean, and Doha in the Arab States (whose commitment to quality of life was highly commended), experts took a critical view of the 42 other surveyed cities on that count. They found public administrations to be generally inefficient and with poor incentives to devise specific quality of life policies, for lack of adequate financial resources, trained staff or political interest.

In describing the evident commitment to quality of life improvement in Ho Chi Minh City, one local expert stated 'investing in human resources is considered to be the best way of seizing more opportunities and turning them into wealth and quality of life to make the city more prosperous'.[13] In Cebu City, a local expert argues that 'it is not only a matter of expanding the pie (i.e., economic development), but also of dividing it and ensuring that

---

Box 2.3.1

Quality of life – the 'spokes' and the 'hub' of the Wheel of Urban Prosperity

Quality of life and productivity
Productivity and quality of life are increasingly associated. Skilled workers and talented people will move to, and concentrate in, livable cities with high quality of life, and firms will follow suit. Consulting firms rank cities based on their 'good living' factors to make informed locational decisions. High human capital, which is a main ingredient of quality of life, attracts firms that cluster in cities to take advantage of common labour pools. Well-planned and designed urban environments, with pedestrian-friendly areas, bicycle paths, mixed land uses and sufficient public goods, attract people and businesses which, in turn, contribute to finance further social amenities and public goods. More and more city leaders are investing in education and the provision of 'commons' and public goods as part of a quality of life. Inversely, cities that do not invest in quality of life tend to feature poor public health, low education, limited mobility, and marginalization of the urban poor, all resulting in low productivity.

Quality of life and infrastructure development
The prosperity of any city largely depends on infrastructure. Physical facilities, such as transportation, power and communications, contribute to economic development, industrialization, trade and mobility of labour. Water supply, sanitation and sewerage, together with education and health facilities, have a direct impact on quality of life. All of these types of infrastructure connect people to people, goods to markets, workers to jobs, families to services, and the poor in rural areas to urban centres – a connectivity process that is essential to induce economic growth, reduce poverty and increase general well-being. More and more cities today are launching into ambitious initiatives to expand/improve infrastructure in a bid to sustain economic growth, prepare for population decline, address climate change issues and/or reduce slum incidence. Conversely, under-developed infrastructure makes life more difficult and more costly: poor facilities discourage industrial development, trade and investment, and reduce competitiveness, not to mention more air pollution and greenhouse gas emissions, wasted time, fuel and safety costs, and noise.

Quality of life and equity
Quality of life and equity are inherent in progress and development. No city can claim to be prosperous when large segments of the population are excluded or live in abject poverty, or are deprived of basic goods or services while others live in affluence. Cities pursuing equity in the distribution of resources and opportunities, in law enforcement, in the rules and relationships that govern institutions and in access to public goods will be those where shared prosperity and quality of life are improved. More equitable cities enhance the prospects for people to take part in democratic processes and participate in a more decisive manner in cultural and political life. The benefits of social participation and political voice extend to other domains such as health, employment and the urban environment.

Quality of life and environmental sustainability
Environmental conditions have an immediate impact on the quality of people's lives. They affect human health both directly (air, water pollution, and noise) and indirectly (climate change, biodiversity). Well-managed urban commons and public goods can improve environmental conditions and quality of life. Conversely, the pursuit of short-term quality of life objectives can be detrimental to the longer-term sustainability objectives that collectively affect the lives of the whole population. Indeed, individual short-term aspirations to quality of life, such as affordable, low-density housing, can act as major factors behind urban sprawl, which in turn is detrimental to the natural environment through higher use of land, energy and water, along with increased greenhouse gas emissions.

Quality of life and the 'hub' of the Wheel of Urban Prosperity
Effective institutions, more appropriate laws and regulations, proper urban planning and new value systems are essential power functions and can make sure that policies, actions and solutions involving any of the 'spokes' of prosperity can have positive effects on the others.

Sources: Glaeser, E. and Berry, C. (2005); Gidwani, V. and Baviskar, A. (2011); European Environment Agency (2009); Stiglitz, Joseph, Sen, Amartya, Fitoussi, Jean-Paul (2009); UN-Habitat (2008/9).

the poor benefit, too (i.e., equity and quality of life)'.[14] Dubai, as other cities in the Arab Gulf, recognizes quality of life as a key competitive advantage that contributes productivity, attracting and retaining highly qualified individuals and prestigious firms and investors. Priority is given to those most easily perceived elements of quality of life such as parks, clean sidewalks, leisure, art and culture amenities as well as hospitals. Although not generalized to all the population, the pursuit of prosperity through quality of life is an interesting connection and entry point to development.

Quality of life: a variety of local responses

UN-Habitat has identified some convergent and divergent forms in which cities address quality of life.

Divergent city responses: Actions to improve quality of life will largely depend on the stage of development of the relevant country or city.

In most poor cities in the developing world, quality of life is strongly associated with the provision of public goods in the form of basic services such as water, sanitation and electricity, along with improvements in slum neighbourhoods.

Tanzania's *National Development Vision 2025* aims at high quality of life for all the population, linking this notion to economic growth and poverty reduction.[15] In Ho Chi Minh City, quality of life is directly linked to improved drainage, sewage collection and treatment systems, and other public infrastructures such as road enlargements.

In middle-income countries, governments link quality of life to various factors, from improved living environments and enhanced material well-being to higher incomes. Experts in cities as diverse as Fort-de-France (Martinique), Habana, Cebu, Davao, and Beirut explicitly refer to the provision of a decent house and a healthy environment as essential elements for improved well-being and quality of life. In other cities – Rosario, Bangalore, Hyderabad, Alexandria and Guarenas (Venezuela) – improved solid waste disposal is perceived as a major condition for better quality of life. Improvements in healthcare services appear as another major factor. In Singapore, Doha, Chongqing and Shenzhen, local experts implicitly refer to good and affordable medical services for all as a good way of improving quality of life. Shenzhen's universal healthcare system and Tehran's *Urban Heart Programme* are good examples.

In rich countries, government responses to the need for quality of life involve access to a number of goods and services and improvements in the domestic living environment. Many European cities emphasize good transport, green open spaces, culture and sports facilities as major factors behind improved quality of life. Although better paid jobs, good levels of education and health facilities always feature in government responses, quality of life is increasingly associated with an inclusive, well-planned, healthy and supportive environment.[16]

With the prospects of population decline, various cities are enhancing quality of life for elderly and disabled populations. Most notable in this regard are the efforts of the Government of Singapore to make the entire built environment disabled-friendly.[17]

Convergent city responses: Beyond local

Experts in 60 per cent of surveyed cities in Africa and Arab States and slightly more than 40 per cent of cities in Asia and Latin America believe that corruption and poor governance conspire against local prosperity and quality of life for all.

POLICY Cities that are committed to quality of life are almost always committed to enhanced productivity and equity, emphasizing the strong relation between these dimensions.

POLICY Equitable cities generalize access to urban commons and public goods, preventing private appropriation and expanding the scope for improved quality of life for all.

Northern European cities such as Copenhagen, Amsterdam and Groningen, Berlin and Muenster promote cycling and walking as part of new urban culture and in the pursuit of better quality of life. Dresden, Vancouver and Los Angeles have launched into urban conversion programmes in cultural and historical neighbourhoods, adapting urban infrastructure and reusing open land areas for better quality of life.

Experts in Beira, Algiers, Praia, Luanda and Addis Ababa, among others, explicitly link improved quality of life to slum upgrading and poverty reduction.

Box 2.3.2

Quality of life, world-class cities and social inclusion

Cities with aspirations to 'world class' status will typically equate this notion with competitiveness. Dubai's *2007–2015 Long-term Strategic Development Plan* declares these two notions as twin objectives that will *'establish the city as a preferred home for current and future residents by improving the well-being of citizens and residents, and helping them live healthier lives enriched with opportunity and choice'*.[18] In Doha, the capital of Qatar, the transition to a diversified knowledge-based economy is seen by public authorities as contingent on the development and upgrading of the education and skills of the population, together

with improved quality of life.[19] Singapore considers quality of life as a key competitive advantage to attract skilled foreign labour and investment.[20] At a different level, a local expert in Beirut noted that 'quality of life' mostly appeared in the advertising brochures of high-end property developments, in response to which non-governmental organizations have used the same notion to draw attention to the lack of public goods in the city, such as public or 'green' spaces.[21] In Santos, Brazil, quality of life is perceived as involving social justice and inclusion, not just economic growth, as a precondition for sustainable development.

In 19 cities out of the 50 surveyed by UN-Habitat, an overwhelming majority of experts (more than 80 per cent) rated security to work and live freely as a major contributor to prosperity. In cities like Praia, Cebu, Algiers, Chongqing, Singapore, La Paz and Amman, nearly all experts rated security as contributing to prosperity.

circumstances, some aspects of quality of life improvements can be found in all types of country. UN-Habitat has identified various areas of intervention which governments with different political orientations and levels of development still consider as priority interventions: safety and security, efficient public transport, public spaces, healthcare and adequate housing, appear to be among the most important.

Public Safety and Quality of Life: A safe and secure life for all is an integral component of a prosperous city. As an expert in Nairobi states, *'quality of life only makes sense when there is adequate security'*.[22] Experts in 50 cities in the developing world agreed that this is the most important factor contributing to a sense of empowerment and a feeling that one is part of a prosperous city. In Lima, for instance, a survey on quality of life conducted by a citizens' observatory found that 73 per cent of the population considers urban insecurity as the main problem that conspires against quality of life and prosperity.[23]

A survey on 'urban lifestyles' conducted in 2010 by the Veolia Observatory in seven cities in both developing and developed nations found that in three of these (Chicago, London and São Paulo) insecurity appears as the most important problem, and in another (Paris) it features as the third most important.[24]

In all these places, urban safety and security means different things to different people: In Latin American cities, this notion is strongly linked to violence and crime.[25] In the Arab world, it is more associated with fear of repression, youth exclusion and gender inequalities. In Africa, in addition to the conventional notion of crime, insecurity is strongly linked to institutional weaknesses, conflict for resources,[26] and lack of tenure in land and housing.[27] In Asia, urban safety is linked to a broader human security notion related to crime and violence, but also to natural risks.[28]

By itself, security may not bring prosperity to any city, but its absence is fatal. Economic inequity and/or instability nurtures high perceptions of crime and violence in various cities around the world, and inadequate urban planning law enforcement drive many high- and middle-class residents into gated communities or other guarded urban and suburban enclaves,[29] creating compounds of prosperity. This type of privilege remains unaffordable to those on low incomes, whose safety is often more at risk. Lack of personal safety is seriously detrimental to freedom, mobility, productivity and public interactions, all of which are crucial to high quality of life.

Crime and violence can hinder, and sometimes paralyze, regional and national economies. High rates of violence and insecurity in Kingston (Jamaica) and Nairobi (Kenya) have stultified the otherwise thriving tourist sectors in these countries.[30]

Even though urban insecurity is, to a large extent, the result of extreme inequalities, it can also

POLICY Effective public safety is a fundamental 'common good' that enhances quality of life for all, and is a major foundation of urban prosperity.

generate further social and spatial disparities that restrain access to employment, resources and opportunities. Recent surveys show that fear for personal safety prohibits an alarming high rate of residents from going out at night in various Mexican cities. In Mexico City, many of those plazas, parks and downtown streets where traditionally the capital's pulse could be felt and public debate and interaction took place, have now become risky.[31] High perceptions of crime and violence reduce investor confidence in the local economy. This in turn can lead to brain drain as people

More than 40 per cent of respondents to the UN-Habitat survey rated the cities of Algiers, Johannesburg, Lahore, Este, Guarenas, La Paz, Lima and Santo Domingo as 'not safe'.

Cultural vitality enhances quality of life: Sinulog Street dancing, an annual event held on the third Sunday in January celebrates Santo Niño, the patron saint of Cebu, Philippines, as well as Cebuano peoples' origins.

© 2012 John Lander/fotoLIBRA.com

Nearly one-third of local experts in Latin America, 25 per cent in African cities and more than 10 per cent in Asia and the Arab States said lack of public security was not properly addressed in their respective cities.

emigrate to safer countries. High perceptions of crime and violence can also engender mistrust and alienation, eventually triggering various forms of social unrest. Recent empirical data in Latin America shows that high crime and violence rates have damaging effects on interpersonal and more general trust, affecting social conviviality and confidence in institutions.[32] Moreover, unsafe cities and perceptions of insecurity also lead to more fragmented, sprawling and motor-dependent urban environments. The fear of crime and violence not only increases reliance on private automobiles through the proliferation of low-density, peri-urban gated communities, it also deters the public from using public transport.

Extensive provision of public goods such as parks, schools, basic services, sports facilities and community centres, particularly in more violent neighbourhoods, together with strong participation from local communities, has enabled Medellín to enhance safety through social cohesion. In addition to contributing to quality of life through culture, recreation and participation, this model also enhanced less tangible dimensions such as dignity, identity and sense of inclusion. These psychological aspects are by now recognized as lying at the core of youth-related crime and violence, more so than the apparent factor of poverty.[33] This is the background against which, in Boston, a scheme known as 'Strategic Approaches to Community Safety' has combined with systematic scrutiny of criminal/ violent incidents to result in reduction in gun-related violence.[34]

Many public spaces are residual urban areas that are exposed to speculation for private profit. In too many cities, public spaces remain concentrated in the more affluent areas.

POLICY Cities that give priority to the notion of the 'public' and thereby provide green areas, parks, recreation facilities and public spaces demonstrate a commitment to improved quality of life. Such cities are also likely to enhance community cohesion and civic identity and quality of life.

Reviving the public space: In a large number of cities, the provision, preservation and improvement of public spaces remains a neglected agenda. According to a local expert in Panama City, *'in practice, the concept of public space does not exist'*.[35] In Cebu City, an expert mentions that *'public parks, playground areas and recreational facilities are grossly inadequate'*.[36] Another in Al-Muharrak (Bahrain) states that *'the city has been losing green areas and today the proportion of gardens is small'*.[37] As with many other public goods, 'green' and open areas tend to be enclosed, restricted, or depleted by unsustainable use. In Amman, city authorities have been converting public areas and parks into developments. In India, confessional groups erect temples in public parks. In Bangladesh, developers construct housing in open public areas. In Nairobi, private interests occupy riparian lands.[38]

In Amman, parks represent 12 per cent of the total land area; however, in the eastern part of the city, where population densities are the highest, open spaces are very scarce.[39] In some other cities, particularly those aiming at 'world-class' status, parks and 'green' spaces have a more ornamental or 'image' role than a real 'public good' one. In Africa, some 40 per cent of surveyed local experts believe that the limited use of public spaces does 'not contribute', or 'somewhat contributes', to the prosperity of their respective

Box 2.3.3

Greenery and quality of life in Asian cities

Many cities across the developing world, especially in Asia and the Arab States, are creating new parks in an effort to meet international standards for green area per capita (i.e., eight square metres per head).[40] In the past five years, Shenzhen has created 435 new parks as part of the 'Eco-city Programme' and the 'Garden City Plan', achieving a ratio of 16.3 m2 in 2009. As a result, the urban ecological environment in Shenzhen has gradually improved and, with it, quality of life.[41] Also in China, Chongqing has expanded the combined green belt and public square surface area by a multiple of 16 in the past 30 years.[42] The city-state of Singapore is a leading example in the world, with greenery over 50 per cent of the surface area and over 450 public parks and gardens. The city is also preserving its rich biodiversity with four nature reserves which cover more than 3,000 ha, and are legally protected to safeguard key indigenous ecosystems. These initiatives contribute to a cleaner environment, shaping the country's landscape and enhancing quality of life. Recently, greenery has been given even more emphasis, with a new plan for a 'City-In-a-Garden'.[43]

cities. In Accra, Beira, Gaborone, Lagos, Lusaka and Ibadan, this percentage reaches 50 per cent. As many as 65 per cent of experts in Asia and 58 per cent in Latin America consider that improvements to pedestrian areas and cycling paths, though relatively minor by themselves, would enhance quality of life to a disproportionately significant extent.

Parks and 'green' spaces have always been associated with better quality of urban life. In Praia, Cape Verde's capital where such spaces are very scarce, a newly opened, small public square has become a major place for recreation, leisure and socialization despite its small dimensions.[44] In Guadalajara, Mexico, temporary

Internet café, Maroc telecom, and teleboutique signs in Morocco. Access to the Internet is now a vital asset for both poor and rich.

© 2012 Alistair Laming/fotoLIBRA.com

appropriation of streets and public spaces for pedestrian and cycling purposes has become extremely popular. As a result, this recreational project, known as *'vía recreativa'*, has been extended from 3.4 km to over 25 km and across four municipal jurisdictions. At national level, the Mexican government has launched an ambitious programme to recover public spaces in a bid to improve quality of life and enhance public security, particularly in marginalized neighbourhoods in various cities.[45] In Cuba, as part of a 'non-discriminatory enjoyment of public spaces' policy, several cultural programmes have been made free or affordable for all, with plazas, avenues and even vacant lots featuring various events that enhance quality of life.[46]

In Europe, public greens which take the form of corner lots, small community parks, street greens, linear or large parks, and river banks are designed for specific types of activity. The liveliness and continuous use of public space as a public good leads, in turn, to urban environments that are well maintained and safe, making the city an attractive place to live and work.[47]

POLICY 'Having access to public spaces does not only improve quality of life, it is a first step to civic empowerment on the way to further institutional and political spaces'.[48]

Box 2.3.4

Internet, information and quality of life

Basic needs are rapidly changing. Access to Internet is increasingly becoming an essential component of quality of life. In many cities today, Internet is used not just to communicate, socialize and learn, but also to promote public participation and to assess citizens' perceptions of urban affairs. Formal recognition of the right to information (i.e., India, 2005; the Philippines, 2008; South Africa, 2000) empowers citizens and encourages participation in governance and government programmes. The cities of Hyderabad, Cebu, and Johannesburg, among many others, are introducing e-governance in a bid to provide many services on-line – issuance of documents, payments, ticketing, applications and complaints – as a major step towards enhanced quality of life. In India more than 500 million cell phones are currently in use, and many with reduced call rates. This improves connectivity for poor and rich alike, enhancing economic opportunities for the urban poor. As stated by a local expert in India, '*Internet is an empowerment tool*'.

Endnotes

1   Stiglitz et al, 2009.

2   *Ibid.*

3   Andrulis et al, 2004.

4   Stiglitz et al, 2009.

5   World Values Survey, 2011.

6   *Ibid.*

7   European Environment Agency, 2009.

8   Mercer's 2011 Quality of Living ranking highlights – Global, http://www.mercer.com/articles/quality-of-living-survey-report-2011; Also targeting business, the Economist Intelligence Unit designed a Quality of Life Index using nine factors: material well-being, health, political stability and security, family life, community life, gender equality, political freedom, climate and geography, and job security, Refer to http://www.economist.com/media/pdf/QUALITY_OF_LIFE.pdf

9   The Economist, 2004.

10 European Environment Agency, 2009.

11 Bodin-Buyle and Hermant-De Callataÿ, 2011.

12 European Environment Agency, 2009.

13 Dzung, 2011.

14 Fernandez, 2011.

15 Lupala, 2011.

16 European Environment Agency, 2009.

17 Centre for Livable Cities, 2011.

18 Al-Bassam and Mouris, 2011.

19 Mena, 2011.

20 Centre for Livable Cities, 2011.

21 Fawaz and Baghdadi, 2011.

22 Omenya, 2011.

23 Lima Como Vamos, 2010.

24 Veolia Environnement, 2010.

25 PNUD, 2010.

26 Commins, 2011.

27 UN-Habitat, 2010b.

28 UN-Habitat and UN ESCAP, 2009

29 Davis, 2007.

30 UN-Habitat, 2007.

31 Davis, 2007.

32 Beltran and Velasquez, 2012.

33 UN-Habitat, 2007.

34 City of Boston ,www.ojp.usdoj.gov/njj/sacsi/

35 Mendoza, 2011.

36 Fernandez, F.L., 2011.

37 Al- Kubaisy, 2011.

38 UN-Habitat, 2010a.

39 Shabou et al, 2011.

40 The agreed international ratio is 8 square metres per capita. For instance, Lima, the capital of Peru, has around 3 square metres, the Mexican border city of Tijuana has around one or two, and Al-Muharrak in Bahrain has less than 1 square metre.

41 Jin and Liu, 2011.

42 Liu and Wang, 2011.

43 Centre for Livable Cities, 2011.

44 Fernandez, C., 2011.

45 SEDESOL, 2007.

46 Coyula, .2011.

47 Shehayeb, 2008.

48 Castellanos, 2011.

© Clive Shirley/Panos Pictures

Equity and the Prosperity of Cities

The past few decades have witnessed a notable surge in economic growth, but one which has been accompanied by an equally daunting degree of inequity under various forms, with wider income gaps and deepening poverty in many cities across the world. In the 1970s, widening income gaps began an unhealthy co-existence with economic growth, with reduced incomes for households in the middle and lower classes and steady increases for the well-off. Economic inequality is seriously detrimental to the equitable distribution among individuals of opportunities to pursue a life of their choosing and be spared from extreme deprivation in outcomes.

Equity involves systematic (re) distribution of the economic benefits of growth or development, with legal frameworks ensuring a 'level playing field' and institutions protecting the rights of the poor, minorities and vulnerable groups. Promotion of equity also involves enhancing socioeconomic equality and providing for civic participation by all in the social, political and cultural spheres.

> Equity has a significant impact on economic performance, since the greater the degree of equity, the greater the chances of a fuller, more efficient use of available resources, including skills and creative talent.[1] urban prosperity thrives on equity, which involves reduction in barriers to individual/collective potential, expansion of opportunities, and strengthening of human agency[2] and civic engagement.

THE UNEQUAL WEALTH OF CITIES: INCREASED INCOME DISPARITIES

> POLICY A prosperous city has the reduction of inequity as its fundamental objective.

The 2011 OECD report *Divided We Stand* stresses that income gaps between rich and poor are expanding in both developed and developing countries. In OECD countries, inequalities are as steep as they have been for over 30 years. The Report shows that, in advanced economies, the average income of the richest 10 per cent of the population is about nine times higher than that of the poorest 10 per cent. In Europe's Nordic countries, the average is a multiple of six but growing, compared with multiples of 10 in Italy, Korea and the United Kingdom, and up to 14 in Israel, Turkey and the United States. These are overshadowed by countries such as Chile and Mexico with multiples of 27, and in Brazil, despite recent declines in inequity (the exception among the BRICs countries), the ratio of incomes between richest and poorest reached a staggering 50:1.[3] In the 34 OECD member countries, Gini coefficients have risen by 10 per cent on average between the 1980s and the late 2000s (from 0.29 to 0.316).[4] In emerging economies (such as Argentina, Brazil, China, India, Indonesia, the Russian Federation and South Africa) income

> Cities generate wealth, but it is not shared equitably. Despite considerable increases in capital and per capita GDP growth along with reductions in extreme poverty, inequality as a whole is growing in most parts of the world – a process that undermines urban prosperity.
>
> In many cities, local experts concur that inequalities are becoming steeper. A review of inequality in cities reveals a steady increase over the long term, as well as in recent decades.[5] Paradoxically, this has occurred as wealth rose enormously around the world.

inequality is significantly steeper than the OECD average. Inequality has increased in all these countries over time, reaching extremes in Argentina, Brazil and South Africa.

EQUITY COMES WITH MULTIPLIER EFFECTS

Equity and lack thereof work in exactly opposite ways. When actively pursued, equity can act as a powerful catalyst for prosperity, exerting multiplier effects on other prosperity factors, optimizing their respective performances and creating linkages among them. Its absence will have the reverse effect, compounding any existing biases, or dysfunctions already hindering prosperity.

Undoubtedly, some cities have demonstrated a capacity to stimulate growth and prosperity even in the absence of equity. However, as has become amply evident in the past three decades, such prosperity, coupled with uneven distribution, remains narrowly confined and is unsustainable. Conversely, cities that have built equity into

Box 2.4.1

Income inequalities in the world's cities: an overview

The UN-Habitat database shows that income inequalities are widening in urban Asia; this is also the case in half of the African countries where urban data is available, while the gap has narrowed slightly in Latin America and the Caribbean.

According to the database, the most unequal cities in the developing world are Hong Kong, Yichan, Shenzhen, Kuala Lumpur, Manila, Davao, Colombo, Bangkok, and Ho Chi Minh City; Bujumbura, Douala, Brazzaville, Addis Ababa, Libreville, Maputo, Lagos, Kigali and several South African cities (the most unequal in the world); and cities in Brazil and Colombia, together with Mexico City, Port-au-Prince, Buenos Aires, Santiago and Quito.

Rising inequity is not limited to the developing world, as the recent banking/financial crisis has had serious socioeconomic effects on the developed countries where it started.

Figure 2.4.1

Urban prosperity, poverty and inequity

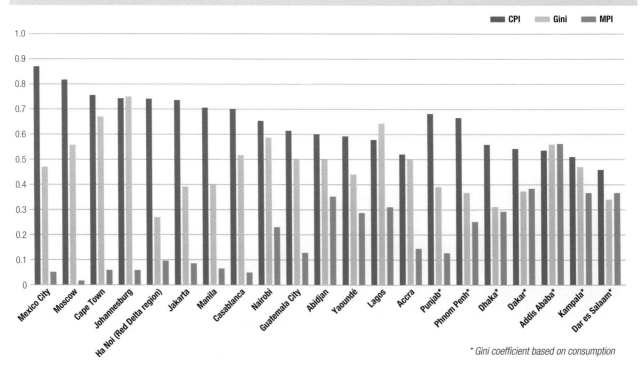

* Gini coefficient based on consumption

This graph shows the difference between poverty and inequity in the context of rising prosperity. In many developing countries, inequity is often concealed in poverty, thus misdirecting policy and strategic interventions which tend to concentrate only on poverty. Chile (Santiago), although not in this chart, is a case in point. Whereas poverty has been reduced by around 20 per cent, the Gini coefficient increased from 0.542 in 1990 to 0.558 in 2009. A typical example of income polarization can be found in Nairobi, which features a Gini coefficient of 0.59, whereby the richest 10 per cent in the city account for 45.2 per cent of income while the poorest 10 per cent account for just 1.6 per cent.

Source: WHO/UNICEF (2010); International Energy Agency (2010); International Road Federation (2009); ITU World Telecommunication / ICT Indicators Database (2010).

their local development strategies are better placed for enhanced prosperity.

Equity reduces alienation and exclusion, paving the way for empowerment and engagement of all social groups, and for the realization of the full potential of the entire population. Indeed, cities that have removed impediments to the full engagement of women, youths and even the elderly have invariably enhanced overall prosperity.

Equity is not simply a normative concern, related to issues of fairness and justice, important as these may be. It is a material factor which directly impinges on the process of social and material sustenance. In fact, through removal of 'unfreedoms', and with the attendant broadening of choices and opportunities, equity enhances the city's transformative capacity while also promoting identity and agency among the population.

POLICY Promoting equity must be a dual endeavour: (i) providing the conditions that enable every individual and social group to realize their full potential and harness the collective benefits and opportunities any city has to offer; and (ii) removing any systemic barriers that discriminate against any individual or social group.

The social process that comes with the opportunities made available to all through public goods, such as quality education and skills, enables the population to remain engaged and to stake a claim on the city. In this respect, the way a city shapes, and is in turn shaped by, its population, will largely depend on whether urban systems provide all residents with equal opportunities for development and the ability to exert agency.

Inequity is inefficient from an economic perspective. As stressed by Sen, 'the primitiveness of social developments (such as widespread illiteracy, malnutrition, lack of health facilities and medical networks) is a barrier to the full realization of the benefits of participatory growth and prosperity.'[6] Remedies here include such public goods as political freedom, economic facilities, social opportunities, transparency and security, with the safeguards against a variety of risks that they ensure for basic capabilities.

Kibera, Nairobi: Looking out ... access to good education is one way out the slum.

© Eduardo Lopez Moreno

POLICY When equity is embedded in urban development strategies, efficiency is enhanced, asset utilization becomes optimal, productivity improves and social cohesion is strengthened.

Box 2.4.2

Spatial divisions exacerbate inequality

Spatial inequalities are not only a forerunner of social and economic divisions; these in turn cause further inequalities and different forms of exclusion and marginalization. In Jordan's capital, for instance, 97 per cent of households in Western Amman have computers while in Eastern Amman the proportion is no more than eight per cent. Not surprisingly, in Western Amman more than 50 per cent of males and 20 per cent of females earn more than US$1,400 monthly, compared with only two per cent for males and less than one per cent for females in Eastern Amman.[7]

The urban divide appears to widen with higher degrees of economic prosperity; at least this is the perception of populations and local experts. In Bangalore, where specialization in computer technologies has brought a fair amount of economic prosperity, a local expert remarked that *'while quality of life is comfortable for "elite Bangalore", it is not so for the "other Bangalore" which comprises the majority of the population'*.[8] In São Paulo, even as municipal authorities strive to integrate *favelas*, informal settlements and rehabilitated urban neighbourhoods into a more inclusive city, wealthy Paulistanos resist the process and gravitate to more exclusive enclaves. The result is what has been dubbed a 'city of walls' where any visible prosperity appears to be largely monopolized by the wealthy. In Lusaka, a local expert reports

that 'increasing degrees of exclusion are reappearing in the city, especially with the new infrastructure under development. Segregation along racial lines is re-emerging.'[9] In Dubai, as in some other Gulf cities, the gap between nationals and non-nationals (access to schooling, public hospitals, health insurance, adequate and affordable housing, labour grievances and rights) is unequal in the extreme.

Research shows that when combined, the physical and social divisions between rich and poor neighbourhoods can generate further exclusion and marginalization, especially when the poor are confined to farther neighbourhoods with inadequate accessibility. The underprivileged people living in these 'lost' areas suffer from a triple jeopardy: long distances, high transport costs and excessive commuting times. This turns into a genuine 'spatial poverty trap' that conspires against shared prosperity through restrictions on jobs, compounding gender differences, limiting social interactions and reducing social capital, increasing the likelihood of crime and violence, with worsening living standards as a result.[10] The spatial inequalities so visible in so many cities are also the outcome of broader and deeply entrenched processes of unplanned urban development, poor governance and institutionalized exclusion and marginalization of specific groups.

THE RISKS OF UNCHALLENGED DIVISION

A growing body of research connects the competitiveness of cities with social cohesion. Analysis increasingly links the importance of tackling inequality at earlier stages of development to the achievement of prosperity. Reducing inequality and poverty has been highlighted as a key aspect of urban quality of life. A UNICEF study on poverty reduction mentioned that 'evidence from India, China and Brazil indicates very clearly that efforts to ease inequalities generate larger dividends for poverty reduction than a more conventional focus on economic growth'.[11] An OECD study has reached similar conclusions: the notion of *social cohesion* includes dimensions of social relationships, social inclusiveness and social equity, which are major components of broader-defined prosperity. 'The key idea that has emerged to link these concerns is that social cohesion improves economic performance. This is a more positive way of saying that

> More and more empirical data suggests a strong connection between equity and economic prosperity, with equity being a cause, not a result, of economic prosperity.

social division and fragmentation undermine long-term economic success'.[12]

However, the absence of social cohesion, particularly in the form of equity, not only challenges economic success: it also jeopardizes prosperity as a whole through the multidimensional, and far-reaching consequences which inequity spreads throughout urban society. UN-Habitat analysis (2010) of urban inequality in 47 developing countries challenged the notion that inequity is an acceptable, inevitable aspect of economic growth.[13] Recently, OECD experts agreed that economic growth and equality were by no means contradictory variables but instead can, and arguably should, act in a complementary way, stressing that 'researchers are increasingly finding that regions marked by higher levels of inequality, in fact, find their economic performance damaged.'[14]

The statement that 'more equal cities are more prosperous cities' is increasingly supported by evidence, and has become a development proposition. Without elaborating on the moral principle that inequality is inherently unacceptable, it would appear that when certain groups of people are repeatedly and disproportionately refrained from taking their fair, full share of the multidimensional benefits of the 'urban advantage', the foregoing statement comes with two interconnected corollaries. First: inequality can be linked to poor economic productivity, and experience shows that more sustainable urban economies are frequently associated with lower inequality. Second: persistent, ever-higher inequality carries direct risks. Stark disparities within cities have proven to be social detonators, as recent revolutions in the Arab world and social unrest in some cities in the developed world have vividly demonstrated.

Take a city anywhere in the world that can boast sustained economic growth thanks to high productivity, adequate infrastructure, a high quality of life and environmental preservation: the more this prosperity is inequitably distributed, the more precarious it is bound to be. All five 'spokes' in the 'prosperity wheel' must be developed in a well-balanced way for a smoother ride on the path of sustainable, shared prosperity.

The recent society-wide upheavals in Tunisia, Libya and Egypt did not occur against a background of extreme poverty or deprivation. In all three countries, national poverty reduction programmes had gained considerable traction. Slum improvement or eradication had been achieved or was on-going. Large infrastructure projects with adequate transport networks had been deployed or were underway and, in terms of education and health, achievements were approaching or surpassing national Millennium Development Goals. Still, Egypt, Libya and Tunisia were shown to have feet of clay. The sobering message from the Arab Spring, though still in a state of flux, is that leaders and societies ignore inequality at their own peril.

A recent report on the East African Community has highlighted a number of remarkable achievements in terms of economic growth over the past decade, propelled by massive increases in trade based on new, all-weather roads and uptake of mobile telephone technology. Still, the actual number of East Africans living below the poverty line has increased from 44 million to 53 million, and income inequality indicators, as measured by Gini coefficients, have also worsened in most countries.[15] As a regional expert put it, 'The reason for this is that inequality is both deepening and widening. Fewer people are enjoying the benefits of economic growth.'[16]

Inequality and criminality appear to be part and parcel of the same equation. This is all the more so when lack of opportunities and rising unemployment are added to the balance. Perceptions of rising criminality, and the fears thereof, may be strong in cities characterised by high inequity, and even stronger than numbers actually state. In one poll, comparing perceptions and expert opinion in São Paulo and London, criminality emerged as a major concern in both cities, even though actual numbers in São Paulo were a multiple of London's.[17] In the same survey, residents of cities as diverse as Mumbai, Chicago, Cairo, London, Paris, Beijing and São Paulo overwhelmingly agreed (89 per cent) that "a non-dangerous city" was their prime criterion for the 'good urban life', a notion that has much to do with prosperity.

LINKING EQUITY TO PROSPERITY

'*Inequalities are increasing day after day*', according to a local expert in Hyderabad. This comment echoes findings from the United Nations General Assembly 2011 Report on Progress towards Millennium Development Goals (MDGs), which stressed that 'despite advances towards achieving the MDGs, insufficient emphasis in the MDG agenda had been given to the issue of inequity which is increasing within and between countries.'[18] Even in those countries that have made progress towards the MDGs, inequalities have grown. Therefore, as suggested by the UN General Assembly, equity must be mainstreamed in the development agenda, based on more inclusive growth.

Evidence showing that equity is a critical dimension of prosperity runs against the conventional development approaches that prevailed before the 2008–09 global financial crisis. A particular case in point is the 'Washington Consensus', which reinforced the notion that economic growth is to take place first before equity

> When prosperity remains an elusive proposition for a majority of the population, the prospects of social unrest or full-blown conflicts increase, since the majority's claims are nothing but demands for effective human dignity.

> **POLICY** If left unaddressed, socioeconomic fragmentation can jeopardize urban prosperity and pose major risks to nationwide political stability.

> **POLICY** Cities should pay more attention to inequity as a critical factor affecting prosperity. Deliberate and conscious policies need to emphasize the importance of equity in urban decision-making.

The impact of inequity has been overlooked in conventional economic and development theory.

issues can be addressed. Although the Consensus promoted pro-poor growth and the provision of primary education along with primary health and infrastructure development, it was based on the premise that poorer sections of society benefit from whatever 'trickles down' the economic and social pyramid, in an environment of free enterprise and deregulation. The dramatic collapse of the banking system in major Western countries in 2008 and the subsequent world economic crisis has seriously discredited the Consensus approach.

Ample evidence suggests that structures and institutions are skewed in favour of dominant groups in society. These groups may legally or otherwise maximize their own benefits, not by chance but by design, and perpetuate and enhance conditions that further benefit themselves or their

POLICY More equitable cities have greater chances to be more prosperous; but prosperity does not happen all by itself, or as a logical consequence of economic growth.

socio-political class. This is particularly true in cities with poor governance arrangements, weak institutions and non-existing or ineffective planning structures – in other words, in cities where the 'hub' of the wheel of prosperity is not properly working and fails to steer growth and development in a more equitable manner.

The UN-Habitat survey on urban prosperity in developing regions has highlighted corruption as the greatest barrier to equity, followed by weak civil society (with its role in rights advocacy) (Figure 2.4.2). This is the case in Lahore, Bangalore, Amman and Beirut. In the survey, local experts also cited poor governance, lack of political will and structural barriers to pro-equity policies as other significant hindrances to equity. Far from being a historic or inevitable phenomenon, urban inequality in this perspective is understood to be the result of deliberate negligence, structural obstacles and weak capacities to counter prevailing conditions.

FOSTERING SOCIAL INCLUSION

Unequal income and unequal opportunities are the two main underlying factors of urban inequity. They derive from biases in distribution at national level as well as dysfunctions at the local urban level. In this sense, inequity

Figure 2.4.2

Factors restricting the scope of greater urban equity

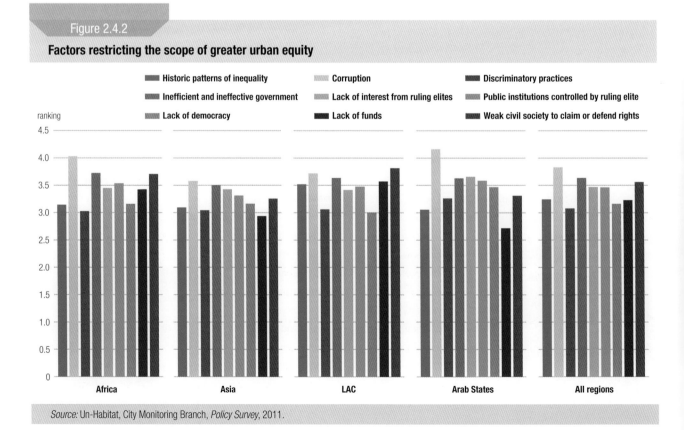

Source: Un-Habitat, City Monitoring Branch, *Policy Survey*, 2011.

reveals a differentiation in the manner in which resources are allocated and facilities and services accessed. The main driver of inequity often tends to be differential access to employment as well as to public goods and services. Inequity in this respect reflects biases in the economic realm which effectively concentrate a disproportionate share of resources, services and opportunities in the hands of certain groups or individuals. A common response is the consolidation of redistributive programmes, mainly in the area of social welfare. In developing countries, this has been complemented with the design of local economic development initiatives as well as poverty alleviation measures. However, it has become increasingly evident that beyond dysfunctions in the distributive systems, in both developed and developing countries, some systemic barriers sustain outright discrimination and alienation.

Transcending poverty and deprivation, social inclusion as both a process and an outcome entails the removal of barriers to access to goods, services and opportunities as well as the improvement of wellbeing and self-fulfilment. This goes to show that social inclusion is not just reactive; rather, it recognizes the importance of differences and diversity, and harnesses the commonality of lived and shared experiences to achieve positive societal ends.

To a substantial degree, the urban protest movements that were referred to earlier in this Report have been about social inclusion (Chapter 1, Part 1). The rallying cry, 'We are the 99 per cent', is more of a reaction to exclusion and alienation than a protest against poverty or deprivation. Whereas equity in its primarily economic dimension is driven by 'macro' and national policies, most interventions in favour of social inclusion take place at the local level. Therefore, urban authorities have a major role to play when it comes to making shared prosperity a reality within their jurisdictions.

In European cities an abundance of initiatives have been introduced to promote social inclusion, and their benefits seem to have registered in the UN-Habitat 'Urban Prosperity Index'. For example, the 'Cities Against Social Exclusion' (CASE) programme illustrates the concerted efforts at local and regional levels to share experiences and improve local action among a network of European cities.

Typical interventions, such as in Stockholm, include removal of barriers to full engagement of women, youths, the homeless, the elderly and the disabled. In Vienna, an elaborate action plan involves systems for non-discrimination at all levels, improved political and social participation of all minority groups including migrants, and measurable monitoring of social diversity and integration. As Vienna's mayor once put it, 'Social cohesion and a climate of respect are particularly important at a time when we all face new challenges. Good neighbourly relations cannot be enacted by law. The people who live in Vienna need to come to an understanding and formulate mutually acceptable solutions.'[19]

Similar noteworthy experiences are emerging in developing countries where Medellín, Dar es Salaam and Kigali, for instance, have found effective ways of enhancing prosperity based on relatively lower productivity, infrastructural development and quality of life. Medellín has resorted to civic architecture and public spaces to further inclusiveness and the empowerment of otherwise marginalized social groups. Such groups benefit from expanded public facilities as infrastructure reaches out to them, improving not just their sense of well-being but also their capacity fully to engage with the urban fabric. In Dar es Salaam, a conscientious plan for socially mixed neighbourhoods has brought more inclusion both in space and in social relations. In Kigali, innovative measures aim to consolidate reconciliation and integration as part of the post-genocide reconstruction process.

PLACING EQUITY ON THE DEVELOPMENT AGENDA
UN-Habitat policy analysis shows that in most developed countries, concerns for socioeconomic equity are typically built into concerted actions from local and national governments. This will usually result in urban policies promoting inclusion, diversity, multi-ethnicity, affirmative

POLICY Equity is also about social and political relations among urban populations as well as among government institutions and individuals and social groups. It is the relational dimension which underlies the degree to which a city operates and sustains as a collective entity.

POLICY At the city level, social inclusion provides an environment where individuals and social groups feel they belong to the larger whole, have access to 'commons' and are free fully to engage in collective affairs.

POLICY Cities willing to embrace shared prosperity must also look beyond equity to ensure the promotion of social inclusion as a whole.

Medellín, Colombia: children enjoy education at a junior school.

© Jez Coulson/Panos Pictures

action, positive discrimination and pro-poor planning. This in turn can take the form of wide-ranging programmes and actions, from strategic positioning of educational and recreational centres to low-cost housing to quota systems to encourage minority engagement in local politics and representation, as well as targeted subsidies and financial support for new businesses. Similar policies and dedicated institutions are found at the municipal level in most developed countries and in some emerging economies.

Local experts in the UN-Habitat survey believe that equity is primarily the responsibility of public authorities; where a failure of political will, or indifference, are to blame for deficient, or total lack of, effective policy. Such failure can be identified at national or local level. In the survey, local experts in Nairobi, Luanda, Kuwait City, Lahore, Lima, Fort-de-France, Erbil and Saida felt that national governments showed little concern for inequity whereas local experts in Alexandria, Algiers, Hyderabad, Guadalajara, Panama City, Beirut and Doha report that it is local policy-makers who show little concern for equity.

> Institutions are not fully contributing to equity. Rulers lack interest and ineffective governments are hampering the potential for more equitable cities.

Elsewhere, local experts report that some cities prioritize equity in planning and policy strategies. Figure 2.4.3 summarizes the types of action they use. In African and Asian cities in the UN-Habitat survey, pro-poor vocational training and skills programmes are emphasized, with some projects explicitly targeting the poor and marginalized. Singapore offers a clear example of repeated commitment by the government to education and training for all in an environment that promotes productivity and social mobility. In Ho Chi Minh City, government-led promotion of the high-tech (IT) and service sectors offers widespread

> POLICY Addressing inequities requires political will, strong institutions and well-targeted policies.

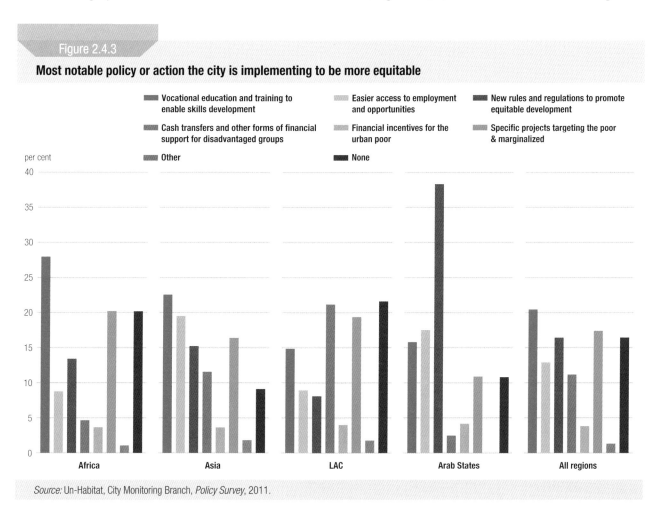

Figure 2.4.3

Most notable policy or action the city is implementing to be more equitable

- Vocational education and training to enable skills development
- Easier access to employment and opportunities
- New rules and regulations to promote equitable development
- Cash transfers and other forms of financial support for disadvantaged groups
- Financial incentives for the urban poor
- Specific projects targeting the poor & marginalized
- Other
- None

Source: Un-Habitat, City Monitoring Branch, *Policy Survey*, 2011.

new opportunities for communities to switch away from conventional manual labour.[20] In Africa, Addis Ababa's *Micro and Small Enterprises Development Strategy* targets the unemployed.[21] Johannesburg enhances the skills of poor communities, expanding access to education and training. In Latin American and Caribbean countries, some experts cited cash transfers and other financial assistance in support of marginalized groups, such as Brazil's '*Bolsa Familia*' and Mexico's '*Oportunidades*' programme. In Arab cities, local experts found that new rules and regulations did promote equitable development.

Box 2.4.3

Making progress on the equity agenda

Today, some cities and national governments in the developing world are beginning to prioritize equity through concerted actions. They understand that working together maximizes their possibilities to make positive changes in the living conditions of the urban poor. They also understand that equity is a fundamental aspect of prosperity. Their interventions are closely linked to pro-poor programmes such as: in Alexandria, the Social Fund for Development, which focuses on small- and medium-size businesses; in Gaziantep, the Social Solidarity Fund whose cash transfers are conditional on children being sent to school; in Lahore, the Benazir Income Support Programme; in Shenzhen, social equity policies have brought large numbers of migrant workers and vulnerable groups into the city's social housing and welfare system; in Ho Chi Minh City, the 'Doimoi' reform process has reduced inequalities in Vietnam's capital.

POLICY There is no substitute for government leadership to address issues of equity. Civil society's complementary role is in advocacy and support.

Cities are also allocating funds and introducing local programmes to promote equity. Some of these interventions are becoming best practices and good examples that are inspiring other cities, and sometimes national governments. Authorities in Chongqing have made social equity a primary goal. Priority public rental housing programmes have improved conditions and rural migrant workers' rights are better protected. In Beirut, vulnerable groups are targeted for special social support as part of a scheme that has significantly reduced homelessness and the number of people (10 per cent in 2009) below the National Poverty line.[22] Faced with very steep income inequality (with Gini coefficients as high as 0.75 in 2005), Johannesburg is responding with pro-poor policies including 'Cash Social Grants'. Singapore integrates equity in national development policies and urban planning. According to a local expert, 'There is room for upward social mobility among the poor and lower-middle class people through adequate opportunities for all in education and the job market'.

Endnotes

1 World Bank, 2006.
2 Gewirth, 1996.
3 OECD, 2011.
4 *Ibid*.
5 UN-Habitat, 2010a
6 Sen, 1999.
7 Shabou et al, 2011.
8 Belliapa, 2011.
9 Hampwaye and Nehito, 2011.
10 UN-Habitat, 2010a.
11 UNICEF, 2010.
12 Turok, 2006.
13 UN-Habitat, 2010a; UN-Habitat, 2008.
14 OECD, 2006.
15 Society for International Development (SID), 2012.
16 SID Programme director Aidan Eyakuze as quoted in the *The East African* [Mungai, C. (2012) 'East Africa Region's Economy Expands Amid Deepening Levels of Poverty and Malnutrition' in *The East African*, April 7, http://www.theeastafrican.co.ke/news/A+richer+East+African+Community+with+more+poor+people/-/2558/1381658/-/v2nkg7/-/index.html]
17 Urban Age, 2009.
18 United Nations General Assembly, 2011.
19 Vienna City Administration (n.d) *Vienna Charter. Shaping the Future Together*, http://www.wien.gv.at/english/living-working/vienna-charter.html
20 Dzung, 2011.
21 Admassie, 2011.
22 UNDP, 2009.

© Edwina Sassoon/fotoLIBRA.com

Environmental Sustainability and the Prosperity of Cities

POLICY Cities can be sources of environmental problems within and beyond their jurisdictions, but they are also best placed to provide most of the solutions. Environmentally sustainable cities are able to strike a healthy balance between economic growth and environmental preservation, in the process facilitating both prosperity and resilience, including to climate change.[6]

The prosperity and environmental sustainability of cities are inextricably linked. Urban areas consume huge amounts of environmental goods and services like food, water, energy, forestry, building materials, and 'green' or open spaces often beyond their boundaries. This undermines the assimilative capacity of the natural environment around urban areas.[1] For example, the cities of the world generate over 720 billion tons of wastes every year, but in developing regions, even in large, presumably more affluent cities, only 25 to 55 per cent of wastes are collected.[2] Demographic and spatial expansion can be so rapid as to outstrip the capacity of cities to provide basic amenities – housing, water and sanitation, etc. – resulting in poor urban conditions.[3]

A key message is that prosperous cities can operate efficiently and productively without necessarily damaging the environment.[4] This is possible only when environmental and social objectives are fully integrated in a city's overall economic goals for the purposes of a sustainable environment.[5] This implies that there is no trade-off between any city's *environmental sustainability* and their *economic growth and prosperity*.

Environmental sustainability is central to the qualitative changes necessary to transform cities and urban lives, particularly the lives of the urban poor. This is due to the fact that environmentally sustainable cities are vibrant, and such cities are more likely to attract the skills and entrepreneurship essential for growth and prosperity, which are necessary to solving urban problems and challenges. However, this will require new arrangements – institutions, technology, financial mechanism, innovative and flexible urban planning process; and above all, tacit commitments and political will to formulate and implement appropriate strategies and policies to drive environmental sustainability, hence prosperity in cities.

ENVIRONMENTAL SUSTAINABILITY IN CITIES

It is generally assumed that any country can preserve the environment while maintaining economic growth.[7] However, a degree of commitment is required from all stakeholders, particularly at local level, if sustainable development is to be achieved.[8] This is in line with the principles of Local Agenda 21, where cities are perceived as both sources and solutions to environmental problems.[9] It is incumbent on cities and their municipal authorities to deploy and maintain local socioeconomic and environmental infrastructures, preside over local planning processes, and formulate and implement environmental policies.[10] A concern for the public interest and shared prosperity will help mobilize the whole population in favour

> Environmentally sustainable cities are likely to be more productive, competitive, innovative and prosperous, which contributes to enhanced quality of life and well-being of the population.

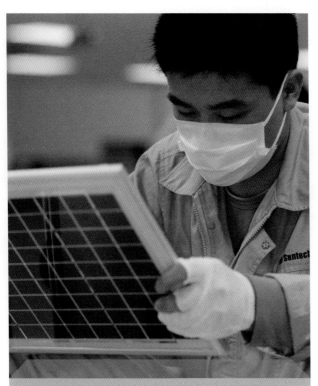

Solar panel assembly at a Suntech factory in Wuxi, China. A high percentage of China's homes use solar-heated water.

© Qilai Shen/Panos Pictures

bring about shared prosperity if it does not go hand in hand with a sustainable environment.

AFRICAN CITIES

Higher oil and commodity prices have enabled Africa's rate of economic growth to outpace the global average over the past decade. Real (i.e., inflation-adjusted) GDP growth has remained steady, particularly south of the Sahara, where it is expected to continue at an annual rate of at least five per cent.[14] However, an overwhelming majority of local experts believe that economic development and related urban activities have unintended effects on the environment in cities such as Nairobi, Lusaka, Praia, Algiers, Dar es Salaam, Ibadan, Accra, Luanda or Lagos. Perceptions are that so far, these cities have been unable to match sustained economic and demographic growth with corresponding expansion in infrastructures and services, with consequent detrimental effects on the natural environment.

In Nairobi, for example, local experts point to extensive pollution of the Nairobi River, not just by industrial effluents but also solid waste.[15] Traffic congestion is also mentioned as a major environmental problem, and apart from the attendant air pollution, the cost to the local economy is enormous.[16] Similar opinions are held by experts in Lusaka, Accra, Algiers, Lagos, Ibadan and Luanda, where rapid urban sprawl and uncontrolled spatial development combine with poor infrastructures and weak regulatory frameworks to undermine quality of life and, more generally, prosperity in their respective cities.

In Praia (Cape Verde), experts point to the inability of infrastructure and services to keep pace with economic growth, particularly inadequate and poor quality housing, as well as proliferating informal settlements. In Accra, the benefits of economic growth (four per cent on an annual average rate) have not been brought to bear on rapid urbanization in the form of new infrastructures and services; these indeed have kept lagging behind, with the collapse of sanitary systems a serious environmental concern.[17] In Dar es Salaam and Beira (Mozambique), local experts also point to the impacts of economic growth, with unsatisfied demand for urban services – housing, water, waste management and

of the many minor changes in individual lifestyles, routines and behaviour that can bring about more sustainable living conditions for all. Participatory governance obviously has a major role to play in this respect, in addition to strengthening the resolve and commitment that are required of urban authorities when faced with the challenge of a sustainable environment.[11]

Nowhere are the commitments of cities to environmental sustainability more vital than in developing countries, where urban demographics are growing rapidly. This underscores the need for growth and prosperity to sustain and fulfil basic needs. Vitally important as economic growth may be, it cannot

> In Europe, many cities stand at the forefront of initiatives in favour of environmental sustainability,[12] as they keep developing and implementing various policies and strategies.[13]

> **POLICY** When pursued in an environmentally sustainable manner, economic development and related urban activities are sure to enhance any city's prosperity.

> In the majority of African cities surveyed, local experts report that economic development and related urban activities have detrimental effects on the natural environment, due to the fact that sustainability concerns are overlooked by policy-makers.

electricity – exacerbating existing problems of informal settlements and urban sprawl. Solid waste management, in particular, is a serious problem,[18] including hazardous wastes in the case of Dar es Salaam.[19]

In 10 of the 14 African cities surveyed for this Report, a large majority of experts perceive a mismatch between economic growth and urban expansion, on the one hand, and environmental preservation on the other hand. In the four remaining African cities in the sample, this view is shared only by a minority of local experts. This comes as no surprise, since these cities seriously pursue environmental sustainability as a matter of policy. This

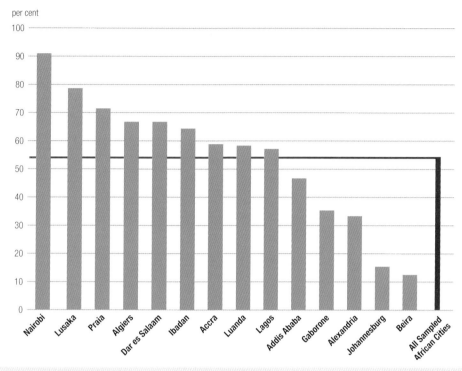

Figure 2.5.1

Environmental impact of growth as perceived by local experts – African cities

Source: UN-Habitat, City Monitoring Branch, *Policy Survey*, 2011.

is not to suggest that these concerns are not shared in the other 10 cities, but rather that Johannesburg,[20] Beira,[21] Alexandria[22] and Gaborone[23] have deployed relatively effective and comprehensive policies in this respect; these include holistic urban management and governance policies combined with appropriate institutional arrangements.

Johannesburg's case is instructive, and has the most holistic approach to urban environmental sustainability in the region. South Africa's economic capital has been systematically promoting the creation and preservation of open spaces, pursuing energy efficiency and the reduction of greenhouse gases, and promoting solar energy, energy-saving bulbs and insulation as part of a retrofitting scheme. Above all, the city promotes sustainable building design and construction through a comprehensive set of planning regulations, whereby a sustainable approach must pervade all planning stages.[24] At the

same time, Johannesburg faces all the problems associated with inequality of access and urban opportunities – with 35 to 40 per cent of the population living in poverty.[25]

In other cities – Accra, Praia, Alexandria and Luanda – the majority of experts report both the serious detrimental effects of economic growth on the environment and a scarcity of environmental policies, but at the same time highlight the huge benefits these policies have brought to the urban population. Accra provides a good illustration of these disproportionate effects, with local experts noting that the environment has been improved by the distribution of energy-efficient electric bulbs to households and commercial facilities, as well as the introduction of waste recycling facilities to tackle the menace of solid wastes, particularly plastics.[26] The case of Alexandria is also instructive, and shows that with effective use of the little capacity available to cities, significant improvements can be made to the urban environment. For instance, cooperation between all stakeholders and more systematic inspection of industrial and tourist facilities (regarding effluents discharge into the environment) have significantly improved water quality in Alexandria.[27]

Johannesburg's approach to environmental sustainability appears to be the most comprehensive and holistic of all African cities.

ASIAN CITIES

Asian cities demonstrate the classic *Environmental Kuznets Curve* scenario where the initial stage of economic development sees environmental quality deteriorate before improving markedly as a certain income level is reached.[28] In practice, polluting heavy and natural resource-intensive industries predominate at the early stages of development. Subsequently, the benefits of economic growth enable industries to deploy less polluting, more resource-efficient technologies. This may explain why, apart from those in Arab States, Asian cities are where the UN-Habitat survey found the lowest numbers of experts claiming that economic development and related urban activities were detrimental to the environment.

However, the local expert survey reveals differences across cities. For instance, economic growth is not perceived to have been matched by adequate infrastructure and services in Ho Chi Minh City, Bangalore, Lahore, and Hyderabad. In Lahore, experts point to ground water pollution, extensive air pollution, traffic congestion and urban sprawl as major effects of economic development and urban activities on the environment, which are compounded by inadequate capacity and weak institutions.[29] Similarly in Bangalore, experts point to poor air quality, depletion of ground water tables and

fast receding lakes as indicative of the environmental consequences of economic development and related urban activities.[30] These perceptions contrast with those of local experts in Singapore, Gaziantep (Turkey) and Shenzhen, where very few local experts view economic growth and urban activities as detrimental to the environment (Figure 2.5.2).

What can be deduced from the perception of experts across Asian cities, just as in the case of Africa, is that cities with policies that promote environmental sustainability are better able to manage the adverse impacts of growth and related urban activities on the environment. In Asia, close to two-thirds of local experts report that this type of policy is at work in their respective cities, especially in Singapore and Ho Chi Minh City. In Asia, close to two-thirds of the experts are of the opinions that cities across the region have policies promoting environmental sustainability. In Singapore and Ho Chi Minh City all local experts believe their respective cities have policies promoting environmental sustainability.

Experts in Singapore point to the strong commitment of the city-State to environmental sustainability. This

POLICY When cities promote environmental sustainability as a matter of policy, they are able to cushion the unintended effects of economic development and urban activities.

POLICY

Environmentally sustainable cities are more compact, energy-efficient, cleaner and less polluted, more accessible, and offer better transport choices.

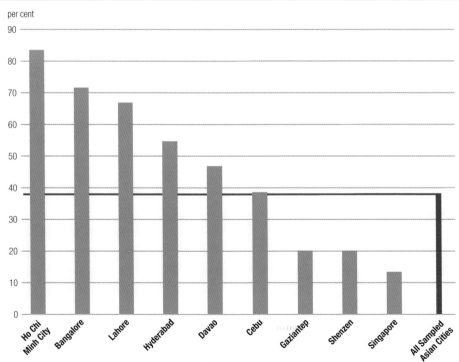

Figure 2.5.2

Environmental impact of growth as perceived by local experts – Asian cities

Source: UN-Habitat, City Monitoring Branch, *Policy Survey*, 2011.

involves an awareness campaign with public authorities working with institutions and grassroots leaders to reach out to the population – with tangible benefits in terms of living standards and prosperity. The 'compact city' initiative favours density and facilitates mass transit, while another initiative promotes walking. As many as 58 per cent of solid wastes are recycled, another 40 per cent produce energy through incineration, and the remaining two per cent goes to a purpose-built off-shore sanitary landfill. The city-State's integrated water management system has allowed it to meet 30 per cent of water needs through water harvesting – with an ambitious plan to increase this to 40 per cent by 2020.[31]

CITIES IN ARAB STATES

Across Arab States, only one-third of local experts consider that economic development and related urban activities have unintended detrimental effects on the environment (Figure 2.5.3). This observation differs markedly from the perception of experts in Africa, Asia, and Latin America, and may be explained by the economic structure of the region that is heavily dependent on crude

oil exports, an activity that, unlike industrial manufacturing, leaves a relatively small ecological footprint in cities, especially where crude oil export processing is kept to a minimum.

However, this favourable overall average conceals sharp differences across cities. Experts that view economic development and related urban activities as having detrimental effects on the environment are an overwhelming majority in Beirut, and 50 per cent in Kuwait City, Shiraz, and Muharrak (Bahrain). The first three of these cities are characterized by relatively large populations and intense economic activity. In Beirut, local experts see a direct link between rapid urban expansion and environmental problems, with one describing the city as '*a metaphor for brutal real estate speculation*', with attendant noise pollution and traffic congestion.[32]

Similarly in Kuwait City, local experts point to the construction boom associated with economic growth and urban expansion. As noted by one, this double boom has placed '*acute pressures on road networks, with traffic becoming a nightmare*'.[33] However, in Iraq, experts in Basra link environmental problems to the vestiges of war, including ordnance with spent uranium which, combined with particulates and fumes from generators and oil installations, pose serious environmental problems.[34]

Some cities are promoting environmental sustainability as a matter of policy. This is the case in Doha, Aqaba and Dubai, according to a

POLICY Across cities, urbanization and economic growth are inevitable; and if matched with appropriate and effective policies and governance, the environmental consequences are manageable.

Figure 2.5.3

Environmental impact of growth as perceived by local experts – Arab cities

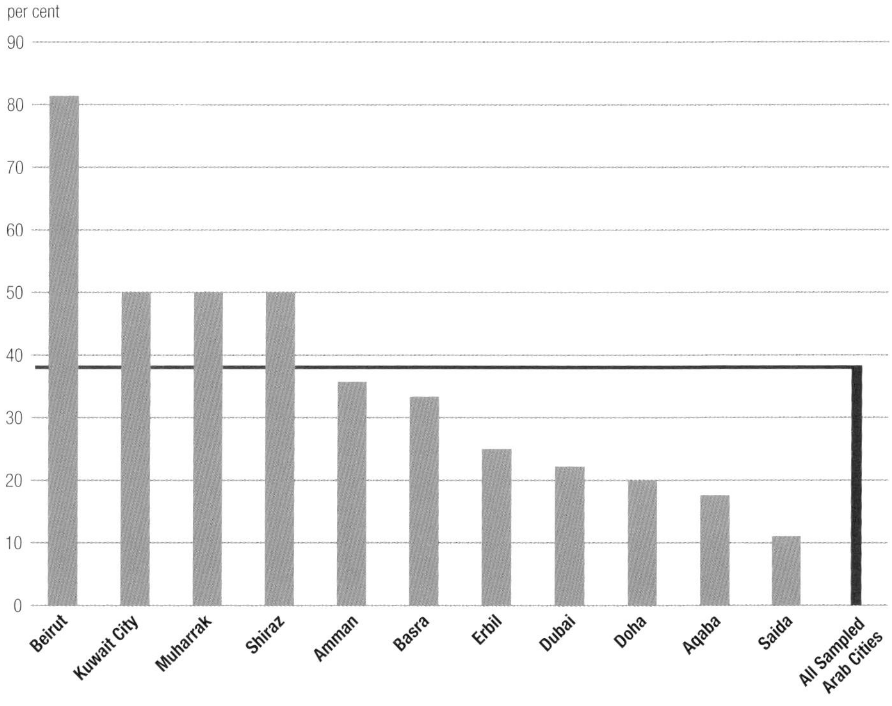

Source: UN-Habitat, City Monitoring Branch, *Policy Survey*, 2011.

majority of local experts. Experts in Doha point to several environmental initiatives and policies jointly implemented by the government, municipalities and civil society. These include keeping the environment clean, energy saving initiatives, protection of wildlife areas, and 'green' and functional infrastructure policies. In Aqaba, local experts mention the sets of laws, by-laws and regulations for the preservation of natural resources and safeguard the highly sensitive marine ecosystem around the harbour.[35] In Dubai, environmental sustainability policies include the Emirates' Energy and Environment Rating and the Air Quality Management Systems, among other robust schemes and governance mechanisms.[36] This is not the case in Saida (Lebanon), Basra and Beirut. In Beirut, *'environmental concerns are rarely considered'*, and this comes within the context of an absence of effective policies for urban planning regardless of pressing needs (e.g., traffic and waste management).[37]

LATIN AMERICA AND THE CARIBBEAN

Latin America and the Caribbean is the region where a greater proportion of local experts believe that economic development and urban activities have (unintended) detrimental effects on the environment. Two distinct phenomena may be at play here: the region's high rates of urban spatial expansion, and relatively high degrees of economic development. The consequences of economic development on the environment are considered as 'serious' or 'very serious' by most local experts in Guadalajara, Lima, Ciudad del Este (Paraguay), Medellín, La Paz and Valparaiso (Figure 2.5.4).

The overall picture in Latin American cities is one of inadequate commitment to environmental sustainability, owing to weak policies and strategies from public authorities. This leaves relatively few opportunities for wider participation in environmental policies, something that can further exacerbate the detrimental effects of economic development and urban activities on the natural environment.

Local experts in Guadalajara and Ciudad del Este mention urban sprawl and related phenomena, which put green and open spaces under pressure, with air pollution as the other major detrimental effect of economic activity on the environment. Heavy industry (cement and smelter plants) ranks among the more prominent culprits.[38, 39] In Ciudad del Este, local experts instead point to pollution from landfills, as well as unplanned urban expansion, with the attending gradual deterioration of natural resources and contamination of streams and water supplies.[40] Waste management is also perceived as a major problem in Valparaiso, where waste once collected is dumped in landfills by the waterfront, causing huge pollution, including release of effluents into the sea.[41]

In Medellín, experts point to the 224,000 tons of pollutants discharged annually into the atmosphere, of which 66 per cent are traceable to traffic in a city that keeps expanding rapidly in both surface area and population.[42] In Santo Domingo, rapid urban sprawl and population expansion are fuelled by natural resource exploitation, and the two combine with weak institutions to compound environmental problems.[43] In Lima, an overwhelming number of local experts concur that environmental sustainability has not been a priority in the management of the city. The few existing initiatives are largely uncoordinated, though all under the responsibility of the central rather than local government.[44] As suggested earlier, the detrimental effect of urban socioeconomic development (and of urbanization more generally) on the environment is seriously compounded by inadequate engagement with sustainability, as indicated by an absence of effective policies or strategies, as well as relatively few opportunities for wider community participation therein.

This finding is further reinforced by the fact that sustainable environmental policies have proved relatively effective in Fort-de-France, Havana and Venezuela's Guarenas. In the case of Fort-de-France, from 2008 onwards, a determined mayor has taken action, challenging environmental misbehaviour, particularly with regard to solid waste, and vigorously enforcing environmental rules and regulations across all sectors (including households and businesses) through so-called 'green' brigades. On top of waste treatment plants, and recycling, the determined drive was supported by educational awareness programmes, daily and public monitoring and reporting of air quality, and promoting public participation in environmental decision-making.[45] Similarly in Medellín, the municipality's environmental department implements a variety of 'sustainable' policies with regard to noise pollution, global warming, water conservation and reforestation. A range of abatement targets and initiatives has been established. These include controls on greenhouse gas emissions and air quality, use of non-polluting fuels and waste treatment/control systems, together with encouraging walking and cycling (dedicated paths). A range of targets have been set

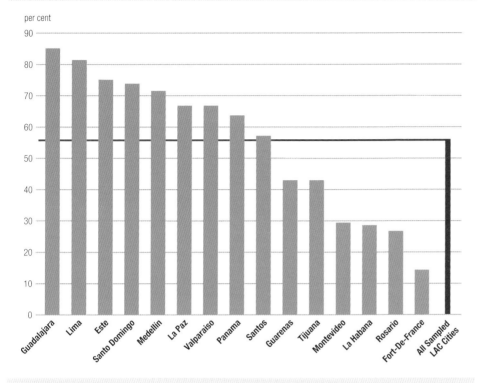

Figure 2.5.4

Environmental impact of grow thas perceived by local experts – Latin American and Caribbean cities

per cent

Source: UN-Habitat, City Monitoring Branch, *Policy Survey*, 2011.

creation is a critical challenge for cities throughout the world. In rapidly growing and developing cities worldwide there is a continuous influx of new residents in search of full-time employment. Within slower growing (or shrinking) cities in Europe, North America, Japan and elsewhere, there is a need to maintain the existing employment base in the face of industrial restructuring, albeit taking advantage of the economic opportunities presented by environmental sustainability to replace obsolescent high-carbon processes and activities. The employment potential of environmental sustainability is huge, deriving mainly from wide ranges of climate-change mitigation and adaptation measures against the threat of the destructive effects of climate change: reducing demand for non-renewable resources, seeking renewable alternatives, recycling and reusing materials.[47] On top of this, huge employment potentials are associated with the production and deployment of new technical systems: renewable energies, sustainable urban transportation, waste recycling, retrofitting old buildings, new sustainable buildings and infrastructures, and environmental services.[48]

involving various greenhouse gas emission controls and air quality. As one local expert put it, '*the municipality is awakening and educating people towards a more responsible environmental behaviour.*'[46]

ENVIRONMENTAL SUSTAINABILITY: A CATALYST FOR CITY PROSPERITY

Environmental sustainability offers cities huge scope for the balanced economic growth that is associated with prosperity. This includes opportunities for new types of employment and investment, poverty alleviation and reduced inequality, together with new types of infrastructures and services. All of these are significant socioeconomic aspects of urban prosperity, along with quality of life and equal access to urban opportunities. Therefore, the relevance of environmental sustainability to urban prosperity cannot be overstated.

THE POTENTIAL FOR JOBS AND INVESTMENT

Unemployment is the bane of most cities and its impacts can dampen the growth and prosperity of cities. Job

POLICY Cities that are environmentally sustainable are likely to increase employment potential in terms of: substitution of renewable alternatives for non-renewable resources, recycling and reusing materials,[49] production and installation of renewable energy systems, sustainable urban transport, waste recycling, retrofitting old buildings, construction of new sustainable buildings and infrastructures, and provision of environmental services.[50]

RENEWABLE ENERGIES

The renewable energy sector – solar, wind, hydroelectric, geothermal and bio-fuel – continues to attract huge investment. By 2010, a total US$243 billion had been committed to this sector worldwide;[51] and this is projected to rise to US$630 billion by 2030, in the process creating as many as 20 million jobs.[52] Although much of this has concentrated on developed countries, investment in renewable energies is beginning to materialize in the developing world as well.[53]

Around the world, about 300,000 workers are employed in the wind power sector alone, and another 100,000 in solar photovoltaic, while some 1.2 million jobs have already been created in the biomass sector in Brazil, China, Germany and the USA.[54] In the UK, 250,000 people are already employed in the various renewable energy sectors estimated to be worth US$53 billion annually.[55]

While developed countries have the lion's share of jobs in the *sustainable* sector around the world, huge opportunities are available to developing countries. India is looking to create no fewer than 100 million jobs in this sector within 10 years, most of which are expected to be in solar energy.[56] In Nigeria, estimates show that a biofuel industry based on cassava and sugar cane crops could generate 200,000 jobs,[57] significant proportions of which would be located in urban areas. South Africa reckons that 98,000 new 'low carbon' jobs are possible in the short term, and close to 717,000 in the medium to long term,[58] to be split into recycling, solar energy and retrofitting of old buildings for energy efficiency.

POLICY Cities that invest in renewable energy can generate more employment and income.

The potential contribution of environmental sustainability to urban prosperity seems to be dawning on urban decision-makers in developing countries. So much transpires from the UN-Habitat survey of local experts, as summarized in Table 2.5.1: where more than half of local experts in Asia, over 40 per cent in Arab States, and over one-third in Africa believe countries in their respective cities have programmes and practices that support the use of renewable energy. This affords huge opportunities to enhance economic growth and prosperity in these cities with no adverse impacts on urban environment, given the carbon neutrality of renewable energy sources.

WASTE MANAGEMENT AND RECYCLING

Waste management provides cities with another major source of employment, and based on the experiences of developed countries, recycling offers huge investment and business opportunities.[59] For example, in Copenhagen only three per cent of waste ends up in landfills, 32 per cent is recycled, while 39 per cent is converted into useful energy sufficient for 70,000 households.[60]

This also applies to cities in developing countries, where an estimated 15 million people are already involved in waste collecting and processing.[61] In Bangladesh, 800,000 of the 3.5 million potential jobs associated with environmental sustainability are in recycling.[62] Besides new jobs, waste management and recycling have also spawned technical innovations, leading to the creation of many specialized small- and medium-sized urban businesses in developing countries.[63] In Ouagadougou, Burkina Faso, a collection/recycling plastic waste project has improved environmental conditions, creating jobs and incomes for local people in either of these two activities.

Table 2.5.1

Environmental sustainability: extant policies, as perceived by local experts (per cent)

Regions	Support to renewable energy use	New parks built in the last 5 years	Encouraging use of recycling facilities	Alternatives to motorized public transport
Africa	33	31	25	41
Arab States	41	70	32	23
Asia	52	77	65	56
Latin America & Caribbean	22	60	33	27
All regions	**36**	**58**	**39**	**37**

Source: UN-Habitat, City Monitoring Branch, *Policy Survey*, 2011.

POLICY Waste recycling and processing offer cities an immense source of employment, as well as investment and business opportunities.

Dhaka, Bangladesh: in a factory producing Polyethylene Terephthalate (PET) flakes, women sort plastic bottles collected from the streets. Bangladesh exports over 20,000 tons of PET flakes made in 3,000 factories across the country. The industry is worth GBP 7 million, and growing by 20% per annum.

© G.M.B. Akash/Panos Pictures

On top of generating US$35,000 in incomes (in a country where average income per capita is US$300), the project has resulted in a cleaner environment in the suburbs.[64]

BUILDINGS

Buildings anywhere in the world have major roles to play in environmental sustainability, including climate change mitigation. This is because of the disproportionate amounts of natural resources, energy waste and pollution involved in buildings. For instance, 60 per cent of the operational energy of a typical building goes to cooling and heating, 18 per cent to water heating, six per cent to refrigeration and three per cent to lighting. This is why buildings offer the greatest potential for reduced greenhouse emissions.[65] Given this situation, two simultaneous avenues are available to cities, in developing as well as in developed countries: construction of new buildings to 'green' standards; and retrofitting existing buildings with energy-saving materials (a major source of additional employment creation).

'Green' construction standards are gaining ground mostly in highly urbanized developed countries. The USA already numbers over 40,000 Leadership in Energy and

Environmental Design (LEED)-accredited professionals involved in design, construction, operation or maintenance of energy-efficient buildings. In Australia, 900 professionals can boast a 'Green Star', and 1,197 Building Research Establishment Environmental Assessment Method (BREEAM)-licensed assessors are at work in the United Kingdom.[66] These numbers have been increasing and are projected to rise further as green building takes over a

The construction industry has the largest potential to create 'green' jobs in urban areas. Building and construction together employ over 111 million worldwide, or an average five to 10 per cent of total employment in every country (75 per cent in developing countries, of which 90 per cent are micro-firms, i.e., those with fewer than 10 employees).[67]

larger share of the construction market. In India, 1,500 professionals are already LEED-accredited.

Developing countries need alternative strategies in the pursuit of 'clean' buildings. This is because they cannot afford the technological solutions at the core of 'intelligent' or energy-efficient buildings in developed countries. A more suitable strategy for these countries is the use of 'passive' technology that combines flexibility, accessible know-how and traditional knowledge through vernacular architectures adapted to local climatic conditions. Urban areas might want to consider combining such 'passive' methods with some features of modern technology taking advantage of their declining cost in recent years (solar photovoltaic/thermal energy, water harvesting, etc.).

URBAN TRANSPORT

In Europe, the average multiplier effect of investment in public transport is 2 to 2.5 jobs for every single direct job created, but the ratio can be as high as 4:1 in some cases. A survey of some 170 cities in the European Union found that 90 per cent of urban bus fleets are made up of inefficient, polluting vehicles.[68] Less-polluting alternatives have been implemented in a number of cities in Europe, the USA, Canada and other developed countries using compressed natural gas (CNG), liquefied petroleum gas (LPG), biodiesel or hybrids. Some developing countries have also introduced low-pollution public transportation systems, particularly in Brazil, but also in India, Colombia, Mexico and other emerging economies.

Retrofitting not just old, polluting buses but also other vehicles used in urban transport will create jobs while reducing air pollution. Motorized two- and three-wheeled vehicles represent a widespread mode of public transport in many developing countries; in the Philippines, pilot projects suggest that retrofits of two-stroke engines cut fuel consumption by as much as 35 to 50 per cent, and emissions of air pollutants by as much as 90 per cent. In this case, retrofitting cuts operational costs on top of creating jobs through installation and maintenance of the kits.[70]

The bicycle industry also offers employment, but only in a few countries. The manufacture of bicycles is dominated by five producers: China, India, the European Union, Taiwan and Japan account for 87 per cent of global production. China alone produces more than half the world's bicycles. Production of electric bicycles is booming, reaching about 12 million units in 2005. Almost all of them were manufactured in China.[71]

DRIVERS AND CAPACITY-BUILDING FOR ENVIRONMENTAL SUSTAINABILITY

Environmentally sustainable urban policies are driven by seven main factors. These include: availability of financial resources, human resources, appropriate technology, specialized institutions, access to information, adequate organizational arrangements, and supportive legal frameworks – none of which can be taken for granted in developing countries.

Approximately one-third of local experts across all surveyed regions are of the view that mechanisms for coordination between city and national authorities regarding environmental sustainability are already in place (Table 2.5.2). Fewer than one-third report that cities are mobilizing investment to support sustainable resource use, or pulling their resources together in order to enhance environmental sustainability.

These efforts can only go so far, it would seem, as experts simultaneously highlight the widespread problem of inadequate capacity. This refers not just to lack of finance, but also of effective arrangements to facilitate partnerships with stakeholders, together with weak institutional frameworks and poor urban governance structures.[72] These conditions exercise drastically restraining effects on cities' ability for effective mitigation and adaptation measures in the face of climate change.

Similarly, cities and local authorities in developing countries may find it difficult to prioritize environmental sustainability issues and challenges over and above unemployment, poverty, housing shortages, infrastructures and services, especially where local political expediency demands this type of action.

This underscores the need for cities to achieve growth and prosperity in order to build the capacity necessary to facilitate environmental sustainability but this requires cities to be innovative and inventive in dealing with historic urban environmental problems while shaping an environmentally sustainable future. This situation highlights the fact that the twin dynamics of sustainability and economic prosperity are inevitably subject to a number of structural constraints that are specific to each and every urban area regardless of size.

Public transport jobs account for one to two per cent of total employment in many countries. In Europe and the USA, some 30 jobs are created for every US$1.4 million invested in public transport infrastructure, and another 57 in transport operations proper.[69]

Cities are best able to combine sustainability and shared prosperity through effective urban governance and transformational leadership. This type of leadership recognizes the complex interactions between urbanization and the environment at the local, regional, and global levels. The next step is to put in place appropriate institutions and build the institutional building capacities required for environmentally sustainable urban systems including transport, energy, waste management, rehabilitation of the built and natural environments, and management of ecosystem services.

The linkages and interactions between the environment and the other four dimensions of prosperity – productivity, infrastructure, equity and quality of life – must be recognized in policy- and decision-making. Mainstreaming environmental concerns into those four other policy dimensions can go a long way towards enhanced sustainability, and urban planning has a major role to play. So have adequate human and financial capacities.

Cities should seek financial and technical assistance from multilateral and unilateral organizations in order to build and enhance their capacities for environmental sustainability.

For example, the Global Environment Facility (GEF), which is an independently operating financial organization, brings together 182 governments in partnership with international and non-governmental organizations, along with the private sector.[73] The GEF provides grants to developing and transition countries for projects related to biodiversity, climate change, international waters, land degradation, the ozone layer, and persistent organic pollutants. These projects benefit the global environment, linking local, national, and global challenges and promoting sustainable livelihoods. So

Kuwait City: the construction industry offers 'green' potential.

© 2012 Wael Hamdan/fotoLIBRA.com

Table 2.5.2

Drivers of environmental sustainability in cities, as perceived by local experts (per cent)

Region	Mechanism for coordination between local and national authorities concerning sustainability	Leveraging investments to support sustainable resource use and lower greenhouse gas emissions	Municipalities in same city/ region combining resources & partnering together for enhanced environmental sustainability
Africa	31	20	20
Arab States	37	35	35
Asia	48	49	48
Latin America & Caribbean	26	18	20
All Regions	**34**	**29**	**29**

Source: UN-Habitat, City Monitoring Branch, *Policy Survey*, 2011.

POLICY Environmental sustainability requires capacity-building and resource availability at the local level.

far, the GEF has allocated a total US$9.2 billion, leveraging more than US$40 billion in complementary co-financing, for more than 2,700 projects in more than 165 countries.

Through its Small Grants Programme, the GEF has also made more than 12,000 direct allocations to non-governmental and community organizations, for a total US$495 million.

As might be expected, Asia and the Arab States appear to be best placed, in terms of financial and institutional capacities to deal with environmental concerns and bring about more sustainable urban environments.

Across all developing regions, local experts confirm the importance of capacity-building and resource availability at local level as crucial for implementing environmental sustainability policies and programmes. Capacity-building comprises human, scientific, technological, organizational, and institutional resources and capabilities.[74] Experts

POLICY Cities should build those financial and other institutions required to achieve environmental sustainability, without which economic growth will fall short of ensuring shared prosperity.

highlight an absence of financial and institutional capacities as a major problem (Table 2.5.3); this may be the reason that, according to an overwhelming majority, no efficient systems are in place in their respective cities to monitor environmental sustainability or develop effective local transport policies. This is an indication of the challenges facing cities. However, more than half of the local experts are of the view that their cities are integrating environmental protection plans and concerns into policies and strategies.

The need for adequate capacity is further underscored by the fact that whereas environmental sustainability is widely recognized as essential, local authorities, when faced with competing demands and budget constraints, consider it to be the least of priorities.[75] This has implications for cities, especially given the role they must play in local environmental issues, including when it comes to responding to the needs of the population at a time when the need for environmental preservation is gaining more recognition in public opinion.[76]

Nevertheless, cities need not wait until full capacity is built before adopting and implementing adequate environmental policies and strategies: indeed, in many cases cities have managed to enhance overall quality of life despite modest financial and institutional capacities – every environmental sustainable effort, no matter how small, will count. Appropriate governance structures, which recognize the capacity of individuals and civil society to deliver, will encourage wider participation in environmental sustainability strategies and policies.

Table 2.5.3

Cities with the capacity to implement environmental sustainability programmes, as perceived by local experts (per cent)

Region	Cities with financial & institutional capacity	Integration of environmental protection concerns into policies and strategies	Efficient monitoring system for environmental sustainability	Cities with local environmental transport policy	Cities making progress towards more sustainable urban environment
Africa	22	48	17	9	36
Arab States	60	46	37	8	4
Asia	64	65	45	31	70
Latin America & Caribbean	24	47	21	8	46
All regions	**39**	**51**	**28**	**36**	**43**

Source: UN-Habitat, City Monitoring Branch, *Policy Survey*, 2011.

Endnotes

1 Mitlin and Satterthwaite, 1996.

2 UNEP, 1996.

3 UN-Habitat, 2003.

4 Cities Alliance, ICLEI and UNEP, 2007.

5 Pacione, 2003.

6 UN-Habitat, 2011a.

7 WCED (World Commission on Environment and Development), 1987.

8 United Nations, 1992.

9 *Ibid.*

10 Redclift, 1996.

11 Lafferty and Eckerberg, 1998.

12 Portney and Berry, 2011.

13 Lafferty and Eckerberg, 1998.

14 African Economic Outlook,2012.

15 Omenya, 2011.

16 *Ibid.*

17 Olokesusi, 2011.

18 Mazembe, 2011.

19 Lupala, 2011.

20 Awuor-Hayanga, 2011.

21 Mazembe, 2011

22 Ayad, 2011.

23 Kalabamu, 2011.

24 Awuor-Hayanga, 2011.

25 Article 13, 2005.

26 Olokesusi, 2011.

27 Ayad, 2011

28 Tierney, 2009.

29 Zaidi, 2011.

30 Belliapa, 2011.

31 Centre for Livable Cities, 2011.

32 Fawaz and Baghdadi, 2011.

33 Khattab, 2011.

34 Karim, 2011.

35 Shabou et al, 2011.

36 Al-Bassam and Mouris, 2011.

37 Fawaz and Baghdadi, 2011.

38 Perez, 2011.

39 Flores, 2011.

40 *Ibid.*

41 Gonzales, 2011.

42 Urán, 2011.

43 Castellanos, 2011.

44 Galimberti, 2011.

45 Yerro, 2011.

46 Urán, 2011.

47 UNEP, 2008.

48 Simon et al, 2011.

49 UNEP, 2008.

50 Simon et al, 2011.

51 UNEP, 2011a

52 UNEP, 2009.

53 Martinot et al, 2002.

54 UNEP, ILO, IOE and ITUC, 2008.

55 Peacock, 2011.

56 Shukla, 2012.

57 UNEP, 2011b.

58 Maia et al, 2011.

59 Simon et al, 2011.

60 *Ibid.*

61 UNEP, ILO, IOE and ITUC, 2008.

62 GHK, 2010.

63 Simon et al, 2011.

64 ILO, 2007.

65 Simon et al, 2011.

66 This British system is claimed to be the world's most widely used environmental assessment method for the rating of buildings (www.breeam.org).

67 Simon et al, 2011.

68 UNEP, 2011b.

69 UNEP, ILO, IOE and ITUC, 2008.

70 *Ibid.*

71 *Ibid.*

72 UN-Habitat, 2011b.

73 Global Environmental Facility, 2012.

74 UNCED, 1992.

75 Hess and Winner, 2006.

76 UNCED, 1992.

Part Three

Policies for Prosperous Cities

© Steve Forrest/Panos Pictures

© Denis Mironov/Shutterstock.com

From Comparative Advantage to Urban Prosperity

Geography has always played an important role in the evolution of cities. Historically, coastal cities and cities in river deltas have been preferred locations – at present, 14 of the world's 19 largest cities are ports. However, with advances in transport and communication technologies and also with increasing specialization, other locational factors, beyond positions along waterways, have accelerated the growth and development of cities. Even when located in the hinterland, cities located close to other major urban centres or to important urban agglomerations have significantly gained from their position and demonstrated relatively higher levels of development. Indeed, new configurations such as mega-regions and urban corridors generate regional economies and trigger the evolution of new patterns of economic activity which contribute to prosperity. Similarly, cities which lie in the vicinity of markets and infrastructure, or close to transnational borders, have also exhibited a tendency to grow and prosper much faster.[1]

The increasing numbers of large and dynamic non-port cities confirms that much as geographic location is an important correlate of a city's prosperity, it does not explain everything. Many cities derive their prosperity from their capacity to harness other advantages, particularly through repositioning themselves in the national, regional or global context. Common among all of them has been their capacity to change and adjust to new circumstances and to build upon their own history and identity. Such cities have been able to envision a new future and to use their different forms of capital and assets. Critical also has been the ability of these cities to build social and political consensus. In essence, many cities today are able to deploy the capacity of human agency and to steer growth in the new direction of choice.

Indeed, the prosperity of any city is no accident. It is the result of innovation, sustained vision and good governance. It is also a result of proper laws, regulations and institutions, as well as reinvigorated planning and adequate policies. Effective use of these instruments and processes has enabled many cities around the world to optimize their comparative advantages and to set themselves along the path of prosperity. They have used a range of avenues and capitalized on different sets of 'spokes' in their drive to shared and sustainable growth and well-being.

Some cities are enhancing prosperity though strategic thinking and conscious planning policies. This is the case with Dubai in the Persian Gulf, which took advantage of its privileged geographic location to become the largest re-exporting centre in the Middle East, and today is emerging as a cosmopolitan centre. Other cities are devising long-term visions with well-defined implementation plans, such as Melbourne's or Rio de Janeiro's strategies for improved quality of life.

Some other cities are enhancing prosperity based on national economic policies and investments with financial support from central government. The Jordanian city of Aqaba on the coastline of the Red Sea was designated the Aqaba Special Economic Zone (ASEZ) in 2001 and

> Geography alone does not determine which cities will grow and which will decline. Other factors such as government policies, corporate strategies, human capital, major political forces and decisions, investments in strategic sectors, all have an influence on the fate of cities.

benefited from a public–private venture that created a duty-free and multi-sectoral development. The Zone contributed to enhanced infrastructure development, restoration of the city's historic core and enhanced prosperity through the development of the tourism industry.[2] Shenzhen, too, has benefited from national economic and industrial policies and related strategic investments. These examples show that success depends on careful design of regional and economic strategies, effective coordination across government tiers, massive infrastructure building, outstanding industrial and entrepreneurial strategies, and pro-equity policies.

Other cities still pursue prosperity through improved provision of goods and services at regional level. Nairobi, the capital of Kenya, is capitalizing on the newly-created East African Common Market and Customs Union to enhance its communications and information technology sector, while at the same time developing its transport infrastructure to improve efficiency and productivity.

Prosperity can also be pursued through other important dimensions such as knowledge development. Doha is developing education and arts as part of the city's new cultural vision. Concepción in Chile, like the Algerian cities of Blida, Tlemcen, Sidi-bel-Abbès and Setif, are growing and becoming more prosperous through education institutions and higher learning.[3]

Some cities showcase their tangible and intangible cultural heritage and identity, in a bid to bring about social and economic transformations.[4] Gaziantep in Eastern Turkey is a case in point, with its efforts to develop cultural heritage tourism. Restoration and rehabilitation works enhance quality of life and at the same time create alternative means of economic development. Valparaiso, Chile's most important seaport and a well-known tourist resort, is repositioning its image as a cultural centre with facilities for entertainment, leisure and tourism.

Many other cities are developing innovative ideas and strategies to shape new urban identity in the pursuit of prosperity. This typically includes revamped public spaces, rehabilitation of architecture and historic landmarks, re-creation of the street as part of the soul of the city, shaping a 'sense of place' with monuments, piazzas, marketplaces and streetscapes as open venues for arts and cultural expression.

All of these achievements testify not just to the creative and innovative powers of municipal and other public authorities; they are also the outcomes of the interplay between the various power functions at work in any city. This driving power behind urban change and transformation acts as the 'hub' at the centre of the 'wheel of prosperity'. Urban power functions are where the public, collective interest is determined, together with the practical rules, plans and actions that are to embed it in a specific area. The hub is where decisions are made to activate any of the five dimensions of prosperity, keeping them well balanced and maintaining the momentum in the wheel.

POLICY Beyond geography, well-managed urbanization stands out as the new comparative advantage in the 21st century.

La Paz, Bolivia: providing public goods for all, irrespective of neighbourhood or income bracket.
© Eduardo Lopez Moreno

Part 2 of this Report detailed the respective roles of the five dimensions of urban prosperity, with the various interlinkages and multipliers involved. Part 3 presents the policy-related factors underlying the prosperity of cities, including drivers and constraints. It also focuses on urban power functions – the 'hub' holding together, activating and controlling the five 'spokes' of the 'wheel of prosperity' across the length and breadth of any urban jurisdiction, regardless of geographic location, size or resources. Just like productivity, infrastructure or a well-preserved natural environment, these urban power functions are human constructs; it is for governments, local and municipal authorities, and society at large to make sure that these power functions work for the benefit of the majority of the population and keep enhancing shared urban prosperity.

Actualizing dreams of prosperity: penthouse in El Alto, Bolivia.

© Eduardo Lopez Moreno

Policy-Related Factors Underlying the Prosperity of Cities: Drivers and Constraints

The policy-related factors underlying the prosperity of cities are multifaceted. They can be described in terms of drivers and constraints. The drivers could be the traditional and nonconventional factors that create an environment conducive to prosperity; they often affect the prosperity of cities in a positive manner. The constraints stand in the way of urban prosperity. These factors are further mediated by the local context, and as such, their effects may vary across cities and regions – one particular factor might be important in one city or region, but not in another. A clear understanding and appreciation of these factors is important in redirecting policies, and supporting structures and mechanisms that can affect the prosperity of cities. It is therefore important to discuss these factors in a comparative manner drawing on examples from cities across various regions.

FACTORS BEHIND A PROSPERITY-INDUCING URBAN ENVIRONMENT

According to the local experts surveyed by UN-Habitat, eight main factors create a favourable environment for cities to prosper, namely: effective urban planning and management; decentralization polices and appropriate institutions; a system that creates equal opportunities for all; participation of civil society; elected local officials; a favourable business environment; access to basic amenities; and public transport and mobility. It is self-evident that, just like the five 'spokes' in the 'wheel of prosperity', these factors are interrelated or complementary and they affect the prosperity of cities both individually and in their various combinations. The importance of these factors with respect to the various regions is presented in Figure 3.1.1. In most cases, similarities can be found in the nature and importance of the factors across regions, with nuance and differences in other cases.

Effective urban planning and management is perceived to be the most important factor behind a favourable environment for the prosperity of cities.

Effective urban planning and management

The perceived importance of urban planning is most pronounced in the Arab States, followed by Africa and Asia. However, in Latin America and the Caribbean, urban planning emerges as the third most important factor. These differences can be attributed to several contextual factors.

Urban planning can contribute to the prosperity of cities in various ways. As a starting point, policy-makers should view urbanization as a positive phenomenon. While there is growing recognition of the benefits, positive contribution and potential opportunities associated with cities, urban planners and policy-makers in some developing countries are still ambivalent about the importance of urbanization, in some cases even showing aversion to the urbanization process. This should not be the case, because cities generate the bulk of GDP; they are the engines of growth and centres of innovation. This suggests that capitalizing on the positive potentials of urban growth should be placed high on the agenda of governments.

Managing urbanization is essential to nurturing the prosperity of cities. There are at least two ways to achieve this. The first is to nurture the growth of high-productivity activities – particularly manufacturing and services, which benefit from agglomeration economies. The second entails managing the negative externalities associated with the economic growth and success of cities – congestion, inequality, crime and violence, and soaring cost of land and housing, among others.[5] Urban planning within the context of rapid urbanization is not a luxury, but a necessity.[6] Rapid urbanization in the absence of effective urban planning has resulted in the proliferation of slum and squatter settlements, spiralling poverty, inadequate infrastructure, and degrading environmental conditions – all of which tend to erode the prosperity of cities. Neglecting cities even in countries with low levels of urbanization can impose significant costs.[7]

POLICY Cities that want to grow and be prosperous in all five dimensions must make urbanization work well.

POLICY When urbanization is planned and well managed, and distributive mechanisms of prosperity are put in place, it can contribute to poverty reduction.

Figure 3.1.1

Factors underlying urban prosperity as perceived by local experts

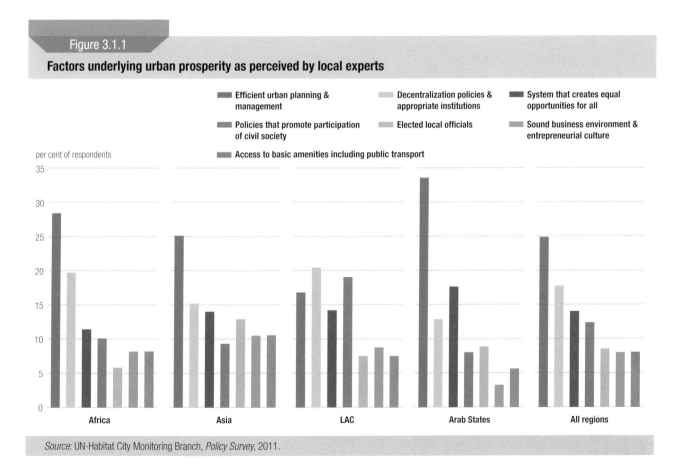

■ Efficient urban planning & management
■ Policies that promote participation of civil society
■ Access to basic amenities including public transport
▨ Decentralization policies & appropriate institutions
▨ Elected local officials
■ System that creates equal opportunities for all
■ Sound business environment & entrepreneurial culture

per cent of respondents

Source: UN-Habitat City Monitoring Branch, *Policy Survey*, 2011.

POLICY Urban planning can bring about more livable cities by tackling slums and informal settlements, as no city can claim to be prosperous when large segments of the population live in slum conditions.

The positive nature of urbanization can be beneficial to the poor if the common deprivations that affect their daily existence are adequately addressed. Such deprivations include limited access to income and employment; inadequate living conditions; poor infrastructure and services; risks associated with living in slums; spatial issues which inhibit mobility and transport; and inequality associated with exclusion.

The global assessment of slums shows that

POLICY Urban planning and appropriately developed institutions and regulations can play major roles in improving urban equity through the capture and redistribution of rising land values.

828 million urban dwellers worldwide reside in slums.[8] In the developing world, 33 per cent of the urban population lives in slums, with sub-Saharan Africa having 62 per cent of its urban population living in slums. Effective urban planning along with political commitment has contributed to the low prevalence of slums in countries such as Argentina, China, Colombia, Egypt, India, Indonesia, Morocco, South Africa and Tunisia. In Tunisia, slum upgrading has been a key component of the country's urban planning programme. This along with massive investments in water and sanitation has contributed to a remarkable decline in the number of slum dwellers from 425,000 in the 1990s to 188,000 in 2005.[9] Since the 1980s, Morocco has used urban planning as a means of implementing large-scale slum upgrading. The programme – *Villes sans Bidonvilles*, which was initiated in 2001 – has the following components of urban planning: in-situ upgrading; extending basic services; land tenure and *post-facto* planning approval; development of serviced resettlement plots; and resettlement housing to assist *bidonville* households that need to be moved.[10]

One positive outcome of urban growth is that it increases urban land values. Components of urban

Kathmandu, Nepal: the relentless urban sprawl of the Kathmandu Valley. The Vishnumati River is surrounded by suburbs which have sprung up in recent years. With few building regulations, the city keeps on growing, as many look for a better life in the city than in the countryside. The result is environmental chaos with severe noise, air and water pollution problems.

© 2012 Jonathan Mitchell/fotoLIBRA.com

planning systems – such as re-zoning, granting of planning permission, and the provision of infrastructure and services – also contribute to higher urban land values. Experience in North and Latin America shows that value capture can be an effective way to link urban planning and land use regulations, as well as to control land use, finance urban infrastructure, and generate local revenue to fund urban management.

Uncontrolled sprawl presents a major challenge for urban planning and has implications for the prosperity of cities. Urban sprawl contributes to high numbers of cars, distances travelled, length of paved roads, fuel consumption, alteration of ecological structures and the conversion of rural land into urban uses – all of which are environmentally unsustainable. Compact urban development has several advantages. It is more efficient, inclusive and sustainable. The cost of providing infrastructure is lower, access to services and facilities is improved since thresholds are higher, the urban poor find that livelihoods are less of a challenge, and social segregation is reduced. Urban planning has played a significant role in Singapore's compact layout and modern, convenient public transportation. The city-State is transit-oriented, with high-density residential and commercial developments integrated into transport nodes, which improve accessibility to public transport.

Decentralization and appropriate institutions

Decentralization refers to the transfer of responsibilities for planning, management and financing from the central to lower tiers of government and other subsidiary units.[11] The most common forms of decentralization are deconcentration, delegation and devolution; in many countries, decentralization is often a combination or hybrid of these forms. Bringing decision-making closer to relevant urban populations can encourage municipal authorities to better focus on prosperity.[12]

In Latin America and the Caribbean, decentralization is perceived to be the most important factor behind enhanced urban prosperity. This is an indication of the effectiveness or higher degree of advancement (particularly in Brazil, Colombia and Mexico) of decentralization policies compared with other regions.

Research on decentralization in sub-Saharan Africa[13] revealed

POLICY Urban planning can encourage more compact, efficient and sustainable development.

that South Africa and Uganda have the highest levels of decentralization; Kenya, Ghana, Nigeria, Rwanda and Namibia have moderate levels, while countries with the lowest levels include Angola, Cameroon, Guinea, Mali, Eritrea, and Zambia. Countries that have done well with respect to decentralization are those that have achieved significant devolution and empowerment of local communities backed by both political will and clear legal mandates.[14]

Many Asian countries have made remarkable progress in instituting decentralization policies. For instance, Indonesia commenced the decentralization process in 2001 as it sought to give greater political and financial autonomy to local authorities[15]. In the Philippines, the enactment of the Local Government Code in 1991 marked a defining moment in decentralization, devolving to municipal authorities the responsibility for basic services such as health, primary education, public works and housing. It also advanced financial autonomy by devolving expenditure responsibilities and expanding local government taxing authority.

Arab States appear to lag behind other regions, as highly centralized governance structures undermine the efficiency of municipal authorities, obstruct political participation and erode the relationship between the citizenry and the level of government closest to them.[16]

Underlying decentralization is the concept of subsidiarity, which implies that decisions regarding the provision of services should rest with the government entity which, being closest to the community, is in a better position to deliver these services in a more cost-effective way. Box 3.1.1 highlights how decentralization can play a key role in the prosperity of cities.

While the responsibilities of municipal governments have increased following reforms in recent years, many have no access to the financial resources needed to undertake these functions. The resulting mismatch between responsibilities and financial resources is a major reason why decentralization has been less than successful in certain countries. National

Decentralization policies emerge as the second important factor enhancing urban prosperity.

POLICY If decentralization is to strengthen urban authorities' commitment to urban prosperity, it must be backed by fiscal devolution.

Box 3.1.1

Decentralization and the prosperity of cities

A major benefit of decentralization as it relates to the prosperity of cities is that delivery of essential services such as water, sanitation and waste management, healthcare and education can be carried out more effectively. Decentralization can make for better urban conditions as it provides greater opportunities for community-based groups to lobby for improved services. Proximity to physical demand for a service encourages effectiveness and promotes a more rational use of resources, while also allowing for closer monitoring by the beneficiary population of any projects intended to serve them.

Devolution of authority can lead to an institutional framework through which various political, religious, social and ethnic groups – together with multiple government/administrative tiers – can participate in making the decisions that will affect them. Residents can make decisions about the location of services and determine priorities. This is why when matched by devolution of taxation powers to municipal authorities, decentralized decision-making can provide a better framework for poverty reduction. Decentralization can also accelerate economic development through active engagement of regional and municipal government units and local enterprises.

Source: UN-Habitat (2012) *Decentralization in Iraq: Challenges and Solutions for Federal and Local Governments,* Nairobi: UN-Habitat

reforms relating to various aspects of decentralization – revenue allocation, community participation, local elections, local planning, pro-urban development strategies – all provide enabling environment for cities to prosper.

POLICY Decentralization works well when backed by strong commitment and support from central government.

A system that guarantees equal opportunities for all is the third most important contributing factor to the prosperity of cities. The more egalitarian a city is, the more prosperous it becomes.

A system that creates equal opportunities

The importance of a system that creates equal opportunities for all is most pronounced in Arab States compared with other regions. Even prior to the uprising in the region, Arab States existed as one of the most egalitarian in terms of income distribution in the developing world. This is reflected in an overall

(low) Gini coefficient of 0.36, which has been declining over time.[17] The low degree of inequality in the region has been attributed to a strong, cohesive social system, and the fact that redistribution constitutes a policy priority in Islamic economies.[18]

A prosperous city is one in which the aspirations of all groups of people are realized. Highly unequal cities are a ticking time bomb waiting to explode. Indeed, '*extreme inequalities can create social and political fractures… that have the potential to increase social unrest or develop into full-blown conflicts, which discourage investment and induce greater government spending on non-productive sectors.*'[19]

A system that creates equal opportunities for all can use redistributive policies that give priority to low-income groups and areas. In Venezuela, the government has used redistributive policies to bring significant improvements to the living standards of the urban poor through massive investment in health and education.[20] With the provision of over 8,000 clinics in the *barrios*, people are able to access health services 24 hours a day at no cost. Similarly, illiteracy has been eliminated, pupils are no longer restricted to elementary school, and those with the required academic qualifications can attend university.

Another form of redistribution policy involves conditional cash transfers. These enhance the human capital of beneficiaries through transfers which are made conditional on certain requirements such as school attendance, visits to clinics and periodic immunization.[21] Brazil's *Bolsa Família* scheme, which benefits 11.1 million families, is the largest of its kind in the world, and has contributed to reducing poverty and inequality.[22] Indeed, 80 per cent of *Bolsa Família* benefits go to families living below the poverty line; the programme also accounted for 21 per cent of the decline in inequality in Brazil between 1995 and 2004[23] – all of which contribute to making cities more prosperous. In Africa, countries such as Botswana, Lesotho, Mauritius and Namibia have universal pension schemes designed to address old-age poverty.

POLICY For a city to be truly prosperous, it must ensure equal opportunities for all, especially the more vulnerable – the poor, women, children, the elderly, youth and the disabled. A prosperous city is one where the aspirations of all segments of the population are realized. Highly unequal cities are ticking time-bombs only waiting to explode.

114

Civil society participation

The perceived importance of participation of civil society varies across regions. It is seen by local experts as the second most important factor in Latin America and the Caribbean, but is ranked only fifth in Arab States. This is not surprising, given that participation of civil society has very strong roots in Latin American cities, where the best-known participatory approaches involve budgeting and planning.

A classic example of participatory planning process in Asia is the People's Campaign for Decentralized Planning, Kerala (India), which was launched in 1996; it aims to strengthen democratic decentralization by identifying local needs and establishing local development options and priorities through local consultation and participation.[24]

An evaluation of the scheme in 2001 revealed several positive features that include:[25] substantial fiscal devolution was achieved in that 35–40 per cent of state development budget was allocated to municipal authorities; structures of participatory governance were created where none previously existed; active participation of disadvantaged groups especially women; institutionalization of participatory governance; positive developmental impacts especially on the poor who are the major beneficiaries; reduction in corruption and greater transparency and accountability of both representatives and officials.

Elected local officials

The election of city officials presupposes the existence of stable democracy through which citizens are empowered to elect and remove their leaders through an open, free and fair ballot. Political institutions like democracy are essential if the conditions for prosperity are to be laid out and nurtured.

Research shows that durable democracy is correlated with economic development.[26] Across the world, the more prosperous cities (at least economically) tend to be located in countries that are stable democracies. Democratically elected local officials owe their mandate to the people, and as such, are best placed to respond to the people's needs, which include providing good conditions for employment, providing adequate infrastructure and urban services, improving the quality of life, making society more equitable, and ensuring environmental sustainability, among others.

Of course, there are instances where non-democratic leadership is associated with a degree of economic prosperity, but this is the exception rather than the rule. Indeed, non-democratic regimes are coterminous with pathologies such as predation and expropriation, and in the long-run undermine the institutions underlying that prosperity.[27]

The election of local officials provides the political incentives and avenue for leaders to respond to the needs and demands of the people.[29] Leaders that are unable to do so risk being voted out at the next available opportunity. It has been noted that autocratic governments often distribute benefits to an elite group, while democratic governments distribute benefits more widely to gain the support of the general public.[30] A study of 44 African countries shows that democratically elected governments spend more on primary education;[31] and in Latin America, democracy is associated with higher spending on education, health and social services.[32] The adaptive efficiencies and institution-building needed to promote economic development and good governance – all of which are crucial to the prosperity of cities – flourish best in democratic societies.

A favourable business environment

Cities with a favourable business environment and entrepreneurial culture are more likely to be prosperous.

> Policies that promote the participation of civil society are perceived by local experts as the fourth most important factor behind enhanced urban prosperity.

> **POLICY** Participation of civil society has the potential to empower communities, build social capital, lead to better design of urban projects, and allow for citizens' concerns to be incorporated into development strategies.

> Lessons from experience suggest that successful civil society participation is dependent upon certain preconditions such as: (i) a political system that encourages active citizenship and is committed to equity and remedial action; (ii) the legal basis for participation; (iii) available resources in terms of skilled and committed professionals, as well as well-resourced and empowered local governments; and (iv) informed and organized communities and stakeholders.[28]

> A system that ensures that local officials are elected is ranked by local experts as the fifth most important policy-related factor that enhances urban prosperity.

A business-conducive environment is needed for a vibrant private sector, attracting and retaining investment (including foreign direct), creating jobs and improving productivity – all of which are important for the promotion of growth and for expanded opportunities for the poor.[33]

Given the role that entrepreneurs play in creating economic opportunities for themselves and others, central governments in conjunction with cities authorities often take steps to improve the investment climate and boost productivity growth.[34] Specifically, countries have undertaken varying degrees of regulatory reforms aimed at making it easier to handle nine crucial steps: starting a business; dealing with construction permits; registering property; obtaining credit; protecting investors; paying taxes; trading across borders; enforcing contracts; and handling insolvency. Based on these reforms, the World Bank shows that the city-State of Singapore – which by all accounts is a prosperous city as indicated in previous chapters – ranks first out of 183 countries.[35] What this shows is that Singapore provides the most favourable environment for business and entrepreneurship, which, in part, accounts for its high levels of prosperity. Other Asian countries that rank high with respect to the ease of doing business include Hong Kong, Korea, Thailand, Malaysia and Japan. This means that the major cities in these countries – Hong Kong, Seoul, Busan, Kuala Lumpur, Tokyo, Yokohama and Osaka – all offer favourable business environments, which ultimately pervade all dimensions of local prosperity.

In Africa, countries such as Mauritius, South Africa, Rwanda, Tunisia and Botswana rank high for favourable business environments. This implies that it is easier to do business in Port Louis, Johannesburg, Kigali, Tunis or Gaborone than in Kinshasa, Conakry, Asmara, N'Djamena or Bangui, whose respective countries rank low for business environment. Generally, cities in the former group of countries tend to be more prosperous than those in the latter.

> In Asia, a favourable business environment is perceived as the most important factor promoting prosperity, highlighting the role played by cities in creating an enabling environment for business and attracting foreign direct investment.

Bogotá, Colombia. Efficient transport systems, well-made streets with lighting, and adequate drainage systems all encourage entrepreneurial activity.

© Gary Yim/Shutterstock.com

Rwanda is a typical example of a country that has consciously created a business-friendly environment, and in the process brought a higher degree of prosperity to its capital, Kigali. In recent years, Rwanda has undertaken reforms to streamline business procedures, create a favourable legal framework, reduce bureaucracy, and improve service delivery in order to promote both domestic and foreign investment.[36] For instance, in Kigali, registering a business takes only three days and costs less than five per cent of the average income in an environment devoid of corruption, making the city 'a very easy place for a global firm to operate.'[37]

Access to basic amenities

The chapter (2.2) on infrastructure clearly shows that access to basic amenities, including improved public transport and information/communication technologies, can deliver major benefits that can make cities more prosperous. For instance, an efficient mass transit system is essential for the seamless movement of people and goods within and between cities, which in turn is vital for the prosperity of cities. Bogotá's bus rapid transport (BRT) provides fast and reliable transport for over 1.4 million passengers per day, and in the process reduces traffic congestion and enhances environmental quality.[38] In Lagos, the BRT system has attracted new patronage, lowering average fares and created 1,000 jobs as well as indirect employment for over 500,000 people.[39] In South Africa, the Gautrain express rail system is expected to reduce road traffic along the all-important Johannesburg– Pretoria axis by 25,000–30,000 cars per day; this is one of the busiest roads in South Africa where traffic increases an average seven per cent every year.[40]

In addition to the foregoing, access to basic amenities can deliver major prosperity-enhancing benefits such as: supporting economic growth; contributing to achievement of Millennium Development Goals through improved health and education; improving quality of life especially for youth and women; enhancing environmental quality through improved access to water and sanitation, which in turn

> Access to basic amenities and infrastructure, including improved public transport and ICTs, is a factor that will enhance the prosperity of any city. This factor is considered as most important in African and Asian cities.

reduces morbidity and mortality, and fosters greater productivity and reduces vulnerability of the poor.

SOME IMPEDIMENTS TO THE PROSPERITY OF CITIES

Based on the UN-Habitat local expert survey, there are seven main impediments to urban prosperity, as follows: poor governance and weak institutions; corruption; lack of appropriate infrastructure; high incidence of slums and poverty; high costs of doing business; low levels of human capital; and high crime rates (Figure 3.1.2). The hard-won prosperity gains made by cities in terms of productivity, infrastructure, quality of life, equity, social inclusion and environmental sustainability can be jeopardized or eroded, either individually or collectively by these impediments.

Poor governance and weak institutions

The impact of poor governance and weak institutions on urban prosperity appears to be more pronounced in African and Arab

> Poor governance and weak institutions act as major impediments to urban prosperity.

cities, where over 40 per cent of experts cite this factor as the single most important impediment. What this implies is that countries in Africa and Arab States should do more to improve urban governance and institutions. Indeed, in many developing countries, the institutions required for urban prosperity, if any, are poorly developed. Proper institutions are crucial, both of a formal (constitution, laws and regulations) and informal nature (social norms, customs and traditions), which together determine how people, organizations and firms make decisions of an economic, social and political nature, maximizing potentials and optimizing resources.[41]

Sound institutions matter for the prosperity of cities, as they provide the superstructure that enables, or otherwise, underlying factors to operate and deliver a maximum of benefits to the largest possible majority of the population. Institutional inadequacies take the form of weak (if not altogether lacking) legal and institutional frameworks,[42] disregard for the rule of law, poor enforcement of property rights, excessive bureaucracy, and proliferation of corrupt practices among others. All these are incompatible with urban prosperity.

> Corruption is considered by local experts as the second most important hindrance to enhanced urban prosperity. It can be detrimental to urban prosperity in a variety of ways.

Corruption

Generally, corruption is defined as the abuse of public office for personal gain. The seriousness of corruption as a hindrance to the prosperity of cities varies across regions. While grand corruption has the most devastating impact, corruption in any form serves to destroy the confidence in the fairness of government, the rule of law and economic stability.[43] In Arab States, corruption is ranked as the joint first factor along with poor governance and weak institutions; in Asia it is the second most serious impediment; in Latin America and the Caribbean, it is the third important obstacle; and in Africa, it is the fourth most serious hindrance. Whatever the case, local experts surveyed by UN-Habitat unanimously concur that corruption is a major threat to the prosperity of cities. This is in line with the view that corruption is the single largest obstacle to development.[44]

Corruption can adversely affect the prosperity of cities in a variety of ways. First, it acts like a tax and a deterrent to foreign direct investment.[45] Several studies have reported a significantly negative correlation between perceived corruption and inflows of foreign direct investment.[46] One of the reasons that foreign firms are attracted to cities such as Bridgetown (Barbados), Santiago (Chile), Gaborone (Botswana), Doha (Qatar), San Juan (Puerto Rico), Port Louis (Mauritius), Kigali (Rwanda) or Victoria (Seychelles) is because all enjoy low levels of corruption.

Second, corruption undermines the ability of city authorities to provide municipal services in a fair way, as it distorts planning and allocation processes. Corruption is a significant factor for those living in squatter settlements as they are usually not recognized by urban authorities as having rights to basic services, such as water, sanitation and electricity. Consequently, access to such amenities can be dependent upon payment of bribes to local officials.

Third, corruption is particularly evident in large-scale urban infrastructure projects, and distorts infrastructure spending in various ways.[47] It can increase public expenditure on new infrastructure, since such capital projects can be easily manipulated by politicians and high-level officials to obtain bribes. Corruption can divert financial resources away from the operation and maintenance of existing infrastructure, reducing relevant budget allocations. It has been shown that the least

Figure 3.1.2

Impediments to the prosperity of cities as perceived by local experts

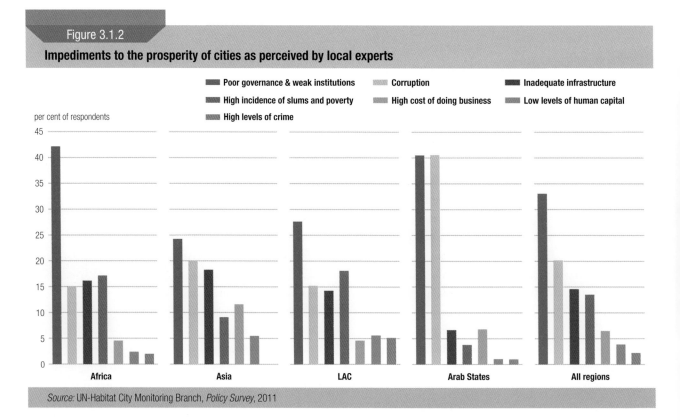

Source: UN-Habitat City Monitoring Branch, *Policy Survey*, 2011

corrupt cities in Africa and Asia spend more on building and maintaining infrastructure.[48] In extreme cases, the maintenance of existing infrastructure may deliberately be neglected so that such infrastructure rapidly falls into disrepair to the point where it must be rebuilt, providing an opportunity for highly placed officials to extract kickbacks from the enterprise that will rebuild the project.

Fourth, corruption can reduce the financial resources available to city authorities for the provision of basic services such as water, sanitation, education, healthcare and recreation, which are all essential for urban prosperity and Millennium Development Goals – many of which are urban-related. Research has shown that in Africa, government spending on education is affected by corruption, with highly corrupt countries devoting only small shares of their budgets to education. This, of course, has implications for the development of human capital and the quality of labour in urban areas.

Finally, corruption can result in shoddy delivery of urban services. When contractors pay bribes to secure contracts, they are likely to cut back and compromise on quality in order to recoup part or all of the bribe paid. The phenomenon partly accounts for the frequent collapse of buildings that have occurred in cities such as Lagos and Nairobi, and substandard roads in these and many other cities that are often washed away or riddled with potholes following innocuous rainfall..

Inadequate infrastructure

Cities with deficient infrastructure will be adversely affected on many fronts; they are less likely to be prosperous, sustainable or productive. For instance, inadequate water and sanitation facilities will lead to deterioration of the urban environment, adding to the burden of disease for the urban poor, particularly in slums and squatter settlements. Deficient infrastructure can drive up the costs of doing business in urban areas and reduce business productivity by as much as 40 per cent;[49] the impact can be as significant as those of crime, bureaucracy, corruption or financial market constraints.[50]

Deficient infrastructure also acts as a major impediment to trade and competitiveness in many developing countries, particularly landlocked and small island States. In the case of Africa, the proportion of paved roads is about five times smaller than in high-income OECD countries; the end-result of this infrastructure bottleneck is that transport costs are 63 per cent higher in Africa compared with developed countries.[51] This has major implications for the competitiveness of African cities on local and international markets. In Africa, transport costs as a share of export values range between 30 and 50 per cent; in landlocked countries, the proportion can be as high as 75 per cent. By comparison, the average for other developing countries is just 17 per cent.[52] These figures are in line with earlier findings whereby congested roads and poor transport infrastructure are among the most pervasive infrastructure problems hampering the prosperity of cities.

High incidence of slums and poverty

Slum prevalence is highest in Sub-Saharan Africa where basic services are lacking not only in informal, but formal settlements. North Africa has the lowest prevalence of slums. In Asia, the proportion of urban population living in slums varies from 25 per cent in Western Asia to 35 per cent in South Asia. In Latin America and the Caribbean, slum prevalence is 24 per cent. To a large extent, regional patterns of slum prevalence reflect different degrees of access to basic services such as water and sanitation, as well as the nature of urban development policies.

Cities where a large number of people live in slum conditions are less likely to be prosperous. This is because slums have the most deplorable living and environmental conditions and are characterized by inadequate water supply, poor sanitation, overcrowded and dilapidated housing, hazardous locations, insecurity of tenure, and vulnerability to serious health risks – all of which have major implications for quality of life. Slums are also known for their atmosphere of fear and the social and economic exclusion of their residents.[53] Slum dwellers are often stigmatized on account of their location and are often discriminated against in terms of access to public and social services, as well as employment.

Large concentrations of slums impose enormous burdens on urban authorities that often lack

> Inadequate infrastructure is another major impediment to the prosperity of cities. The effects of deficient infrastructure appear to be more pronounced in Asian and African cities and less so in Arab States.

> Slums are the physical negation of everything that shared urban prosperity stands for, what with lack of infrastructure, appalling quality of life and inequitable socio-economic conditions, low-productivity, informal economies and a variety of environmental hazards.

POLICY Cities with large concentration of slums should adopt proactive approaches to urban development, rather than antagonistic or fragmentary approaches.

Mumbai, India: where there is inadequate access to, or provision of, resources, people will improvise dwellings using whatever comes to hand.

© 2012 Nicola Barranger/fotoLIBRA.com

the political will and resources to provide even the most basic services, with implications for the prosperity of cities. Rather than being proactive in their approach to urban development, cities with large concentrations of slums are likely to adopt a reactionary and fragmentary approach to urban development, which tends to be expensive in the long run.

High costs of doing business

The high cost of doing business can serve as an impediment to cities becoming more prosperous. A high cost of doing business has obvious implications for investment, productivity, employment, income generation, taxation and poverty reduction – all of which impact on the prosperity of cities.

In Africa, countries like Mauritania, Cameroon, Burundi, Benin, Eritrea, and Guinea Bissau are ranked low in terms of the ease of doing business.[54] This means that their major cities – Nouakchott, Yaoundé, Bujumbura, Porto Novo, Asmara and Bissau, will be characterized by a high cost of doing business and, thus, likely to be less prosperous compared to other African cities located in countries where the cost of doing business is low.

In Latin America and the Caribbean, Brazil, Honduras, Bolivia, Haiti and Suriname are ranked relatively low on ease of doing business. In the case of Brazilian cities, the business environment is bogged down by the labyrinth of bureaucracy. For instance, it takes an average of 119 days and 13 procedures to register a business.[55] Anyone wishing to start a business will require approval from no less than 12 different government agencies.[56] As one store owner lamented: 'You need a document. But to have that document, you need to hand in seven documents. And to get each of these seven, there's a different demand.'[57] Similarly in Jamaica, the private sector is held hostage by the web of bureaucracy. Filing of taxes involves 72 steps, which takes up 400 hours in a year.[58] It takes manufacturers three months to get connected

> The myriad of laws, taxes and regulations and bureaucracy involved in registering or running a business has been cited as one of the main reasons why 40 per cent of Brazilian startup businesses hardly survive for more than two years. The cost of bureaucracy is staggering; in 2010 bureaucracy cost the Brazilian economy 46.3 billion reals.[59] This has implications for the prosperity of cities in Brazil.

to electricity, and costs five times more than in Trinidad and Tobago. Crime is also a major problem that drives up the cost of doing business in Jamaica, as many hotels spend up to US$100,000 a year on security guards. All these impact negatively on the prosperity of Jamaican cities.

Poorly developed human capital

Education is essential not just for nurturing, but also for attracting talents and bolstering innovation. The development of Boston, Silicon Valley, Oxford and Cambridge (UK) clearly benefited from the presence of reputed universities.[60] Availability of highly-skilled human capital in turn attracts and generates innovative and knowledge-based industries.

Within the OECD, the productivity of some metropolitan areas has been attributed to human resource endowments. For instance in Montreal, the relatively low productivity of high value-added sectors has been linked to lower educational attainment and inadequate investment, particularly in small and medium-sized enterprises.[61] Similarly, in Istanbul and Mexico City, productivity, and hence prosperity, is hampered by low skills, as well as by the extent of the informal sector, where adult education and skill upgrading are difficult to provide.[62]

> **POLICY** Low levels of human capital and skilled labour can hinder urban prosperity.

Attracting and cultivating talents has become common practice for cities in the pursuit of prosperity. From New York to London, Boston to Vienna, Dubai to Singapore, or Bangalore to Shenzhen, many cities can illustrate this phenomenon. Munich's experience with vocational education can be particularly inspiring. The capital of Bavaria (as well as the economic, cultural, technological and transportation centre of South Germany), Munich is one of Europe's most prosperous cities. It ranked 8th for technological innovation (as measured by international patent applications) among the 500-strong sample in the *2010 Global Urban Competitiveness Ranking*; GDP per capita was US$58,197 in 2007 with three per cent economic growth on an annual average basis in 2001–2007.[63] Munich's manufactured products (including motor cars) enjoy a good international reputation and export competitiveness. The city's large proportion of high-skilled workers, nurtured through its vocational education system, has been crucial to the city's prosperity.

High crime rates

Safeguarding people and property against crime and other insecurity is a prerequisite for urban prosperity, which involves a shared sense of mutual confidence for both the present and the future. Crime is a major deterrent to domestic and foreign investment and can cause capital flight. In Africa, more than 29 per cent of business people report that crime is a significant investment constraint.[64] Investors generally worry about violent crime for fear of direct losses to business and lack of security for staff. High crime rates can have a crippling effect on the prosperity of cities.

> Crime emerges as a major impediment to the prosperity of cities. No city can claim to be truly prosperous if it is crime-ridden and the population lives in a perpetual state of insecurity.

In Lusaka, for instance, fear of crime in the poverty-stricken community of Chawama can prevent teachers from showing up at work.[65] In South Africa, a survey of major cities showed that over a quarter of respondents would not consider opening a business due to fear of crime, with more than 25 per cent saying they were reluctant to allow their children to walk to school, while 30 per cent gave up on public transportation.[66]

In Jamaica, crime has a pernicious effect on national tourism and is often cited as a major reason for the country's weak economy. In large cities in Latin America, high numbers of murders deter people from working evenings and at night.[67] All these have implications for local economies, quality of life and the attractiveness of public spaces, on top of lost opportunities for socioeconomic advancement that is so crucial for the prosperity of cities.

Endnotes

1   UN-Habitat, 2008.
2   Shabou et al, 2011.
3   UN-Habitat, 2008.
4   Costas, 2011.
5   Spence et al, 2008.
6   Bloom and Khanna, 2007.
7   Annez and Buckley, 2008.
8   UN-Habitat, 2010a.
9   UN-Habitat, 2006.
10 Cities Alliance, 2003.
11 UN-Habitat, 2010b.
12 Ni, 2011.
13 Ndegwa, 2002.
14 *Ibid.*
15 UN-Habitat, 2006.
16 UN-Habitat, 2012.
17 UN-Habitat (2004) *State of the World's Cities 2004/05: Globalization and Urban Culture:* Earthscan, London.
18 *Ibid.*
19 UN-Habitat, 2008.
20 Scipes, 2006.
21 Hailu and Soares, 2008.
22 Britto, 2008.
23 Soares et al, 2006.
24 UN-Habitat, 2009.
25 Heller et al, 2007.
26 Sharma, 2005.
27 *Ibid.*
28 UN-Habitat, 2009.
29 Sharma, 2005.
30 Holcombe, 2012.
31 Stasavage, 2005.
32 Avelino et al, 2005.
33 World Bank and International Finance Corporation, 2011.

34 World Bank (2012).
35 *Ibid.*
36 Rwanda Development Board, 2012.
37 The Economist, 2012.
38 Hidalgo, 2008.
39 World Bank, 2009b.
40 BBC, 2011.
41 Sharma, 2005.
42 Oyeyinka, 2012.
43 UNODC, 2004.
44 UN-Habitat, 2007.
45 Dong and Torgler, 2010.
46 Wei, 2000 ; Smarzynska and Wei, 2000; Habib and Zurawicki, 2002.
47 Arimah, 2005.
48 *Ibid.*
49 Escribano et al, 2008.
50 Foster and Briceno-Garmendia, 2010.
51 African Economic Outlook, 2012.
52 *Ibid.*
53 Bloom et al, 2008.
54 World Bank and International Finance Corporation, 2011.
55 *Ibid.*
56 Gomes, 2012.
57 *Ibid.*
58 The Economist, 2012.
59 Gomes, 2012.
60 Ni, 2011.
61 OECD, 2006.
62 *Ibid.*
63 Ni, 2011.
64 UNODC, 2005.
65 Moser and Holland, 1997.
66 UNODC, 2005.
67 Hamermesh, 1998.

Chapter 3.2

© Jon Spaull/Panos Pictures

Innovating to Support the Transition to the City of the 21st Century

Throughout history, cities have played a major role in creativity and innovation. Creative people and systems, innovative milieus, knowledge creation mechanisms and new technological developments have all primarily happened in cities and all contributed to societal development and prosperity.

Creativity and innovation involve a variety of areas that range from technology to institutions, organizations and modes of operation to information and knowledge, finance and human development. Innovation also comes under a variety of forms, including improved design and quality, changes in organization and management, higher efficiency, high- and medium-technological industrial development, new linkages and coordination mechanisms, scientific research and the commercialization of technical knowledge.[1] This goes to show that, to a large extent, creativity and innovation are already embedded in economic functions and, as such, under the control of financial capital.[2] In technologies and the arts alike, innovation is increasingly dominated by the private sector.

Creativity and innovation are largely influenced by six main types of factors: (i) locational advantages (i.e., economies of agglomeration and 'positive externalities' at regional scale); (ii) knowledge networks; (iii) cultural factors; (iv) the economic environment; (v) organizational factors; and (vi) State/government interventions (i.e., policies, incentives, institutions).

'Innovation', as glorified in association with 'creative cities', the 'creative class' and 'city competition', more often than not is in the sole benefit of business and economic elites,[4] and it fails to integrate the various dimensions of prosperity, particularly equitable development and environmental sustainability.

Innovation is a creative capital that is brought to bear on various dimensions of development and prosperity, in the process unleashing undeveloped potential and making fuller use of local resources and assets. The culture of creativity must be embedded in the way

Creativity and innovation can flourish in many areas such as developing and managing urban life, renewal of social institutions, improved urban policies, development of knowledge networks, etc.

POLICY The cities and countries best placed for economic growth and prosperity are those that invest in building knowledge and innovation institutions and related systems with strong support from public authorities and the private sector.[3]

Innovation should be seen as a broader notion that has to do with creative approaches to planning, the economy, social inclusion, the environment, culture and local identity.[5]

POLICY A creative city must establish a balance between 'hardware' factors – infrastructure and technology – and 'software' factors (including mind-set, dynamics of place, the connection between thinkers and doers, and a change-friendly environment).[6]

123

Box 3.2.1

Measuring innovation and creativity

The 'Creative City Index' was recently developed to measure 'the imaginative pulse of cities', combining a variety of indicators including political and public frameworks, diversity, vitality and expression, openness and tolerance, entrepreneurship, vision, liveability, learning and professionalism, among 10 specific dimensions. In 2007, Melbourne-based '2thinkNow' developed an 'Innovation Cities Program' along with an 'Innovation Cities Index' in a bid to enhance understanding of the links between innovation and the way cities operate. The measure also uses a large variety of indicators, involving cultural assets, infrastructure and networked markets in areas such as commerce, finance, food, the arts, health, technology, religion, the media, etc. On this basis, cities are classified in five categories: 'nexus' (cities featuring critical innovations),'hub' (cities that are influential in key areas), 'node' (cities combining broad-ranging performance and imbalances), 'influencer' (cities that are competitive but unbalanced on the whole), and 'upstart' (cities with potential for future performance).

Sources: www.charleslandry.com; www.2thinknow.com.

cities operate.[7] Therefore, it is not just for government or business, but also for communities and the public at large, to contribute their own powers of imagination. And this has to be not just encouraged but legitimized as well, in a bid to broaden the range of available solutions to urban issues.

THE FACTORS BEHIND URBAN INNOVATIVENESS

Innovation can emanate from a creative worker, a community leader, a business person, an artist, a public servant or a scientist, etc. Innovation can respond to a specific problem, reduce risks, anticipate challenges, result in new products or processes, or harness existing or emerging opportunities. For the purposes of urban prosperity, innovation has a clear role in improved conditions for populations and the way they live, work, move, relax and more generally make the most of the urban advantage.

If its existing creative capital is to be enhanced, or activated where dormant, a city should become a locus where sociocultural diversity can be staged, and where links can flourish among both individuals and institutions. In practice, all of this requires well-adapted

POLICY The culture of creativity must be embedded in the way cities operate.[8]

physical environments, which in turn have to do with urbanization economies[9] and better urban planning. From a more institutional point of view, support to knowledge exchange and networking is another way of stimulating creative capital, along with favourable conditions for research and development. As for the productive sector, creative stimulation can also derive from economies of agglomeration and an entrepreneur-friendly environment.

It may come as no surprise that in Asia, most local experts see a strong link between research and development (R&D), on the one hand, and enhanced prosperity on the other, with public authorities and other stakeholders playing significant roles in the areas of business, industry and technology.

This was the case in Singapore, in Hyderabad and Bangalore (India), Shenzhen and Chongqing (China), Gaziantep (Turkey) and Cebu (the Philippines). In Singapore, gross expenditure on R&D increased from 1.9 per cent in 1990 to 2.8 per cent in 2008 and three per cent in 2010,[10] with the focus on applied research, technology, sustainable urban living and 'clean' energy.[11] In Bangalore, the emergence of the city as a knowledge hub is a visible outcome of policy, entrepreneurship and innovation all combined. With more than 66 engineering colleges and 55 polytechnics, the city has developed as a centre for scientific innovation and research in aeronautics and electronics, with strong public research facilities.[12] Biotechnologies and computer/communications also feature highly in Hyderabad, India's pharmaceutical capital, with support from central government and more than 40 research and educational institutions.[13] Shenzhen has developed a State-led endogenous innovation strategy with investments from government agencies, industrial firms and universities. In just a few years, the city has developed a high-tech, modern service industry, actively promoting industrial transformation and upgrading, which focuses on electronics, biological engineering and new material technology. The city has also made important innovations in the service industry (finance, logistics and culture) in a further effort to sustain economic growth and prosperity.[14] Still in China, Chongqing has

The UN-Habitat survey of local experts shows that five main factors are at play when cities innovate: creative urban management; entrepreneurial capacity; the promotion of the arts and culture; the emergence of industrial clusters; and research and development (R&D).

Karnataka, Bangalore, India: A road sign hangs over the entrance to 'Electronics City', an industrial complex dedicated to the IT and electronics industries. Located ten miles (16km) outside Bangalore, the complex has been hugely successful in attracting foreign investment.

© Chris Stowers/Panos Pictures

In contrast to Asia, the share of Research and Development expenditure in GDP in Africa and Latin America is low, where not next to nil. In the absence of any systematic public sector involvement, creativity and innovation largely remain the purview of the private sector.

used State-led investment to stimulate the economy and improve social welfare, optimizing endogenous development through research and technology. Chongqing's strategy, known as 'Three Centers, Two Hubs, and One Base', connects business, finance and education with strong support for infrastructure, communications and a modern base of high-tech industries.[15] In southeast Turkey, Gaziantep – one of the oldest inhabited cities in the world – has deliberately embraced R&D and innovation, with various educational institutions explicitly supporting entrepreneurship. Business has cooperated with public authorities to launch a number of initiatives known as Trademark City, Smart Industry, Teknopark, Innovation Valley and R&D Movement in a bid to open up markets, diversify the economy and promote employment in the pursuit of prosperity.[16]

In contrast to Asia, the share of R&D expenditure in GDP in Africa and Latin America is low at around 0.6 per cent on average. In some African countries, such as Mali, Mozambique, Nigeria, Senegal, Uganda, Zambia, among many others, this share was under 0.4 per cent. In the two regions, the highest expenditure – about one per cent of GDP in 2008 – was recorded in South Africa and Brazil, with central government playing a strong role.[17]

South Africa's national R&D strategy is based on so-called 'Triple Helix' cooperation among business, government and higher education centres, focusing on engineering, the natural sciences, and medicine/health.[18] As might be expected, the Gauteng and Cape Town regions appear to be particularly innovation-friendly with more highly trained graduates involved in research and making the more significant contribution to scientific excellence.[19] It does not come as a surprise either that in Johannesburg, the consistency between the city-region's

own science/technology policies and the national Growth and Development Strategy is deliberate.

A VARIETY OF SOCIAL AND INSTITUTIONAL INNOVATIONS

Many factors stand in the way of urban innovation, especially in developing countries. Not all these factors have been sufficiently identified, understood or addressed. Still, seven major types of deficiency seem to play significant roles: (i) poor physical and knowledge infrastructure; (ii) an absence of appropriate innovation policies (due to lack of interest or understanding); (iii) limited financial resources; (iv) weak local institutions (formal or informal); (v) inadequacy of human resources (number and qualification of personnel); (vi) lack of stakeholder participation and coordination in the elaboration and implementation of innovation policies; and (vii) poor incentives (where any).

In other cases, the problems instead lie in technology transfer and poor adaptation to local know-how.[20] But then 'home-made' innovations, too, can be poorly related to local and national conditions, or overlook the needs of the underprivileged, when they fail 'to take into due consideration the plurality of knowledge and technological options' that are locally available.[21]

The city of Johannesburg has adopted an innovative governance model to rebuild local government and improve service delivery. Bangalore, too, has launched technology-based public–private experiments in governance in a bid to deliver better public services. In Latin America and the Caribbean, Rosario, just like Santo Domingo, has introduced significant institutional innovations in terms of participatory governance. In Nairobi, the private sector has launched a new Internet/ cellphone-based virtual payment platform enabling low- and middle-income residents to conduct e-commerce transactions and even to pay school fees.

Many other social and institutional innovations involve the creation of new systems and models to meet the needs of underserved populations in a more efficient, effective, and sustainable manner. In Tehran, the scope of the WHO-UN-Habitat 'Urban HEART' Programme has been extended to assess

Innovations are often duplicated or transferred from abroad. More often than not, though, this causes problems when foreign innovation runs against the grain of the social or cultural features of the target communities.

POLICY It is in the best interest of cities to promote social and institutional innovations in response to local problems, in a necessary effort to address social needs and improve the efficiency and quality of urban management.

equity under not just the health dimension but also a more general social perspective. Shenzhen has created a multilevel social security system that includes basic social insurance, poverty insurance, compensation for job seekers, and special care for patients and the disabled. These innovative schemes redistribute the benefits of prosperity among migrant workers (up to 75 per cent of Shenzhen's population) under the form of social security, working conditions, rights, education and access to public services.[22] Chongqing has created investment companies to mobilize public capital in order to accelerate construction of infrastructure and public facilities, using a combination of innovative funding mechanisms: taxes, land reserves, fees, and government bonds.[23]

Apart from new, dedicated schemes, social and institutional innovation can take the form of enlightened rules or legislation. In Cebu, the Philippines, an ordinance now encourages those employed in outsourced business processing services to enrol in (post)graduate studies, in a bid to expand the pool of highly skilled people. Rosario,

Argentina, has declared itself a 'Human Rights City', with a commitment to openness, transparency and accountability.[24] Some other institutional innovations connect urban planning and design with the use of social public space. In Colombia, Bogotá has improved many diverse public spaces (sidewalks, public parks and libraries) in a bid to rebuild social cohesion. Singapore's 'Skyway' is a spectacular aerial walkway among giant man-made trees that collect rainwater and generate solar energy, and is an invitation to view the city from a different perspective. In Korea, the municipality of Seoul resorts to urban design to improve the efficiency and enhance the attractiveness of the city with innovative projects, such as the 'Han River Renaissance' scheme and the 'City in the Park' initiative.[25]

THE TRANSFORMATIVE POWER OF INNOVATIONS

Almost by definition, innovation processes are not linear, nor are they easily controllable. However, as far as urban innovation is concerned, a consistent basic pattern seems to be at work. Whether in response to new risks or immediate emergencies, or in more ordinary circumstances, urban innovation seems to result from cooperation and dialogue among a broad variety of stakeholders. Such dialogue acts as a catalyst, bringing together a variety of perspectives, resources, capacities and types of human capital.[26]

Nairobi, Kenya: children play in a schoolyard in Kibera. The newly introduced Pesapal system enables school fees to be paid by the Internet or mobile telephone.

© Meunierd/Shutterstock.com

POLICY It is in cities' best interests to strengthen the links between policy-makers, business, academia, civil society and a variety of practitioners to promote urban innovations.

Innovations introduce knowledge, products, processes and programmes that change the ways of doing business or using resources, or even social attitudes and preferences. Innovations lie at the core of all economic processes and they contribute to knowledge generation and information flows.[27] Innovations of a technological nature have added value and helped transform the urban space (e.g., connectivity, proximity and distance, outsourcing of

manufacturing). Although innovations take place mainly in major metropolitan centres, they are not restricted to those.

The transformative power of innovation is closely linked to the various components of prosperity – productivity, infrastructure, quality of life, equity and environmental sustainability. Innovation can contribute to any of these dimensions, or respond to the supporting institutions and policies at the core of these dimensions (see the 'Wheel of Urban Prosperity', Chapter 1.1), steering the course of the city along the path of prosperity and sustainable development. From this more general, strategic perspective, innovation can bring four major types of benefits: (i) reviving and sustaining the social economy (e.g., better policies for human needs satisfaction); (ii) changes in social relations (e.g., new societal arrangements, new social pact); (iii) reinforcing existing, or creating new, institutions for improved urban management and governance (e.g., regulation of land or social conflicts, new legislation); and (iv) forward-looking changes to the urban space (e.g., resource redistribution, expanded access to services and public goods). Any value added by all these social and institutional innovations will accrue primarily to society as a whole, rather than private individuals or groups,[28] enhancing the prospects of prosperity and giving its full meaning to the notion of 'spatial justice'.[29]

Being a social construct, any city can be steered and shaped towards higher levels of prosperity. A fresh, different vision of urban planning and design can combine with new, more insightful change narratives and development ideas. As urban risks and challenges keep changing over space and time, existing safeguards, instruments or mechanisms must come under review and be adjusted as and where required. Innovation must also help reduce the costs of urban living. Innovative rules and legislation must support the transformation of the existing urban model. The current model is unsustainable for several reasons: endless physical expansion, intensive energy use, alarming and dangerous contributions to climate change, multiple forms of inequality and exclusion, and inability to provide decent jobs and livelihoods.[30] If ongoing urbanization is to usher in the city of the 21st century, then this transformation must be grounded in a more effective and sustainable use of urban space. More compact cities can preserve

A pedestrian bridge (part of the railing stolen for scrap) near Cape Town, South Africa

© 2012 Rodger Shagam/fotoLIBRA.com

Local authorities should be aware that promoting interactions, synergies and adequate environments can enhance local creative capital and prosperity.

open spaces and reduce the costs of transport and service delivery, while encouraging economies of agglomeration and urbanization. These in turn help reduce the overall costs of societal transactions and harness regional potential. Innovation is a catalyst of productivity, which has a major role to play in urban transformation. As demonstrated at their own modest level by innovative, entrepreneurial youth in African, Latin American or Asian slums, urban socioeconomic dynamics calls for optimization of all local assets, potentials and opportunities. At the same time, this 'endogenous growth' process positions the city against the broader background of regional, national and global development. The city of the 21st century is a reinvented city that is more productive, equitable and sustainable. It is a more prosperous city.

Urban Prosperity Through Planning and Design

In the midst of ongoing demographic, socioeconomic or environmental cross-currents, cities must reassert control over their destinies with reinvigorated urban planning and design for the sake of shared prosperity and harmonious development.

This imperative comes as a reminder of the fact that so far, in most cities of the developing world, modern urban planning (where any) has proved unable to nurture shared socioeconomic advancement. For all the paraphernalia of legislation, complex regulations and spatial design plans, a majority of those cities have continued with the flawed models which, as 'advanced' countries have finally found out, are unsustainable in a variety of ways.

Cities have found themselves woefully unprepared in the face of the spatial and demographic challenges associated with urbanization, not

> From Asia to Africa to Latin America, 'master', 'blueprint' and layout plans have had similar, harmful consequences in cities: spatial segregation, social exclusion, excessive mobility needs and consumption of energy, together with poor regard for the potential economies of scale and agglomeration that any city can offer.[31]

to mention those of an environmental nature. With a few commendable exceptions, modern urban planning has failed to integrate the urban poor in the socioeconomic fabric of the city. As an expert in Bangalore put it, '*The poor have survived* despite *master planning.*'[32] Understood primarily as a technical tool, planning has been unable to address the power relations that have been at work to the detriment of the great majorities of urban populations. Planning has also proved unable to prevent environmental degradation or the formation of slums, and is notable for serious shortcomings in terms of transport and urban mobility.

Conceived as a comprehensive, long-term strategy, a master plan – the quintessence of modern planning – typically represents an ideal end-state for a particular city, but with serious gaps between the initial vision and actual results. This brought a scholar in 1996 to talk of '*the dark side of planning*',[33] something an expert in Montevideo has referred to as '*urban plans that are at odds with the notion of prosperity*'.[34]

The shortcomings of modern urban planning have triggered significant reform since the 1980s and 1990s, in an effort to move away from comprehensive plans, top-down decision-making and broad-ranging regulation.[35] A more flexible approach was adopted to improve conditions in cities, through 'strategic planning' and other methods that are more pragmatic, incremental and typically focused on 'getting things done'. However, too many 'strategic urban plans' have effectively imposed an entrepreneurial view of the city, promoting mostly *economic* prosperity and often turning into marketing gimmicks in all but name, complete with oversized architectural designs and mega-developments. In emerging or developing countries, these initiatives typically favour the gentrification of entire areas and, at times, massive displacement in order to make room for highways, skyscrapers, luxury compounds, shopping malls, etc., at the expense of the habitat and livelihoods of the poor.[36]

UN-Habitat policy analysis in 50 cities in Asia, Africa, Latin America and the Arab States (2011) shows that up to 80 per cent of local experts believe that the benefits of economic prosperity mainly serve the interests of the wealthy and

> Whatever the planning approach, powerful political and economic interests keep interfering with the design and implementation of strategic plans and the pursuit of urban prosperity for all.

Today, the Global Standard Urbanization Model of the 20th century appears to be predominant across the world, being largely driven by land speculation and real estate interests that build cities according to financial and economic parameters often radically at odds with shared prosperity.[37]

politicians (a view shared by up to 90 per cent of African experts). Through political influence, bribery and corruption, these powerful interest groups manage to distort urban plans, dodge spatial or legal rules, reduce the production of public goods and manipulate the power of eminent domain; in the process they capture unfair shares of a city's potential, resources and prosperity to the detriment of large, poor majorities of urban populations.

The New Urbanism Movement of the early 1980s broke with conventional master-planning and introduced a number of welcome innovations: livable, pedestrian-friendly cities, dense neighbourhoods with mixes of housing and job-creating commercial and business sites, together with mixed land uses having a diversity of buildings in terms of style, size, price and function – all of this with a strong focus on local communities.[38] For all these fresh efforts, though, a conventional approach to urban development has remained dominant to this day. In developing and emerging countries alike, cities are still hostages to a mix of homogeneous forms or functions on the one hand, and spatial/social segregation on the other hand. Urban areas continue to expand across endless peripheries, with serious, pervasive problems of traffic congestion, enhancing the dependence on motor vehicles

POLICY If urban planning is to be in a better position to address the shortcomings of the Global Standard Urbanization Model of the 20th century, both theory and practice must come under serious review to 'rescue' the discipline from its role as a mere technical tool, restoring it to its rightful position in the public sphere.

POLICY As a decision-making tool, urban planning must better defend the 'public' against the menace of ever-expanding 'private' interests and its consequences: shrinking public spaces and reduced provision of public goods, which affect more collective, intangible dimensions like quality of life, social interaction, cultural identity and social values.

and intensive use of expensive fossil fuels. This dominant type of city is detrimental to the built heritage and the environment, including surrounding agricultural land, as well as biodiversity. This is the pattern which UN-Habitat refers to as the 'Global Standard Urbanization Model of the 20th Century' (GS20C),[39] which privileges individualism, consumerism, new (artificial) values and lifestyles, excessive mobility and privatization of the public space.

RE-POSITIONING URBAN PLANNING AT THE HUB OF THE WHEEL OF PROSPERITY

'The city has many scars to treat and many wounds to cure; urban planning is powerless to do that',[40] claims an expert in Santo Domingo (Dominican Republic). Still, in the 50 cities surveyed by UN-Habitat in 2011, efficient urban planning and urban management are perceived as the most important conditions for shared prosperity.[41]

However, efficient urban planning requires a reinvigorated notion that can really contribute to the pursuit of shared prosperity, and for that purpose four conditions must be met: (i) restoration of public confidence; (ii) repositioning of urban planning in decision-making; (iii) deployment of the fullness of its functions across the five dimensions of shared prosperity; and (iv) support for these functions with adequate financing.

Restoration of confidence: Public confidence must be restored in the capacity of urban planning (alongside other urban power functions) to represent the interests of all the population – including the poor, women, children, youth, elderly or disabled people, immigrants and ethnic minorities – so that the *public, collective* interest prevails at all times and across the whole jurisdiction over any other, and more particularly the vested or special interests of the rich and powerful.

Repositioning: If it is to play this stronger role to the full, urban planning must be re-positioned. No longer a mere technical functionality, urban planning must sit at the core of urban power. As the expression of the collective agreement on interests and vision, urban planning can only be as good as the values it represents and the governance mechanisms that frame it.

Very often, planning has failed correctly to represent collective values and agreements, instead of contributing to the perpetuation of the urban divide with excessive, outdated, irrelevant requirements.

Working on the five 'spokes': Interdependencies and interactions among the five 'spokes' in the 'wheel of urban prosperity' (productivity, infrastructure, quality of life, equity and environmental sustainability) can be deliberately enhanced (as opposed to being allowed to occur all by themselves) through the strategies and interventions that are part and parcel of urban planning. For example, the process of designing a street which supports multimodal transport as part of the infrastructure development of the city leads also to the improvement of productivity, quality of life and social inclusion (see Table 3.2.1.).

Financial support: For urban planning to work more efficiently as an urban power function, it must be reinforced from a financial and legal point of view. Cities need more permanent funding mechanisms to support the provision of public goods and the design and implementation of sustainable technical solutions if their performance and functionality are to be improved.

Few cities or countries are in a proper legal position to do that, and where they are, they find themselves faced with systematic interference by special interest groups

or political expediency.[42] Here again, the public interest must prevail, and governments must look to improve and enforce the mechanisms that enable local authorities to capture urban land and site values, in the process generating the revenues needed to extend prosperity to the poorest areas.[43]

POLICY Restoring urban planning at the central point of the 'wheel', where a solid and efficient institutional 'hub' holds together, controls and activates the five 'spokes', can only enhance the conditions for sustained, shared prosperity.

POLICY Land legislation and planning must combine to put municipal authorities in a better position to extract land values and related capital gains, with the additional revenue available for the funding of infrastructure extensions and other projects.

Box 3.2.2

Streetwise *versus* petrol-powered prosperity

In Peru's capital Lima, it has taken 'only' an open-air public staircase all the way downhill to the city centre to change the name of an informal settlement from fearful 'Quick Sands' to 'The Belt of Hope'. This goes to show the regenerating power of planning for urban public spaces and their decisive role in shared prosperity – well away from the constraints of the outdated automobile-based model of urban development.

Indeed, public spaces, as symbolized by 'the street', can make significant contributions to socioeconomic prosperity, if only they are adequately configured. The street acts as the interface between public and private spaces, with retail businesses and jobs dependent on the quality of the pedestrian environment. In British towns, customers have been found to spend nearly twice as much when walking instead of driving. In Mexico, research has shown that 'walkability' improves home and land values.

Public spaces provide the physical support for urban infrastructure. However, and particularly in the developing world, streets are designed mainly for motorized traffic, overlooking the human dimension and only adding to congestion with more or wider streets. The resulting huge imbalance in transport options damages other aspects of urban functionality. A number of cities

have sought to counter this trend in a variety of ways. As early as 1962 motor vehicles were banned from Copenhagen's main street and bicycle commuting was facilitated. In Melbourne, improved sidewalks, new pedestrian streets, squares and urban design have together increased pedestrian traffic by 39 per cent in daytime and 100 per cent at night. Combined with other modes of popular transport like biking and walking, Bus Rapid Transport (BRT) has spread from Curitiba (Brazil) to Jakarta to Bogotá, Guatemala City, Guangzhou, Istanbul, Mexico City, Brisbane and Los Angeles, among others.

Upgraded and better designed public spaces have the potential to improve overall quality of life. In Cape Town under the Dignified Places Programme, more than 40 projects have brought dignity, beauty and better functionality to various areas, in the process demonstrating that after decades of repression it was once again` possible to meet and talk in a shared space. Finally, planning can make public spaces more compatible with a healthier, less polluted environment. Once one of the most polluted capitals in the world (with a 70 per cent contribution from public transport), Delhi in 2008 combined a popular, low-cost transport with an alternative source of energy to substitute hybrid for petrol-powered rickshaws.

POLICY UN-Habitat calls for a fresh, different type of urban planning and design – one that has the power to transform city landscapes and expand existing enclaves of prosperity to the entire city.

EXPANDING PROSPERITY: CHANGING CITY LANDSCAPES

In many cities, urban planning has been instrumentalized by the real estate business. Cities that respond to the interests of the better-off or only focus on strategic economic interventions in specific spaces tend to create enclaves of prosperity for a select few. Urban planning can be so unrealistic or over-ambitious as to overlook the need to steer and control spatial expansion, with large parts of the city ignoring existing plans or regulations. '*The city falls out of the map, making it irrelevant*', deplores an expert in Panama City.[44] More often than not, these are divided cities, splitting the 'South' from the 'North', and the 'high part' from the 'low part', as these partitions are known colloquially in many parts of the developing world, creating patches of prosperity surrounded by middle-class and deprived areas. Either by action or omission, this type of urban planning contributes to the production of spatial inequities, rather than better shared prosperity.

POLICY The 21st century is in a position to ensure equitable development, preserve the natural environment, promote inexpensive energy sources, provide necessary infrastructures and ensure inclusive economic growth.

UN-Habitat proposes a reinvigorated notion of urban planning, one that comes with a new value system that relies on effective institutions, well-adapted laws and regulations, sustainable urban solutions and active civic involvement in public affairs. This type of planning signals a paradigm shift towards a new urban pattern – the city of the 21st century: a city that can better respond to the challenges of our age, optimizing resources to harness the potentialities of the future; a people-centred city, one that is capable of transcending the inefficient, unsustainable GS20C model, in the process

POLICY UN-Habitat's reinvigorated notion of urban planning involves sustainable use of, and equitable access to, the 'commons' through appropriate policies and schemes.

integrating and nurturing the five dimensions of urban prosperity as defined in this Report.

However, if urban planning is to be reinvigorated, it must shift away from the 'spoke' of productivity, where it has been predominantly operating these past several decades, to the centre of the 'wheel', right in the 'hub': indeed this is where, as an urban power function, planning will be in a better position to make its beneficial influence felt across all five 'spokes', enhancing the scope of shared prosperity across the whole of the city. This will, of course, involve political choices and commitments, which must be turned into tools, regulations and sustainable technical solutions, which will be all the better accepted by society at large as they are seen to embed shared prosperity across the whole urban space.

FACILITATING ACCESS TO 'COMMONS', PROVIDING PUBLIC GOODS, IMPLEMENTING SUSTAINABLE SOLUTIONS

Facilitating access to 'commons': A prosperous city facilitates equitable access to the 'commons'. These include water, air, biodiversity, knowledge and other shared resources, including public infrastructure, together with more intangible forms such as a better environment, a sense of identity and cultural and symbolic spaces that in principle belong to everyone.

Cities with islands of prosperity tend to enclose the 'commons', restrict their use to a select few, or deplete them through unsustainable use.

Prosperous cities require 'commons resource pools', which can take the form of institutional arrangements where conflicts are solved through negotiation, and consensus is built for decision-making. 'Commons' also include any legal or statutory provisions facilitating community participation in planning decisions, available quality information, transparency as well as cultural norms and social compacts.

Some public goods, such as community civic centres, will often be found to function as 'space commons', facilitating the integration of marginal and voiceless groups, in the process promoting pluralism and diversity, which are inseparable from shared prosperity. Contrary to conventional

In general, the production and enjoyment of public goods rely on a set of preconditions such as better connectivity, public security and safety, predictability, property rights under their various forms, street nomenclature, etc.

wisdom, not all '*commons are tragic*',[45] i.e., free access and unrestricted use do not necessarily deplete existing 'stocks' of 'commons'. Rather, fresh evidence shows that under certain circumstances, collective responsibility for some 'commons' creates sustainable conditions, and can even be more efficient than individual property rights.[46]

Providing public goods:[47] A prosperous city makes a profusion of public goods available to all: efficient public transport, educational opportunities, healthcare, quality public spaces such as libraries, recreation areas, parks and open spaces, etc. A substantial part of urban well-being is derived from access to and consumption of these public goods, which in principle must be 'non-excludable' (everyone can enjoy their benefits) and 'non-rivalry' (individual consumption of the good does not decrease the amount available for consumption by others).[48]

Enclaves of prosperity 'fence in' or restrict availability of public goods, concentrating public investment in selected areas only, limiting access and privatizing control over a number of such goods.

The provision of public goods contributes to economic advancement with environmental preservation and quality of life, which, incidentally, are fundamental 'smart growth' concerns, too.[49] Bogotá has transformed its own landscape with a variety of public goods such as multi-modal transport, social infrastructure and quality public spaces that have contributed to sharing more of the benefits of prosperity with poor and middle-income neighbourhoods. Still in Colombia, Medellín has resorted to bold civic architecture, public spaces and other public goods in a bid to enhance collective prosperity. Involvement of urban planning with education, culture, infrastructure, safety and community development has enabled the municipality to connect poor *barrios* (which, according to the head of municipal planning, '*always had lots of energy, but were disconnected from the city*') with more affluent neighbourhoods in the process planting the seeds of mutual trust and expanding shared prosperity.[50]

A public good is typically produced by the public sector, but it can also be provided by public agencies, private enterprises or community organizations, although with a degree of government support to ensure universal access. Production of public goods can be requested from a private developer in exchange for the right to develop and benefit from the surroundings where they want to locate a project. It is for appropriate planning to secure such participation from private developers (land owners, real estate developers, etc.) in the production of public

POLICY A reinvigorated notion of urban planning would give any city tighter public control over the use of land, change the form and function of cities based on sustainable development principles, as well as expand the provision of, and access to, public goods.

goods, quantifying the amounts required, vetting values and development plans, and ensuring orderly deployment across space.

Acting from the 'hub' of the 'wheel for prosperity', urban planning can identify strategies and plan for optimal production of public goods, in the process contributing to social capital, enhancing sense of place, safety and security, integrating social groups (e.g., youth), and increasing the economic value of the areas where these goods are provided. This strategy can generate widespread benefits to all urban residents, expanding prosperity across different areas. Such prosperity in turn can be leveraged for maintenance and further enhancement of public goods.

Implementing sustainable solutions: Prosperous cities must plan and implement a variety of technical solutions to improve functionality and achieve sustainable urban forms. Although solutions can vary according to local conditions, UN-Habitat has identified a number of key interventions in various areas to assist the transition away from the current 'Global Standard Urbanization Model of the 20th Century' (GS20C), which is unsustainable on many accounts, to the city of the 21st century. As suggested earlier, it is in the power of well-calibrated planning rules and interventions to help embed the five dimensions of shared prosperity across the length and breadth of any urban jurisdiction.

Making the city more functional, preserving access to the commons and producing useful public goods can be achieved through five different, sustainable types of intervention:

Increase population density to sustainable levels: More intense land occupation and activities result in sustainable population densities which contain or reduce urban sprawl and depletion of limited resources. Greater proximity will, in turn,

POLICY As it manages space (the form and function of the city), urban planning can steer the overall functioning of the 'wheel', modulating each dimension of prosperity and ensuring synergies between them in order to maintain overall balance and sustainable growth.

facilitate supply and distribution of goods and services. An efficient layout (together with adequate land legislation and policies) can reduce the cost of infrastructure. In addition to suburban densification and sprawl remediation, land use can be intensified through area redevelopment, planning for new areas with higher densities, 'brownfield' development (i.e., decontaminating and developing land previously used for industrial or certain commercial purposes), building conversions, and transit-oriented developments.

Encourage social diversity and mixed land-use: Land planning can bring about clusters of land uses in appropriate locations, with the flexibility needed to adapt to the changing requirements of the population. Urban planning must facilitate the deployment of common spaces that allow encounter, interaction and dialogue between different social-ethnic groups. Moreover, physical urban structure facilitates communication between economic activities and residential areas, providing employment and services on a neighbourhood scale, with positive repercussions on productivity, infrastructure, equity, quality of life and the environment. Urban design strengthens and empowers structures through infrastructure and facilities (education, healthcare, commerce, manufacturing and culture/entertainment).

Devise multimodal mobility strategies: Urban planning can provide alternatives to the current widespread dependency on private motorized vehicles and reinforce use of public transport in combination with non-motorized modes and proper sidewalks. An integrated urban transport strategy generates immediate effects on productivity, including reductions in travel times. Improved transport systems come with environmental

benefits such as better air quality due to reduced exhaust fumes. Accessibility for all potential users is essential to ensure equal mobility opportunities.

Plan infill development and guided expansion: Urban planning must combine both of these for the sake of proper density and provision of affordable urban land. Infill development can revitalize dilapidated areas in the city. In those developing countries where urbanization continues apace, new areas must be developed for the benefit of newcomers if further slum expansion is to be avoided. Properly planned spatial patterns can reduce pressure on land, provide for urban services and alleviate the burden

London, UK: the Olympic Park for the 2012 Olympics was constructed on brownfield sites in Stratford, an area of east London that had been previously rundown. After the Olympic games, the site is to be used to accommodate low-cost housing as well as leisure activities.

© 2012 Alistair Laming/fotoLIBRA.com

Table 3.2.1
Urban planning/design and prosperity

Prosperity Dimensions	Urban Planning	Commons/Goods/ Sustainable Solutions
Productivity	Harness the benefits of agglomeration economies.	Commons
	Improve access to productive advantage (knowledge, quality of the environment, etc.).	Commons
	Provide sufficient public space for circulation of goods and people and deploy adequate infrastructure. Provide efficient transport systems for people and goods.	Public goods
	Encourage polycentric urban development, allowing synergies between centres and sub-centres. Promote mixed-land use to enhance economies of agglomeration and scale with better clustering. Intensify urban nodes and corridors to maximize the benefits of concentration.	Sustainable solutions
Infrastructure development	Provide 'clean' infrastructure, closing 'energy waste loops' to preserve climate, air and water quality; improve connectivity.	Commons
	Expand multimodal transport systems with sidewalks and bicycle infrastructure. Provide social infrastructure such as civic centres, libraries, sports facilities, etc.	Public goods
	Ensure eco-efficiency of infrastructural systems. Support density through integrated infrastructure development, enhancing efficiency and access.	Sustainable solutions
Quality of life	Enhance identity and culture through symbolic spaces and heritage preservation. Improve safety and security. Support place-making through urban design.	Commons
	Ensure high quality of public spaces that engage interaction among communities. Promote green spaces.	Public goods
	Enhance the role of the street as a multi-functional urban space and integrate natural spaces and recreational areas.	Sustainable solutions
Equity and social inclusion	Enhance freedom of movement.	Commons
	Provide well-located, adequate public infrastructure and amenities (incl. education, healthcare, recreation, etc.).	Public goods
	Create mixed neighbourhoods with the diversity of jobs and housing options. Plan infill development and guided expansions. Promote mixed-used land development, ensuring involvement from marginalized groups. Improve connectivity between neighbourhoods and access to services. Turn land and development thereof into a revenue source.	Sustainable solutions
Environmental sustainability	Ensure clean air, unpolluted water and preservation of biodiversity. Act on climate change adaptation/mitigation. Maximize the natural benefits of the site (sunlight, water bodies, winds, etc.). Plan for restoration of ecosystems.	Commons
	Enhance public parks, waterfront and 'green' areas for recreational and productive purposes.	Public goods
	Use 'passive urban design' to reduce carbon emissions. Plan for urban density to reduce energy consumption and settlements footprint. Reduce fragmentation of natural systems; reduce spatial footprint through careful design of infrastructure networks and settlements.	Sustainable solutions

on existing infrastructure. In addition, forward-looking planning can put a halt to land speculation while facilitating access to affordable housing and urban services.

Promote livable public spaces and vibrant streets: Public spaces and streets must be seen as multifunctional areas for social interaction, economic exchange and cultural expression among a wide diversity of participants. It is for planning to organize for those public spaces, and for design to encourage their use, in the process enhancing a sense of identity and belonging. Safety and security are important dimensions to be considered in any such design, together with vital underground infrastructure (water, energy and communications).

Empowering Laws and Institutions for Urban Prosperity

Laws, regulations and institutions are a critical factor in determining the success of cities in achieving holistic and integrated prosperity. In almost all cases of prosperous cities cited in this report, progress along the five dimensions of prosperity is either accelerated or impeded by existing bodies of laws and regulations, the strength of enforcement, as well as by the configuration, capacity and flexibility of the institutions responsible for steering urban development. Laws and institutions provide the normative and organizational underpinnings of urban change and it is no wonder that in recent years, there

> As the proximate reflection of society's values, and as representing political and social relations, laws and institutions serve as the most powerful instruments available to shape urban development.

> **POLICY** Promoting prosperity involves deployment of proper laws, regulations and institutions which have a direct or indirect bearing on equity, productivity, infrastructures and living standards, and which extend across the length and breadth of the whole jurisdiction of the relevant urban authority.

has been a resurgence of policy reviews and scholarly studies striving to address these aspects.

Laws and institutions provide the power and rigour for enabling action, granting authority, defining relations and generally sustaining continuity or triggering change. At a time when so many crisis-struck nations find that a fresh start on the path of prosperity depends more than ever on cities, these elements of the process of urban development must be mobilized to their full potential.[51] Business, academia, civil society – non-governmental and grassroots organizations, trade unions and professional associations, political parties, etc. – are all the legitimate expressions of the various forms which a city's specific potential can take; and the needs to which these stakeholders give 'voice' relate to the preservation and further development of their respective potentials. More than ever, cities need *empowering*, not *forbidding*, legal and institutional systems for their prosperity. Amartya Sen emphasizes this point when he argues a city does not need to be deemed fit for a prosperity-oriented legal and institutional system; rather, *it must become fit through such a system* – which, again, is needed *now*, and for *the city as a whole*.[52]

Indeed, cities do need such systems *now* – and they are at hand's reach, if only public authorities can find the political will (as this chapter will show, some do). Addressing legal and institutional dimension fosters integrated prosperity by promoting the universal demand for justice, fairness and legitimacy. It is a process which transcends cultural barriers and it can be met in a variety of ways as determined by local urban power functions. It forms part of the hub that drives the 'wheel of urban prosperity', which supports and shapes the five 'spokes', adjusting them over time as conditions, needs and fresh risks may require. At the same time, in all parts of the world, laws and institutions have always been shaped by the complex interactions of socio-cultural factors, with new forces constantly bringing their own influences to bear.[53]

As shown in this chapter, urban power functions – governance, urban planning, legal and regulatory frameworks and strong institutions – form the 'hub' that controls the 'wheel of urban prosperity' and give it direction, pace and momentum (see Chapter 1.1). Shared prosperity requires the

> In the cities of the world today, the power to be mobilized against the crisis emanates from a variety of stakeholders, not just public authorities, although these retain a decisive role.

predominance of the *public interest* as embodied in public authorities[54] to ensure that none of the five 'spokes' gain prevalence to the detriment of the others. Abstract values and norms are institutions because they guide individual and collective action.[55] Box 3.2.4 shows how, in China and in Europe centuries ago, the State imposed the prevalence of the *public* over other interests and needs, treating them all equitably for the sake of shared prosperity.

The importance of laws and institutions in urban settings is manifested in a variety of ways. This includes the delineation of powers and functions in the governance structure of a city, which often derive from promulgated city charters, local government frameworks, or directly from the national constitution. Similarly, the rights and responsibilities granted to individuals and firms in cities are all dictated by prevailing legal frameworks. Also, the interaction among urban residents as well as the modalities of production, distribution and consumption of urban space have always been regulated by explicit and implicit codes of behaviour and practice. The transformative potential of any city has, therefore, always been a function of the enabling scope of its laws, regulations and institutions. The degree to which such instruments can be deployed as they are, or consolidated, or even reformed will determine a city's degree of prosperity.

In the metaphor of the *'Prosperity Wheel'*, the legal and institutional framework as a whole acts as the 'hub' which steers the development of the five dimensions ('spokes') of prosperity, modulating momentum, relaying its energy to the other dimensions, and maintaining the overall balance of the 'wheel'. Internal dysfunctions in the legal and institutional framework, or any disconnect between the hub and the spokes, interferes with the operation of the 'wheel' and makes any existing momentum unsustainable (for example, if based on only one of the five dimensions).

THE LEGAL-INSTITUTIONAL BASIS OF THE 20TH-CENTURY CITY

Advances in industrial development, consolidation of the market economy and the permeating influence of liberal democracy (both in its origin in the West and the post-colonial variant in the developing world) have created a shared legal and regulatory foundation in much of the urban world. The legal, regulatory and institutional fundamentals of the contemporary city tend to be identical, differing only in levels of development, institutional characteristics and performance ability. Indeed, the legal-institutional basis of the 20th-century city is fairly uniform; and this explains the

> Laws and the associated institutional set-up have determined the very genesis of the modern city, both in its essence as well as its functionality.

similarities not only in functional modalities but also in the all-too-visible imbalances characterizing the 20th-century city in its generic sense (i.e., spatial segregation, social exclusion, a predominance of motorized mobility, high energy consumption and poor regard for the potential for agglomeration economies).

Driven by the dominant paradigm of the pursuit of individual interests and sustained by a vigorous quest for ever-maximized exchange values, the pivotal dynamics of the 20th-century city has been its age-old accumulation function. Cities have become places of transactions realized through the Weberian formal rational-legal systems. This feature has evolved from the institutional traditions of Western European states that were devised to

> Although the 20th-century city tends to exhibit fair degrees of vibrancy and dynamism, whatever attendant prosperity it experiences is often skewed and unsustainable – and therefore ridden with perennial crises.

Box 3.2.3

Individual *versus* collective interests

The legal foundation of the 20th-century city lies in the ancient tenets of Roman Law and the Napoleonic Code, together with the subsequent elaboration into modern civil and common law. The gist of this legal corpus is the pre-eminence of the individual, who is considered as possessed of inherent rights as represented in the 18th-century French Revolution's *Declaration of the Rights of Man and the Citizen*. Within this individualistic legal tradition, property rights reign supreme, with the emphasis on the rights of owners to the detriment of their social implications and other, broader, collective interests, including duties and responsibilities. With particular regard to urban settings, 'land and property are conceived largely as commodities whose economic value is determined by the owners' interests.'[56] In this system, the role of the State at all levels is relegated to harmonizing and mediating these interests, and to overseeing those assets and facilities that require collective use.

provide predictable conditions for market transactions and to facilitate investment and economic growth.

The community dimension of the city, which has played a major role in the genesis of urbanism, is granted only marginal treatment, while the harnessing of opportunity provides the central impetus for development in general, and urbanisation in particular. As a result, in the words of Lawrence Haworth, '*societies that not very long ago cultivated relationships, conversation, and reasonably vibrant public forums, now cultivate disconnectedness, [and have become] self-absorbed, narcissistic individuals.*'[57]

TOWARDS A NEW LEGAL-URBAN ORDER FOR HOLISTIC PROSPERITY

During the past two decades, the pitfalls of the conventional urban development model have become more glaring. As shown in the previous section (*Urban Prosperity through Planning and Design*) the potential of cities has not been fully harnessed, a more common trend has developed where urban development tends to be spatially fragmented and the benefits of prosperity remain socially segmented.

The financial centre of Rio de Janeiro, Brazil.

© Publio Furbino/Shutterstock.com

In contrast, over the past two decades there are a few cities in the world that have undertaken a major re-examination of the prevailing urban legal order, and initiated bold practical schemes inspired by a set of alternative, radical urban doctrines and jurisprudence which depart from the classical liberal legalism exalting individualism and private property. Among these are cities in Brazil, which, in 2001, after a long period of consultations and negotiations, adopted a nationwide *City Statute* which enshrined the notion of a *Right to the City*. The Statute makes an important contribution to urban law, facilitating shared prosperity, particularly in the context of a developing country. The Statute also 'broke with the long-standing tradition of civil law and set the basis of a new legal-political paradigm for urban land use and development control'.[58]

A prominent scholar highlights four dimensions of Brazil's 2001 *City Statute*: 'A conceptual one, providing elements for the interpretation of the constitutional principle of the social functions of urban property and of the city; the regulation of new instruments for the construction of a different urban order by the municipalities; the indication of processes for the democratic management of cities; and the identification of legal instruments for the comprehensive regularisation of informal settlements in private and public urban areas.'[59] This new urban legal order has had highly visible effects. As a nation and at macro-economic level, Brazil is among a handful of countries in the world that has been able to achieve remarkable growth rates for much of the early years of this century, despite the global economic turbulence. More significantly, Brazilian cities have been able to expand the middle-class segments of their populations and to improve economic and living conditions for substantial numbers of poor residents. Although still very high, cities are reducing income inequalities, as measured by the Gini coefficient, which decreased from 0.606 in 1990 to 0.569 in 2009.[60]

The experience of Diadema, in the São Paulo metropolitan region (the main hub of Brazil's motor industry), is a case in point. At the beginning of the 1980s, the city was effectively a dormitory town, with a majority of residents living in slum conditions. Only 22 per cent of the road and street network was up to urban standards, on top of a general lack of drainage, surfacing, water and sewerage networks. Around 30 per cent of the population lived in *favelas* without any attention from local public authorities. Education, health, cultural and leisure services and amenities were in very short supply. The city was among those with the highest child mortality rates in Brazil (83/1,000 live births).

A generation or so later, by 2009, only three per cent of Diadema's population were still residing in *favelas*. The municipality has incorporated some of the instruments and mechanisms provided in the 2001 *City Statute* in its own urban planning and participatory management. A proper infrastructure has been put in place, the local economy is dynamic and the city has demonstrated its capacity to mobilize the population. On top of productivity, infrastructure and quality of life, Diadema has also promoted equitable standards in spatial development.[61]

REVITALIZED 'RIGHTS TO THE COMMONS' AND EXPANSION OF THE PUBLIC REALM

'Commons' reinforce the social function of property and that of the city as a whole, while recognizing the dynamism of private assets. Laws, regulations and institutions as factors of restraint, opportunity and action act as the levers that can optimize the social function of property and balance it out with private rights and assets. It must be stressed here that this social function is not about ownership rights or their transactional implications. Rather, it is essentially about user rights for enhanced human value.

The 'Right to the Commons' is an ancient concept in legal jurisprudence originating in feudal England, where it referred to the extension of user rights for all on a manor's grazing land. Lately, the notion has resurfaced in urban settings (including public goods, societal institutional arrangements, public culture, and heritage sites), where it is perceived as an effective way of countering not just rampant enclosures and appropriations, but also the rise of duality under the form of inequity and segregation.

The relevance of the 'commons' concept to the legal-institutional dimensions of urban prosperity lies in its ability to emphasize and materialize the inherent collective dimension of urbanism. In this respect,

Those few cities featuring balanced and sustainable prosperity have effectively deployed adequate laws, regulations and institutions in support of their transformation.

POLICY Shared urban prosperity is about enhancing the public realm, equitable sharing of public goods and consolidating rights to the commons for all.

POLICY As cities work on the five dimensions of prosperity, there also occurs a progressive expansion in the size of the commons. More amenities are brought into collective use and more access is provided, enabling larger numbers of urban residents to use and enjoy shared spaces, services and facilities.

The capacity for a city to maintain extensive and quality shared spaces and facilities provides a good indication of its degree of prosperity.

In this era of enclosures, privatization and even invasion of the traditional urban commons (including beaches, river banks, forests, school yards and even pavements), the size and quality of a city's overall public space acts as a good indicator of shared prosperity.

cities such as Helsinki, Toronto and Barcelona, which achieve high rankings on the UN-Habitat City Prosperity Index (CPI), feature more extensive public realms than Monrovia, Nairobi or Dakar, or similar cities with low CPI readings.

In essence, the extended public realm, with its negation of any spatial, social or functional duality, fills a two-way function as both a cause and a consequence of the cumulative operation and interaction of the five 'spokes' of the 'wheel of shared urban prosperity'.

Legal and regulatory instruments exert a major bearing on the origination and preservation of the commons, and also in ensuring indiscriminate access. Statutes, ordinances and regulations are the bases for the guidelines and standards regulating spatial layouts and construction designs. The same applies to institutional relationships, functional allocations and authority designation, besides resource distribution. The legal framework in turn enables civic organizations and community activities. Equally significant is the overall manner in which legal-regulatory and institutional frameworks delineate the public and private spheres and guide the interaction between and within them in the everyday workings of the city.

One component of the commons that lately has attracted a lot of attention is the management of public spaces.[62] In Panama City, one of the local experts surveyed by UN-Habitat put it as follows: 'The more degraded public space, the more degraded the citizen, because public space is not only about quality of life but also the expression of citizenship'.[63] Another local expert, in Santo Domingo, underscored the same point perhaps more incisively: 'Citizens need to gain positive empowerment, to defend space enclaves where public life is still alive and where laws and norms for doing so are available.'[64]

REVISITING URBAN CODES FOR SHARED PROSPERITY

Rules and regulations constitute a key instrument in urban management and development. That is why appropriate institutions are required to ensure implementation and enforcement as well as awareness building and mobilization. Whereas *laws must empower both spaces* (e.g., serviced land) *and stakeholders* (e.g., secure tenure) for shared prosperity, it is for *rules and regulations to embed the public interest on the ground* (when effectively enforced). Supporting institutions in this endeavour include programme implementation, education and training, as well as awareness building and mobilization. Rules and regulations have significant roles to play, as they generally steer and circumscribe planning and construction. One author has even gone so far as to ascribe the *'shaping and misshaping of American cities'* to poor planning regulations.[65] Indeed, zoning regulations, building codes, utility standards, deed restrictions and the many other instruments that shape the urban built environment, will determine not only the pattern, use and form of spaces and structures, but will also strongly influence the quality of life in cities.

The review of regulatory frameworks is of particular importance for those cities in the developing world that have long operated with externally derived standards and codes, who must also tend to effective implementation and enforcement capacities. Revisiting the codes developed for formerly colonial or apartheid cities like Nairobi, Dar es Salaam or Johannesburg in a bid to achieve an inclusive urban form is a challenging endeavour. This calls not only for major institutional restructuring, but also a revision of zoning and

POLICY Laws, rules and institutions must be kept alert, not inert, to current and evolving needs and risks if a city's whole human potential is to be harnessed, not repressed – empowering the whole population with 'basic capabilities' or 'generic conditions of agency' at the service of today's and tomorrow's prosperity.

building codes to support urban reforms, not to mention squatter regulation and slum upgrading. In addition, cities today must provide accommodative measures, allowing for progressive construction, smaller plot sizes and multiple variants of land tenure. Similarly, utility standards must be adjusted, and new development financing channels devised, in the face of inequity and exclusion.

Indeed, the need for revisiting rules and regulations for shared prosperity applies across all the five 'spokes' of the prosperity wheel. The on-going transformations in Hong Kong and China show that even in an aspect such as environment there is an urgent need to pay attention to the legal and regulatory implications of change. Adequate rules and regulations[66] are required not just for the purposes of improved quality of life, or climate change adaptation, but also because in developing countries the poor are heavily reliant on natural capital for their subsistence.[67] At the same time, urban rule-makers must remain well aware of the inter-linkages between environmental protection and slum/poverty reduction.

INSTITUTIONAL TRANSFORMATION

Some of the real-life experiences outlined in this chapter suggest that when it comes to structuring the urban power functions that form the hub of the 'prosperity wheel', it is for every city to make its own choices. Indeed, many choices have already been made; but common to all is the adaptation and consolidation of key institutions which harness the energy and engagement of all stakeholders in a city. Major stakeholders, such as business, professionals, civic organizations, besides neighbourhood associations, must be provided with an institutional avenue for effective engagement with urban prosperity – how it is generated and how it is shared. Such engagement transcends the traditional participatory practices of forums and consultative mechanisms; it turns socioeconomic conditions into levers of enhanced prosperity, with every household and business considered as an asset to be safeguarded, optimized and promoted – empowered – for the benefit of all.

An exemplary case of institutional innovation for shared prosperity is that of Medellín. During the past decade, the Colombian city's prosperity has experienced major turnaround, as it endeavoured to overcome the combined challenges of poverty, inequality, exclusion and informality, besides rampant violence, through a whole new social dispensation. Conditions have been put in place for civic mobilization, bringing together politicians, the private sector, professionals and communities, with the aim of

> As some cities have discovered, shared prosperity involves a serious review of regulatory frameworks.

> **POLICY** Shared and integrated prosperity is a socio-political project, involving a commitment by all stakeholders and entailing a re-examination of laws, regulations, and the corresponding institutional framework.

building a future that benefits everyone. The collective energy behind this compact reconstructs the foundations of shared prosperity in all socioeconomic spheres.

It strives to expand the civic order through cooperative endeavours, using local economic development as the entry point. It is in this regard, for example, that the limitations of the informal economy (locally known as the '*chasita economy*' (*chasita* being small trolleys the poor use to peddle wares around the community) have been addressed and measures taken to create more sustainable business enterprises. Well-adapted, modern financial institutions have been established, such as the strengthening of '*Banco de las Oportunidades*', which is a microfinance initiative, along with networks of business development agencies (*CEDEZOs*). All these are targeting growth-oriented, small and medium-sized enterprises in a bid to generate momentum for systemic transformation in favour of growth and inclusiveness.

Furthermore, as a way of enabling the municipality to cater for the overall needs of its residents the local authority enhanced its resource disposition by consolidating a community-owned agency – *Empresas Públicas de Medellín (EPM)*. It is now acknowledged that owing to its effective management, not only does the Agency contribute about 30 per cent of its net revenue into the city budget, but it has also provided close to 99 per cent utility connections to the city residents. Recent reviews have confirmed that the funding from EPM has enabled the city to ensure a minimum income floor to the poorest residents.[68]

Helsinki, a city that features prominently in the UN-Habitat City Prosperity Index, has optimized on

> **POLICY** Shared prosperity is not accidental, nor is it an automatic outcome of economic growth or market forces. It is a human, collective construct which requires vision, leadership and a coherent programme of action.

In Helsinki, the enabling potential of legal and regulatory instruments is used to build a dynamic institutional framework which enhances shared prosperity.

partnerships, and vertical linkages as well as system modernization. The main accent of its prosperity building strategy has been through investing in human capital by promoting innovation. The city uses a multi-pronged approach to building prosperity, thus it is not surprising that it remains in the top category of the prosperity index.[69]

Barcelona and Toronto have similarly managed to enhance prosperity by a comprehensive deployment of legal, regulatory and institutional frameworks. Making full use of the stronger powers vested into it, the municipality of Barcelona was able to use physical improvements to public spaces to rebuild *social* and *political* cohesion among the population. The nexus between regulations and institutions, on the one hand, and the social and political sphere on the other hand, has played a crucial role in Barcelona's success. The same applies to Toronto, which has been consistently meticulous in organizational performance. Using its rich diversity as an asset, the city has been able to utilize effectively its metropolitan status, an engaging relationship with the province and federal government to maintain its economic competitiveness and a high level of quality of life for its residents.[70]

The case of Dubai brings out an institutional factor which is common to most of the above cities, but somewhat more prominent in this city-state. This is the aspect of vision and leadership. The transformation from a desolate desert land to a global business hub is an outstanding achievement, notwithstanding its current poor performance in the equity dimension. The city's prosperity has been driven by institutional modernization,

A metro train downtown in Dubai, United Arab Emirates. The driverless system opened in 2009.
© Philip Lange /Shutterstock.com

and also a judicious application of rules and regulations in planning and management. Being a state in itself and also very small in size, much of the progress achieved is led by the central government.[71] While in the case of Dubai, the overall national leadership and the royal family is credited with the city's success, for many others the role of particular mayors is also recognized.[72]

At this juncture it is worth noting that most of the cities that can be called 'prosperous' are impacted by development forces which operate beyond the boundaries of single municipalities. There is an increasing process of metropolitization in triggering the dynamic of prosperity to the extent that metros are described as the building blocks of prosperity.[73] At the same time, complementarities

---

Box 3.2.4

Law, institutions and the public interest

Urban space is shaped by laws, rules and institutions (or lack thereof) in response to the needs and requirements of varying numbers of stakeholders. In this sense, the prosperity of a city is also a *legal* and *institutional* construct, and the past has some lessons for early 21st-century central and municipal governments. Major legal systems around the world have long recognized that far from being just an abstract norm, law and institutions have the capacity to shape up a variety of interests across ethnic, cultural and other divides. They do so within the spatial confines of their jurisdictions, and with a long-term view.[75]

This is the background against which the state has historically emerged as the apex body of an interdependent network of powerful repositories of different kinds of power – legal, religious, bureaucratic, economic, etc.[76] In this role, the state has gradually built a monopoly over universality. This went hand in hand with the constitution of bureaucratic functions independent of particular interests – family, religion, the economy – with agents that were mandated to embody the public interest. Along with this came the constitution of a new, 'public' kind of resources that embodied universality, or at any rate a degree of universality that was superior to that of previously existing resources. This public realm gradually stood out against particular interests, and also against private appropriation of public functions through patronage or nepotism.

As the state evolved into '*the geometric focal point of all perspectives*' and a principle of public order, it established a unified space – imposing *spatial* over social, genealogical or other types of proximity. In the process, public authority has gained more recognition from the various segments of society, which further consolidates both its privileged position and its efficiency. As a result, the notion of 'public interest' can pave the way for consensus and mobilization; at any rate, it sheds light on reality and becomes a shared evaluation criterion.

Historically, in China as in Europe, the city has served as the privileged locus of the emergence of the state and the public interest as we know them today. In 11th-century Western Europe,[77] it fell to municipal authorities to control violence as well as economic and political relations. Although the poor were effectively left out of some functions, they were equal members of the assemblies in charge of endorsing municipal officials and laws (including those on economic activities). Moreover, purchase, sale and mortgaging of land and buildings were open to all. At the time, the protections and safeguards provided by cities also aimed at preserving their prosperity from heavy-handed monarchs or emperors.

---

of higher levels of government – State and national – are needed for the prosperity project to succeed. The balance of this relationship has not always been easy, with fears about the erosion of municipal power, particularly in the United States.[74]

Legal and institutional transformation for the sake of prosperity is not confined to the cities of the developed world. Despite the formidable challenges facing them, a number of Asian and African cities are taking significant steps, with some already achieving visibly higher degrees of prosperity. Cities such as Bangalore and Hyderabad, South Africa's Gauteng urban region, Nairobi, Dakar and Dar es Salaam are all engaged in the pursuit of shared, sustainable prosperity through effective legal, regulatory and institutional frameworks. Bangalore clearly demonstrates the challenges of a higher prosperity path against a

developing country background; but the city benefits from strong institutional synergies, with investment by national, state and local government, including Greater Bangalore authority. The private–public partnership model seems to be the driving factor behind the city's enhanced prosperity, together with a well-adapted regulatory framework for Information Technology Parks, an attractive environment for highly skilled labour, and facilitation of the establishment of training and research institutions.

POLICY Shared and integrated prosperity in cities is about the reclaiming of a sense of community and sustainability through urban power functions. It is about regaining the very objective of people converging in cities – the 'urban advantage', with the notions of shared social and cultural values attached to it.

A pedestrian footbridge at night in the modern city of Shenzhen, China.

© Fuyu Liu/Shutterstock.com

Endnotes

1 Oyelaran-Oyeyinka and Sampath, 2010.

2 Kratke, 2011.

3 Oyelaran-Oyeyinka and Sampath, 2010.

4 Kratke, 2011.

5 Landry, 2000.

6 *Ibid.*

7 *Ibid.*

8 *Ibid.*

9 'Urbanization economies' refer to the advantages gained from a specific urban location: proximity to markets, available labour force, communications, and auxiliary business services.

10 Government of Singapore, 2010.

11 Centre for Livable Cities, 2011.

12 Belliapa, 2011.

13 Vejella, 2011.

14 Jin and Liu, 2011.

15 The city's GDP rose from 136.024 billion Yuan in 1997 to 789.424 billion Yuan in 2010. Even during the serious financial crisis of 2008 and 2009, Chongqing maintained a high growth rate of GDP of 14% [Liu and Wang, 2011] Kurtul, 2011.

16 Kurtul, 2011.

17 World Bank, 2012.

18 Gabara, 2008.

19 Lorentzen et al, 2010.

20 SET-DEV, 2011.

21 *Ibid.*

22 Jin and Liu, 2011.

23 In ten years of reform and development, the total assets of state-owned enterprises increased from 160 billion Yuan to one trillion Yuan, nearly seven-fold increase [Liu and Wang, 2011.

24 UN-Habitat, 2010a.

25 UN-Habitat, 2010c.

26 James et al, 2008.

27 Castells, 1996.

28 James et al, 2008.

29 Soja, 2010.

30 Cohen, 2012.

31 Clos, 2012.

32 Belliapa, 2011.

33 Flyvbjerg, 1996.

34 Viana, 2011.

35 López, 2011.

36 Kothari and Chaudhry , 2009.

37 Buhigas, 2012.

38 Briney, 2009.

39 Clos, 2012; This 'global standardization process' is also referred by professionals like David Mangin [Mangin, 2004]

40 Castellanos, 2011.

41 A highest percentage of respondents in all regions found that planning and management is the most important factor, while the majority of respondents in LAC opined that decentralization of policies and appropriate laws and regulation plays a more important role.

42 ONU-HÁBITAT, 2012.

43 Earth Right Institute, 2011.

44 Mendoza, 2011.

45 The "Tragedy of the Commons' refers to a dilemma arising from the situation in which multiple individuals, acting independently and rationally consulting their own self-interest, will ultimately deplete a shared limited resource, even when it is clear that it is not in anyone's long-term interest for this to happen. This dilemma was described in an influential article, "The Tragedy of the Commons", by ecologist Garrett Hardin and first published in Science in 1968. (http://en.wikipedia.org/wiki/Tragedy_of_the_commons)

46 Ostrom, 1990.

47 The notion of fixed social capital, which encompasses all assets of society that are not mobile (or soft) but are solid and owned by the public is equivalent to the 'public goods' mentioned in this chapter.

48 UNIDO, 2008.

49 The CLEAR Network, 2006.

50 Kimmelman, 2012.

51 'Cities have always been exposed to brutal economic pressures from overseas; the nation state has always, to a greater or smaller extent, tried to cushion these pressures.' [Pierre, 2011]

52 Sen, 1999.

53 Menski, 2006.

54 'It could well be argued that the growing significance of non-elected actors in urban politics in many countries only increases the need for political control and accountability.' [Pierre, 2011]

55 Pierre, 2011.

56 Fernandes and Copello , 2009.

57 Haworth, 1963.

58 Fernandes, 2007a.

59 Fernandes, 2007b.

60 UN-Habitat database (2012).

61 Reali and Alli, 2010.

62 See, for instance, Gehl, J. (2010) *Cities for People*, Island Press, Washington DC.

63 Mendoza, 2011.

64 Castellanos, 2011.

65 Talen, 2012.

66 Kremzner, 1998; Chan and Yung, 2004; Waldman, 2012

67 World Bank, 2006.

68 Bateman, 2012; McGuirk, 2012.

69 Karvinen, M. (2005) *Innovation and creativity strategies in Helsinki Metropolitan Area – reinvention of regional governance*, proceedings of the 41st ISoCaRP Congress 2005, Bilbao, Spain.

70 City of Toronto (n.d) *How Toronto Ranks*, http://www.toronto.ca/progress/world_rankings.htm

71 Cooper, 2003.

72 IIED (2009) 'What Role for Mayors in Good City Governance?' in *Environment & Urbanization* Vol 21, No 1, April 2009. Brief.

73 Peirce et al (eds.), 2008.

74 European Commission, 1998; Creedy et al, 2007; Jaffe, 2012; Peirce et al (eds.), 2012.

75 Berman, 1983; Menski, 2006.

76 Bourdieu, 2012.

77 Berman, 1983; Sassen, 2006.

Statistical Annex

GENERAL DISCLAIMER
The designations employed and presentation of the data in the Statistical Annex do not imply the expression of any opinion whatsoever on the part of the Secretariat of the United Nations concerning the legal status of any country, city or area of its authorities, or concerning the delimitation of its frontiers or boundaries.

Table 1: City Prosperity Index and components

Table 2: Proportion of urban population living in slums and urban slum population, by country, 1990–2009

Table 3: Urban population, proportion of urban population living in slum area and urban slum population, by region, 1990–2012

Table 4: City population and city population growth rate of urban agglomerations with 750,000 inhabitants or more in 2009, by country, 1950–2025 (thousands)

Table 5: Urban population and urbanization by country, 1990–2030

Table 1

City Prosperity Index and components

Country	City	City Prosperity Index (CPI) with 5 Dimensions	City Prosperity Index (CPI) with 4 Dimensions*	Productivity Index	Quality of Life Index	Infrastructure Index	Enivronment Index	Equity Index
Austria	Vienna	0.925	0.936	0.939	0.882	0.996	0.932	0.883
United States	New York	0.825	0.934	0.940	0.866	0.994	0.941	0.502
Canada	Toronto	0.890	0.934	0.874	0.907	0.997	0.963	0.733
United Kingdom	London	0.904	0.934	0.923	0.898	0.997	0.920	0.793
Sweden	Stockholm	0.898	0.934	0.896	0.925	0.995	0.921	0.767
Finland	Helsinki	0.924	0.933	0.890	0.905	0.997	0.944	0.890
Ireland	Dublin	0.913	0.929	0.901	0.867	0.996	0.958	0.850
Norway	Oslo	0.924	0.929	0.870	0.914	0.997	0.939	0.903
France	Paris	0.897	0.927	0.895	0.925	0.996	0.895	0.788
Japan	Tokyo	0.905	0.925	0.850	0.931	0.989	0.936	0.828
Australia	Melbourne	0.903	0.925	0.867	0.875	0.996	0.967	0.820
New Zealand	Auckland	0.862	0.922	0.854	0.889	0.994	0.958	0.657
Netherlands	Amsterdam	0.895	0.915	0.866	0.872	0.995	0.933	0.818
Switzerland	Zurich	0.884	0.914	0.868	0.858	0.997	0.941	0.772
Denmark	Copenhagen	0.913	0.911	0.855	0.871	0.997	0.928	0.922
Belgium	Brussels	0.883	0.910	0.862	0.864	0.997	0.922	0.783
Spain	Barcelona	0.876	0.909	0.829	0.912	0.995	0.908	0.755
Italy	Milan	0.870	0.908	0.868	0.895	0.997	0.876	0.733
Poland	Warsaw	0.883	0.901	0.846	0.864	0.990	0.911	0.817
Portugal	Lisbon	0.853	0.899	0.827	0.867	0.995	0.916	0.692
Hungary	Budapest	0.881	0.894	0.808	0.867	0.990	0.921	0.833
Greece	Athens	0.862	0.889	0.800	0.885	0.996	0.884	0.762
Czech Republic	Prague	0.871	0.882	0.855	0.771	0.992	0.926	0.827
Republic of Korea	Seoul	0.861	0.876	0.801	0.903	0.989	0.822	0.807
Russia	Moscow	0.793	0.870	0.806	0.813	0.960	0.908	0.550
Mexico	Guadalajara	0.801	0.839	0.787	0.759	0.922	0.899	0.667
Brazil	São Paulo	0.757	0.836	0.742	0.803	0.918	0.894	0.507
Kazakhstan	Almaty	0.830	0.833	0.751	0.822	0.872	0.897	0.818

Table 1

City Prosperity Index and components

Country	City	City Prosperity Index (CPI) with 5 Dimensions	City Prosperity Index (CPI) with 4 Dimensions*	Productivity Index	Quality of Life Index	Infrastructure Index	Enivronment Index	Equity Index
China	Shanghai	0.826	0.832	0.671	0.836	0.900	0.950	0.800
Romania	Bucharest	0.836	0.821	0.707	0.767	0.968	0.867	0.900
Mexico	Mexico City	0.709	0.816	0.743	0.764	0.900	0.866	0.405
Turkey	Ankara	0.780	0.806	0.699	0.802	0.842	0.891	0.683
Jordan	Amman	0.771	0.796	0.697	0.790	0.887	0.824	0.680
Thailand	Bangkok	0.733	0.794	0.719	0.747	0.871	0.850	0.533
Colombia	Bogotá	0.699	0.791	0.672	0.767	0.970	0.785	0.427
Colombia	Medellín	0.667	0.789	0.600	0.718	0.959	0.812	0.394
Ukraine	Kyiv	0.798	0.781	0.579	0.757	0.968	0.874	0.873
Viet Nam	Hà Noi	0.756	0.776	0.712	0.761	0.912	0.733	0.683
Armenia	Yerevan	0.779	0.769	0.635	0.850	0.870	0.745	0.817
China	Beijing	0.799	0.762	0.667	0.836	0.911	0.663	0.967
South Africa	Cape Town	0.590	0.758	0.628	0.645	0.933	0.875	0.217
Indonesia	Jakarta	0.769	0.743	0.636	0.733	0.741	0.881	0.885
South Africa	Johannesburg	0.479	0.742	0.654	0.645	0.880	0.816	0.083
Philippines	Manila	0.723	0.737	0.676	0.647	0.775	0.868	0.669
Egypt	Cairo	0.722	0.730	0.679	0.743	0.916	0.616	0.692
Morocco	Casablanca	0.647	0.700	0.634	0.513	0.827	0.891	0.472
Honduras	Tegucigalapa	0.652	0.694	0.541	0.729	0.709	0.829	0.510
Moldova	Chisinau	0.698	0.693	0.340	0.850	0.895	0.894	0.717
India	Mumbai	0.694	0.688	0.645	0.739	0.745	0.632	0.715
Kenya	Nairobi	0.593	0.673	0.481	0.559	0.860	0.889	0.357
Cambodia	Phnom Penh	0.677	0.666	0.544	0.613	0.728	0.809	0.722
Mongolia	Ulaanbaatar	0.675	0.664	0.493	0.777	0.632	0.804	0.722
Guatemala	Guatemala City	0.614	0.646	0.440	0.556	0.823	0.866	0.502
Cameroon	Yaoundé	0.618	0.623	0.492	0.555	0.666	0.827	0.600
India	New Delhi	0.635	0.617	0.596	0.690	0.786	0.448	0.712
Côte d'Ivoire	Abidjan	0.578	0.599	0.452	0.440	0.767	0.842	0.500
Nepal	Kathmandu	0.598	0.594	0.385	0.621	0.740	0.704	0.617
Bangladesh	Dhaka	0.633	0.593	0.545	0.539	0.673	0.627	0.817
Uganda	Kampala	0.581	0.590	0.512	0.486	0.507	0.956	0.550
Nigeria	Lagos	0.496	0.582	0.475	0.634	0.576	0.659	0.262
Ghana	Accra	0.560	0.576	0.347	0.592	0.737	0.728	0.500
Bolivia	La Paz	0.551	0.565	0.363	0.621	0.745	0.606	0.502
Ethiopia	Addis Ababa	0.501	0.564	0.503	0.534	0.521	0.724	0.313
Senegal	Dakar	0.581	0.552	0.510	0.384	0.794	0.596	0.712
Zimbabwe	Harare	0.493	0.542	0.246	0.451	0.899	0.864	0.338
United Republic of Tanzania	Dar es Salaam	0.571	0.530	0.427	0.371	0.607	0.822	0.767
Zambia	Lusaka	0.434	0.507	0.316	0.463	0.590	0.766	0.233
Niger	Niamey	0.482	0.456	0.402	0.426	0.485	0.521	0.602
Mali	Bamako	0.491	0.452	0.401	0.416	0.544	0.460	0.683
Madagascar	Antananarivo	0.465	0.446	0.171	0.558	0.511	0.812	0.552
Guinea	Conakry	0.449	0.416	0.133	0.461	0.607	0.809	0.612
Liberia	Monrovia	0.313	0.285	0.048	0.381	0.411	0.886	0.457

*The CPI with 4 dimensions does not include the equity index

Source: United Nations Human Settlements Programme (UN-Habitat), Global Urban Indicators Database 2012.

Table 2

Proportion of urban population living in slums and urban slum population, by country, 1990–2009

Major area, region, country or area	Proportion of urban population living in slum area[a]						Urban slum population at mid-year by major area, region and country (thousands)					
	1990	1995	2000	2005	2007	2009	1990	1995	2000	2005	2007	2009
AFRICA												
Angola				86.5	76.2	65.8				7,756	7,466	7,019
Benin	79.3	76.8	74.3	71.8	70.8	69.8	1,311	1,616	1,897	2,260	2,423	2,595
Burkina Faso	78.8	72.4	65.9	59.5	59.5		960	1,109	1,374	1,762	2,029	
Burundi				64.3	64.3					452	508	
Cameroon	50.8	49.6	48.4	47.4	46.6	46.1	2,532	3,160	3,826	4,585	4,870	5,188
Central African Republic	87.5	89.7	91.9	94.1	95.0	95.9	943	1,113	1,296	1,470	1,551	1,642
Chad	98.9	96.4	93.9	91.3	90.3	89.3	1,257	1,507	1,844	2,312	2,509	2,714
Comoros	65.4	65.4	65.4	68.9	68.9		80	91	101	119	124	
Congo				53.4	51.7	49.9				1,098	1,119	1,134
Côte d'Ivoire	53.4	54.3	55.3	56.2	56.6	57.0	2,674	3,366	4,158	5,066	5,496	5,979
Democratic Republic of Congo				76.4	69.1	61.7				14,491	14,375	14,079
Egypt	50.2	39.2	28.1	17.1	17.1	17.1	12,607	10,704	8,447	5,677	5,903	6,143
Equatorial Guinea				66.3						157		
Ethiopia	95.5	95.5	88.6	81.8	79.1	76.4	5,819	7,562	8,653	9,729	10,067	10,427
Gabon				38.7						443		
Gambia				45.4	34.8					373	313	
Ghana	65.5	58.8	52.1	45.4	42.8	40.1	3,571	4,070	4,473	4,755	4,817	4,848
Guinea	80.4	68.8	57.3	45.7	45.7		1,385	1,517	1,490	1,390	1,489	
Guinea-Bissau				83.1						362		
Kenya	54.9	54.8	54.8	54.8	54.8	54.7	2,343	2,859	3,400	4,069	4,396	4,762
Lesotho				35.1	44.4	53.7				163	223	290
Liberia						68.3						1,282
Madagascar	93.0	88.6	84.1	80.6	78.0	76.2	2,470	2,997	3,486	4,046	4,225	4,460
Malawi	66.4	66.4	66.4	66.4	67.7	68.9	725	893	1,192	1,572	1,786	2,027
Mali	94.2	84.8	75.4	65.9	65.9	65.9	1,902	2,066	2,247	2,496	2,743	3,009
Morocco	37.4	35.2	24.2	13.1	13.1	13.1	4,490	4,904	3,713	2,205	2,308	2,416
Mozambique	75.6	76.9	78.2	79.5	80.0	80.5	2,161	3,216	4,381	5,714	6,311	6,940
Namibia	34.4	34.1	33.9	33.9	33.6	33.5	135	165	200	239	254	272
Niger	83.6	83.1	82.6	82.1	81.9	81.7	1,016	1,219	1,475	1,787	1,944	2,121
Nigeria	77.3	73.5	69.6	65.8	64.2	62.7	26,549	31,538	36,951	42,783	45,195	47,612
Rwanda	96.0	87.9	79.7	71.6	68.3	65.1	372	397	874	1,129	1,165	1,208
Senegal	70.6	59.8	48.9	43.3	41.1	38.8	2,071	2,051	1,955	2,010	2,030	2,048
Sierra Leone				97.0						1,824		
Somalia				73.5	73.6	73.6				2,161	2,316	2,486
South Africa	46.2	39.7	33.2	28.7	23.0	23.0	8,834	8,950	8,475	8,179	6,814	7,055
Togo				62.1						1,486		
Uganda	75.0	75.0	75.0	66.7	63.4	60.1	1,473	1,833	2,214	2,403	2,487	2,578
United Republic of Tanzania	77.4	73.7	70.1	66.4	65.0	63.5	3,719	4,539	5,335	6,271	6,713	7,200
Zambia	57.0	57.1	57.2	57.2	57.3	57.3	1,778	1,930	2,083	2,350	2,483	2,633
Zimbabwe	4.0	3.7	3.3	17.9	21.0	24.1	121	138	140	801	963	1,141
ASIA												
China	43.6	40.5	37.3	32.9	31.0	29.1	13,1670	151,437	169,102	183,544	182,934	180,560
Mongolia	68.5	66.7	64.9	57.9	57.9		866	860	882	878	915	
Bangladesh	87.3	84.7	77.8	70.8	66.2	61.6	19,999	23,535	25,819	27,831	27,770	27,542

Table 2

Proportion of urban population living in slums and urban slum population, by country, 1990–2009

Major area, region, country or area	Proportion of urban population living in slum area[a]						Urban slum population at mid-year by major area, region and country (thousands)					
	1990	1995	2000	2005	2007	2009	1990	1995	2000	2005	2007	2009
India	54.9	48.2	41.5	34.8	32.1	29.4	121,022	122,231	119,698	112,913	109,102	104,679
Nepal	70.6	67.3	64.0	60.7	59.4	58.1	1,194	1,585	2,100	2,630	2,850	3,075
Pakistan	51.0	49.8	48.7	47.5	47.0	46.6	18,054	20,688	23,890	27,158	28,529	29,965
Cambodia				78.9						2,052		
Indonesia	50.8	42.6	34.4	26.3	23.0	23.0	27,559	29,017	29,691	24,777	22,456	23,255
Lao People's Democratic Republic				79.3						1,277		
Myanmar				45.6						6,701		
Philippines	54.3	50.8	47.2	43.7	42.3	40.9	16,479	17,158	17,613	17,972	18,134	18,302
Thailand				26.0	26.5	27.0				5,539	5,841	6,146
Viet Nam	60.5	54.6	48.8	41.3	38.3	35.2	8,118	8,852	9,395	9,491	9,396	9,224
Iraq	16.9	16.9	16.9	52.8	52.8	52.8	2,131	2,439	2,828	9,974	10,361	10,759
Jordan				15.8	17.7	19.6				689	824	971
Lebanon				53.1						1,877		
Saudi Arabia				18.0						3,442		
Syrian Arab Republic				10.5	22.5					1,080	2,516	
Turkey	23.4	20.7	17.9	15.5	14.1	13.0	7,773	7,859	7,714	7,422	7,022	6,728
Yemen				67.2	76.8					4,088	5,140	
LATIN AMERICA AND THE CARIBBEAN												
Argentina	30.5	31.7	32.9	26.2	23.5	20.8	8,622	9,772	10,953	9,274	8,521	7,737
Belize				18.7							28	
Bolivia	62.2	58.2	54.3	50.4	48.8	47.3	2,305	2,590	2,794	2,972	3,030	3,080
Brazil	36.7	34.1	31.5	29.0	28.0	26.9	40,527	42,789	44,604	45,428	45,309	44,947
Chile				9.0						1,285		
Colombia	31.2	26.8	22.3	17.9	16.1	14.3	7,077	6,884	6,404	5,670	5,306	4,899
Costa Rica				10.9						291		
Dominican Republic	27.9	24.4	21.0	17.6	16.2	14.8	1,135	1,143	1,145	1,100	1,067	1,024
Ecuador				21.5						1,786		
El Salvador				28.9						1,079		
French Guiana				10.5						16		
Grenada				6.0						2		
Guadeloupe				5.4						24		
Guatemala	58.6	53.3	48.1	42.9	40.8	38.7	2,146	2,301	2,438	2,572	2,619	2,660
Guyana				33.7	33.5	33.2				73	73	72
Haiti	93.4	93.4	93.4	70.1	70.1	70.1	1,893	2,393	2,876	2,908	3,230	3,557
Honduras				34.9						1,170		
Jamaica				60.5						840		
Mexico	23.1	21.5	19.9	14.4	14.4		13,760	14,457	14,800	11,574	11,906	
Nicaragua	89.1	74.5	60.0	45.5	45.5		1,929	1,860	1,676	1,388	1,437	
Panama				23.0						526		
Paraguay				17.6						608		
Peru	66.4	56.3	46.2	36.1	36.1		9,964	9,566	8,776	7,540	7,801	
Saint Lucia				11.9						5		
Suriname				3.9						13		
Trinidad and Tobago				24.7						40		
Venezuela (Bolivarian Republic of)				32.0						7,861		

Note: (a) Computed from country household data using the four components of slum (improved water, improved sanitation, durable housing and sufficient living area).

Source: United Nations Human Settlements Programme (UN-Habitat), Global Urban Indicators Database 2012.

Table 3

Urban population, proportion of urban population living in slum area and urban slum population, by region, 1990–2012

Urban population at mid-year by major area, region (thousands)[a]

Major region or area	1990	1995	2000	2005	2007	2010	2012
Developing Regions	1,406,473	1,658,909	1,930,248	2,228,145	2,341,589	2,514,583	2,634,197
Northern Africa	58,552	66,491	73,996	82,209	85,843	91,590	95,602
Sub-Saharan Africa	146,640	181,532	220,535	266,848	287,548	321,300	345,564
Latin America and the Caribbean	311,042	352,267	393,420	432,646	447,430	468,757	482,496
Eastern Asia	352,808	429,924	512,043	619,535	652,715	699,813	731,647
Southern Asia	317,857	369,356	424,294	481,719	506,248	545,479	573,698
South-eastern Asia	138,996	165,445	197,360	220,814	230,851	246,701	257,677
Western Asia	79,005	92,146	106,691	122,294	128,796	138,654	145,126
Oceania	1,572	1,748	1,908	2,080	2,158	2,289	2,387

Proportion of urban population (per cent)

Major region or area	1990	1995	2000	2005	2007	2010	2012
Developing Regions	34.5	37.2	39.9	42.7	43.7	45.0	45.9
Northern Africa	48.5	50.0	51.2	52.4	53.0	54.0	54.6
Sub-Saharan Africa	28.3	30.6	32.7	34.9	35.8	37.2	38.2
Latin America and the Caribbean	70.3	73.0	75.5	77.7	78.5	79.6	80.3
Eastern Asia	29.1	33.4	38.0	44.5	46.3	48.7	50.3
Southern Asia	26.5	27.7	29.0	30.2	30.8	31.7	32.4
South-eastern Asia	31.6	34.5	38.2	39.9	40.6	41.8	42.7
Western Asia	60.5	62.1	63.7	65.2	65.7	66.6	67.1
Oceania[c]	24.4	24.1	23.5	23.0	22.9	22.8	22.9

Notes: (a) United Nations Department of Economic and Social Affairs Population Division – World Urbanization Prospects: The 2009 Revision

(b) Population living in household that lack either improved water, improved sanitation, sufficient living area (more than three persons per room), or durable housing

(c) Trends data are not available for Oceania. A constant figure does not mean there is no change

Source: United Nations Human Settlements Programme (UN-Habitat), Global Urban Indicators Database 2012.

Urban slum population at mid-year by region (thousands)[b]

Major region or area	1990	1995	2000	2005	2007	2010	2012
Developing Regions	650,444	711,832	759,915	793,723	803,280	819,969	862,569
Northern Africa	20,126	18,798	15,054	10,984	11,463	12,226	12,762
Sub-Saharan Africa	102,641	122,635	143,255	168,005	179,538	198,168	213,134
Latin America and the Caribbean	104,794	110,871	114,993	110,129	110,412	110,194	113,424
Eastern Asia	154,175	174,363	191,563	204,253	202,809	197,529	206,515
Southern Asia	181,667	190,758	194,364	192,842	192,325	190,647	200,510
South-eastern Asia	68,852	74,049	78,246	75,443	73,744	76,540	79,945
Western Asia	17,810	19,936	21,980	31,565	32,470	34,112	35,704
Oceania	379	421	460	501	520	552	575

Proportion of urban population living in slum (per cent)

Major region or area	1990	1995	2000	2005	2007	2010	2012
Developing Regions	46.2	42.9	39.4	35.6	34.3	32.6	32.7
Northern Africa	34.4	28.3	20.3	13.4	13.4	13.3	13.3
Sub-Saharan Africa	70.0	67.6	65.0	63.0	62.4	61.7	61.7
Latin America and the Caribbean	33.7	31.5	29.2	25.5	24.7	23.5	23.5
Eastern Asia	43.7	40.6	37.4	33.0	31.1	28.2	28.2
Southern Asia	57.2	51.6	45.8	40.0	38.0	35.0	35.0
South-eastern Asia	49.5	44.8	39.6	34.2	31.9	31.0	31.0
Western Asia	22.5	21.6	20.6	25.8	25.2	24.6	24.6
Oceania[c]	24.1	24.1	24.1	24.1	24.1	24.1	24.1

Notes: (a) United Nations Department of Economic and Social Affairs Population Division – World Urbanization Prospects: The 2009 Revision

(b) Population living in household that lack either improved water, improved sanitation, sufficient living area (more than three persons per room), or durable housing

(c) Trends data are not available for Oceania. A constant figure does not mean there is no change

Source: United Nations Human Settlements Programme (UN-Habitat), Global Urban Indicators Database 2012.

Table 4

City population and city population growth rate of urban agglomerations with 750,000 Inhabitants or more in 2009, by country, 1950–2025 (thousands)

Country/City	City population of urban agglomerations ('000)								City population growth rate of urban agglomerations (%)						
	1990	1995	2000	2005	2010	2015	2020	2025	1990–1995	1995–2000	2000–2005	2005–2010	2010–2015	2015–2020	2020–2025
AFGHANISTAN															
Kabul	1,282	1,616	1,963	2,994	3,731	4,616	5,665	6,888	4.63	3.90	8.44	4.41	4.26	4.09	3.91
ALGERIA															
El Djazaïr (Algiers)	1,815	2,023	2,254	2,512	2,800	3,099	3,371	3,595	2.17	2.17	2.17	2.17	2.03	1.68	1.29
Wahran (Oran)	647	675	705	736	770	827	902	970	0.86	0.86	0.86	0.90	1.43	1.73	1.47
ANGOLA															
Huambo	326	444	578	775	1,034	1,305	1,551	1,789	6.17	5.25	5.87	5.78	4.64	3.46	2.85
Luanda	1,568	1,953	2,591	3,533	4,772	6,013	7,080	8,077	4.39	5.66	6.20	6.01	4.62	3.27	2.63
ARGENTINA															
Buenos Aires	10,513	11,154	11,847	12,551	13,074	13,401	13,606	13,708	1.18	1.21	1.15	0.82	0.49	0.30	0.15
Córdoba	1,200	1,275	1,348	1,423	1,493	1,552	1,601	1,638	1.21	1.11	1.09	0.96	0.78	0.61	0.46
Mendoza	759	802	838	876	917	956	990	1,016	1.11	0.88	0.88	0.91	0.84	0.68	0.53
Rosario	1,084	1,121	1,152	1,186	1,231	1,280	1,322	1,354	0.68	0.55	0.58	0.75	0.78	0.64	0.48
San Miguel de Tucumán	611	666	722	781	831	868	899	924	1.71	1.63	1.58	1.23	0.89	0.70	0.54
ARMENIA															
Yerevan	1,175	1,142	1,111	1,104	1,112	1,120	1,132	1,143	-0.55	-0.55	-0.14	0.14	0.15	0.22	0.18
AUSTRALIA															
Adelaide	1,046	1,074	1,102	1,133	1,168	1,214	1,263	1,307	0.53	0.51	0.55	0.61	0.78	0.79	0.68
Brisbane	1,329	1,471	1,603	1,780	1,970	2,096	2,178	2,245	2.04	1.71	2.10	2.03	1.24	0.76	0.61
Melbourne	3,117	3,257	3,433	3,641	3,853	4,022	4,152	4,261	0.88	1.05	1.17	1.13	0.86	0.64	0.51
Perth	1,160	1,273	1,373	1,484	1,599	1,687	1,753	1,810	1.87	1.51	1.56	1.49	1.07	0.77	0.64
Sydney	3,632	3,839	4,078	4,260	4,429	4,592	4,733	4,852	1.11	1.21	0.87	0.78	0.72	0.61	0.50
AUSTRIA															
Wien (Vienna)	1,539	1,544	1,549	1,642	1,706	1,753	1,779	1,801	0.06	0.07	1.17	0.76	0.55	0.30	0.25
AZERBAIJAN															
Baku	1,733	1,766	1,806	1,867	1,972	2,082	2,190	2,291	0.37	0.45	0.67	1.09	1.08	1.01	0.90
BANGLADESH															
Chittagong	2,023	2,578	3,308	4,180	4,962	5,680	6,447	7,265	4.85	4.99	4.68	3.43	2.70	2.53	2.39
Dhaka	6,621	8,332	10,285	12,555	14,648	16,623	18,721	20,936	4.60	4.21	3.99	3.08	2.53	2.38	2.24
Khulna	985	1,133	1,285	1,464	1,682	1,933	2,211	2,511	2.79	2.53	2.60	2.79	2.78	2.69	2.54
Rajshahi	521	606	678	764	878	1,013	1,164	1,328	3.02	2.27	2.39	2.77	2.86	2.78	2.63
BELARUS															
Minsk	1,607	1,649	1,700	1,775	1,852	1,905	1,917	1,917	0.52	0.61	0.85	0.86	0.56	0.12	0.01
BELGIUM															
Antwerpen	893	906	925	945	965	979	984	985	0.28	0.43	0.43	0.42	0.28	0.10	0.02
Bruxelles-Brussel	1,680	1,715	1,776	1,840	1,904	1,941	1,948	1,948	0.41	0.70	0.70	0.69	0.39	0.07	0.00
BENIN															
Cotonou	504	577	642	720	844	1,016	1,217	1,445	2.73	2.13	2.28	3.19	3.69	3.62	3.44
BOLIVIA															
La Paz	1,062	1,267	1,390	1,524	1,673	1,840	2,005	2,156	3.53	1.85	1.85	1.87	1.90	1.72	1.45
Santa Cruz	616	833	1,054	1,325	1,649	1,916	2,103	2,261	6.04	4.69	4.59	4.37	3.01	1.86	1.45

Table 4

City population and city population growth rate of urban agglomerations with 750,000 Inhabitants or more in 2009, by country, 1950–2025 (thousands)

Country/City	City population of urban agglomerations ('000)								City population growth rate of urban agglomerations (%)						
	1990	1995	2000	2005	2010	2015	2020	2025	1990–1995	1995–2000	2000–2005	2005–2010	2010–2015	2015–2020	2020–2025
BRAZIL															
Aracaju	453	527	606	691	782	849	883	902	2.99	2.83	2.60	2.49	1.63	0.79	0.42
Baixada Santista	1,184	1,319	1,468	1,638	1,819	1,949	2,014	2,045	2.15	2.14	2.18	2.10	1.39	0.66	0.30
Belém	1,129	1,393	1,748	1,963	2,191	2,351	2,427	2,460	4.20	4.54	2.32	2.19	1.41	0.64	0.27
Belo Horizonte	3,548	4,093	4,659	5,237	5,852	6,260	6,420	6,463	2.86	2.59	2.34	2.22	1.35	0.50	0.13
Brasília	1,863	2,257	2,746	3,292	3,905	4,296	4,433	4,474	3.84	3.92	3.62	3.42	1.91	0.63	0.19
Campinas	1,693	1,975	2,264	2,533	2,818	3,018	3,109	3,146	3.08	2.74	2.24	2.14	1.37	0.60	0.24
Cuiabá	510	606	686	728	772	813	843	861	3.43	2.49	1.18	1.16	1.04	0.72	0.42
Curitiba	1,829	2,138	2,494	2,951	3,462	3,791	3,913	3,953	3.12	3.07	3.37	3.19	1.82	0.63	0.20
Florianópolis	503	609	734	882	1,049	1,162	1,210	1,233	3.85	3.72	3.67	3.48	2.04	0.81	0.37
Fortaleza	2,226	2,554	2,875	3,280	3,719	4,011	4,130	4,170	2.75	2.37	2.63	2.51	1.51	0.58	0.20
Goiânia	1,132	1,366	1,635	1,880	2,146	2,327	2,405	2,439	3.75	3.60	2.80	2.65	1.62	0.66	0.27
Grande São Luís	672	844	1,066	1,173	1,283	1,367	1,415	1,440	4.54	4.68	1.90	1.79	1.28	0.68	0.35
Grande Vitória	1,052	1,221	1,398	1,613	1,848	2,008	2,078	2,109	2.97	2.72	2.85	2.72	1.66	0.69	0.30
João Pessoa	652	741	827	918	1,015	1,089	1,129	1,151	2.54	2.21	2.09	2.01	1.39	0.73	0.38
Londrina	491	554	613	709	814	889	925	944	2.39	2.04	2.89	2.78	1.75	0.80	0.41
Maceió	660	798	952	1,068	1,192	1,282	1,329	1,353	3.77	3.55	2.30	2.19	1.46	0.72	0.36
Manaus	955	1,159	1,392	1,577	1,775	1,913	1,979	2,009	3.87	3.68	2.49	2.36	1.50	0.67	0.30
Natal	692	800	910	1,099	1,316	1,460	1,519	1,545	2.89	2.58	3.79	3.60	2.08	0.78	0.34
Norte/Nordeste Catarinense	603	709	815	936	1,069	1,162	1,207	1,230	3.22	2.78	2.78	2.66	1.67	0.76	0.37
Pôrto Alegre	2,934	3,236	3,505	3,791	4,092	4,316	4,428	4,469	1.96	1.59	1.57	1.53	1.07	0.51	0.18
Recife	2,690	2,958	3,230	3,542	3,871	4,107	4,219	4,259	1.90	1.76	1.84	1.78	1.18	0.54	0.19
Rio de Janeiro	9,595	10,174	10,803	11,368	11,950	12,404	12,617	12,650	1.17	1.20	1.02	1.00	0.75	0.34	0.05
Salvador	2,331	2,644	2,968	3,422	3,918	4,243	4,370	4,411	2.53	2.31	2.84	2.71	1.60	0.59	0.19
São Paulo	14,776	15,948	17,099	18,647	20,262	21,300	21,628	21,651	1.53	1.39	1.73	1.66	1.00	0.31	0.02
Teresina	614	706	789	843	900	950	984	1,004	2.77	2.24	1.32	1.30	1.09	0.70	0.40
BULGARIA															
Sofia	1,191	1,168	1,128	1,169	1,196	1,211	1,215	1,215	-0.38	-0.70	0.71	0.46	0.25	0.06	0.00
BURKINA FASO															
Ouagadougou	537	667	921	1,328	1,908	2,643	3,457	4,332	4.32	6.45	7.32	7.25	6.52	5.37	4.51
CAMBODIA															
Phnum Pénh (Phnom Penh)	615	836	1,160	1,354	1,562	1,803	2,093	2,427	6.14	6.55	3.10	2.87	2.86	2.99	2.96
CAMEROON															
Douala	931	1,155	1,432	1,767	2,125	2,478	2,815	3,131	4.30	4.30	4.20	3.69	3.07	2.55	2.13
Yaoundé	754	948	1,192	1,489	1,801	2,103	2,392	2,664	4.59	4.59	4.45	3.80	3.11	2.57	2.15
CANADA															
Calgary	738	809	953	1,056	1,182	1,262	1,315	1,364	1.84	3.26	2.06	2.27	1.30	0.82	0.73
Edmonton	831	859	924	1,017	1,113	1,178	1,227	1,274	0.67	1.47	1.92	1.80	1.14	0.81	0.74
Montréal	3,154	3,305	3,471	3,603	3,783	3,925	4,048	4,165	0.94	0.98	0.74	0.98	0.74	0.62	0.57
Ottawa-Gatineau	918	988	1,079	1,119	1,182	1,236	1,285	1,333	1.48	1.74	0.75	1.09	0.89	0.78	0.74
Toronto	3,807	4,197	4,607	5,035	5,449	5,706	5,875	6,029	1.95	1.86	1.78	1.58	0.92	0.59	0.52
Vancouver	1,559	1,789	1,959	2,093	2,220	2,318	2,400	2,479	2.75	1.81	1.33	1.18	0.86	0.70	0.65

Table 4

City population and city population growth rate of urban agglomerations with 750,000 Inhabitants or more in 2009, by country, 1950–2025 (thousands)

Country/City	City population of urban agglomerations ('000)								City population growth rate of urban agglomerations (%)						
	1990	1995	2000	2005	2010	2015	2020	2025	1990–1995	1995–2000	2000–2005	2005–2010	2010–2015	2015–2020	2020–2025
CHAD															
N'Djaména	477	565	647	732	829	960	1,170	1,445	3.38	2.72	2.48	2.48	2.93	3.96	4.23
CHILE															
Santiago	4,616	4,964	5,275	5,605	5,952	6,237	6,408	6,503	1.46	1.21	1.21	1.20	0.94	0.54	0.29
Valparaíso	733	771	803	837	873	911	946	973	1.02	0.83	0.83	0.83	0.86	0.76	0.57
CHINA															
Anshan, Liaoning	1,234	1,307	1,384	1,515	1,663	1,827	1,990	2,120	1.15	1.15	1.81	1.86	1.89	1.71	1.27
Anyang	410	556	753	1,033	1,130	1,220	1,326	1,417	6.07	6.08	6.32	1.79	1.53	1.67	1.32
Baoding	471	645	884	1,042	1,213	1,385	1,524	1,628	6.28	6.29	3.30	3.03	2.67	1.91	1.32
Baotou	1,044	1,212	1,406	1,826	1,932	2,072	2,243	2,388	2.98	2.98	5.23	1.13	1.41	1.58	1.25
Beijing	6,788	8,138	9,757	11,455	12,385	13,335	14,296	15,018	3.63	3.63	3.21	1.56	1.48	1.39	0.99
Bengbu	447	554	687	794	914	1,037	1,142	1,222	4.29	4.29	2.91	2.80	2.53	1.91	1.36
Benxi	759	807	857	911	969	1,044	1,136	1,215	1.22	1.22	1.22	1.22	1.50	1.68	1.35
Changchun	2,192	2,446	2,730	3,143	3,597	4,046	4,409	4,673	2.19	2.19	2.81	2.70	2.35	1.72	1.16
Changde	275	450	735	801	849	913	994	1,064	9.82	9.82	1.73	1.16	1.47	1.69	1.36
Changsha, Hunan	1,089	1,504	2,077	2,197	2,415	2,655	2,885	3,066	6.45	6.46	1.12	1.89	1.89	1.66	1.22
Changzhou, Jiangsu	730	883	1,068	1,876	2,062	2,267	2,466	2,624	3.81	3.81	11.27	1.89	1.90	1.68	1.24
Chengdu	2,955	3,403	3,919	4,467	4,961	5,441	5,886	6,224	2.82	2.82	2.62	2.10	1.85	1.57	1.12
Chifeng	345	483	677	761	842	931	1,020	1,092	6.74	6.74	2.33	2.02	2.03	1.81	1.37
Chongqing	3,123	4,342	6,039	7,266	9,401	9,850	10,514	11,065	6.59	6.60	3.70	5.15	0.93	1.30	1.02
Cixi	207	367	650	725	781	850	928	994	11.44	11.44	2.16	1.50	1.70	1.75	1.38
Dalian	1,884	2,311	2,833	3,060	3,306	3,599	3,896	4,132	4.08	4.08	1.54	1.54	1.70	1.59	1.17
Dandong	543	607	679	736	795	867	947	1,014	2.24	2.24	1.60	1.56	1.73	1.75	1.37
Daqing	757	905	1,082	1,294	1,546	1,797	1,981	2,112	3.58	3.58	3.58	3.56	3.00	1.96	1.28
Datong, Shanxi	917	981	1,049	1,141	1,251	1,375	1,500	1,602	1.34	1.34	1.68	1.84	1.89	1.74	1.31
Dongguan, Guangdong	553	1,416	3,631	4,692	5,347	5,971	6,483	6,852	18.82	18.83	5.13	2.61	2.21	1.64	1.11
Dongying	395	498	628	773	949	1,123	1,246	1,334	4.64	4.64	4.14	4.09	3.37	2.09	1.36
Foshan	429	569	754	4,033	4,969	5,455	5,903	6,242	5.63	5.63	33.53	4.17	1.86	1.58	1.12
Fushun, Liaoning	1,289	1,323	1,358	1,368	1,378	1,434	1,544	1,647	0.52	0.52	0.16	0.15	0.79	1.49	1.29
Fuxin	600	633	667	739	821	912	999	1,070	1.06	1.06	2.05	2.12	2.09	1.83	1.37
Fuyang	142	265	695	804	874	957	1,045	1,119	12.42	19.30	2.91	1.69	1.81	1.76	1.36
Fuzhou, Fujian	875	1,316	1,978	2,368	2,787	3,201	3,509	3,727	8.15	8.15	3.59	3.26	2.77	1.84	1.20
Guangzhou, Guangdong	3,072	4,745	7,330	8,165	8,884	9,669	10,409	10,961	8.69	8.70	2.16	1.69	1.69	1.48	1.03
Guilin	561	652	757	867	991	1,120	1,231	1,317	2.99	2.99	2.71	2.68	2.45	1.89	1.35
Guiyang	1,080	1,417	1,860	2,015	2,154	2,325	2,519	2,679	5.44	5.44	1.60	1.33	1.53	1.60	1.23
Haerbin	2,392	2,860	3,419	3,789	4,251	4,473	4,800	5,080	3.57	3.57	2.06	2.30	1.02	1.41	1.14
Haikou	331	494	738	1,410	1,586	1,772	1,937	2,065	8.02	8.02	12.96	2.35	2.21	1.78	1.28
Handan	525	653	811	1,007	1,249	1,488	1,652	1,764	4.33	4.34	4.33	4.32	3.50	2.09	1.32
Hangzhou	1,476	1,887	2,411	3,516	3,860	4,145	4,470	4,735	4.91	4.91	7.55	1.87	1.42	1.51	1.15
Hefei	1,100	1,298	1,532	2,065	2,404	2,626	2,850	3,029	3.32	3.32	5.97	3.04	1.76	1.64	1.22
Hengyang	504	632	793	936	1,099	1,263	1,393	1,488	4.53	4.53	3.31	3.22	2.79	1.95	1.33
Hohhot	635	798	1,005	1,264	1,589	1,907	2,118	2,258	4.59	4.59	4.59	4.57	3.66	2.09	1.28
Huai'an	330	520	818	914	998	1,095	1,195	1,278	9.06	9.06	2.24	1.76	1.85	1.75	1.34
Huaibei	290	423	617	775	962	1,147	1,275	1,364	7.53	7.53	4.55	4.32	3.52	2.12	1.35
Huainan	724	872	1,049	1,212	1,396	1,583	1,738	1,854	3.71	3.71	2.88	2.82	2.52	1.86	1.30

Table 4

City population and city population growth rate of urban agglomerations with 750,000 Inhabitants or more in 2009, by country, 1950–2025 (thousands)

Country/City	City population of urban agglomerations ('000)								City population growth rate of urban agglomerations (%)						
	1990	1995	2000	2005	2010	2015	2020	2025	1990–1995	1995–2000	2000–2005	2005–2010	2010–2015	2015–2020	2020–2025
Huizhou	205	336	551	1,212	1,384	1,562	1,713	1,828	9.90	9.91	15.77	2.66	2.42	1.84	1.30
Huludao	351	431	529	648	795	940	1,045	1,120	4.09	4.09	4.08	4.07	3.36	2.11	1.38
Jiamusi	469	539	619	711	817	927	1,020	1,092	2.78	2.78	2.78	2.77	2.52	1.92	1.37
Jiangmen	190	314	519	977	1,103	1,236	1,355	1,448	10.02	10.02	12.67	2.42	2.28	1.84	1.33
Jiaozuo	395	500	631	755	900	1,045	1,155	1,236	4.68	4.68	3.59	3.50	2.99	2.01	1.36
Jieyang	176	327	608	732	855	980	1,081	1,158	12.36	12.37	3.73	3.10	2.73	1.96	1.37
Jilin	1,090	1,251	1,435	1,647	1,888	2,135	2,338	2,489	2.75	2.75	2.75	2.74	2.46	1.81	1.25
Jinan, Shandong	1,923	2,134	2,592	2,951	3,237	3,522	3,813	4,044	2.08	3.89	2.59	1.85	1.69	1.59	1.18
Jingzhou	301	479	761	899	1,039	1,183	1,302	1,392	9.25	9.26	3.33	2.91	2.59	1.91	1.34
Jining, Shandong	343	542	856	972	1,077	1,193	1,304	1,394	9.15	9.16	2.53	2.06	2.04	1.79	1.33
Jinjiang	98	212	456	636	858	1,080	1,216	1,303	15.38	15.38	6.64	5.99	4.61	2.37	1.37
Jinzhou	592	675	770	814	857	918	998	1,068	2.63	2.63	1.12	1.02	1.38	1.67	1.36
Jixi, Heilongjiang	650	732	823	927	1,042	1,166	1,278	1,366	2.36	2.36	2.36	2.36	2.24	1.83	1.34
Kaohsiung	1,372	1,431	1,488	1,548	1,611	1,711	1,850	1,971	0.83	0.79	0.79	0.80	1.20	1.56	1.27
Kunming	1,100	1,679	2,561	2,857	3,116	3,405	3,691	3,915	8.45	8.45	2.19	1.73	1.78	1.61	1.18
Lanzhou	1,290	1,561	1,890	2,085	2,285	2,507	2,724	2,896	3.82	3.82	1.96	1.83	1.85	1.66	1.23
Lianyungang	344	442	567	732	878	1,002	1,105	1,183	4.99	4.99	5.12	3.63	2.65	1.94	1.36
Linyi, Shandong	260	542	1,130	1,297	1,427	1,571	1,713	1,827	14.67	14.67	2.76	1.91	1.93	1.73	1.29
Liuzhou	637	809	1,027	1,183	1,352	1,527	1,675	1,788	4.78	4.78	2.82	2.68	2.43	1.85	1.30
Lufeng	275	391	556	706	889	1,069	1,192	1,276	7.05	7.05	4.78	4.60	3.70	2.17	1.37
Luoyang	725	938	1,213	1,373	1,539	1,716	1,875	1,999	5.14	5.14	2.48	2.29	2.17	1.78	1.28
Luzhou	273	421	649	751	850	955	1,049	1,123	8.67	8.67	2.90	2.49	2.33	1.88	1.37
Maoming	173	327	617	717	803	896	983	1,053	12.69	12.70	2.98	2.28	2.20	1.85	1.37
Mianyang, Sichuan	289	468	758	883	1,006	1,133	1,244	1,331	9.62	9.62	3.07	2.59	2.39	1.87	1.34
Mudanjiang	479	564	665	724	783	855	933	1,000	3.29	3.29	1.69	1.58	1.75	1.76	1.38
Nanchang	912	1,226	1,648	2,380	2,701	2,978	3,236	3,436	5.92	5.92	7.35	2.53	1.95	1.66	1.20
Nanchong	279	411	606	705	808	914	1,006	1,078	7.74	7.74	3.05	2.71	2.48	1.91	1.37
Nanjing, Jiangsu	2,497	2,944	3,472	3,966	4,519	5,076	5,524	5,845	3.30	3.30	2.66	2.61	2.33	1.69	1.13
Nanning	759	1,118	1,445	1,826	2,096	2,306	2,508	2,669	7.74	5.13	4.68	2.76	1.91	1.68	1.24
Nantong	470	534	607	767	1,423	1,586	1,734	1,850	2.55	2.55	4.70	12.36	2.17	1.78	1.29
Nanyang, Henan	228	392	672	774	867	967	1,060	1,135	10.79	10.80	2.83	2.26	2.18	1.84	1.36
Neijiang	415	533	685	781	883	991	1,088	1,165	5.00	5.00	2.63	2.46	2.31	1.87	1.36
Ningbo	634	909	1,303	1,897	2,217	2,536	2,782	2,959	7.20	7.20	7.51	3.12	2.69	1.85	1.23
Panjin	367	467	593	696	813	932	1,028	1,101	4.79	4.79	3.22	3.10	2.73	1.97	1.37
Pingdingshan, Henan	431	606	852	942	1,024	1,120	1,222	1,307	6.81	6.81	2.01	1.68	1.79	1.74	1.34
Puning	76	214	603	763	911	1,060	1,172	1,255	20.76	20.76	4.71	3.55	3.02	2.02	1.36
Putian	311	370	439	1,052	1,085	1,147	1,241	1,327	3.43	3.43	17.48	0.62	1.11	1.58	1.33
Qingdao	1,332	1,882	2,659	3,029	3,323	3,622	3,923	4,159	6.91	6.91	2.61	1.85	1.72	1.59	1.17
Qinhuangdao	358	501	702	800	893	993	1,088	1,165	6.74	6.74	2.61	2.21	2.12	1.82	1.36
Qiqihaer	1,115	1,218	1,331	1,453	1,588	1,740	1,894	2,019	1.77	1.77	1.76	1.77	1.83	1.70	1.28
Quanzhou	174	356	728	898	1,068	1,238	1,367	1,462	14.34	14.34	4.19	3.46	2.95	1.99	1.34
Rizhao	248	390	613	715	816	922	1,014	1,086	9.03	9.03	3.08	2.65	2.44	1.90	1.37
Shanghai	7,823	10,171	13,224	15,184	16,575	17,840	19,094	20,017	5.25	5.25	2.76	1.75	1.47	1.36	0.94
Shantou	724	950	1,247	3,375	3,502	3,704	3,983	4,222	5.43	5.43	19.91	0.74	1.12	1.46	1.16

Table 4

City population and city population growth rate of urban agglomerations with 750,000 Inhabitants or more in 2009, by country, 1950–2025 (thousands)

| Country/City | City population of urban agglomerations ('000) | | | | | | | | City population growth rate of urban agglomerations (%) | | | | | | |
	1990	1995	2000	2005	2010	2015	2020	2025	1990–1995	1995–2000	2000–2005	2005–2010	2010–2015	2015–2020	2020–2025
Shaoguan	237	350	517	766	845	914	995	1,066	7.79	7.80	7.86	1.96	1.56	1.71	1.37
Shaoxing	181	332	608	731	853	977	1,077	1,153	12.09	12.09	3.69	3.08	2.71	1.96	1.37
Shenyang	3,651	4,081	4,562	4,788	5,166	5,650	6,108	6,457	2.23	2.23	0.96	1.52	1.79	1.56	1.11
Shenzhen	875	2,304	6,069	7,931	9,005	9,827	10,585	11,146	19.36	19.37	5.35	2.54	1.75	1.49	1.03
Shijiazhuang	1,372	1,621	1,914	2,192	2,487	2,789	3,044	3,235	3.33	3.33	2.71	2.52	2.30	1.75	1.22
Suzhou, Jiangsu	689	952	1,316	1,992	2,398	2,619	2,842	3,021	6.47	6.47	8.29	3.71	1.76	1.64	1.22
Taian, Shandong	367	577	910	1,073	1,239	1,409	1,548	1,653	9.09	9.09	3.30	2.88	2.57	1.89	1.31
Taichung	765	864	978	1,106	1,251	1,403	1,538	1,642	2.45	2.47	2.47	2.46	2.30	1.83	1.31
Tainan	669	697	723	750	777	825	895	959	0.79	0.76	0.71	0.72	1.19	1.64	1.38
Taipei	2,737	2,698	2,630	2,627	2,633	2,725	2,921	3,102	-0.29	-0.51	-0.02	0.04	0.68	1.39	1.20
Taiyuan, Shanxi	1,637	2,024	2,503	2,819	3,154	3,504	3,812	4,043	4.25	4.25	2.38	2.24	2.11	1.68	1.18
Taizhou, Jiangsu	158	290	535	662	795	928	1,028	1,101	12.23	12.24	4.24	3.66	3.10	2.05	1.38
Taizhou, Zhejiang	912	1,042	1,190	1,259	1,338	1,442	1,566	1,671	2.66	2.66	1.13	1.21	1.49	1.64	1.30
Tangshan, Hebei	996	1,177	1,390	1,614	1,870	2,130	2,335	2,487	3.33	3.33	2.99	2.95	2.59	1.85	1.26
Tianjin	4,558	5,513	6,670	7,278	7,884	8,559	9,216	9,713	3.81	3.81	1.75	1.60	1.64	1.48	1.05
Ürümqi (Wulumqi)	1,149	1,399	1,705	2,025	2,398	2,767	3,040	3,231	3.95	3.95	3.43	3.39	2.86	1.88	1.22
Weifang	634	885	1,235	1,457	1,698	1,941	2,131	2,271	6.67	6.67	3.31	3.06	2.67	1.87	1.27
Wenzhou	1,111	1,318	1,565	2,187	2,659	3,119	3,436	3,650	3.43	3.43	6.69	3.90	3.19	1.94	1.21
Wuhan	3,417	4,763	6,638	7,204	7,681	8,253	8,868	9,347	6.64	6.64	1.64	1.28	1.44	1.44	1.05
Wuhu, Anhui	442	529	634	759	908	1,057	1,169	1,252	3.60	3.60	3.60	3.59	3.04	2.02	1.36
Wuxi, Jiangsu	992	1,182	1,409	2,435	2,682	2,951	3,206	3,405	3.51	3.51	10.94	1.93	1.91	1.66	1.20
Xiamen	639	952	1,416	1,765	2,207	2,641	2,926	3,112	7.95	7.95	4.40	4.47	3.59	2.04	1.24
Xi'an, Shaanxi	2,157	2,821	3,690	4,382	4,747	5,038	5,414	5,726	5.37	5.37	3.43	1.60	1.19	1.44	1.12
Xiangfan, Hubei	554	685	847	1,278	1,399	1,536	1,674	1,786	4.25	4.25	8.21	1.81	1.87	1.72	1.30
Xiangtan, Hunan	456	564	698	806	926	1,050	1,155	1,236	4.25	4.25	2.88	2.78	2.52	1.91	1.36
Xianyang, Shaanxi	317	500	790	908	1,019	1,138	1,247	1,334	9.14	9.14	2.77	2.32	2.21	1.83	1.34
Xining	592	707	844	1,032	1,261	1,488	1,649	1,761	3.55	3.55	4.00	4.02	3.31	2.05	1.31
Xinxiang	450	586	762	884	1,016	1,152	1,267	1,355	5.26	5.26	2.96	2.79	2.52	1.90	1.34
Xuzhou	781	1,033	1,367	1,715	2,142	2,559	2,833	3,015	5.60	5.60	4.54	4.44	3.56	2.04	1.24
Yancheng, Jiangsu	392	513	671	1,071	1,289	1,474	1,622	1,731	5.38	5.38	9.33	3.72	2.68	1.91	1.31
Yangzhou	455	565	702	871	1,080	1,287	1,430	1,529	4.33	4.33	4.33	4.31	3.50	2.10	1.34
Yantai	422	717	1,218	1,383	1,526	1,684	1,836	1,958	10.59	10.59	2.55	1.97	1.97	1.73	1.28
Yichang	492	583	692	879	959	1,039	1,132	1,210	3.40	3.40	4.79	1.74	1.61	1.71	1.35
Yichun, Heilongjiang	855	835	815	796	779	795	856	917	-0.47	-0.47	-0.47	-0.45	0.43	1.47	1.37
Yinchuan	384	468	571	720	911	1,099	1,225	1,312	3.97	3.97	4.66	4.69	3.76	2.18	1.36
Yingkou	458	535	624	728	848	972	1,072	1,148	3.08	3.08	3.08	3.07	2.71	1.96	1.37
Yiyang, Hunan	191	360	678	760	820	892	974	1,043	12.69	12.69	2.26	1.52	1.70	1.74	1.37
Yueyang	305	518	881	997	1,096	1,206	1,317	1,408	10.62	10.62	2.47	1.89	1.93	1.76	1.33
Zaozhuang	303	508	853	1,014	1,175	1,339	1,473	1,574	10.36	10.36	3.45	2.95	2.62	1.90	1.32
Zhangjiakou	558	667	797	913	1,043	1,178	1,294	1,384	3.56	3.56	2.72	2.66	2.43	1.88	1.34
Zhanjiang	486	630	818	908	996	1,097	1,198	1,281	5.21	5.21	2.08	1.86	1.92	1.77	1.34
Zhengzhou	1,134	1,663	2,438	2,715	2,966	3,245	3,519	3,734	7.65	7.65	2.16	1.76	1.80	1.62	1.19
Zhenjiang, Jiangsu	328	472	679	832	1,007	1,181	1,308	1,399	7.27	7.27	4.06	3.82	3.19	2.04	1.35
Zhongshan	393	736	1,376	1,768	2,211	2,643	2,927	3,114	12.51	12.52	5.02	4.47	3.57	2.04	1.24

Table 4

City population and city population growth rate of urban agglomerations with 750,000 Inhabitants or more in 2009, by country, 1950–2025 (thousands)

Country/City	City population of urban agglomerations ('000)								City population growth rate of urban agglomerations (%)						
	1990	1995	2000	2005	2010	2015	2020	2025	1990–1995	1995–2000	2000–2005	2005–2010	2010–2015	2015–2020	2020–2025
Zhuhai	220	419	799	1,224	1,252	1,315	1,420	1,516	12.89	12.90	8.55	0.44	0.98	1.54	1.31
Zhuzhou	430	593	819	923	1,025	1,137	1,244	1,330	6.45	6.45	2.39	2.10	2.07	1.80	1.34
Zibo	777	1,207	1,874	2,168	2,456	2,752	3,004	3,192	8.80	8.80	2.92	2.49	2.28	1.75	1.22
Zigong	368	467	592	847	918	982	1,067	1,142	4.75	4.75	7.17	1.62	1.35	1.65	1.35
Zunyi	250	368	541	679	843	1,005	1,118	1,198	7.72	7.72	4.55	4.31	3.52	2.14	1.37
CHINA, HONG KONG SAR															
Hong Kong	5,677	6,214	6,667	6,883	7,069	7,398	7,701	7,969	1.81	1.41	0.64	0.54	0.91	0.80	0.68
COLOMBIA															
Barranquilla	1,229	1,363	1,531	1,719	1,867	2,015	2,145	2,255	2.06	2.32	2.32	1.65	1.53	1.25	1.00
Bogotá	4,740	5,494	6,356	7,353	8,500	9,521	10,129	10,537	2.95	2.92	2.91	2.90	2.27	1.24	0.79
Bucaramanga	650	759	855	964	1,092	1,213	1,303	1,375	3.08	2.39	2.39	2.49	2.11	1.43	1.08
Cali	1,552	1,757	1,950	2,164	2,401	2,627	2,800	2,938	2.48	2.08	2.08	2.08	1.80	1.28	0.97
Cartagena	561	645	737	842	962	1,076	1,158	1,223	2.77	2.68	2.67	2.66	2.23	1.47	1.10
Cúcuta	506	571	632	700	774	848	910	963	2.41	2.04	2.03	2.03	1.82	1.41	1.13
Medellín	2,135	2,372	2,724	3,127	3,594	4,019	4,294	4,494	2.11	2.76	2.76	2.78	2.24	1.33	0.91
CONGO															
Brazzaville	704	830	986	1,172	1,323	1,504	1,703	1,878	3.31	3.44	3.46	2.42	2.55	2.49	1.95
COSTA RICA															
San José	737	867	1,032	1,232	1,461	1,655	1,799	1,923	3.25	3.48	3.54	3.41	2.50	1.67	1.33
CÔTE D'IVOIRE															
Abidjan	2,102	2,535	3,032	3,564	4,125	4,788	5,550	6,321	3.74	3.58	3.24	2.92	2.98	2.95	2.60
Yamoussoukro	136	218	348	556	885	1,273	1,559	1,797	9.36	9.37	9.36	9.32	7.27	4.06	2.83
CUBA															
La Habana (Havana)	2,108	2,151	2,187	2,187	2,130	2,100	2,095	2,094	0.40	0.33	0.00	-0.53	-0.28	-0.05	-0.00
CZECH REPUBLIC															
Praha (Prague)	1,212	1,194	1,172	1,164	1,162	1,165	1,168	1,173	-0.29	-0.38	-0.14	-0.02	0.04	0.06	0.08
DEM. PEOPLE'S REPUBLIC OF KOREA															
P'yongyang	2,526	2,749	2,777	2,805	2,833	2,859	2,894	2,941	1.70	0.20	0.20	0.20	0.18	0.24	0.33
DEMOCRATIC REPUBLIC OF CONGO															
Kananga	353	451	552	705	878	1,087	1,324	1,583	4.92	4.03	4.89	4.40	4.26	3.95	3.57
Kinshasa	3,564	4,590	5,611	7,106	8,754	10,668	12,788	15,041	5.06	4.02	4.72	4.17	3.96	3.62	3.25
Kisangani	362	450	535	664	812	1,002	1,221	1,461	4.34	3.45	4.32	4.03	4.19	3.96	3.58
Lubumbashi	655	826	995	1,252	1,543	1,899	2,304	2,744	4.62	3.73	4.60	4.17	4.15	3.87	3.49
Mbuji-Mayi	580	749	924	1,190	1,488	1,838	2,232	2,658	5.09	4.20	5.06	4.48	4.22	3.88	3.50
DENMARK															
København (Copenhagen)	1,035	1,048	1,077	1,125	1,186	1,228	1,238	1,238	0.25	0.54	0.87	1.05	0.70	0.16	0.01
DOMINICAN REPUBLIC															
Santo Domingo	1,522	1,661	1,813	1,981	2,180	2,381	2,552	2,691	1.74	1.76	1.77	1.92	1.76	1.39	1.06
ECUADOR															
Guayaquil	1,572	1,808	2,077	2,386	2,690	2,941	3,153	3,328	2.80	2.78	2.77	2.39	1.79	1.39	1.08
Quito	1,088	1,217	1,357	1,593	1,846	2,035	2,188	2,316	2.25	2.18	3.20	2.95	1.95	1.45	1.13

Table 4

City population and city population growth rate of urban agglomerations with 750,000 Inhabitants or more in 2009, by country, 1950–2025 (thousands)

| Country/City | City population of urban agglomerations ('000) | | | | | | | | City population growth rate of urban agglomerations (%) | | | | | | |
	1990	1995	2000	2005	2010	2015	2020	2025	1990–1995	1995–2000	2000–2005	2005–2010	2010–2015	2015–2020	2020–2025
EGYPT															
Al-Iskandariyah (Alexandria)	3,063	3,277	3,592	3,973	4,387	4,791	5,201	5,648	1.35	1.83	2.02	1.98	1.76	1.64	1.65
Al-Qahirah (Cairo)	9,061	9,707	10,170	10,565	11,001	11,663	12,540	13,531	1.38	0.93	0.76	0.81	1.17	1.45	1.52
EL SALVADOR															
San Salvador	970	1,112	1,248	1,401	1,565	1,691	1,789	1,891	2.73	2.32	2.32	2.21	1.55	1.13	1.10
ETHIOPIA															
Addis Ababa	1,791	2,144	2,376	2,633	2,930	3,365	3,981	4,757	3.60	2.05	2.05	2.13	2.77	3.36	3.56
FINLAND															
Helsinki	871	943	1,019	1,067	1,117	1,153	1,170	1,174	1.58	1.56	0.92	0.91	0.65	0.28	0.07
FRANCE															
Bordeaux	698	730	763	799	838	875	899	913	0.88	0.89	0.93	0.95	0.86	0.55	0.29
Lille	961	984	1,004	1,015	1,033	1,066	1,092	1,107	0.47	0.41	0.22	0.35	0.62	0.50	0.26
Lyon	1,265	1,313	1,362	1,412	1,468	1,523	1,559	1,575	0.74	0.73	0.73	0.77	0.74	0.46	0.21
Marseille-Aix-en-Provence	1,305	1,331	1,363	1,413	1,469	1,524	1,560	1,577	0.39	0.48	0.73	0.77	0.74	0.46	0.21
Nice-Cannes	854	874	899	936	977	1,018	1,045	1,059	0.46	0.56	0.82	0.86	0.81	0.52	0.27
Paris	9,330	9,510	9,739	10,105	10,485	10,777	10,880	10,884	0.38	0.48	0.74	0.74	0.55	0.19	0.01
Toulouse	654	714	778	844	912	962	989	1,003	1.75	1.72	1.63	1.55	1.07	0.55	0.28
GEORGIA															
Tbilisi	1,224	1,160	1,100	1,093	1,120	1,136	1,138	1,138	-1.07	-1.07	-0.12	0.48	0.28	0.05	0.00
GERMANY															
Berlin	3,422	3,471	3,384	3,391	3,450	3,489	3,498	3,499	0.29	-0.51	0.04	0.34	0.23	0.05	0.00
Hamburg	1,639	1,707	1,710	1,739	1,786	1,818	1,825	1,825	0.81	0.04	0.34	0.53	0.35	0.08	0.00
Köln (Cologne)	950	965	963	976	1,001	1,015	1,018	1,018	0.31	-0.04	0.28	0.50	0.26	0.06	0.00
München (Munich)	1,218	1,241	1,202	1,254	1,349	1,401	1,412	1,413	0.37	-0.62	0.85	1.46	0.75	0.17	0.01
GHANA															
Accra	1,197	1,415	1,674	1,985	2,342	2,722	3,110	3,497	3.35	3.35	3.41	3.30	3.01	2.66	2.35
Kumasi	696	909	1,187	1,519	1,834	2,139	2,448	2,757	5.34	5.34	4.94	3.76	3.08	2.70	2.38
GREECE															
Athínai (Athens)	3,070	3,122	3,179	3,230	3,257	3,283	3,312	3,346	0.34	0.37	0.31	0.17	0.16	0.17	0.21
Thessaloniki	746	771	797	821	837	853	868	886	0.66	0.67	0.60	0.40	0.36	0.37	0.40
GUATEMALA															
Ciudad de Guatemala (Guatemala City)	803	839	908	984	1,104	1,281	1,481	1,690	0.89	1.57	1.62	2.30	2.97	2.90	2.64
GUINEA															
Conakry	895	1,045	1,219	1,411	1,653	2,004	2,427	2,906	3.11	3.08	2.92	3.17	3.84	3.83	3.61
HAITI															
Port-au-Prince	1,134	1,427	1,693	2,171	2,143	2,481	2,868	3,246	4.60	3.42	4.96	-0.25	2.93	2.90	2.48
HONDURAS															
Tegucigalpa	578	677	793	901	1,028	1,181	1,339	1,493	3.16	3.16	2.57	2.63	2.77	2.51	2.18
HUNGARY															
Budapest	2,005	1,893	1,787	1,698	1,706	1,711	1,711	1,711	-1.15	-1.15	-1.02	0.09	0.05	0.01	0.00

Table 4

City population and city population growth rate of urban agglomerations with 750,000 Inhabitants or more in 2009, by country, 1950–2025 (thousands)

Country/City	City population of urban agglomerations ('000)								City population growth rate of urban agglomerations (%)						
	1990	1995	2000	2005	2010	2015	2020	2025	1990–1995	1995–2000	2000–2005	2005–2010	2010–2015	2015–2020	2020–2025
INDIA															
Agra	933	1,095	1,293	1,511	1,703	1,886	2,089	2,313	3.20	3.32	3.13	2.38	2.04	2.04	2.04
Ahmadabad	3,255	3,790	4,427	5,122	5,717	6,277	6,892	7,567	3.04	3.11	2.92	2.20	1.87	1.87	1.87
Aligarh	468	554	653	763	863	960	1,068	1,189	3.39	3.29	3.11	2.44	2.14	2.14	2.14
Allahabad	830	928	1,035	1,152	1,277	1,415	1,570	1,742	2.23	2.17	2.15	2.06	2.05	2.08	2.08
Amritsar	726	844	990	1,152	1,297	1,439	1,597	1,771	3.00	3.20	3.02	2.37	2.08	2.08	2.08
Asansol	727	891	1,065	1,258	1,423	1,579	1,751	1,941	4.06	3.56	3.33	2.47	2.08	2.07	2.06
Aurangabad	568	708	868	1,049	1,198	1,331	1,478	1,641	4.38	4.09	3.79	2.65	2.12	2.09	2.09
Bangalore	4,036	4,744	5,567	6,465	7,218	7,913	8,674	9,507	3.23	3.20	2.99	2.20	1.84	1.84	1.83
Bareilly	604	664	722	787	868	963	1,072	1,192	1.87	1.67	1.73	1.95	2.09	2.14	2.13
Bhiwandi	362	479	603	745	859	957	1,066	1,186	5.62	4.60	4.23	2.84	2.18	2.14	2.14
Bhopal	1,046	1,228	1,426	1,644	1,843	2,039	2,257	2,497	3.21	3.00	2.85	2.28	2.02	2.03	2.03
Bhubaneswar	395	504	637	790	912	1,017	1,131	1,258	4.90	4.69	4.30	2.86	2.17	2.13	2.13
Chandigarh	564	667	791	928	1,049	1,166	1,296	1,440	3.36	3.40	3.20	2.46	2.11	2.11	2.11
Chennai (Madras)	5,338	5,836	6,353	6,919	7,547	8,253	9,043	9,909	1.78	1.70	1.71	1.74	1.79	1.83	1.83
Coimbatore	1,088	1,239	1,420	1,619	1,807	1,999	2,212	2,449	2.60	2.73	2.62	2.20	2.02	2.03	2.03
Delhi	9,726	12,407	15,730	19,493	22,157	24,160	26,272	28,568	4.87	4.75	4.29	2.56	1.73	1.68	1.68
Dhanbad	805	915	1,046	1,189	1,328	1,472	1,633	1,812	2.56	2.67	2.58	2.21	2.06	2.08	2.07
Durg-Bhilainagar	670	780	905	1,044	1,172	1,301	1,445	1,604	3.03	2.98	2.84	2.32	2.09	2.10	2.09
Guwahati (Gauhati)	564	675	797	932	1,053	1,170	1,300	1,445	3.60	3.32	3.14	2.43	2.11	2.11	2.11
Gwalior	706	779	855	940	1,039	1,152	1,280	1,423	1.97	1.88	1.90	1.99	2.07	2.11	2.11
Hubli-Dharwad	639	705	776	855	946	1,050	1,168	1,299	1.95	1.93	1.95	2.02	2.08	2.13	2.12
Hyderabad	4,193	4,825	5,445	6,117	6,751	7,396	8,110	8,894	2.81	2.42	2.33	1.97	1.83	1.85	1.84
Indore	1,088	1,314	1,597	1,914	2,173	2,405	2,659	2,939	3.77	3.91	3.62	2.54	2.03	2.01	2.00
Jabalpur	879	981	1,100	1,231	1,367	1,514	1,679	1,862	2.19	2.29	2.25	2.09	2.04	2.07	2.07
Jaipur	1,478	1,826	2,259	2,748	3,131	3,458	3,813	4,205	4.23	4.26	3.91	2.61	1.99	1.96	1.95
Jalandhar	502	588	694	811	917	1,020	1,134	1,262	3.16	3.31	3.13	2.44	2.13	2.13	2.13
Jammu	356	458	588	739	857	956	1,064	1,184	5.00	5.01	4.58	2.97	2.19	2.14	2.14
Jamshedpur	817	938	1,081	1,239	1,387	1,537	1,705	1,891	2.75	2.84	2.72	2.26	2.06	2.07	2.07
Jodhpur	654	743	842	951	1,061	1,177	1,308	1,454	2.54	2.51	2.44	2.18	2.09	2.11	2.11
Kanpur	2,001	2,294	2,641	3,020	3,364	3,706	4,084	4,501	2.73	2.82	2.68	2.16	1.93	1.94	1.94
Kochi (Cochin)	1,103	1,229	1,340	1,464	1,610	1,779	1,971	2,184	2.17	1.73	1.76	1.90	2.00	2.05	2.05
Kolkata (Calcutta)	10,890	11,924	13,058	14,284	15,552	16,924	18,449	20,112	1.82	1.82	1.79	1.70	1.69	1.73	1.73
Kota	523	604	692	789	884	982	1,093	1,216	2.89	2.71	2.62	2.26	2.12	2.14	2.13
Kozhikode (Calicut)	781	835	875	924	1,007	1,115	1,240	1,378	1.33	0.94	1.10	1.71	2.05	2.12	2.11
Lucknow	1,614	1,906	2,221	2,567	2,873	3,169	3,497	3,858	3.33	3.06	2.89	2.25	1.96	1.97	1.97
Ludhiana	1,006	1,183	1,368	1,572	1,760	1,947	2,156	2,387	3.24	2.91	2.78	2.26	2.03	2.04	2.03
Madurai	1,073	1,132	1,187	1,255	1,365	1,509	1,674	1,856	1.07	0.95	1.11	1.68	2.00	2.07	2.07
Meerut	824	975	1,143	1,328	1,494	1,656	1,836	2,035	3.36	3.18	3.00	2.35	2.06	2.06	2.06
Moradabad	436	520	626	744	845	941	1,048	1,166	3.53	3.68	3.45	2.56	2.15	2.14	2.14
Mumbai (Bombay)	12,308	14,111	16,086	18,205	20,041	21,797	23,719	25,810	2.73	2.62	2.48	1.92	1.68	1.69	1.69
Mysore	640	708	776	853	942	1,045	1,163	1,293	2.01	1.85	1.88	1.99	2.08	2.13	2.12
Nagpur	1,637	1,849	2,089	2,351	2,607	2,875	3,175	3,505	2.44	2.44	2.36	2.07	1.96	1.98	1.98
Nashik	700	886	1,117	1,381	1,588	1,763	1,954	2,165	4.71	4.63	4.24	2.79	2.09	2.05	2.05

Table 4

City population and city population growth rate of urban agglomerations with 750,000 Inhabitants or more in 2009, by country, 1950–2025 (thousands)

Country/City	City population of urban agglomerations ('000)								City population growth rate of urban agglomerations (%)						
	1990	1995	2000	2005	2010	2015	2020	2025	1990–1995	1995–2000	2000–2005	2005–2010	2010–2015	2015–2020	2020–2025
Patna	1,087	1,331	1,658	2,030	2,321	2,569	2,839	3,137	4.05	4.40	4.04	2.68	2.03	2.00	1.99
Pune (Poona)	2,430	2,978	3,655	4,412	5,002	5,505	6,050	6,649	4.07	4.09	3.76	2.51	1.92	1.89	1.89
Raipur	453	553	680	824	943	1,050	1,167	1,298	4.00	4.13	3.83	2.69	2.15	2.13	2.12
Rajkot	638	787	974	1,186	1,357	1,508	1,672	1,855	4.21	4.26	3.93	2.69	2.11	2.07	2.07
Ranchi	607	712	844	990	1,119	1,243	1,380	1,533	3.21	3.39	3.19	2.45	2.11	2.10	2.10
Salem	574	647	736	834	932	1,035	1,152	1,281	2.38	2.58	2.51	2.22	2.11	2.13	2.12
Solapur	613	720	853	1,002	1,133	1,258	1,398	1,552	3.20	3.41	3.21	2.45	2.10	2.10	2.10
Srinagar	730	833	954	1,088	1,216	1,349	1,497	1,662	2.62	2.72	2.62	2.23	2.07	2.09	2.09
Surat	1,468	1,984	2,699	3,558	4,168	4,607	5,071	5,579	6.01	6.16	5.53	3.16	2.01	1.92	1.91
Thiruvananthapuram	801	853	885	927	1,006	1,114	1,239	1,377	1.25	0.73	0.93	1.65	2.04	2.12	2.11
Tiruchirappalli	705	768	837	916	1,010	1,120	1,245	1,383	1.71	1.74	1.79	1.95	2.07	2.12	2.11
Tiruppur	299	392	523	678	795	888	989	1,101	5.43	5.73	5.19	3.19	2.22	2.15	2.15
Vadodara	1,096	1,273	1,465	1,676	1,872	2,071	2,292	2,536	2.99	2.81	2.69	2.22	2.02	2.03	2.03
Varanasi (Benares)	1,013	1,106	1,199	1,303	1,432	1,584	1,756	1,947	1.75	1.62	1.67	1.88	2.02	2.07	2.06
Vijayawada	821	914	999	1,095	1,207	1,337	1,484	1,647	2.14	1.79	1.82	1.95	2.05	2.09	2.09
Visakhapatnam	1,018	1,168	1,309	1,465	1,625	1,798	1,992	2,206	2.73	2.29	2.25	2.07	2.02	2.05	2.05
INDONESIA															
Bandar Lampung	454	578	743	790	799	842	903	972	4.84	5.01	1.22	0.23	1.03	1.41	1.47
Bandung	2,035	2,097	2,138	2,280	2,412	2,568	2,739	2,925	0.59	0.39	1.29	1.13	1.25	1.29	1.31
Bogor	596	668	751	880	1,044	1,162	1,251	1,344	2.26	2.36	3.17	3.41	2.14	1.48	1.43
Jakarta	8,175	8,322	8,390	8,795	9,210	9,709	10,256	10,850	0.36	0.16	0.94	0.92	1.05	1.10	1.13
Malang	689	725	757	773	786	830	891	959	1.03	0.88	0.40	0.35	1.08	1.42	1.48
Medan	1,718	1,816	1,912	2,023	2,131	2,266	2,419	2,586	1.11	1.03	1.13	1.04	1.23	1.30	1.33
Palembang	1,130	1,287	1,459	1,331	1,244	1,271	1,356	1,456	2.59	2.51	-1.83	-1.35	0.43	1.30	1.41
Pekan Baru	389	481	588	699	769	834	898	967	4.26	4.02	3.47	1.89	1.63	1.47	1.48
Semarang	1,243	1,333	1,427	1,359	1,296	1,334	1,424	1,528	1.40	1.36	-0.98	-0.94	0.57	1.31	1.41
Surabaya	2,467	2,544	2,611	2,623	2,509	2,576	2,738	2,923	0.62	0.51	0.09	-0.89	0.53	1.22	1.31
Ujung Pandang	816	918	1,031	1,159	1,294	1,409	1,512	1,621	2.35	2.34	2.34	2.21	1.69	1.41	1.40
IRAN (ISLAMIC REPUBLIC OF)															
Ahvaz	685	784	868	960	1,060	1,160	1,249	1,317	2.69	2.03	2.01	1.99	1.80	1.48	1.07
Esfahan	1,094	1,230	1,382	1,553	1,742	1,914	2,056	2,161	2.33	2.33	2.34	2.29	1.89	1.43	1.00
Karaj	693	903	1,087	1,317	1,584	1,796	1,937	2,038	5.30	3.70	3.84	3.69	2.52	1.52	1.01
Kermanshah	608	675	729	781	837	905	974	1,029	2.11	1.55	1.36	1.40	1.55	1.48	1.10
Mashhad	1,680	1,854	2,073	2,348	2,652	2,919	3,128	3,277	1.97	2.23	2.50	2.43	1.92	1.38	0.94
Qom	622	744	843	938	1,042	1,143	1,232	1,299	3.56	2.49	2.14	2.11	1.85	1.49	1.07
Shiraz	946	1,030	1,115	1,203	1,299	1,406	1,510	1,590	1.70	1.58	1.52	1.54	1.58	1.42	1.04
Tabriz	1,058	1,165	1,264	1,369	1,483	1,606	1,724	1,814	1.91	1.64	1.59	1.60	1.60	1.41	1.02
Tehran	6,365	6,687	6,880	7,044	7,241	7,614	8,059	8,387	0.99	0.57	0.47	0.55	1.00	1.14	0.80
IRAQ															
Al-Basrah (Basra)	474	631	759	837	923	1,023	1,139	1,267	5.71	3.68	1.96	1.96	2.05	2.15	2.14
Al-Mawsil (Mosul)	736	889	1,056	1,236	1,447	1,676	1,885	2,092	3.78	3.44	3.15	3.15	2.94	2.35	2.08
Baghdad	4,092	4,598	5,200	5,327	5,891	6,614	7,321	8,043	2.34	2.46	0.48	2.01	2.32	2.03	1.88
Irbil (Erbil)	536	644	757	874	1,009	1,158	1,301	1,447	3.65	3.23	2.88	2.88	2.74	2.33	2.13
Sulaimaniya	402	483	580	696	836	988	1,121	1,249	3.66	3.66	3.66	3.66	3.34	2.52	2.17

Table 4

City population and city population growth rate of urban agglomerations with 750,000 Inhabitants or more in 2009, by country, 1950–2025 (thousands)

Country/City	City population of urban agglomerations ('000)								City population growth rate of urban agglomerations (%)						
	1990	1995	2000	2005	2010	2015	2020	2025	1990–1995	1995–2000	2000–2005	2005–2010	2010–2015	2015–2020	2020–2025
IRELAND															
Dublin	916	946	989	1,037	1,099	1,179	1,261	1,337	0.65	0.87	0.96	1.15	1.42	1.34	1.17
ISRAEL															
Hefa (Haifa)	582	775	888	992	1,036	1,089	1,144	1,195	5.74	2.73	2.22	0.87	0.98	0.99	0.87
Jerusalem	522	610	651	712	782	850	901	944	3.12	1.31	1.76	1.89	1.66	1.17	0.92
Tel Aviv-Yafo (Tel Aviv-Jaffa)	2,026	2,442	2,752	3,012	3,272	3,515	3,689	3,823	3.73	2.39	1.81	1.65	1.44	0.96	0.71
ITALY															
Milano (Milan)	3,063	3,020	2,985	2,956	2,967	2,980	2,981	2,981	-0.28	-0.23	-0.19	0.07	0.09	0.00	0.00
Napoli (Naples)	2,208	2,218	2,232	2,248	2,276	2,292	2,293	2,293	0.09	0.13	0.14	0.24	0.14	0.01	0.00
Palermo	844	850	855	861	875	887	891	896	0.14	0.12	0.15	0.32	0.27	0.10	0.09
Roma (Rome)	3,450	3,425	3,385	3,352	3,362	3,375	3,376	3,376	-0.14	-0.24	-0.20	0.06	0.08	0.00	0.00
Torino (Turin)	1,775	1,733	1,694	1,662	1,665	1,678	1,679	1,680	-0.48	-0.45	-0.38	0.03	0.15	0.02	0.01
JAPAN															
Fukuoka-Kitakyushu	2,487	2,619	2,716	2,771	2,816	2,833	2,834	2,834	1.04	0.73	0.40	0.33	0.12	0.01	0.00
Hiroshima	1,986	2,040	2,044	2,063	2,081	2,088	2,088	2,088	0.54	0.04	0.19	0.17	0.06	0.01	0.00
Kyoto	1,760	1,804	1,806	1,805	1,804	1,804	1,804	1,804	0.49	0.02	-0.01	-0.01	-0.00	-0.00	—
Nagoya	2,947	3,055	3,122	3,199	3,267	3,292	3,295	3,295	0.71	0.44	0.49	0.42	0.15	0.02	0.00
Osaka-Kobe	11,035	11,052	11,165	11,258	11,337	11,365	11,368	11,368	0.03	0.20	0.17	0.14	0.05	0.01	0.00
Sapporo	2,319	2,476	2,508	2,601	2,687	2,718	2,721	2,721	1.31	0.26	0.73	0.65	0.23	0.02	0.00
Sendai	2,021	2,135	2,184	2,284	2,376	2,410	2,413	2,413	1.09	0.46	0.90	0.79	0.28	0.03	0.00
Tokyo	32,530	33,587	34,450	35,622	36,669	37,049	37,088	37,088	0.64	0.51	0.67	0.58	0.21	0.02	0.00
JORDAN															
Amman	851	973	1,007	1,042	1,105	1,186	1,272	1,364	2.67	0.68	0.68	1.19	1.41	1.39	1.40
KAZAKHSTAN															
Almaty	1,080	1,109	1,159	1,267	1,383	1,482	1,554	1,612	0.52	0.90	1.78	1.75	1.38	0.95	0.72
KENYA															
Mombasa	476	572	687	830	1,003	1,216	1,479	1,795	3.65	3.67	3.79	3.78	3.86	3.91	3.87
Nairobi	1,380	1,755	2,230	2,814	3,523	4,303	5,192	6,246	4.81	4.79	4.65	4.50	4.00	3.76	3.69
KUWAIT															
Al Kuwayt (Kuwait City)	1,392	1,190	1,499	1,888	2,305	2,592	2,790	2,956	-3.13	4.62	4.61	3.99	2.35	1.47	1.16
KYRGYZSTAN															
Bishkek	635	703	770	820	864	912	967	1,034	2.03	1.82	1.27	1.03	1.08	1.17	1.36
LAO PEOPLE'S DEMOCRATIC REPUBLIC															
Vientiane	451	533	612	702	831	1,035	1,270	1,501	3.32	2.75	2.75	3.39	4.39	4.08	3.35
LEBANON															
Bayrut (Beirut)	1,293	1,268	1,487	1,777	1,937	2,033	2,090	2,135	-0.39	3.19	3.57	1.72	0.97	0.55	0.42
LIBERIA															
Monrovia	1,042	464	836	1,202	827	728	807	932	-16.18	11.76	7.27	-7.47	-2.56	2.06	2.88
LIBYAN ARAB JAMAHIRIYA															
Tarabulus (Tripoli)	862	984	1,022	1,059	1,108	1,192	1,286	1,364	2.64	0.77	0.71	0.89	1.48	1.51	1.17
MADAGASCAR															
Antananarivo	948	1,169	1,361	1,590	1,879	2,235	2,658	3,148	4.20	3.04	3.10	3.34	3.47	3.46	3.39

Table 4

City population and city population growth rate of urban agglomerations with 750,000 Inhabitants or more in 2009, by country, 1950–2025 (thousands)

Country/City	City population of urban agglomerations ('000)								City population growth rate of urban agglomerations (%)						
	1990	1995	2000	2005	2010	2015	2020	2025	1990–1995	1995–2000	2000–2005	2005–2010	2010–2015	2015–2020	2020–2025
MALAWI															
Blantyre-Limbe	370	446	538	667	856	1,103	1,407	1,766	3.73	3.74	4.30	4.99	5.06	4.87	4.55
Lilongwe	266	362	493	662	865	1,115	1,422	1,784	6.17	6.17	5.89	5.35	5.08	4.87	4.54
MALAYSIA															
Johore Bharu	417	516	630	797	999	1,175	1,295	1,382	4.28	4.01	4.68	4.53	3.25	1.94	1.31
Klang	345	466	631	849	1,128	1,361	1,503	1,603	6.01	6.07	5.93	5.68	3.75	1.99	1.29
Kuala Lumpur	1,120	1,213	1,306	1,405	1,519	1,670	1,820	1,938	1.58	1.47	1.47	1.56	1.89	1.72	1.26
MALI															
Bamako	746	910	1,110	1,368	1,699	2,086	2,514	2,971	3.96	3.97	4.19	4.32	4.11	3.73	3.35
MEXICO															
Aguascalientes	552	631	734	829	926	995	1,039	1,073	2.69	3.02	2.42	2.23	1.43	0.86	0.66
Chihuahua	539	625	683	760	840	899	939	971	2.94	1.77	2.15	2.00	1.36	0.87	0.67
Ciudad de México (Mexico City)	15,312	16,811	18,022	18,735	19,460	20,078	20,476	20,713	1.87	1.39	0.78	0.76	0.62	0.39	0.23
Ciudad Juárez	809	997	1,225	1,308	1,394	1,470	1,528	1,575	4.19	4.11	1.32	1.28	1.05	0.77	0.60
Culiacán	606	690	749	791	836	881	918	950	2.60	1.63	1.10	1.11	1.04	0.84	0.68
Guadalajara	3,011	3,431	3,703	4,051	4,402	4,648	4,796	4,902	2.61	1.53	1.80	1.66	1.08	0.63	0.44
Hermosillo	454	552	616	697	781	840	878	909	3.89	2.19	2.48	2.28	1.46	0.89	0.68
León de los Aldamas	961	1,127	1,290	1,429	1,571	1,673	1,739	1,791	3.19	2.70	2.04	1.90	1.26	0.78	0.58
Mérida	664	765	848	931	1,015	1,081	1,127	1,164	2.83	2.06	1.85	1.74	1.25	0.83	0.65
Mexicali	607	690	770	851	934	997	1,040	1,075	2.57	2.21	1.99	1.86	1.30	0.85	0.66
Monterrey	2,594	2,961	3,266	3,579	3,896	4,118	4,253	4,351	2.65	1.96	1.83	1.70	1.11	0.65	0.46
Puebla	1,686	1,692	1,907	2,109	2,315	2,460	2,551	2,620	0.07	2.40	2.02	1.86	1.22	0.72	0.53
Querétaro	561	671	795	911	1,031	1,111	1,160	1,198	3.58	3.39	2.71	2.47	1.51	0.86	0.64
Saltillo	491	577	643	720	801	859	897	928	3.21	2.16	2.28	2.11	1.40	0.88	0.68
San Luis Potosí	665	774	858	952	1,049	1,120	1,168	1,206	3.04	2.06	2.09	1.94	1.32	0.84	0.64
Tampico	563	609	659	709	761	806	842	871	1.54	1.60	1.46	1.41	1.16	0.86	0.69
Tijuana	760	1,017	1,287	1,472	1,664	1,789	1,861	1,915	5.82	4.71	2.69	2.44	1.45	0.79	0.58
Toluca de Lerdo	835	981	1,417	1,498	1,582	1,661	1,725	1,776	3.22	7.35	1.11	1.10	0.98	0.75	0.59
Torreón	882	954	1,014	1,105	1,199	1,273	1,325	1,367	1.55	1.22	1.73	1.63	1.19	0.81	0.62
MONGOLIA															
Ulaanbaatar	572	661	764	873	966	1,050	1,129	1,202	2.90	2.90	2.67	2.03	1.66	1.47	1.25
MOROCCO															
Agadir	403	536	609	693	783	869	948	1,020	5.70	2.58	2.57	2.44	2.07	1.75	1.46
Dar-el-Beida (Casablanca)	2,682	2,951	3,043	3,138	3,284	3,537	3,816	4,065	1.91	0.62	0.62	0.91	1.49	1.52	1.26
Fès	685	785	870	963	1,065	1,173	1,277	1,371	2.72	2.04	2.04	2.02	1.92	1.70	1.42
Marrakech	578	681	755	837	928	1,023	1,114	1,198	3.26	2.07	2.07	2.06	1.95	1.72	1.44
Rabat	1,174	1,379	1,507	1,647	1,802	1,973	2,139	2,288	3.22	1.77	1.77	1.80	1.81	1.62	1.35
Tanger	423	510	591	686	788	877	958	1,030	3.73	2.98	2.98	2.75	2.16	1.75	1.46
MOZAMBIQUE															
Maputo	776	921	1,096	1,341	1,655	1,994	2,350	2,722	3.43	3.47	4.03	4.21	3.73	3.29	2.94
Matola	319	401	504	636	793	961	1,139	1,326	4.55	4.56	4.68	4.41	3.84	3.39	3.04

Table 4

City population and city population growth rate of urban agglomerations with 750,000 Inhabitants or more in 2009, by country, 1950–2025 (thousands)

Country/City	City population of urban agglomerations ('000)								City population growth rate of urban agglomerations (%)						
	1990	1995	2000	2005	2010	2015	2020	2025	1990–1995	1995–2000	2000–2005	2005–2010	2010–2015	2015–2020	2020–2025
MYANMAR															
Mandalay	636	718	810	915	1,034	1,176	1,331	1,484	2.43	2.43	2.43	2.45	2.57	2.48	2.18
Nay Pyi Taw	—	—	—	57	1,024	1,185	1,344	1,499	—	—	—	57.77	2.92	2.52	2.18
Yangon	2,907	3,213	3,553	3,928	4,350	4,873	5,456	6,022	2.01	2.01	2.01	2.04	2.27	2.26	1.98
NEPAL															
Kathmandu	398	509	644	817	1,037	1,295	1,589	1,915	4.92	4.70	4.76	4.78	4.44	4.10	3.73
NETHERLANDS															
Amsterdam	936	988	1,005	1,023	1,049	1,076	1,097	1,110	1.09	0.34	0.37	0.49	0.50	0.40	0.23
Rotterdam	951	981	991	1,000	1,010	1,026	1,044	1,057	0.62	0.19	0.19	0.19	0.31	0.36	0.24
NEW ZEALAND															
Auckland	870	976	1,063	1,189	1,404	1,566	1,631	1,671	2.30	1.71	2.24	3.33	2.17	0.82	0.48
NICARAGUA															
Managua	735	865	887	909	944	1,015	1,103	1,192	3.26	0.50	0.50	0.74	1.46	1.67	1.54
NIGER															
Niamey	432	542	680	848	1,048	1,302	1,643	2,105	4.54	4.55	4.42	4.22	4.35	4.65	4.96
NIGERIA															
Aba	484	545	614	691	785	914	1,058	1,203	2.38	2.38	2.38	2.55	3.04	2.93	2.57
Abuja	330	526	832	1,315	1,995	2,563	2,977	3,361	9.31	9.16	9.16	8.33	5.01	3.00	2.43
Benin City	689	845	975	1,124	1,302	1,523	1,758	1,992	4.08	2.85	2.85	2.95	3.13	2.88	2.50
Ibadan	1,739	1,993	2,236	2,509	2,837	3,276	3,760	4,237	2.73	2.30	2.30	2.46	2.88	2.75	2.39
Ilorin	515	580	653	735	835	972	1,125	1,279	2.38	2.38	2.38	2.55	3.03	2.92	2.56
Jos	493	556	627	706	802	934	1,081	1,229	2.39	2.39	2.39	2.56	3.04	2.93	2.57
Kaduna	961	1,083	1,220	1,375	1,561	1,811	2,087	2,362	2.39	2.39	2.39	2.55	2.97	2.84	2.48
Kano	2,095	2,360	2,658	2,993	3,395	3,922	4,495	5,060	2.38	2.38	2.38	2.52	2.89	2.73	2.37
Lagos	4,764	5,966	7,233	8,767	10,578	12,427	14,162	15,810	4.50	3.85	3.85	3.76	3.22	2.61	2.20
Maiduguri	598	673	758	854	970	1,127	1,303	1,480	2.37	2.37	2.37	2.54	3.01	2.90	2.54
Ogbomosho	622	704	798	904	1,032	1,201	1,389	1,576	2.49	2.49	2.49	2.65	3.04	2.90	2.53
Port Harcourt	680	766	863	972	1,104	1,283	1,482	1,681	2.38	2.38	2.38	2.55	3.00	2.88	2.52
Zaria	592	667	752	847	963	1,120	1,295	1,471	2.39	2.39	2.39	2.56	3.02	2.90	2.54
NORWAY															
Oslo	684	729	774	818	888	946	985	1,019	1.28	1.19	1.12	1.64	1.25	0.82	0.68
PAKISTAN															
Faisalabad	1,520	1,804	2,140	2,496	2,849	3,252	3,704	4,200	3.43	3.41	3.08	2.64	2.65	2.60	2.51
Gujranwala	848	1,019	1,224	1,441	1,652	1,893	2,165	2,464	3.69	3.67	3.26	2.74	2.72	2.68	2.59
Hyderabad	950	1,077	1,222	1,394	1,590	1,822	2,084	2,373	2.51	2.52	2.64	2.64	2.73	2.68	2.60
Islamabad	343	452	595	737	856	985	1,132	1,295	5.54	5.47	4.28	3.00	2.83	2.77	2.68
Karachi	7,147	8,467	10,021	11,618	13,125	14,818	16,693	18,725	3.39	3.37	2.96	2.44	2.43	2.38	2.30
Lahore	3,970	4,653	5,449	6,294	7,132	8,087	9,150	10,308	3.17	3.16	2.88	2.50	2.51	2.47	2.38
Multan	953	1,097	1,263	1,453	1,659	1,901	2,174	2,474	2.82	2.83	2.80	2.66	2.72	2.68	2.59
Peshawar	769	905	1,066	1,242	1,422	1,632	1,868	2,128	3.27	3.27	3.05	2.72	2.74	2.70	2.61
Quetta	414	504	614	729	841	968	1,113	1,272	3.96	3.93	3.45	2.85	2.82	2.78	2.69
Rawalpindi	1,087	1,286	1,520	1,772	2,026	2,318	2,646	3,008	3.36	3.34	3.07	2.68	2.69	2.65	2.56

Table 4

City population and city population growth rate of urban agglomerations with 750,000 Inhabitants or more in 2009, by country, 1950–2025 (thousands)

Country/City	City population of urban agglomerations ('000)								City population growth rate of urban agglomerations (%)						
	1990	1995	2000	2005	2010	2015	2020	2025	1990–1995	1995–2000	2000–2005	2005–2010	2010–2015	2015–2020	2020–2025
PANAMA															
Ciudad de Panamá (Panama City)	847	953	1,072	1,216	1,378	1,527	1,652	1,758	2.36	2.36	2.51	2.51	2.04	1.59	1.24
PARAGUAY															
Asunción	1,091	1,287	1,507	1,762	2,030	2,277	2,505	2,715	3.32	3.15	3.13	2.83	2.30	1.91	1.61
PERU															
Arequipa	564	628	678	732	789	848	903	953	2.17	1.52	1.52	1.52	1.43	1.25	1.09
Lima	5,837	6,582	7,294	8,081	8,941	9,659	10,145	10,530	2.40	2.05	2.05	2.02	1.55	0.98	0.75
PHILIPPINES															
Cebu	612	661	721	787	860	945	1,046	1,162	1.53	1.75	1.76	1.77	1.89	2.04	2.09
Davao	854	1,001	1,152	1,325	1,519	1,701	1,881	2,080	3.17	2.81	2.80	2.72	2.27	2.02	2.01
Manila	7,973	9,401	9,958	10,761	11,628	12,587	13,687	14,916	3.30	1.15	1.55	1.55	1.58	1.68	1.72
Zamboanga	444	509	605	721	854	973	1,082	1,201	2.71	3.47	3.50	3.38	2.61	2.13	2.09
POLAND															
Kraków (Cracow)	735	748	756	757	756	756	756	756	0.35	0.21	0.04	-0.03	-0.01	-0.00	-0.00
Warszawa (Warsaw)	1,628	1,652	1,666	1,693	1,712	1,720	1,722	1,722	0.29	0.17	0.33	0.22	0.09	0.02	0.00
PORTUGAL															
Lisboa (Lisbon)	2,537	2,600	2,672	2,747	2,824	2,907	2,973	3,009	0.49	0.55	0.55	0.55	0.58	0.45	0.24
Porto	1,164	1,206	1,254	1,303	1,355	1,407	1,448	1,473	0.72	0.77	0.77	0.77	0.76	0.57	0.35
PUERTO RICO															
San Juan	1,539	1,855	2,237	2,601	2,743	2,763	2,763	2,763	3.74	3.74	3.01	1.07	0.14	0.00	—
REPUBLIC OF KOREA															
Bucheon	651	771	763	833	909	948	960	961	3.39	-0.23	1.77	1.73	0.85	0.24	0.03
Busan	3,778	3,813	3,673	3,533	3,425	3,407	3,409	3,409	0.18	-0.75	-0.78	-0.62	-0.11	0.01	0.00
Daegu	2,215	2,434	2,478	2,466	2,458	2,474	2,481	2,481	1.88	0.36	-0.10	-0.06	0.12	0.06	0.00
Daejon	1,036	1,256	1,362	1,438	1,509	1,550	1,562	1,562	3.85	1.62	1.09	0.97	0.54	0.15	0.01
Goyang	241	493	744	859	961	1,012	1,025	1,026	14.28	8.25	2.88	2.23	1.03	0.25	0.02
Gwangju	1,122	1,249	1,346	1,413	1,476	1,513	1,524	1,525	2.16	1.49	0.97	0.86	0.50	0.15	0.01
Incheon	1,785	2,271	2,464	2,527	2,583	2,621	2,630	2,631	4.82	1.62	0.51	0.43	0.29	0.07	0.00
Seongnam	534	842	911	934	955	974	983	984	9.10	1.59	0.48	0.45	0.39	0.19	0.02
Seoul	10,544	10,256	9,917	9,825	9,773	9,767	9,767	9,767	-0.55	-0.67	-0.19	-0.11	-0.01	-0.00	-0.00
Suweon	628	748	932	1,037	1,132	1,180	1,193	1,194	3.50	4.42	2.13	1.74	0.84	0.21	0.01
Ulsan	673	945	1,011	1,047	1,081	1,106	1,116	1,117	6.80	1.36	0.69	0.65	0.45	0.18	0.02
ROMANIA															
Bucuresti (Bucharest)	2,040	2,018	1,949	1,931	1,934	1,947	1,959	1,963	-0.21	-0.69	-0.19	0.03	0.12	0.13	0.05
RUSSIAN FEDERATION															
Chelyabinsk	1,129	1,104	1,082	1,094	1,094	1,095	1,095	1,095	-0.45	-0.40	0.21	0.01	0.01	0.00	0.00
Kazan	1,092	1,092	1,096	1,112	1,140	1,159	1,164	1,164	-0.01	0.07	0.29	0.49	0.35	0.08	0.00
Krasnoyarsk	910	911	911	920	961	991	998	999	0.02	0.02	0.18	0.88	0.62	0.14	0.01
Moskva (Moscow)	8,987	9,201	10,005	10,418	10,550	10,641	10,662	10,663	0.47	1.67	0.81	0.25	0.17	0.04	0.00
Nizhniy Novgorod	1,420	1,375	1,331	1,286	1,267	1,256	1,253	1,253	-0.65	-0.65	-0.69	-0.29	-0.19	-0.04	-0.00
Novosibirsk	1,430	1,428	1,426	1,400	1,397	1,397	1,398	1,398	-0.03	-0.03	-0.38	-0.04	0.00	0.00	0.00
Omsk	1,144	1,140	1,136	1,140	1,124	1,114	1,112	1,112	-0.07	-0.07	0.08	-0.28	-0.18	-0.04	-0.00
Perm	1,076	1,044	1,014	992	982	974	972	972	-0.59	-0.59	-0.43	-0.20	-0.16	-0.04	-0.00
Rostov-na-Donu (Rostov-on-Don)	1,022	1,041	1,061	1,056	1,046	1,040	1,038	1,038	0.38	0.38	-0.10	-0.19	-0.12	-0.03	-0.00

Table 4

City population and city population growth rate of urban agglomerations with 750,000 Inhabitants or more in 2009, by country, 1950–2025 (thousands)

Country/City	City population of urban agglomerations ('000)								City population growth rate of urban agglomerations (%)						
	1990	1995	2000	2005	2010	2015	2020	2025	1990–1995	1995–2000	2000–2005	2005–2010	2010–2015	2015–2020	2020–2025
Samara	1,244	1,208	1,173	1,146	1,131	1,121	1,119	1,119	-0.58	-0.58	-0.48	-0.27	-0.16	-0.04	-0.00
Sankt Peterburg (Saint Petersburg)	4,989	4,836	4,719	4,598	4,575	4,561	4,557	4,557	-0.62	-0.49	-0.52	-0.10	-0.06	-0.01	-0.00
Saratov	901	890	878	853	822	802	798	797	-0.25	-0.25	-0.60	-0.74	-0.49	-0.11	-0.01
Ufa	1,078	1,063	1,049	1,032	1,023	1,017	1,016	1,016	-0.27	-0.27	-0.33	-0.18	-0.10	-0.02	-0.00
Volgograd	999	1,005	1,010	994	977	967	965	964	0.11	0.11	-0.32	-0.34	-0.21	-0.05	-0.00
Voronezh	880	867	854	847	842	839	838	838	-0.30	-0.30	-0.17	-0.12	-0.07	-0.02	-0.00
Yekaterinburg	1,350	1,326	1,303	1,307	1,344	1,370	1,376	1,377	-0.35	-0.35	0.06	0.56	0.39	0.09	0.00
RWANDA															
Kigali	219	278	497	775	939	1,138	1,392	1,690	4.77	11.63	8.86	3.85	3.84	4.02	3.88
SAUDI ARABIA															
Ad-Dammam	409	533	639	766	902	1,013	1,109	1,197	5.30	3.63	3.62	3.26	2.33	1.80	1.53
Al-Madinah (Medina)	529	669	795	944	1,104	1,236	1,351	1,456	4.69	3.45	3.45	3.12	2.27	1.77	1.50
Ar-Riyadh (Riyadh)	2,325	3,035	3,567	4,193	4,848	5,373	5,809	6,196	5.33	3.23	3.23	2.90	2.06	1.56	1.29
Jiddah	1,742	2,200	2,509	2,860	3,234	3,569	3,868	4,138	4.66	2.63	2.62	2.46	1.97	1.61	1.35
Makkah (Mecca)	856	1,033	1,168	1,319	1,484	1,642	1,789	1,924	3.76	2.45	2.45	2.35	2.02	1.72	1.46
SENEGAL															
Dakar	1,405	1,688	2,029	2,434	2,863	3,308	3,796	4,338	3.67	3.68	3.64	3.25	2.89	2.75	2.67
SERBIA															
Beograd (Belgrade)	1,130	1,128	1,122	1,116	1,117	1,131	1,149	1,168	-0.03	-0.11	-0.11	0.03	0.25	0.31	0.32
SIERRA LEONE															
Freetown	529	603	688	785	901	1,046	1,219	1,420	2.62	2.63	2.62	2.76	2.99	3.06	3.05
SINGAPORE															
Singapore	3,016	3,480	4,018	4,267	4,837	5,059	5,219	5,362	2.86	2.88	1.20	2.51	0.90	0.63	0.54
SOMALIA															
Muqdisho (Mogadishu)	1,035	1,147	1,201	1,415	1,500	1,795	2,156	2,588	2.04	0.92	3.28	1.17	3.59	3.67	3.66
SOUTH AFRICA															
Cape Town	2,155	2,394	2,715	3,091	3,405	3,579	3,701	3,824	2.10	2.52	2.59	1.93	1.00	0.67	0.65
Durban	1,723	2,081	2,370	2,638	2,879	3,026	3,133	3,241	3.77	2.60	2.15	1.75	1.00	0.69	0.68
Ekurhuleni (East Rand)	1,531	1,894	2,326	2,824	3,202	3,380	3,497	3,614	4.26	4.11	3.88	2.51	1.08	0.68	0.66
Johannesburg	1,898	2,265	2,732	3,263	3,670	3,867	3,996	4,127	3.53	3.75	3.55	2.35	1.05	0.66	0.64
Port Elizabeth	828	911	958	1,002	1,068	1,126	1,173	1,222	1.93	1.00	0.90	1.27	1.06	0.83	0.82
Pretoria	911	951	1,084	1,274	1,429	1,514	1,575	1,637	0.85	2.61	3.24	2.29	1.16	0.79	0.77
Vereeniging	743	800	897	1,029	1,143	1,211	1,262	1,313	1.48	2.30	2.75	2.09	1.16	0.82	0.81
SPAIN															
Barcelona	4,101	4,318	4,560	4,815	5,083	5,315	5,443	5,477	1.03	1.09	1.09	1.09	0.89	0.48	0.12
Madrid	4,414	4,688	5,014	5,409	5,851	6,213	6,379	6,412	1.20	1.35	1.52	1.57	1.20	0.53	0.10
Valencia	776	785	795	804	814	832	857	873	0.25	0.24	0.24	0.24	0.44	0.58	0.38
SUDAN															
Al-Khartum (Khartoum)	2,360	3,242	3,949	4,518	5,172	6,046	7,005	7,953	6.35	3.95	2.69	2.70	3.12	2.95	2.54
SWEDEN															
Stockholm	1,038	1,138	1,206	1,248	1,285	1,309	1,327	1,345	1.83	1.16	0.69	0.59	0.36	0.28	0.26
SWITZERLAND															
Zürich (Zurich)	1,006	1,048	1,078	1,114	1,150	1,177	1,196	1,217	0.83	0.56	0.65	0.64	0.45	0.32	0.35

Table 4

City population and city population growth rate of urban agglomerations with 750,000 Inhabitants or more in 2009, by country, 1950–2025 (thousands)

Country/City	City population of urban agglomerations ('000)								City population growth rate of urban agglomerations (%)						
	1990	1995	2000	2005	2010	2015	2020	2025	1990–1995	1995–2000	2000–2005	2005–2010	2010–2015	2015–2020	2020–2025
SYRIAN ARAB REPUBLIC															
Dimashq (Damascus)	1,691	1,854	2,063	2,294	2,597	2,918	3,213	3,534	1.85	2.13	2.13	2.48	2.33	1.93	1.90
Halab (Aleppo)	1,554	1,864	2,204	2,605	3,087	3,510	3,864	4,244	3.64	3.35	3.35	3.39	2.57	1.92	1.88
Hamah	309	361	495	676	897	1,060	1,180	1,307	3.12	6.27	6.26	5.65	3.34	2.14	2.05
Hims (Homs)	565	684	856	1,072	1,328	1,536	1,702	1,881	3.83	4.49	4.49	4.29	2.91	2.06	1.99
THAILAND															
Krung Thep (Bangkok)	5,888	6,106	6,332	6,614	6,976	7,399	7,902	8,470	0.73	0.73	0.87	1.07	1.18	1.31	1.39
TOGO															
Lomé	619	795	1,020	1,310	1,667	2,036	2,398	2,763	5.00	5.00	5.00	4.82	4.00	3.27	2.84
TUNISIA															
Tunis	644	682	711	734	767	814	864	911	1.16	0.84	0.63	0.87	1.21	1.19	1.04
TURKEY															
Adana	907	1,011	1,123	1,245	1,361	1,465	1,556	1,635	2.18	2.10	2.06	1.79	1.46	1.21	0.99
Ankara	2,561	2,842	3,179	3,572	3,906	4,174	4,401	4,591	2.08	2.25	2.33	1.79	1.33	1.06	0.85
Antalya	370	471	595	736	838	909	969	1,022	4.83	4.67	4.26	2.62	1.61	1.28	1.06
Bursa	819	981	1,180	1,413	1,588	1,711	1,816	1,906	3.62	3.69	3.60	2.33	1.50	1.19	0.97
Gaziantep	595	710	844	992	1,109	1,197	1,274	1,341	3.54	3.47	3.22	2.22	1.53	1.24	1.02
Istanbul	6,552	7,665	8,744	9,710	10,525	11,164	11,689	12,108	3.14	2.63	2.10	1.61	1.18	0.92	0.70
Izmir	1,741	1,966	2,216	2,487	2,723	2,917	3,083	3,224	2.43	2.39	2.31	1.81	1.38	1.11	0.90
Konya	508	610	734	871	978	1,057	1,125	1,186	3.66	3.69	3.42	2.31	1.56	1.26	1.04
UGANDA															
Kampala	755	912	1,097	1,318	1,598	1,982	2,504	3,189	3.79	3.68	3.68	3.85	4.31	4.67	4.83
UKRAINE															
Dnipropetrovsk	1,162	1,119	1,077	1,052	1,004	974	967	967	-0.77	-0.77	-0.47	-0.93	-0.61	-0.14	-0.01
Donetsk	1,097	1,061	1,026	997	966	946	941	941	-0.67	-0.67	-0.57	-0.64	-0.41	-0.09	-0.01
Kharkiv	1,586	1,534	1,484	1,464	1,453	1,446	1,444	1,444	-0.66	-0.66	-0.28	-0.15	-0.10	-0.02	-0.00
Kyiv (Kiev)	2,574	2,590	2,606	2,673	2,805	2,894	2,914	2,915	0.13	0.13	0.51	0.96	0.63	0.14	0.01
Odesa	1,092	1,064	1,037	1,007	1,009	1,010	1,011	1,011	-0.52	-0.52	-0.57	0.04	0.02	0.01	0.00
Zaporizhzhya	873	847	822	797	775	761	758	758	-0.60	-0.60	-0.61	-0.56	-0.36	-0.08	-0.00
UNITED ARAB EMIRATES															
Dubayy (Dubai)	473	650	906	1,264	1,567	1,772	1,934	2,076	6.36	6.64	6.67	4.30	2.46	1.76	1.42
Sharjah	229	311	444	637	809	926	1,016	1,096	6.11	7.12	7.22	4.78	2.69	1.86	1.51
UNITED KINGDOM															
Birmingham	2,301	2,291	2,285	2,283	2,302	2,337	2,375	2,415	-0.09	-0.05	-0.02	0.17	0.30	0.32	0.33
Glasgow	1,217	1,186	1,171	1,160	1,170	1,193	1,218	1,245	-0.52	-0.26	-0.19	0.17	0.39	0.42	0.43
Liverpool	831	829	818	811	819	837	857	878	-0.05	-0.26	-0.18	0.21	0.44	0.47	0.48
London	7,654	7,908	8,225	8,506	8,631	8,693	8,753	8,816	0.65	0.79	0.67	0.29	0.14	0.14	0.14
Manchester	2,282	2,264	2,248	2,237	2,253	2,287	2,325	2,364	-0.16	-0.14	-0.10	0.14	0.30	0.33	0.33
Newcastle upon Tyne	877	883	880	880	891	911	932	954	0.14	-0.07	-0.01	0.26	0.43	0.46	0.47
West Yorkshire	1,449	1,468	1,495	1,521	1,547	1,575	1,606	1,637	0.27	0.36	0.34	0.34	0.37	0.38	0.39
UNITED REPUBLIC OF TANZANIA															
Dar es Salaam	1,316	1,668	2,116	2,680	3,349	4,153	5,103	6,202	4.75	4.75	4.73	4.46	4.30	4.12	3.90

Table 4

City population and city population growth rate of urban agglomerations with 750,000 Inhabitants or more in 2009, by country, 1950–2025 (thousands)

Country/City	City population of urban agglomerations ('000)								City population growth rate of urban agglomerations (%)						
	1990	1995	2000	2005	2010	2015	2020	2025	1990–1995	1995–2000	2000–2005	2005–2010	2010–2015	2015–2020	2020–2025
UNITED STATES OF AMERICA															
Atlanta	2,184	2,781	3,542	4,306	4,691	4,886	5,036	5,153	4.84	4.84	3.90	1.72	0.81	0.60	0.46
Austin	569	720	913	1,107	1,215	1,277	1,329	1,373	4.73	4.73	3.87	1.85	1.00	0.80	0.65
Baltimore	1,849	1,962	2,083	2,206	2,320	2,421	2,508	2,579	1.19	1.19	1.15	1.01	0.85	0.70	0.56
Boston	3,428	3,726	4,049	4,363	4,593	4,773	4,920	5,034	1.66	1.66	1.49	1.03	0.77	0.61	0.46
Bridgeport-Stamford	714	799	894	987	1,055	1,108	1,154	1,193	2.25	2.25	1.99	1.32	0.98	0.82	0.67
Buffalo	955	966	977	1,000	1,045	1,096	1,142	1,181	0.23	0.23	0.45	0.89	0.95	0.82	0.67
Charlotte	461	596	769	946	1,043	1,098	1,144	1,183	5.10	5.10	4.16	1.94	1.03	0.82	0.67
Chicago	7,374	7,839	8,333	8,818	9,204	9,513	9,758	9,936	1.22	1.22	1.13	0.86	0.66	0.51	0.36
Cincinnati	1,335	1,419	1,508	1,600	1,686	1,764	1,831	1,887	1.22	1.22	1.19	1.05	0.90	0.75	0.60
Cleveland	1,680	1,734	1,789	1,856	1,942	2,029	2,104	2,166	0.63	0.63	0.73	0.90	0.87	0.73	0.58
Columbus, Ohio	950	1,040	1,138	1,236	1,313	1,376	1,432	1,478	1.81	1.81	1.65	1.21	0.95	0.79	0.64
Dallas-Fort Worth	3,219	3,665	4,172	4,657	4,951	5,145	5,301	5,421	2.59	2.59	2.20	1.22	0.77	0.60	0.45
Dayton	616	659	706	754	800	841	878	909	1.37	1.37	1.33	1.17	1.01	0.86	0.71
Denver-Aurora	1,528	1,747	1,998	2,240	2,394	2,501	2,590	2,662	2.68	2.68	2.29	1.33	0.87	0.70	0.55
Detroit	3,703	3,804	3,909	4,036	4,200	4,363	4,500	4,608	0.54	0.54	0.64	0.80	0.76	0.62	0.47
El Paso	573	623	678	732	779	820	856	887	1.67	1.67	1.56	1.23	1.02	0.86	0.71
Hartford	783	818	853	894	942	989	1,031	1,067	0.86	0.86	0.93	1.04	0.98	0.83	0.68
Honolulu	635	676	720	767	812	854	891	923	1.27	1.27	1.25	1.14	1.00	0.85	0.71
Houston	2,922	3,353	3,849	4,322	4,605	4,789	4,937	5,051	2.76	2.76	2.32	1.27	0.78	0.61	0.46
Indianapolis	921	1,063	1,228	1,387	1,490	1,562	1,623	1,674	2.87	2.87	2.45	1.42	0.94	0.77	0.62
Jacksonville, Florida	742	811	886	962	1,022	1,074	1,119	1,157	1.78	1.78	1.63	1.23	0.98	0.82	0.67
Kansas City	1,233	1,297	1,365	1,438	1,513	1,584	1,645	1,697	1.02	1.02	1.04	1.02	0.91	0.77	0.62
Las Vegas	708	973	1,335	1,721	1,916	2,011	2,086	2,147	6.34	6.34	5.08	2.14	0.97	0.73	0.58
Los Angeles-Long Beach-Santa Ana	10,883	11,339	11,814	12,303	12,762	13,156	13,463	13,677	0.82	0.82	0.81	0.73	0.61	0.46	0.32
Louisville	757	810	866	925	979	1,028	1,071	1,108	1.34	1.34	1.30	1.14	0.98	0.83	0.68
McAllen	268	377	532	701	789	833	870	901	6.87	6.87	5.51	2.36	1.10	0.86	0.71
Memphis	829	899	976	1,053	1,117	1,173	1,221	1,262	1.64	1.64	1.52	1.19	0.97	0.81	0.66
Miami	3,969	4,431	4,946	5,436	5,750	5,967	6,142	6,275	2.20	2.20	1.89	1.12	0.74	0.58	0.43
Milwaukee	1,228	1,269	1,311	1,362	1,428	1,495	1,554	1,603	0.65	0.65	0.76	0.94	0.91	0.77	0.63
Minneapolis-St. Paul	2,087	2,236	2,397	2,557	2,693	2,808	2,905	2,984	1.38	1.39	1.30	1.03	0.84	0.68	0.54
Nashville-Davidson	577	660	755	848	911	958	999	1,034	2.69	2.69	2.32	1.44	1.01	0.84	0.69
New Orleans	1,039	1,024	1,009	996	858	921	984	1,044	-0.30	-0.30	-0.26	-2.99	1.43	1.33	1.18
New York-Newark	16,086	16,943	17,846	18,727	19,425	19,968	20,374	20,636	1.04	1.04	0.96	0.73	0.55	0.40	0.26
Oklahoma City	711	729	748	773	812	854	891	923	0.51	0.51	0.67	0.98	0.99	0.85	0.71
Orlando	893	1,020	1,165	1,306	1,400	1,468	1,526	1,575	2.66	2.66	2.29	1.38	0.95	0.78	0.63
Philadelphia	4,725	4,938	5,160	5,395	5,626	5,833	6,004	6,135	0.88	0.88	0.89	0.84	0.72	0.58	0.43
Phoenix-Mesa	2,025	2,437	2,934	3,418	3,684	3,840	3,965	4,063	3.71	3.71	3.05	1.50	0.83	0.64	0.49
Pittsburgh	1,681	1,717	1,755	1,807	1,887	1,971	2,045	2,106	0.43	0.43	0.58	0.87	0.87	0.73	0.59
Portland	1,181	1,372	1,595	1,811	1,944	2,035	2,110	2,173	3.01	3.01	2.54	1.42	0.91	0.73	0.58
Providence	1,047	1,111	1,178	1,249	1,317	1,380	1,435	1,482	1.18	1.18	1.16	1.07	0.93	0.79	0.64
Raleigh	310	413	549	692	769	812	848	879	5.71	5.71	4.63	2.11	1.08	0.86	0.71
Richmond	696	757	822	888	944	991	1,034	1,070	1.66	1.66	1.54	1.21	0.99	0.83	0.68

Table 4

City population and city population growth rate of urban agglomerations with 750,000 Inhabitants or more in 2009, bycountry, 1950–2025 (thousands)

Country/City	City population of urban agglomerations ('000)								City population growth rate of urban agglomerations (%)						
	1990	1995	2000	2005	2010	2015	2020	2025	1990–1995	1995–2000	2000–2005	2005–2010	2010–2015	2015–2020	2020–2025
Riverside-San Bernardino	1,178	1,336	1,516	1,691	1,807	1,891	1,962	2,021	2.53	2.53	2.18	1.32	0.91	0.74	0.59
Rochester	621	658	696	738	780	820	857	888	1.14	1.14	1.15	1.12	1.01	0.86	0.71
Sacramento	1,104	1,244	1,402	1,555	1,660	1,739	1,805	1,861	2.39	2.39	2.08	1.30	0.92	0.75	0.60
Salt Lake City	792	840	890	944	997	1,047	1,091	1,129	1.17	1.17	1.17	1.10	0.97	0.83	0.68
San Antonio	1,134	1,229	1,333	1,436	1,521	1,593	1,655	1,707	1.62	1.62	1.49	1.15	0.92	0.77	0.62
San Diego	2,356	2,514	2,683	2,853	2,999	3,125	3,231	3,316	1.30	1.30	1.23	1.00	0.82	0.67	0.52
San Francisco-Oakland	2,961	3,095	3,236	3,386	3,541	3,683	3,804	3,900	0.89	0.89	0.91	0.89	0.79	0.64	0.50
San Jose	1,376	1,457	1,543	1,632	1,718	1,797	1,865	1,922	1.14	1.14	1.13	1.03	0.90	0.75	0.60
Seattle	2,206	2,453	2,727	2,991	3,171	3,305	3,415	3,504	2.12	2.12	1.85	1.17	0.83	0.66	0.51
St. Louis	1,950	2,014	2,081	2,160	2,259	2,357	2,442	2,511	0.65	0.65	0.74	0.89	0.85	0.71	0.56
Tampa-St. Petersburg	1,717	1,886	2,072	2,253	2,387	2,492	2,581	2,653	1.88	1.88	1.68	1.15	0.86	0.70	0.55
Tucson	582	649	724	798	853	898	936	970	2.18	2.18	1.94	1.33	1.01	0.85	0.70
Virginia Beach	1,286	1,341	1,397	1,461	1,534	1,605	1,668	1,720	0.83	0.83	0.89	0.97	0.91	0.76	0.62
Washington, D.C.	3,376	3,651	3,949	4,239	4,460	4,635	4,779	4,891	1.57	1.57	1.42	1.01	0.77	0.61	0.46
URUGUAY															
Montevideo	1,546	1,584	1,605	1,622	1,635	1,644	1,653	1,657	0.49	0.26	0.21	0.16	0.11	0.11	0.04
UZBEKISTAN															
Tashkent	2,100	2,116	2,135	2,169	2,210	2,279	2,420	2,616	0.15	0.17	0.32	0.37	0.62	1.20	1.55
VENEZUELA (BOLIVARIAN REPUBLIC OF)															
Barquisimeto	742	838	946	1,067	1,180	1,273	1,350	1,413	2.42	2.43	2.39	2.02	1.52	1.17	0.92
Caracas	2,767	2,816	2,864	2,929	3,090	3,292	3,467	3,605	0.35	0.34	0.45	1.07	1.27	1.03	0.78
Maracaibo	1,303	1,501	1,724	1,973	2,192	2,357	2,488	2,593	2.82	2.77	2.70	2.10	1.45	1.08	0.83
Maracay	760	831	898	973	1,057	1,138	1,208	1,266	1.77	1.56	1.59	1.67	1.48	1.19	0.93
Valencia	1,053	1,213	1,392	1,592	1,770	1,905	2,014	2,103	2.82	2.76	2.69	2.12	1.48	1.11	0.86
VIET NAM															
Da Nang - CP	388	470	570	692	838	997	1,146	1,291	3.86	3.86	3.85	3.85	3.47	2.78	2.38
Hà Noi	1,136	1,344	1,631	2,144	2,814	3,516	4,056	4,530	3.35	3.88	5.46	5.44	4.45	2.86	2.21
Hai Phòng	1,474	1,585	1,704	1,831	1,970	2,164	2,432	2,722	1.45	1.45	1.45	1.46	1.88	2.34	2.25
Thành Pho Ho Chí Minh (Ho Chi Minh City)	3,411	3,802	4,336	5,264	6,167	7,140	8,067	8,957	2.17	2.63	3.88	3.17	2.93	2.44	2.09
YEMEN															
Sana'a'	653	1,034	1,365	1,801	2,342	2,934	3,585	4,296	9.18	5.55	5.54	5.26	4.51	4.01	3.62
ZAMBIA															
Lusaka	757	902	1,073	1,265	1,451	1,666	1,941	2,267	3.49	3.49	3.29	2.74	2.77	3.05	3.10
ZIMBABWE															
Harare	1,047	1,255	1,379	1,513	1,632	1,856	2,170	2,467	3.62	1.89	1.85	1.51	2.57	3.13	2.57

Source: United Nations Department of Economic and Social Affairs, Population Division (2010) World Urbanization Prospects: The 2009 Revision, United Nations, New York.

Table 5

Urban population and urbanization by country, 1990–2030

Country	Urban population ('000)					Level of urbanization (%)				
	1990	2000	2010	2020	2030	1990	2000	2010	2020	2030
AFRICA										
Algeria	13,168	18,246	23,555	29,194	34,097	52.1	59.8	66.5	71.9	76.2
Angola	3,960	6,995	11,112	16,184	21,784	37.1	49.0	58.5	66.0	71.6
Benin	1,654	2,553	3,873	5,751	8,275	34.5	38.3	42.0	47.2	53.7
Botswana	567	917	1,209	1,506	1,769	41.9	53.2	61.1	67.6	72.7
Burkina Faso	1,218	2,083	4,184	7,523	11,958	13.8	17.8	25.7	34.4	42.8
Burundi	356	536	937	1,524	2,362	6.3	8.3	11.0	14.8	19.8
Cameroon	4,981	7,910	11,655	15,941	20,304	40.7	49.9	58.4	65.5	71.0
Cape Verde	156	235	313	394	468	44.1	53.4	61.1	67.4	72.5
Central African Republic	1,078	1,410	1,755	2,268	2,978	36.8	37.6	38.9	42.5	48.4
Chad	1,271	1,964	3,179	5,054	7,843	20.8	23.4	27.6	33.9	41.2
Comoros	122	155	195	259	356	27.9	28.1	28.2	30.8	36.5
Congo	1,329	1,770	2,335	3,118	3,883	54.3	58.3	62.1	66.3	70.9
Côte d'Ivoire	5,011	7,524	10,906	15,574	20,873	39.7	43.5	50.6	57.8	64.1
Democratic Republic of Congo	10,299	15,168	23,887	36,834	53,382	27.8	29.8	35.2	42.0	49.2
Djibouti	424	555	670	798	956	75.7	76.0	76.2	77.6	80.2
Egypt	25,124	30,032	36,664	45,301	56,477	43.5	42.8	43.4	45.9	50.9
Equatorial Guinea	132	205	275	379	527	34.7	38.8	39.7	43.3	49.4
Eritrea	499	650	1,127	1,845	2,780	15.8	17.8	21.6	27.5	34.4
Ethiopia	6,095	9,762	14,158	20,800	31,383	12.6	14.9	16.7	19.3	23.9
Gabon	641	989	1,292	1,579	1,853	69.1	80.1	86.0	88.8	90.6
Gambia	343	639	1,018	1,449	1,943	38.3	49.1	58.1	65.0	71.0
Ghana	5,454	8,584	12,524	17,274	22,565	36.4	44.0	51.5	58.4	64.7
Guinea	1,723	2,603	3,651	5,580	8,219	28.0	31.0	35.4	41.4	48.6
Guinea-Bissau	288	387	494	678	979	28.1	29.7	30.0	32.8	38.6
Kenya	4,271	6,204	9,064	13,826	20,884	18.2	19.7	22.2	26.6	33.0
Lesotho	224	377	560	775	999	14.0	20.0	26.9	34.5	42.4
Liberia	887	1,252	1,961	2,739	3,725	40.9	44.3	47.8	52.1	57.6
Libyan Arab Jamahiriya	3,305	4,083	5,098	6,181	7,060	75.7	76.4	77.9	80.3	82.9
Madagascar	2,657	4,143	6,082	8,953	13,048	23.6	27.1	30.2	34.9	41.4
Malawi	1,093	1,796	3,102	5,240	8,395	11.6	15.2	19.8	25.5	32.4
Mali	2,018	2,982	4,777	7,325	10,491	23.3	28.3	35.9	43.7	51.3
Mauritania	789	1,041	1,395	1,859	2,478	39.7	40.0	41.4	45.4	51.7
Mauritius	464	510	542	595	681	43.9	42.7	41.8	43.4	48.0
Mayotte	33	71	100	129	168	36.1	47.7	50.1	51.6	55.7
Morocco	12,005	15,375	18,859	23,158	27,157	48.4	53.3	58.2	64.0	69.2
Mozambique	2,857	5,601	8,996	13,208	18,199	21.1	30.7	38.4	46.3	53.7
Namibia	392	590	840	1,161	1,541	27.7	32.4	38.0	44.4	51.5
Niger	1,215	1,785	2,719	4,417	7,641	15.4	16.2	17.1	19.3	23.5
Nigeria	34,343	53,078	78,818	109,859	144,116	35.3	42.5	49.8	56.8	63.6
Réunion	491	650	787	891	972	81.2	89.9	94.0	95.7	96.3
Rwanda	387	1,096	1,938	2,993	4,550	5.4	13.8	18.9	22.6	28.3
Saint Helena	2	2	2	2	2	41.6	39.7	39.7	41.7	46.4
São Tomé and Príncipe	51	75	103	136	173	43.6	53.4	62.2	69.0	74.0
Senegal	2,932	3,995	5,450	7,524	10,269	38.9	40.3	42.4	46.5	52.5
Seychelles	35	41	47	54	62	49.3	51.0	55.3	61.1	66.6
Sierra Leone	1,345	1,501	2,241	3,134	4,384	32.9	35.5	38.4	42.8	49.0

Table 5

Urban population and urbanization by country, 1990–2030

Country	Urban population ('000)					Level of urbanization (%)				
	1990	2000	2010	2020	2030	1990	2000	2010	2020	2030
Somalia	1,956	2,458	3,505	5,268	7,851	29.7	33.2	37.4	43.0	49.9
South Africa	19,121	25,528	31,155	35,060	39,032	52.0	56.9	61.7	66.6	71.3
Sudan	7,211	11,661	17,322	24,804	33,267	26.6	33.4	40.1	47.4	54.5
Swaziland	198	244	257	307	400	22.9	22.6	21.4	22.3	26.2
Togo	1,182	1,917	2,945	4,261	5,795	30.1	36.5	43.4	50.5	57.3
Tunisia	4,760	5,996	6,980	8,096	9,115	57.9	63.4	67.3	71.2	75.2
Uganda	1,964	2,952	4,493	7,381	12,503	11.1	12.1	13.3	15.9	20.6
United Republic of Tanzania	4,807	7,614	11,883	18,945	29,190	18.9	22.3	26.4	31.8	38.7
Western Sahara	190	264	434	606	704	86.2	83.9	81.8	83.9	85.9
Zambia	3,117	3,643	4,733	6,584	9,340	39.4	34.8	35.7	38.9	44.7
Zimbabwe	3,033	4,205	4,837	6,839	9,086	29.0	33.8	38.3	43.9	50.7
ASIA										
Afghanistan	2,277	4,148	6,581	10,450	16,296	18.1	20.2	22.6	26.4	32.2
Armenia	2,390	1,989	1,984	2,087	2,186	67.4	64.7	64.2	65.7	69.0
Azerbaijan	3,876	4,158	4,639	5,332	6,044	53.7	51.2	51.9	54.2	58.6
Bahrain	434	574	715	852	984	88.1	88.4	88.6	89.4	90.6
Bangladesh	22,908	33,208	46,149	62,886	83,408	19.8	23.6	28.1	33.9	41.0
Bhutan	90	143	246	348	451	16.4	25.4	34.7	42.4	50.0
Brunei Darussalam	169	237	308	379	450	65.8	71.1	75.7	79.3	82.3
Cambodia	1,221	2,157	3,027	4,214	5,870	12.6	16.9	20.1	23.8	29.2
China	301,995	453,029	635,839	786,761	905,449	26.4	35.8	47.0	55.0	61.9
China, Hong Kong SAR	5,677	6,667	7,069	7,701	8,185	99.5	100.0	100.0	100.0	100.0
China, Macao SAR	371	441	548	588	611	99.8	100.0	100.0	100.0	100.0
Cyprus	454	540	619	705	797	66.8	68.6	70.3	72.7	75.7
Dem. People's Republic of Korea	11,760	13,581	14,446	15,413	16,633	58.4	59.4	60.2	62.1	65.7
Georgia	3,005	2,498	2,225	2,177	2,218	55.0	52.6	52.7	54.7	58.7
India	220,260	288,430	364,459	463,328	590,091	25.5	27.7	30.0	33.9	39.7
Indonesia	54,252	86,219	102,960	122,257	145,776	30.6	42.0	44.3	48.1	53.7
Iran (Islamic Republic of)	31,958	42,952	53,120	63,596	71,767	56.3	64.2	70.8	75.9	79.8
Iraq	12,602	16,722	20,822	26,772	33,930	69.7	67.8	66.2	66.6	69.4
Israel	4,079	5,563	6,692	7,673	8,583	90.4	91.4	91.9	92.4	93.1
Japan	77,726	82,633	84,875	85,848	85,700	63.1	65.2	66.8	69.4	73.0
Jordan	2,350	3,798	5,083	5,998	7,063	72.2	78.3	78.5	79.8	82.0
Kazakhstan	9,301	8,417	9,217	10,417	11,525	56.3	56.3	58.5	62.3	66.8
Kuwait	2,100	2,188	3,001	3,637	4,218	98.0	98.2	98.4	98.6	98.7
Kyrgyzstan	1,660	1,744	1,918	2,202	2,625	37.8	35.2	34.5	35.7	40.1
Lao People's Democratic Republic	649	1,187	2,136	3,381	4,699	15.4	22.0	33.2	44.2	53.1
Lebanon	2,472	3,244	3,712	4,065	4,374	83.1	86.0	87.2	88.6	90.0
Malaysia	9,014	14,424	20,146	25,128	28,999	49.8	62.0	72.2	78.5	82.2
Maldives	56	75	126	186	242	25.8	27.7	40.1	51.5	60.1
Mongolia	1,264	1,358	1,675	2,010	2,316	57.0	56.9	62.0	67.0	71.6
Myanmar	10,092	12,956	16,990	22,570	28,545	24.7	27.8	33.6	40.7	48.1
Nepal	1,692	3,281	5,559	8,739	12,902	8.9	13.4	18.6	24.8	31.7
Occupied Palestinian Territory	1,462	2,267	3,269	4,447	5,810	67.9	72.0	74.1	76.6	79.4
Oman	1,218	1,719	2,122	2,645	3,184	66.1	71.6	73.0	75.7	78.7
Pakistan	35,400	49,088	66,318	90,199	121,218	30.6	33.1	35.9	39.9	45.6
Philippines	30,333	37,283	45,781	57,657	72,555	48.6	48.0	48.9	52.6	58.3

Table 5

Urban population and urbanization by country, 1990–2030

Country	Urban population ('000)					Level of urbanization (%)				
	1990	2000	2010	2020	2030	1990	2000	2010	2020	2030
Qatar	431	586	1,445	1,679	1,891	92.2	94.9	95.8	96.5	96.9
Republic of Korea	31,740	36,967	40,235	42,362	43,086	73.8	79.6	83.0	85.6	87.7
Saudi Arabia	12,451	16,615	21,541	26,617	31,516	76.6	79.8	82.1	84.2	86.2
Singapore	3,016	4,018	4,837	5,219	5,460	100.0	100.0	100.0	100.0	100.0
Sri Lanka	3,217	2,971	2,921	3,360	4,339	18.6	15.8	14.3	15.5	19.6
Syrian Arab Republic	6,224	8,577	12,545	15,948	19,976	48.9	51.9	55.7	60.2	65.4
Tajikistan	1,679	1,635	1,862	2,364	3,121	31.7	26.5	26.3	28.0	32.5
Thailand	16,675	19,417	23,142	27,800	33,624	29.4	31.1	34.0	38.9	45.8
Timor-Leste	154	198	329	538	848	20.8	24.3	28.1	33.2	39.9
Turkey	33,204	43,027	52,728	62,033	70,247	59.2	64.7	69.6	74.0	77.7
Turkmenistan	1,653	2,062	2,562	3,175	3,793	45.1	45.8	49.5	54.6	60.4
United Arab Emirates	1,476	2,599	3,956	4,915	5,821	79.1	80.3	84.1	86.8	88.8
Uzbekistan	8,241	9,273	10,075	11,789	14,500	40.2	37.4	36.2	37.8	42.7
Viet Nam	13,418	19,263	27,046	36,269	46,585	20.3	24.5	30.4	37.0	44.2
Yemen	2,577	4,776	7,714	12,082	17,844	20.9	26.3	31.8	38.2	45.3
EUROPE										
Albania	1,198	1,280	1,645	2,027	2,301	36.4	41.7	51.9	60.7	67.4
Andorra	50	61	76	85	96	94.7	92.4	88.0	84.9	85.1
Austria	5,045	5,267	5,666	6,003	6,372	65.8	65.8	67.6	70.3	73.8
Belarus	6,769	7,030	7,162	7,219	7,070	66.0	69.9	74.7	79.2	82.6
Belgium	9,573	9,899	10,421	10,792	11,070	96.4	97.1	97.4	97.7	97.9
Bosnia and Herzegovina	1,691	1,597	1,828	2,028	2,170	39.2	43.2	48.6	55.2	61.7
Bulgaria	5,854	5,516	5,357	5,215	5,012	66.4	68.9	71.5	74.3	77.5
Channel Islands	45	45	47	52	59	31.4	30.5	31.4	34.2	39.1
Croatia	2,441	2,504	2,546	2,657	2,781	54.0	55.6	57.7	61.5	66.5
Czech Republic	7,750	7,565	7,656	7,929	8,202	75.2	74.0	73.5	75.0	78.0
Denmark	4,361	4,540	4,761	4,923	5,058	84.8	85.1	86.9	88.6	90.1
Estonia	1,115	951	931	942	955	71.1	69.4	69.5	70.7	73.4
Faeroe Islands	14	17	20	23	26	30.6	36.3	40.3	42.2	46.6
Finland	3,958	4,252	4,549	4,805	4,947	79.4	82.2	85.1	87.4	89.2
France	42,095	45,466	53,398	58,267	61,043	74.1	76.9	85.3	89.7	91.8
Germany	58,080	59,970	60,598	60,827	60,993	73.1	73.1	73.8	75.6	78.3
Gibraltar	28	29	31	32	31	100.0	100.0	100.0	100.0	100.0
Greece	5,979	6,537	6,868	7,307	7,785	58.8	59.7	61.4	64.8	69.3
Holy See	1	1	1	1	1	100.0	100.0	100.0	100.0	100.0
Hungary	6,824	6,596	6,791	7,011	7,180	65.8	64.6	68.1	71.8	75.5
Iceland	231	260	308	349	372	90.8	92.4	93.4	94.3	95.0
Ireland	2,000	2,250	2,842	3,370	3,889	56.9	59.1	61.9	65.5	69.8
Isle of Man	36	40	41	41	43	51.7	51.8	50.6	51.2	53.9
Italy	38,032	38,395	41,083	42,840	44,395	66.7	67.2	68.4	70.9	74.6
Latvia	1,844	1,616	1,517	1,471	1,453	69.3	68.1	67.7	68.4	70.9
Liechtenstein	5	5	5	6	7	16.9	15.1	14.3	15.0	18.0
Lithuania	2,499	2,345	2,181	2,096	2,080	67.6	67.0	67.0	68.5	71.5
Luxembourg	309	366	419	480	547	80.9	83.8	85.2	87.4	89.1
Malta	325	359	388	405	413	90.4	92.4	94.7	96.0	96.6
Monaco	29	32	33	34	35	100.0	100.0	100.0	100.0	100.0
Montenegro	282	387	384	394	417	48.0	58.5	61.5	62.4	65.7

Table 5

Urban population and urbanization by country, 1990–2030

Country	Urban population ('000)					Level of urbanization (%)				
	1990	2000	2010	2020	2030	1990	2000	2010	2020	2030
Netherlands	10,270	12,222	13,799	14,824	15,501	68.7	76.8	82.9	86.5	88.6
Norway	3,052	3,411	3,856	4,297	4,700	72.0	76.1	79.4	82.6	85.2
Poland	23,351	23,719	23,187	23,135	23,481	61.3	61.7	61.0	61.7	64.9
Portugal	4,782	5,563	6,515	7,148	7,585	47.9	54.4	60.7	66.4	71.4
Republic of Moldova	2,041	1,828	1,679	1,833	1,938	46.8	44.6	47.0	54.2	60.9
Romania	12,350	11,734	12,177	12,839	13,296	53.2	53.0	57.5	63.0	68.2
Russian Federation	108,670	107,582	102,702	100,892	99,153	73.4	73.4	73.2	74.5	76.9
San Marino	22	25	30	31	32	90.4	93.4	94.1	94.4	94.9
Serbia	4,822	5,369	5,525	5,871	6,252	50.4	53.0	56.1	60.0	64.8
Slovakia	2,969	3,025	2,975	3,031	3,168	56.5	56.2	55.0	55.7	59.2
Slovenia	971	1,008	1,002	1,035	1,110	50.4	50.8	49.5	50.4	54.5
Spain	29,266	30,707	35,073	38,542	40,774	75.4	76.3	77.4	79.4	81.9
Sweden	7,112	7,445	7,870	8,333	8,799	83.1	84.0	84.7	85.8	87.3
Switzerland	4,914	5,268	5,591	5,922	6,336	73.2	73.3	73.6	75.2	77.8
TFYR Macedonia	1,103	1,194	1,212	1,260	1,331	57.8	59.4	59.3	61.6	66.0
Ukraine	34,435	32,814	31,252	30,860	30,243	66.8	67.1	68.8	71.9	75.3
United Kingdom	44,726	46,331	49,295	53,001	56,901	78.1	78.7	79.6	81.4	83.7
LATIN AMERICA AND THE CARIBBEAN										
Anguilla	8	11	15	18	19	100.0	100.0	100.0	100.0	100.0
Antigua and Barbuda	22	25	27	32	40	35.4	32.1	30.3	32.5	38.4
Argentina	28,268	33,291	37,572	41,554	44,726	87.0	90.1	92.4	93.8	94.6
Aruba	32	42	50	54	59	50.3	46.7	46.9	48.8	52.5
Bahamas	204	250	291	331	367	79.8	82.0	84.1	86.1	87.9
Barbados	85	97	114	134	151	32.7	38.3	44.5	51.1	57.9
Belize	90	120	164	213	268	47.5	47.8	52.2	56.9	62.3
Bolivia	3,707	5,143	6,675	8,265	9,799	55.6	61.8	66.5	71.0	75.2
Brazil	110,565	141,416	169,098	187,104	197,874	73.9	81.2	86.5	89.5	91.1
British Virgin Islands	6	8	10	11	14	37.8	39.4	41.0	45.2	51.6
Cayman Islands	26	40	57	61	65	100.0	100.0	100.0	100.0	100.0
Chile	10,984	13,252	15,251	16,958	18,247	83.3	85.9	89.0	91.0	92.3
Colombia	22,670	28,666	34,758	40,800	46,357	68.3	72.1	75.1	78.0	81.0
Costa Rica	1,560	2,321	2,989	3,643	4,259	50.7	59.0	64.4	69.4	73.9
Cuba	7,767	8,382	8,429	8,462	8,550	73.4	75.6	75.2	75.6	77.6
Dominica	47	46	45	47	50	67.7	67.2	67.2	69.4	73.1
Dominican Republic	4,072	5,452	7,074	8,560	9,793	55.2	61.7	69.2	74.8	78.8
Ecuador	5,662	7,423	9,222	11,152	12,813	55.1	60.3	66.9	72.5	76.8
El Salvador	2,624	3,503	3,983	4,583	5,287	49.2	58.9	64.3	69.3	73.7
Falkland Islands (Malvinas)	2	2	2	2	3	74.2	67.6	73.6	78.2	81.6
French Guiana	87	124	177	229	288	74.5	75.1	76.4	78.6	81.4
Grenada	32	37	41	48	55	33.4	35.9	39.3	44.5	51.2
Guadeloupe	381	422	460	476	485	98.6	98.4	98.4	98.5	98.6
Guatemala	3,664	5,068	7,111	9,893	13,153	41.1	45.1	49.5	54.7	60.6
Guyana	222	217	218	233	265	29.6	28.7	28.6	31.3	37.2
Haiti	2,026	3,079	5,307	7,546	9,450	28.5	35.6	52.1	64.4	71.6
Honduras	1,983	2,832	3,930	5,263	6,656	40.5	45.5	51.6	57.6	63.4
Jamaica	1,169	1,330	1,420	1,521	1,660	49.4	51.8	52.0	53.7	57.8
Martinique	310	345	362	370	376	86.3	89.7	89.0	89.1	90.0
Mexico	59,566	74,372	86,113	96,558	105,300	71.4	74.7	77.8	80.7	83.3

Table 5

Urban population and urbanization by country, 1990–2030

Country	Urban population ('000)					Level of urbanization (%)				
	1990	2000	2010	2020	2030	1990	2000	2010	2020	2030
Montserrat	1	1	1	1	1	12.5	11.0	14.3	16.9	21.6
Netherlands Antilles	163	163	187	199	200	85.6	90.2	93.2	94.7	95.5
Nicaragua	2,166	2,792	3,337	4,077	4,860	52.3	54.7	57.3	61.0	65.8
Panama	1,300	1,941	2,624	3,233	3,751	53.9	65.8	74.8	80.3	83.6
Paraguay	2,069	2,960	3,972	5,051	6,102	48.7	55.3	61.5	67.1	71.9
Peru	15,004	18,994	22,688	26,389	29,902	68.9	73.0	76.9	80.3	83.0
Puerto Rico	2,546	3,614	3,949	4,112	4,178	72.2	94.6	98.8	99.5	99.6
Saint Kitts and Nevis	14	15	17	21	26	34.6	32.8	32.4	35.4	41.6
Saint Lucia	41	44	49	58	74	29.3	28.0	28.0	30.6	36.1
Saint Vincent and the Grenadines	44	49	54	60	68	41.4	45.2	49.3	54.6	60.7
Suriname	244	303	364	418	466	60.0	64.9	69.4	73.5	77.3
Trinidad and Tobago	104	140	186	250	328	8.5	10.8	13.9	18.1	23.7
Turks and Caicos Islands	9	16	31	35	38	74.3	84.6	93.3	96.5	97.4
United States Virgin Islands	91	101	104	102	96	87.7	92.6	95.3	96.5	97.0
Uruguay	2,767	3,033	3,119	3,264	3,382	89.0	91.3	92.5	93.4	94.3
Venezuela (Bolivarian Republic of)	16,638	21,940	27,113	31,755	35,588	84.3	89.9	93.4	95.0	95.8
NORTHERN AMERICA										
Bermuda	60	63	65	66	66	100.0	100.0	100.0	100.0	100.0
Canada	21,214	24,389	27,309	30,426	33,680	76.6	79.5	80.6	82.0	84.0
Greenland	44	46	48	49	49	79.7	81.6	84.2	86.5	88.4
Saint Pierre and Miquelon	6	6	5	6	6	88.9	89.1	90.6	91.8	92.8
United States of America	191,914	227,651	261,375	293,732	321,698	75.3	79.1	82.3	84.9	87.0
OCEANIA										
American Samoa	38	51	64	76	87	80.9	88.8	93.0	94.8	95.6
Australia	14,596	16,710	19,169	21,459	23,566	85.4	87.2	89.1	90.6	91.9
Cook Islands	10	11	15	17	19	57.7	65.2	75.3	81.4	84.9
Fiji	301	384	443	501	566	41.6	47.9	51.9	56.4	61.7
French Polynesia	109	124	140	160	186	55.9	52.4	51.4	52.7	56.6
Guam	122	144	168	188	208	90.8	93.1	93.2	93.5	94.2
Kiribati	25	36	44	54	67	35.0	43.0	43.9	46.5	51.7
Marshall Islands	31	36	45	56	65	65.1	68.4	71.8	75.3	78.8
Micronesia (Fed. States of)	25	24	25	29	38	25.8	22.3	22.7	25.1	30.3
Nauru	9	10	10	11	11	100.0	100.0	100.0	100.0	100.0
New Caledonia	102	127	146	169	200	59.5	59.2	57.4	58.5	62.7
New Zealand	2,869	3,314	3,710	4,058	4,382	84.7	85.7	86.2	86.9	88.1
Niue	1	1	1	1	1	30.9	33.1	37.5	43.0	49.4
Northern Mariana Islands	39	62	81	96	111	89.7	90.2	91.3	92.4	93.3
Palau	10	13	17	20	23	69.6	70.0	83.4	89.6	92.0
Papua New Guinea	619	711	863	1,194	1,828	15.0	13.2	12.5	14.1	18.2
Pitcairn	—	—	—	—	—	—	—	—	—	—
Samoa	34	39	36	38	46	21.2	22.0	20.2	20.5	24.0
Solomon Islands	43	65	99	152	230	13.7	15.7	18.6	23.0	29.2
Tokelau	—	—	—	—	—	—	—	—	—	—
Tonga	21	23	24	28	35	22.7	23.0	23.4	25.6	30.4
Tuvalu	4	4	5	6	7	40.7	46.0	50.4	55.6	61.5
Vanuatu	28	41	63	95	140	18.7	21.7	25.6	31.0	38.0
Wallis and Futuna Islands	—	—	—	—	—	—	—	—	—	—

Source: United Nations Department of Economic and Social Affairs, Population Division (2010) World Urbanization Prospects: The 2009 Revision, United Nations, New York.

Bibliography

A

ActiveUKChina (2012) *Business and economic distributions and clusters*, http://www.activeukchina.com/business-environment/business-and-economic-distributions-and-clusters/

Adebowale, B. A. (2011) *Industrial Clusters and Prosperity of Cities*, background paper for this Report.

Admassie, Y. (2011) *City Report on Addis Ababa*, Unpublished UN-Habitat background study for this Report.

Africa Economic Outlook (2012) *Macroeconomic Prospects*, http://www.africaneconomicoutlook.org/en/outlook/forecast/

African Economic Outlook (2011) *Mauritius*, http://www.africaneconomicoutlook.org/en/countries/southern-africa/mauritius/

African Economic Outlook (2012) *Progress in Infrastructure Developments*, http://www.africaneconomicoutlook.org/en/outlook/trade_policies/progress-in-infrastructure-developments/

Aker, J. C. and I. M. Mbiti (2010) 'Mobile telephones and economic development in Africa', *Journal of EconUN-Habitatomic Perspectives*, Vol. 24(3), pp. 207-232.

Al-Bassam, D. and J. Mouris (2011) *City Report on Dubai*, Unpublished UN-Habitat background study for this Report.

Al- Kubaisy, F. (2011) *City Report on Al-Muharrak*, Unpublished UN-Habitat background study for this Report.

Al-Rawashdeh, A. (2011) 'New Bus System Aims to Reduce Amman's traffic congestion', *Al-Shorfa.com*, January 26, http://al-shorfa.com/en_GB/articles/meii/features/main/2011/01/26/feature-02

Andrulis, D.P., H.M. Reid, L. M. Duchon (2004), *Quality of Life in the Nation's 100 Largest Cities and Their Suburbs: New and Continuing Challenges for Improving Health and Well-Being*, The Social and Health Landscape of Urban and Suburban America Report Series, USA.

Annez, P.C. and R. Buckley (2008) 'Urbanization and growth: Setting the context', in Spence M., P.C. Annez., and R. Buckley (eds.) *Urbanization and Growth*, Commission on Growth and Development, World Bank, Washington DC.

Arimah, B. C. (2005) 'What Drives Infrastructure Spending in Cities of Developing Countries?', *Urban Studies*, Vol 42 (8), pp. 1345–1368.

Article 13 (2005) 'EcoCity: Johannesburg, South Africa', *CSR Best Practice*, http://www.article13.com/A13_ContentList.asp?

Assaad, R. and F. Roudi-Fahimi (2007) *Youth in the Middle East and North Africa: Demographic opportunity or challenge?* Population Reference Bureau, Washington, DC.

Astroman (2011) *City Government and IBM Close Partnership to Make Rio de Janeiro a Smarter City*, January 3, http://www.astroman.com.pl/index.php?mod=magazine&a=read&id=871

Avelino, G., Brown, D. and Hunter, W. (2005) "The Effects of Capital Mobility, Trade Openness and Democracy on Social Spending In Latin America, 1980-1999," *American Journal of Political Science*, Vol. 49 (3), pp. 625-641.

Awuor-Hayanga, R. (2011) *City Report on Johannesburg*. Unpublished UN-Habitat background study for this Report.

Ayad, H. M. (2011) *City Report on Alexandria*. Unpublished UN-Habitat background study for this Report.

B

Banco De España (2012) 'Indicadores del mercado de la vivienda', *Síntesis de Indicadores,* http://www.bde.es/webbde/es/estadis/infoect/3i_1_6.pdf

Barboza, D. (2010) 'Chinese City Has Many Buildings, but Few People', *New York Times*, October 19, http://www.nytimes.com/2010/10/20/business/global/20ghost.html?adxnnl=1&pagewanted=all&adxnnlx=1322738684-BC+hgnWy4oSrvl8Fhggx3A

Bateman, M. (2012) 'Medellín Emerges as a Latin American Trailblazer for Local Economic Growth', *The Guardian*, April 3, http://www.guardian.co.uk/global-development/poverty-matters/2012/apr/03/medellin-trailblazer-local-economic-growth

BBVA (2011) *Situación inmobiliaria México. Análisis económico. Julio 2011.* Servicio de estudios económicos del BBVA, BBVA Research,http://www.bbvaresearch.com/KETD/fbin/mult/1107_SituacionInmobiliariaMexico_20_tcm346-262669.pdf?ts=29112011

Beijing Traffic Management Bureau (2010), Statistical Analysis on China's Vehicles and Drivers in the First Half of 2009, http://www.bjjtgl.gov.cn/publish/portal1/tab165/info12857.htm

Belliapa, S.G. (2011) *City Report on Bangalore*. Unpublished UN-Habitat background study for this Report.

Beltran, I. and E. Velasquez (2012) 'Cohesion Social, Confianza y Seguridad en America Latina: Un estudio exploratorio', in *Violencia y Cohesion Social en America Latina*, Diaz, F. and P. Meller (ed.). CIEPLAN, Santiago de Chile.

Berman, H. J. (1983) *Law and Revolution: The formation of the Western Legal Tradition*, Harvard University Press, Cambridge, MA.

Bloom, D. E. and T. Khanna (2007) 'The Urban Revolution', *Finance & Development*, Vol. 44 (3).

Bloom, D. E., D. Canning, and G. Fink (2008) 'Urbanization and the Wealth of Nations', *Science*, Vol. 319, pp. 772–775.

Bourdieu, P. (ed.) (1993) *La Misère du monde*, Seuil, Paris.

Bourdieu, P. (2012) *Sur l'Etat – Cours au Collège de France 1989–1992*, Raisons d'Agir/Seuil, Paris.

Briney, A. (2009) *New Urbanism is Taking Planning to a New Level*, http://geography.about.com/od/urbaneconomicgeography/a/newurbanism.htm

British Broadcasting Corporation (2010) *'Audit shows 33,000 "ghost" houses in the Republic'*, BBC NEWS, October 21, http://www.bbc.co.uk/news/world-europe-11596357

British Broadcasting Corporation (2011) 'South Africa Gautrain opens Johannesburg-Pretoria route', *BBC News*, August 2, http://www.bbc.co.uk/news/world-africa-14371113

Britto, T (2008) 'Brazil's Bolsa Família: Understanding its Origins and Challenges', *Poverty in Focus*, Number 15, International Policy Centre for Inclusive Growth, Brasilia, pp. 6–7.

Buckley, R. and A. Kallergis (2011) *The Wealth of Cities and Equitable Growth*, background paper for this Report.

Buhigas, M. (2012), *Efficient Urban Planning and Management*, background paper for this Report.

Buyle-Bodin, Z., and C. Hermant-De Callataÿ (2011) *Urban Prosperity and Quality of Life in European cities – Beyond GDP*, Background paper prepared for this Report.

C

Calafati, A. (2011) *The Economic Prosperity of European Cities*, Brussels, background paper produced for this Report.

Calderón, C. (2008) 'Infrastructure and growth in Africa', *Policy Research Working Paper* 4914, World Bank, Washington, DC.

Calderón, C. and L. Servén (2003) 'The Output Cost of Latin America's Infrastructure Gap.' in W. Easterly and L. Servén, Eds., *The Limits of Stabilization: Infrastructure, Public Deficits and Growth in Latin America.* pp. 95–118. Stanford University Press: Palo Alto and the World Bank: Washington D.C.

Canassa, H. (2008) 'São Paulo Traffic Jams Mean Lost Business, Stress, Helicopters', *Bloomberg*, July 14, http://www.bloomberg.com/apps/news?pid=newsarchive&sid=aAwzOeXmlxgk

Castellanos, G. (2011) *City Report on Santo Domingo*, Unpublished UN-Habitat background study for this Report.

Castells, M. (1996) *The Information Age: Economy, Society and Culture – Volume 1 – The Rise of the Network Society*, Blackwell, Oxford.

Centre for Livable Cities (2011) *City Report on Singapore*, Unpublished UN-Habitat background study for this Report.

Chan, E.H.W and E. H.K. Yung (2004) 'Is The Development Control Legal Framework Conducive to a Sustainable Dense Urban Development In Hong Kong?', *Habitat International*: 28. pp. 409–426.

Choguill, C. (1996) 'Ten steps to sustainable infrastructure', *Habitat International*, Vol. 20(3), pp. 389–4044.

Cities Alliance (2003) *2003 Annual Report*, Cities Alliance, Washington DC, http://www.citiesalliance.org/sites/citiesalliance.org/files/Anual_Reports/03-annual-report.pdf

Cities Alliance (2006) *Guide to City Development Strategies: Improving Urban Performance*, Cities Alliance, Washington, D.C., http://www.citiesalliance.org/ca/sites/citiesalliance.org/files/CA_Docs/resources/cds/cds-guidelines/role_of_cities.pdf

Cities Alliance, ICLEI and UNEP (2007) *Liveable Cities: The Benefits of Urban Environmental Planning. A Cities Alliance Study on Good Practices and Useful Tools*, Cities Alliance, Washington DC.

City of Cape Town (2011) *Community Satisfaction Survey 2010/11*, http://www.capetown.gov.za/en/Pages/CommunitySatisfactionSurvey201011.aspx

City of Dublin (2009) *Economic Development Action Plan for the Dublin Region*, http://www.dublincity.ie/YourCouncil/CouncilPublications/Documents/Dublin_Region_Economic_Action_Plan_-_Lo_Res.pdf

City of Toronto (n.d) *How Toronto Ranks*, http://www.toronto.ca/progress/world_rankings.htm

Clos, J. (2012) *Urbanization Challenges of the 21st Century*, Unpublished document, UN-Habitat, Nairobi.

Cohen, M. (2012) *Reinventing the Future: Designing Urban 3.0*, Unpublished proposal for UN-Habitat Habitat 3 Summit.

Commins, S. (2011) 'Urban fragility and security in Africa' In *Africa Security Brief*, Nr 12. Africa Center for Strategic Studies, Washington D.C.

Cooper, M. (2010) 'Cities face tough choices as US slashes block grants program', *New York Times*, http://www.nytimes.com/2011/12/22/us/cities-struggle-as-us-slashes-block-grants-program.html

Cooper, P. J. (2003) 'Why Dubai? Anatomy of a Business Success Story', *AMEInfo.com*, September 10, http://www.ameinfo.com/28046.html

Costas, S. (2011) *Urban Tourism and Urban Change: Cities in a Global Economy*, New York, Routledge.

Coyula, M. (2011) *City Report on Havana*, Unpublished UN-Habitat background study for this Report.

Creedy, A., C. Zuidema, G. Porter, G. de Roo (2007) *Towards Cities and Towns. Guidance for Sustainable Urban Management*, EUROCITIES.

D

Davis, D. (2007) 'Urban Violence, Quality of Life, and the Future of Latin American Cities,' in Garland, A.M., M. Massoumi and B. A. Ruble (eds.) *Global Urban Poverty: Setting the Agenda*. Woodrow Wilson International Center for Scholars, Comparative Urban Studies Project, Washington D.C, pp. 57-87.

de la Torre, A., P. Fajnzylbe, and J. Nash (2009) *Low Carbon, High Growth: Latin American Responses to Climate Change: An Overview*, World Bank, Washington, DC.

Dickinson, E. (2011) 'GDP: A Brief History', *Foreign Policy*, January/February 2011, http://www.foreignpolicy.com/articles/2011/01/02/gdp_a_brief_history.

Dong, B, and B. Torgler (2010) *The Consequences of Corruption: Evidence from China*, Center for Economics, Management and the Arts Working Paper No. 2010-06, http://www.crema-research.ch/papers/2010-06.pdf

Duranton, G. and D. Puga (2004) 'Micro-foundations of urban agglomeration economies', in Henderson, V. and Thisse, J. (eds) *Handbook of Urban and Regional Economics*, vol. 4, North Holland, Amsterdam.

Dzung, D. D. (2011) *City Report on Ho Chi Minh City*, Unpublished UN-Habitat background study for this Report.

E

Earth Right Institute (2011), *Land Rights and Land Value Capture*, http://www.earthrights.net/docs/long_form_brochure_lrlvc.html;UN-Habitat (2008), *Municipal financing and urban development*, UN-Habitat, Nairobi.

Easterlin, R. A. (1973) 'Does Money Buy Happiness?' *The Public Interest* 30 (Winter): 3-10.

Easterlin, R. A. (1974) 'Does Economic Growth Improve the Human Lot? Some Empirical Evidence', In David, P. A. and M. W. Reder (eds.) *Nations and Households in Economic Growth: Essays in Honor of Moses Abramowitz*, Academic Press, New York, pp. 89-125.

Escribano, A., J.L. Guasch, and J. Pena (2008) *Impact of Infrastructure Constraints on Firm Productivity in Africa*, Africa Infrastructure Diagnostic Study Working Paper 9, World Bank, Washington, DC.

ESCWA (2009) Transport for Sustainable Development in the Arab Region: Measures, Progress Achieved, Challenges and Policy Framework, United Nations, New York, http://www.uncclearn.org/sites/www.uncclearn.org/files/unescwa14.pdf

European Commission (1998) *Sustainable Urban Development in the European Union: A Framework for Action*, Communication from the Commission, http://ec.europa.eu/environment/urban/pdf/framework_en.pdf

European Commission (2009) *Promoting Sustainable Urban Development in Europe: Achievements and Opportunities*. European Commission, Brussels.

European Environment Agency (2009) *Ensuring quality of life in Europe's cities and towns: Tackling the environmental challenges driven by European and global change*, EEA Report 5/2009,Office for Official Publications of the European Communities, Luxembourg.

Eurostat (2008) 'Ageing Characterizes the Demographic Perspectives of the European societies', *Eurostat - Statistics in focus, 72/2008*, Author: Konstantinos Giannakouris. European Commission, Brussels.

F

Fawaz, M. and N. Baghdadi (2011) *City Report on Beirut*, Unpublished UN-Habitat background study for this Report.

Fay, M. and M. Morrison (2005) *Infrastructure in Latin America and the Caribbean: Recent Developments and Key Challenges*, World Bank, Washington, DC.

Fernandes, E. (2007a) 'Implementing the Urban Reform Agenda in Brazil', *Environment & Urbanization*, Vol 19(1), pp. 177–189.

Fernandes, E. (2007b) 'Constructing the `Right to the City' in Brazil', *Social & Legal Studies*, Vol. 16(2), pp. 201–219.

Fernandes, E. and M.M.M. Copello (2009) 'Law and Land Policy in Latin America: Shifting Paradigms and Possibilities for Action', *Land Lines*, Lincoln Institute of Land Policy, Cambridge, MA.

Fernandez, C. (2011) *City Report on Cape Verde*, Unpublished UN-Habitat background study for this Report.

Fernandez, F.L. (2011) *City Report on Cebu*, Unpublished UN-Habitat background study for this Report.

Fernández-Ardèvol, M. (2010) 'Household access to mobile telephony in Latin America', in Sevensson, J. and G. Wicander (eds.) *Proceedings of the 2nd International Conference on M4D, Mobile Communication Technology for Development*, 10-11 November, Kampala, Uganda.

Finaccess (2009) *Finaccess 2009 Survey Results*, http://www.fsdkenya.org/finaccess/documents/09-06-10%20FinAccess%20FA09%20Report%20Contents.pdf

Flores, A. R. (2011) *City Report on Ciudad Del Este*. Unpublished UN-Habitat background study for this Report.

Flyvbjerg, B. (1996) 'The Dark Side of Planning: Rationality and Realrationalität,' in Seymour, M., Mazza, L., and R. Burchell (eds.) *Explorations in Planning Theory*, Center for Urban Policy Research Press, New Brunswick, NJ. pp. 383–394.

Foster, V., and C. Briceno-Garmendia (2010) *Africa's Infrastructure: A Time for Transformation*, World Bank, Washington DC.

G

Gabara, N. (2008) 'South Africa Increases R&D spend', *SouthAfrica.info*, September 18, http://www.southafrica.info/about/science/rnd-180908.htm#ixzz1wdPBQMvx.

Galiani, S., P. Gertler and E. Schargrodsky (2005) "Water for life: The Impact of the Privatization of Water Services on Child Mortality", *Journal of Political Economy*, Vol. 113 (1), pp. 83–120.

Galimberti, L. D. (2011) *City Report on Lima*, Unpublished UN-Habitat background study for this Report.

Gehl, J. (2010) *Cities for People*, Island Press, Washington DC.

General Electric Power and Water (2010) *Africa's Largest Seawater Desalination Plant Eases Water Scarcity for City of Algiers, Algeria*, http://www.gewater.com/pdf/Case%20Studies_Cust/Americas/English/CS1338EN.pdf

Gewirth, A. (1996) *The Community of Rights*, Chicago: University of Chicago Press.

GHK (2010) *Estimating green jobs in Bangladesh: A GHK report for the ILO*, http://www.ilo.org/wcmsp5/groups/public/---ed_emp/---emp_ent/documents/publication/wcms_159433.pdf

Gidwani, V. and A. Baviskar (2011) 'Urban Commons,' *Economic and Political Weekly*, 46 (50), pp. 42–43.

Glaeser, E. and C. Berry (2005) *The Divergence of Human Capital Levels across Cities*. Harvard Institute of Economic Research, Discussion Paper Number 2091, http://post.economics.harvard.edu/hier/2005papers/2005list.html

Global Environmental Facility (2012) *What is GEF*, http://www.thegef.org/gef/whatisgef

Gomes, L . (2012) 'Brazil's Labyrinth of Bureaucracy', *BBC News*, May 16, http://www.bbc.co.uk/news/business-18020623

Gonzales, V. M. (2011) *City Report on Valparaiso*. Unpublished UN-Habitat background study for this Report.

Goodman, J., M. Laube, and J. Schwenk (2006) "Curitiba's bus System is model for rapid transit", *Race, Poverty and Environment*, Winter 2005/2006, pp. 75–76.

Government of Karnataka (2008) *Advantage Karnataka: The Gateway of Innovative Ideas*, http://www.indianhcabuja.com/docs/events/Jun-07-08-2012/Advantage_Karnataka.pdf

Government of Karnataka (2011) *Economic Survey of Karnataka 2010-11*, http://www.planning.kar.nic.in/sites/planning.kar.nic.in/files/ES_Final_Printing_English_13-3-11_5.30.pdf

Government of Karnataka (n.d) *Bangalore Urban: the Silicon Valley of India*, http://advantagekarnataka.com/images/district-profiles/Bangalore-Urban-District-Profile.pdf

Government of Singapore (2010) *Singapore Budget 2010 - Towards an Advanced Economy: Superior Skills, Quality Jobs, Higher Incomes*, http://www.mof.gov.sg/budget_2010/speech_toc/pd.html.

Greater Bangalore Municipal Corporation (n.d) *Bengaluru City Profile*, http://bbmp.gov.in/

GSM Association (2011a) *Africa Mobile Observatory 2011*, GSMA, London.

GSM Association (2011b) *Asia Pacific Mobile Observatory 2011*, GSMA, London.

GSM Association (2011c) *Latin American Mobile Observatory 2011*, GSMA, London.

Gulf Talent (2007) *Dubai overtakes Cairo in traffic congestion*, June 2007, http://www.gulftalent.com/home/Dubai-Overtakes-Cairo-in-Traffic-Congestion-Article-23.html

Gulyani, S. and E. M. Bassett (2007) 'Retrieving the baby from the bathwater: Slum upgrading in Sub-Saharan Africa', *Environment and Planning C*, 25, pp. 486–515.

H

Habib, M. and L. Zurawicki, (2002) 'Corruption and foreign direct investment' *Journal of International Business Studies*, Vol. 33, pp. 291–307.

Hailu, D. and F. V. Soares (2008) 'Cash transfers in Africa and Latin America: An overview', *Poverty in Focus*, Number 15, International Policy Centre for Inclusive Growth, Brasilia, pp. 3–5.

Hamermesh, D. S. (1998) *Crime and the Timing of Work*, National Bureau of Economic Research Working Paper 6613, NBER, Boston.

Hampwaye, G. and W. Nchito (2011) *City Report on Lusaka*, Unpublished UN-Habitat background study for this Report.

Harris, C. (2008) "India Leads Developing Nations in Private Sector Investment", *Gridlines*, No.3, March 2008, http://www.pppinindia.com/pdf/gridlines.pdf

Haworth, L.L. (1963) *The Good City*, Indiana University Press, Bloomington.

Heller, P., K. N. Harilal and S. Chaudhuri (2007) 'Building local democracy: Evaluating the impact of decentralization in Kerala, India', *World Development*, Vol 35(4), pp. 626–648.

Hess, D. and L. Winner (2006) *Enhancing Justice and Sustainability at Local Level: Affordable Policies for Urban Governments*, http://www.davidjhess.org/PolicyPaper.pdf

Hidalgo, D. (2008) 'Why is TransMilenio still so special?', *The City Fix*, August 5, http://thecityfix.com/blog/why-is-transmilenio-still-so-special/

Holcombe, R. G. (2012) 'Democracy and Prosperity', in Young, B. C. (ed.) *Institutional Economics and National Competitiveness*, Routledge, London.

HPEC (2011) *Report on Indian Urban Infrastructure and Services*, National Institute of Urban Affairs, New Delhi.

I

IIED (2009) 'What Role for Mayors in Good City Governance?' in *Environment & Urbanization*, Vol 21 (1), April 2009 Brief.

IIHS (2011) *Urban India 2011: Evidence*, Brief for the India Urban Conference 2011: Evidence and Experience, Indian Institute for Human Settlements, New Delhi.

ILO (2007) *Green jobs initiative in Burkina Faso: From waste to wages*, http://www.ilo.org/global/about-the-ilo/press-and-media-centre/insight/WCMS_084547/lang--en/index.htm

IMF (2011) *Regional Economic Outlook. Sub-Saharan Africa October 2011*, International Monetary Fund, Washington DC.

INFONAVIT (2011a) *Síntesis INFONAVIT Nacional*, 7 de Julio, http://portal.infonavit.org.mx/pdfs/110707.pdf

INFONAVIT (2011b) *Síntesis INFONAVIT Nacional*, 8 de Agosto. http://portal.infonavit.org.mx/pdfs/110808.pdf

Instituto Brasileiro de Geografia e Estadistica (2010) *Censo 2010: população do Brasil é de 190.732.694 pessoas*, http://www.ibge.gov.br/home/presidencia/noticias/noticia_visualiza.php?id_noticia=1766

International Labor Organization (2003) *Key Indicators of Labour Market*, Third Edition, International Labor Office, Genève.

International Telecommunication Union (2010) *World Telecommunication/ICT Indicators Database*, http://www.itu.int/ITU-D/ict/statistics/

Inurrieta Beruete, I. (2007) *Mercado de vivienda en alquiler en España: más vivienda social y más Mercado profesional*, documento de trabajo 113/2007, Laboratorio de alternativas (Fundación Alternativas).

ISMU Foundation – Projects and Studies on Multiethnicity (2010), *The 16th Italian Report on Migrations 2010*, ISTAT, www.istat.it http://demo.istat.it/index_e.html

J

Jackson T. (2009 *Prosperity without Growth: Economics for a Finite Planet*, Earthscan, London and New York.

Jacobs, J. (1969) *The Economy of Cities*, Jonathan Cape, London.

Jacobs, J. (1984) *Cities and the Wealth of Nations*, Random House, New York.

Jaffe, E. (2012) 'Are Cities Losing it to States', in *The Atlantic Cities*, May 30, http://www.theatlanticcities.com/politics/2012/05/are-us-cities-losing-power-states/2138

James, P.A., K. Deiglmeier and D. T. Miller (2008) 'Rediscovering Social Innovations', *Stanford Social Innovation Review*, http://www.ssireview.org/articles/entry/rediscovering_social_innovation/

Jeddah Municipality (2009) *Jeddah Strategic Plan: Building our future, preserving our heritage and values*, http://www.jeddah.gov.sa/Strategy/English/JSP/index.php

Jin, L. and Y. Liu (2011) *City Report on Shenzhen*, Unpublished UN-Habitat background study for this Report.

K

Kalabamu, F. T. (2011) *City Report on Gaborone*. Unpublished UN-Habitat background study for this Report.

Karim, S. S.A. (2011) *City Report on Basra*. Unpublished UN-Habitat background study for this Report.

Karvinen, M. (2005) *Innovation and creativity strategies in Helsinki Metropolitan Area – reinvention of regional governance*, proceedings of the 41st ISoCaRP Congress 2005, Bilbao, Spain.

Khattab, O. (2011) *City Report on Kuwait City*, Unpublished UN-Habitat background study for this Report.

Kimmelman, M. (2012), 'A City Rises, Along With Its Hopes', *New York Times*, May 18, http://www.nytimes.com/2012/05/20/arts/design/fighting-crime-with-architecture-in-medellin-colombia.html?_r=1&pagewanted=all.

Kitchin, R., J. Gleeson, K. Keaveney, and C. O'Callaghan (2010) *A Haunted Landscape: Housing and Ghost Estates in Post-Celtic Tiger Ireland*, National Institute for Regional and Spatial Analysis (NIRSA) Working Paper 59, http://www.nuim.ie/nirsa/research/documents/WP59-A-Haunted-Landscape.pdf

Kollock, P. (2010) 'Still Sitting in Beirut Traffic', *NOW Lebanon*, May 5 http://www.nowlebanon.com/NewsArchiveDetails.aspx?ID=166121

Kothari, M. and S. Chaudhry (2009) *Taking the right to the city forward: Obstacles and promise*, background paper for this Report.

Kratke, S. (2011) *The Creative Capital of Cities: Interactive Knowledge Creation and The Urbanization Economies of Innovation*, Wiley-Blackwell, Chichester.

Kremzner. M. T. (1998) 'Managing Urban Land in China: The Emerging Legal Framework and its Role in Development', *Pacific Rim Law & Policy Journal*, Vol. 7 (3) pp. 611–655.

Kumar, A. (2011) *Understanding the Emerging Role Of Motorcycles in African Cities: A Political Economy Perspective*, Sub-Saharan Africa Transport Policy Program Discussion Paper No. 13, World Bank, Washington, DC.

Kumar, A., and F. Barrett (2008) *Stuck in Traffic: Urban Transport in Africa*, World Bank, Washington, DC.

Kurtul, P. F. (2011) *City Report on Gaziantep*. Unpublished UN-Habitat background study for this Report.

L

Lafferty, W.M and K. Eckerberg, (1998) *From the Earth Summit to Local Agenda 21: Working Towards Sustainable Development*, Earthscan, London.

176

Lagos Metropolitan Transport Authority (n.d) *Bus Rapid Transit*, http://www.lamata-ng.com/brt.htm

Lall, R., R. Anand and A. Rastogi (2010) 'Developing Physical Infrastructure: A Comparative Perspective on the Experience Of China And India', in Gerhaeusser K., Iwasaki, Y. and V. B. Tulasidhar, (eds.) *Resurging Asian Giants*, Asian Development Bank, Manila, pp.57–114.

Landry, C. (2000) *The Creative City*, Earthscan, London.

Latin American Herald Tribune (2011) 'Cuban Capital Faces Worst Water Shortage in 50 Years', *Latin American Herald Tribune*, http://laht.com/article.asp?ArticleId=391553&CategoryId=14510

Lennert, M. (2011) *Cities in Networks*, Unpublished background study for this Report.

Leung, K. L. (2009) 'Reducing CO2 Emissions Through the Development of a Sustainable Urban Transportation System: The Trinidad Case Study', paper presented at the 45th ISOCARP Congress 2009.

Lima Como Vamos (2010) *Lima Según sus Ciudadanos*, Observatorio Ciudadano, Informe de Percepción sobre la Calidad de Vida, Lima.

Liu, Y. and Y. Wang (2011) *City Report on Chongqing*, Unpublished UN-Habitat background study for this Report.

López, M. (2011) *Water Distribution as an Indicator of Social Inequality: The Case of Medellín, Colombia*, http://www.centrodametropole.org.br/static/uploads/marcela_l.pdf

López Moreno, E. (2010) *Addressing New Forms of Poverty and Exclusion*, World and European Sustainable Cities: Insights from EU Research, European Commission, Brussels.

López, E. M. (2011), *New Urban Planning: Going Back to Basics*, Unpublished document, UN-Habitat, Nairobi.

Lorentzen, J., T. Mugadza and S. Robinson (2010) *Innovation in South African City Regions: Can We Explain It?*, Georgia Institute of Technology,http://smartech.gatech.edu/bitstream/handle/1853/35257/1238509150_JL.pdf?sequence=1

Luoma, J., M. Sivak and S. Zielinski (2010) *The Future of Personal Transportation in Megacities of the World*, Transportation Research Institute, University of Michigan, Ann Arbor.

Lupala, A. (2011) *City Report on Dar es Salaam*. Unpublished UN-Habitat background study for this Report.

M

Maddison, A. (2001) *The World Economy: A Millennial Perspective*, Paris, OECD.

Maia, J., T. Giordano,N. Kelder, G. Bardien, M. Bodibe, P. Du Plooy, X. Jafta, D. Jarvis, E. Kruger-Cloete, G. Kuhn, R. Lepelle, L. Makaulule. K. Mosoma, S. Neoh, N. Netshitomboni, T. Ngozo, and J. Swanepoel, (2011) *Green Jobs: An Estimate Of The Direct Employment Potential Of A Greening South African Economy*. IDC/DBSA, Trade and Industrial Policy strategies.

Mangin, D. (2004) *La Ville franchisée: Formes et structures de la ville contemporaine*, Editions de la Villette, Paris.

Marshall, A. (1920) *Principles of Economics* (8th edition), Macmillan, London.

Martinot, E. , A. Chaurey , D. Lew, J. R. Moreira, and N. Wamukonya (2002) 'Renewable Energy Markets in Developing Countries', *Annual Review of Energy and Environment*, vol. 27, pp. 309–348.

Mazembe, A. (2011) *City Report on Beira*. Unpublished UN-Habitat background study for this Report.

McGuirk, J. (2012) Colombia's Architectural Tale of Two Cities, in *The Guardian*, April 11, http://www.guardian.co.uk/artanddesign/2012/apr/11/colombia-architecture-bogota-medellin

McKinsey Global Institute (2009) *Preparing for China's Urban Billion*, McKinsey and Company.

Mena, A. (2011) *City Report on Doha*, Unpublished UN-Habitat background study for this Report.

Mendoza, I. R. (2011) *City Report on Panama City*, Unpublished UN-Habitat background study for this Report.

Menski, W. (2006) *Comparative Law in a Global Context: The Legal Systems of Asia and Africa*, Cambridge University Press, Cambridge.

Mitlin, D., and S. Satterthwaite (1996) 'Sustainable Development and Cities', In Pugh, C. (ed.) *Sustainability, the Environment and Urbanisation*, Earthscan, London.

Mohan, R. (2006) *Asia's Urban Century: Emerging Trends*, Key note address delivered at the Conference of Land and Policies and Urban Development, Lincoln Institute of Land Policy, Cambridge, Massachusetts, June 5, http://www.bis.org/review/r060705e.pdf

Morawczynski, O and Pickens, M (2009) *Poor People Using Mobile Financial Services: Observations on Customer Usage and Impact from M-PESA*. CGAP Brief, http://www.cgap.org/gm/document1.9.36723/BR_Poor_People_Using_Mobile_Financial_Services.pdf

Moser, C. O. N. and J. Holland (1997) 'Confronting Crisis in Chawama, Lusaka Zambia', *Household Responses to Poverty and Vulnerability*, Vol 4, Urban Programme Management Policy Paper 24, World Bank, Washington, DC.

Mungai, C. (2012) 'East Africa Region's Economy Expands Amid Deepening Levels of Poverty and Malnutrition' in *The East African*, April 7 , http://www.theeastafrican.co.ke/

N

Ndegwa, S. N. (2002) 'Decentralization in Africa: A stocktaking survey', *Africa Region Working Paper Series No. 40*, World Bank: Washington, DC.

Ni, P. (2011) *Driving factors of Prosperity: An Empirical Analysis Global Cities*, background paper for this Report.

O

OECD (2001) *OECD Manual: Measuring Productivity: Measurement of Aggregate and Industry-Level Productivity Growth*, OECD Publishing, Paris.

OECD (2006) *OECD Territorial Reviews Competitive Cities in the Global Economy*, OECD Publishing, Paris.

OECD (2011) *Divided We Stand: Why Inequality Keeps Rising*, OECD Publishing, Paris.

Olokesusi, F. (2011) *City Report on Accra*. Unpublished UN-Habitat background study for this Report.

Omenya, A. (2011) *City Report on Nairobi*, Unpublished UN-Habitat background study for this Report.

ONU-HÁBITAT (2012) *El estado de las ciudades de América Latina y el Caribe 2012*, ONU-HÁBITAT ,Rio de Janeiro.

ONU-HABITAT and SEDESOL (2011), *El Estado de las Ciudades de México*, ONU-HABITAT (Oficina Regional para América Latina y el Caribe), Rio de Janeiro.

OSEC and Rainbow Unlimited GMBH (2010) *Opportunities in Infrastructure. A review of South and Southern Africa*, http://www.osec.ch/en/filefield-private/files/6543/field_blog_public_files/7952

Ostrom, E. (1990), *Governing the Commons: The Evolution of Institutions for Collective Action*, Cambridge University Press, Cambridge (UK).

Oyelaran-Oyeyinka, B. and P.G. Sampath (2010) *Latecomer Development: Innovation and Knowledge for Economic Growth*, Routledge, London and New York.

Oyeyinka, B. O. (2012) 'Institutional capacity and policy for latecomer technology development', *International Journal of Technological Learning, Innovation and Development*, Vol. 5, (1/2), pp. 85–110.

P

Pacific Institute (2011) *The World's Water Volume 7: The Biennial Report on Freshwater Resources*, Table 21, http://www.worldwater.org/data.html

Pacione, M. (2003) 'Urban Environmental Quality and Human Wellbeing; A Social Geographical Perspective', *Landscape and Urban Planning*, vol.65, pp.19–30.

Peacock, L. (2011) 'Future of jobs: Green Industry to Create Thousands of Roles', *The Telegraph*, September 15, http://www.telegraph.co.uk/finance/jobs/8765695/Future-of-jobs-Green-industry-to-create-thousands-of-roles.html

Peirce, N., and C. Johnson with F. Peters (2012) *America's Metro Regions Take Center Stage: 8 Reasons Why*, Citistates Group- Community Growth Education Foundation, Alexandria, Va.

Peirce, N.R., and C.W. Johnson with F. M. Peters (eds) (2008) *Century of the City: No Time to Lose*, The Rockefeller Foundation, New York.

Perez, F. (2011) *City Report on Guadajara*. Unpublished UN-Habitat background study for this Report.

Philip, J. T. (2009) 'Average Urban Teledensity Crosses 100% Mark', *The Economic Times*, December 12, http://articles.economictimes.indiatimes.com/2009-12-12/news/28416388_1_cent-mark-mobile-connections-teledensity

Pierre, J. (2011) *The Politics of Urban Governance*, Palgrave Macmillan, Basingstoke.

PNUD (2010) *Abrir espacios a la seguridad ciudadana y al desarrollo humano Informe de Desarrollo Humano para America Central, IDHAC 2009-2010*, http://hdr.undp.org/en/reports/regional/latinamericathecaribbean/Central_America_RHDR_2009-10_ES.pdf

Porter, M. (1998) 'Clusters and the new economics of competitiveness', *Harvard Business Review*, December.

Portney, K. E. and J.M. Berry (2011) *Civil Society and Sustainable Cities*, Paper prepared for the Princeton Conference on Environmental Politics: Research Frontiers in Comparative and International Environmental Politics, Niehaus Center for Globalization and Governance, Princeton University, December 2–3, 2011.

PricewaterhouseCoopers (2009) 'Global city GDP rankings 2008-2025' *PricewaterhouseCoopers UK Economic Outlook, November 2009*, London. http://www.ukmediacentre.pwc.com/ Media-Library/Global-city-GDP-rankings-2008-2025-61a.aspx

PricewaterhouseCoopers (2010) *Cities of opportunities*, PricewaterhouseCoopers/ The Partnership for New York City Inc., http://www.pwc.com/us/en/cities-of-opportunity/2011/pdfdownload.jhtml

Pucher, J., N. Korattyswaropam, N. Mittal, and N. Ittyerah (2005) "Urban Transport Crisis in India", *Transport Policy*, Vol. 12, pp. 185–198.

Pucher, J., Z. Peng, N. Mittal, Y. Zhu, and N. Korattyswaroopam (2007) 'Urban Transport Trends and Policies in China and India: Impacts of Rapid Economic Growth', *Transport Reviews*, Vol. 27 (4), pp. 379–410.

Q

Quantisoft (2012) *Municipal Opinion Surveys/Municipal Satisfaction Survey*, http://www.quantisoft.com/Industries/ Municipal.htm

Quartly, J. (2010) 'Ordos rises from the grassland', *China Daily*, September 16, http://www.chinadaily.com.cn/usa/2010-09/16/content_11313108.htm

R

Railway-technology.com (n.d) *Gautrain rapid rail link, South Africa*, http:// www.railway-technology.com/projects/ gautrain/

Raouf, M. A. (2009) 'Towards Sustainable Transportation', *Gulf News*, September 18, http://gulfnews.com/opinions/ columnists/towards-sustainable-transportation-1.539872

Reali, M. and S. Alli (2010) *The City of Diadema and the City Statute*, http://www.citiesalliance.org/sites/ citiesalliance.org/files/CA_Images/ CityStatuteofBrazil_English_Ch3.pdf

Redclift, M. (1996) *Wasted: Counting the Costs of Global Consumption*, Earthscan, London.

Regional Plan Association and America 2050 (2012) *Landscapes: Improving Conservation Practice in the Northeast Megaregion*, http://www.rpa.org/ northeastlandscapes/

Roberts, B.H.(2011) *City Clusters and Prosperity*, Unpublished UN-Habitat background study for this Report.

Roudi-Fahimi, F., L. Creel and R. M. De Souza (2002) *Finding the Balance: Population and Water Scarcity in the Middle East and North Africa*, MENA Policy Brief, Population Reference Bureau, Washington, DC.

Rwanda Development Board (2012) *Doing Business 2012 report: Rwanda 3rd Easiest Place to Do Business in Africa and 2nd Five Year Top Global Reformer*, http://gov.rw/Doing-Business-2012-report-Rwanda-3rd-easiest-place-to-do-business-in-Africa-and-2nd-five-year-top-global-reformer

S

Safar Zitoun, M. and A. Tabti-Talamali (2009) *La Mobilité Urbaine dans l'Agglomération d'Alger: Evolutions et Perspectives*, Plan Bleu, Algiers.

Safaricom (2010) *Annual Report & Group Accounts 2010*, http://www.safaricom. com/

Safaricom (2011) *Half- Year Results Presentation, 9th November*, http://www. safaricom.co.ke/

Sassen, S. (2006) *Territory, Authority, Rights: From Medieval to Global Assemblages*, Princeton University Press, Princeton.

Schifferes, S. (2007) 'Multinationals lead India's IT Revolution', *BBC News*, January 24, http://news.bbc.co.uk/2/hi/ business/6288247.stm

Schrank, D., T. Lomax, and B. Eisele (2011) *2011 Urban Mobility Report*, Texas Transportation Institute, http://mobility. tamu.edu/ums/report/

Scipes, K. (2006) 'Venezuela and South Africa: Redistributive Policies *vs.* Neo-Liberal Economic Policies', *Third World Traveler*, http://www.thirdworldtraveler. com/Venezuela_page/Venez_SAfrica_ EconPolicies.html

SEDESOL (2007) *Guia de Diseno del Espacio Publico Seguro, Incluente y Sustentable*. Secretaria de Desarrollo Social, México.

Sen, A.(1979) 'Issues in the Measurement of Poverty,' Scandinavian *Journal of Economics*, Wiley Blackwell, vol. 81(2), pp. 285-307.

Sen, A. (1999) *Development as Freedom*, Oxford University Press, Oxford.

Sen, A. K.(1999) 'Democracy as a Universal Value', *Journal of Democracy*, vol 10 (3), pp. 3–17.

SEPA and NBS (2006) China Green National Accounting Study Report 2004.

SET-DEV (2011) *Technological Responsibility:Guidelines For A Shared Governance Of The Processes of Socialisation of Scientific Research and Innovation, Within an Interconnected World*, http://www.set-dev.eu/images/pdf/ setdev-pg2110728?e6227e3a1ee01ab67 932453dd186b586=fe92758461b42841 8da8873e8a9fc566

Shabou, A., N. Soboh, K. Jalouka, and D. A. Thaib (2011) *City Report on Amman*. Unpublished UN-Habitat background study for this Report.

Shariff, O. (2007) 'Dubai Traffic Woes Inflict Losses of Dh4.6b a Year', *Gulf News*, December 13, http://gulfnews. com/business/shipping/dubai-traffic-woes-inflict-losses-of-dh4-6b-a-year-1.75892

Sharma, S. (2005) 'Democracy, Good Governance, and Economic Development', *Taiwan Journal of Democracy*, Vol. 3 (1), pp. 29–62.

Shehayeb, D. (2008) 'Safety and Security in Public Space' in *International Report on Crime Prevention and Community Safety: Trends and Perspectives*, ICPC, Montreal, pp. 107–112

Shlomo, A, J.Parent, D. L. Civco, and A. M. Blei (2010) *The Persistent Decline in Urban Densities: Global and Historical Evidence of 'Sprawl'* (Working Paper), Lincoln Institute of Land Policy, Cambridge (USA).

Shukla, A. (2012) 'India to create 100 million green jobs', *One World South Asia*, February 13, http://southasia.oneworld. net/todaysheadlines/india-to-create-100-million-green-jobs/?searchterm=100%20 million%20green%20jobs

Simon, D., M. Fragkias, R.Leichenko , R. Sánchez-Rodríguez, K. Seto and B.Solecki (2011) *The Green Economy and the Prosperity of Cities*, background paper for this Report

Smarzynska, B.K. and S.J. Wei (2000) *Corruption and the Composition of Foreign Direct Investment: Firm-Level Evidence*, World Bank Discussion Paper no. 2360, World Bank, Washington, DC.

Soares, F. V., S. Soares, M .Medeiros, , and R. G. Osório, (2006) *Cash transfer programmes in Brazil: Impacts on inequality and poverty*, International Policy Centre for Inclusive Growth working Paper No. 21, International Poverty Centre Brasilia

Society for International Development (SID) (2012) *The State of East Africa Report 2012: Deepening Integration, Intensifying Challenges*, http://www.sidint. net/docs/SoEAR2012_final.pdf

Soja, E. W. (2010), *Seeking Spatial Justice*, University of Minnesota Press, Minneapolis.

Spector, J. (2011) 'New York struggles to bridge $80 billion chasm for infrastructure needs', *lohud.com*, September 25, http:// www.lohud.com/article/20110925/ NEWS05/109250332/New-York-struggles-bridge-80-billion-chasm-infrastructure-needs

Spence, M., P. C. Annez, and R. Buckley (eds) (2008) *Urbanisation and Growth*, Commission on Growth and Development, World Bank, Washington DC.

Spirou, C. (2011) *Urban Tourism and Urban Change: Cities in a Global Economy*, New York, Routledge.

Stasavage, D. (2005) "Democracy and Education Spending in Africa," *American Journal of Political Science*, Vol. 49 (2), pp. 343–358.

Statistics Canada (2001) *2001 Census Analysis Series - A profile of the Canadian population: Where we live*, http:// prod.library.utoronto.ca:8090/datalib/ codebooks/c/cc01/doc/article.pdf

Statistics Canada (2005), *The Rural and Small Town Canada*, Analysis Bulletin, Vol. 6, no. 3, http://www.statcan.gc.ca/ daily-quotidien/050531/dq050531b-eng. htm

Stiglitz, J.E., A. Sen, and J. P. Fitoussi (2009) *Report by the Commission on the Measurement of Economic Performance and Social Progress*, The Commission, Paris.

T

Takechi, A. (2010) *Basrah Water Supply from viewpoint of Its Water Sources*, http://www.waterforum.jp/jpn/iraq/doc/ expert_meeting/session/4_2.pdf

Talen, E. (2012) *City Rules: How Regulations Affect Urban Form*, Island Press, Washington DC.

Telecommunications and Regulatory Authority (2011) *UAE Telecommunications Sector Developments and Indicators, 2007 –2010*, http://www.tra.gov.ae

Teriman, S., T. Yigitcanlar, and S. Mayere (2010) 'Sustainable Urban Infrastructure Development in South East Asia: Evidence from Hong Kong, Kuala Lumpur and Singapore' in Yigitcanlar, T. (ed.) *Sustainable Urban and Regional Infrastructure Development: Technologies, Applications and Management*, IGI Global, Hershey, Pennsylvania.

The CLEAR Network (2006) *Urban Planning and Smart Growth*, http://www.clear.london.ca/Urban_Planning.html

The Economist (2004) *The World In 2005: Quality of Life Index*, http://www.economist.com/media/pdf/QUALITY_OF_LIFE.pdf

The Economist (2012) 'Business in Rwanda: Africa's Singapore?' *The Economist*, February 25, http://www.economist.com/node/21548263

The Economist (2012) 'Jamaica at 50: On your marks, get set…oh', *The Economist*, July 21, http://www.economist.com/node/21559348

Tierney, J. (2009) 'The Richer-Is-Greener Curve' *The New York Times*, April 20, http://tierneylab.blogs.nytimes.com/2009/04/20/the-richer-is-greener-curve/

Toteng, E. (2008) 'The effects of water management frameworks and the role of domestic consumers on urban water consumption in Botswana', *Water International*, Vol. 33(4), pp. 475–487.

Turok, I (2006) 'The Connection between Social Cohesion and City Competitiveness', in *OECD Territorial Reviews Competitive Cities in the Global Economy*, OECD publishing, Paris.

Turok, I. (2011) *Urban Employment and the Prosperity of Cities*. Background paper prepared for this Report.

U

Uddin, A. (2009) *Traffic Congestion in Indian Cities: Challenges of a Rising Power*, paper presented at the conference: Kyoto of the Cities, Naples, March 26-28, 2009.

UNCED (1992) *Capacity Building: Agenda 21's definition* (Chapter 37), United Nations, New York.

UNDP (2002) *Arab Human Development Report: Creating opportunities for Future Generations*, UNDP, New York.

UNDP (2009) *Arab Human Development Report: Challenges to Human Security in the Arab Countries*, UNDP , New York.

UNDP (2010) *The Real Wealth of Nations: Pathways to Human Development*. New York, UNDP.

UNEP (1996) *Taking Action: Environmental Guide for You and Your Community*, UNEP, Nairobi.

UNEP (2008) *UNEP Background Paper on Green Jobs*, UNEP, Nairobi.

UNEP (2009) *Global Green New Deal*, UNEP Policy Brief, http://www.unep.org/pdf/A_Global_Green_New_Deal_Policy_Brief.pdf

UNEP (2011a) *Renewable Energy: Investing in Energy and Resource efficiency*, http://www.unep.org/greeneconomy/Portals/88/documents/ger/GER_6_RenewableEnergy.pdf

UNEP, (2011b) *Towards a Green Economy: Pathways to Sustainable Development and Poverty Eradication: A synthesis for Policy Makers*, http://www.unep/greeneconomy

UNEP, ILO, IOE and ITUC (2008) *Green Jobs: Towards Decent Work in a Sustainable, Low-Carbon World*, UNEP, Nairobi.

UN-Habitat (2003) *The Challenge of Slums: Global Report on Human Settlements 2003*, Earthscan, London.

UN-Habitat (2004) *State of the World's Cities 2004/05: Globalization and Urban Culture*, Earthscan, London.

UN-Habitat (2006) *State of the World's Cities 2006/2007: The Millennium Development Goals and Urban Sustainability*, Earthscan, London.

UN-Habitat (2007) *Enhancing Urban Safety and Security: Global Report on Human Settlements 2007*, Earthscan, London.

UN-Habitat (2008) *State of the World's Cities Report 2008/09: Harmonious Cities*, Earthscan, London.

UN-Habitat (2010a) *State of the World's Cities 2010/2011: Bridging the Urban Divide*, Earthscan, London.

UN-Habitat (2010b) *The State of African Cities 2010: Governance Inequality and Urban Land Markets*, UN-Habitat, Nairobi.

UN-Habitat (2010c) 'Scaling New Heights: New Ideas in Urban Planning', *Urban World*, Vol. 1, Issue, 4, October. Nairobi.

UN-Habitat (2011a) *Cities and Climate Change: Policy Directions*, Abridged edition, Earthscan, London.

UN-Habitat (2011b) *Cities and Climate Change: Global Report on Human Settlements 2011*, Earthscan, London.

UN-Habitat (2011c) 'Cairo: A City in Transition', *Cities and Citizens Series-Bridging the Urban Divide*, The American University in Cairo / UN-Habitat, Nairobi.

UN-Habitat (2012) *Decentralization in Iraq: Challenges and Solutions for Federal and Local Governments*, UN-Habitat, Nairobi.

UN-Habitat (2012) *The State of Arab Cities 2012: Challenges of Urban Transition*, UN-Habitat, Nairobi.

UN-Habitat and UNESCAP (2009) *Urban Safety and Poverty in Asia and the Pacific: Key findings from sub-regional studies on South Asia, South-East Asia and the Pacific*, UNON, Nairobi.

UN-Habitat and ESCAP (2010) *The State of Asian Cities 2010/11*, Fukuoka, Japan.

UNICEF (2010) *Understanding Urban Inequalities in Bangladesh: A Prerequisite for Achieving Vision 2021*, UNICEF Bangladesh, Dhaka.

UNIDO (2008) *Public Goods for Economic Development*, UNIDO, Vienna,

United Nations (1992) *Agenda 21: Programme of Action for Sustainable Development*, United Nations, New York.

United Nations (1999) *The World at Six Billion*, United Nations Department of Economic and Social Affairs, Population Division, New York.

United Nations (2010a) *World Economic and Social Survey 2010: Retooling Global Development*, United Nation (DESA),New York.

United Nations (2010b) *World Population Policies 2009*, United Nations, Department of Economic and Social Affairs, Population Division, New York.

United Nations General Assembly (2011) *Accelerating progress towards the Millennium Development Goals: options for sustained and inclusive growth and issues for advancing the United Nations development agenda beyond 2015*, Annual report of the Secretary-General (A/66/126), July 2011.

United Nations, Department of Economic and Social Affairs, Population Division (2012). *World Urbanization Prospects: The 2011 Revision*, CD-ROM Edition.

UNODC (2004) *The Global Programme against Corruption: UN Anti-Corruption Toolkit*, 3rd edition, United Nations Office on Drugs and Crime, Vienna.

UNODC (2005) *Crime and Development in Africa*, http://www.unodc.org/pdf/African_report.pdf

Urán, H. B. (2011) *City Report on Medellín*, Unpublished UN-Habitat background study for this Report.

Urban Age (2009) *Cities and Social Equity: Inequality, Territory and Urban Form*, Summary report, http://downloads0.cloud.lsecities.net/downloads/2009/09/SouthAmericaReport/CSE_Summary_Report.pdf

U.S. Census Bureau (n.d.) *U.S. Census Bureau: State and County QuickFacts*, http://quickfacts.census.gov/qfd/index.html

U.S. Department of Commerce (2011) 'Residential Vacancies and Homeownership in the Third Quarter 2011', *U.S. Census Bureau News*, http://www.census.gov/hhes/www/housing/hvs/qtr311/files/q311press.pdf

V

Vassalli, C. P. and M. Y. Sánchez (2009) 'Producción Masiva De Vivienda En Ciudad De México: Dos Políticas En Debate', *Centro-h, Revista de la Organización Latinoamericana y del Caribe de Centros Históricos*, No. 3, pp. 15–26.

Vaughan, P. (2010) *The growth of Mobile Money Transfer Service: The Case of M-PESA*, http://aitec.usp.net/

Vejella, S. (2011) *City Report on Hyderabad*, Unpublished UN-Habitat background study for this Report.

Venables, A. J. (2010) 'Economic geography and African development', *Papers in Regional Science*, Vol. 89(3).

Veolia Environnement (2010) *Villes à Vivre 2010*, Observatoire Veolia des Modes de Vie Urbains, Paris.

Viana, I. (2011) *City Report on Montevideo*, Unpublished UN-Habitat background study for this Report.

Vicentini, V. L. (2010) 'Lessons from urban transport in Latin America and the Caribbean', Presentation at the *2010 ADB Transport Forum*, May 25-27, Manila.

Vienna City Administration (n.d) *Vienna Charter. Shaping the Future Together*, http://www.wien.gv.at/english/living-working/vienna-charter.html

W

Waldman, S. R. (2012) 'Zoning Laws and Property Rights', in *The Berkeley Daily Planet*, March 27, http://www.berkeleydailyplanet.com/issue/2012-03-27/article/39504?headline=Zoning-Laws-and-Property-Rights--By-Steve-Randy-Waldman

WCED (World Commission on Environment and Development) (1987) *Our Common Future*, Oxford University Press, Oxford.

Wei, S.J. (2000) 'How Taxing is Corruption on International Investors' *Review of Economics and Statistics*, Vol. 82, pp. 1–11

World Bank (2002) *Cities on the Move: A World Bank Urban Transport Strategy Review*, World Bank, Washington, DC.

World Bank (2005) *World Development Report 2006: Equity and Development*, Oxford University Press, New York.

World Bank (2006) *Where is the Wealth of Nations? Measuring Capital for the 21st Century*, World Bank, Washington DC.

World Bank (2009a) *World Development Report 2009: Reshaping Economic Geography*, World Bank, Washington, DC.

World Bank (2009b) *Getting People and Traffic Moving Again in Lagos*, http://www.worldbank.org/

World Bank (2010) *Kenya Economic Update: Kenya at the Tipping Point? with a special focus on the ICT Revolution and Mobile Money*, December 2010 Edition No.3,http://siteresources.worldbank.org/KENYAEXTN/Resources/KEU-Dec_2010_with_cover_e-version.pdf

World Bank (2011) *World Development Indicators*, World Bank: Washington, DC.

World Bank (2012) *Doing Business 2012: Doing Business in a More Transparent*, World Bank, Washington, DC.

World Bank (2012) *World Bank Data: World Development Indicators & Global Development Finance*, Online database last updated July 9 2012, http://data.worldbank.org

World Bank and International Finance Corporation (2011) *Doing Business 2012: Doing Business in a More Transparent World*, World Bank, Washington DC.

World Values Survey (2011) *Values That Change the World*, http://www.worldvaluessurvey.org/wvs/articles/folder_published/article_base_110/files/WVSbrochure6-2008_11.pdf

Y

Yerro, A. P. (2011) *City Report on Fort-De-France*. Unpublished UN-Habitat background study for this Report.

Yu, S. (2011) 'Why Roubini May be Wrong on China's Property Doom' *Financial Times*. May 12, http://blogs.ft.com/beyond-brics/2011/05/12/why-roubini-may-be-wrong-on-china%E2%80%99s-property-doom/#axzz1mXDFChfj

Z

Zaidi, S.S.H. (2011) *City Report on Lahore*. Unpublished UN-Habitat background study for this Report.

Index

Note: Page numbers in *italics* refer to maps, figures, tables, boxes and illustrations. Those followed by 'n' refer to notes.